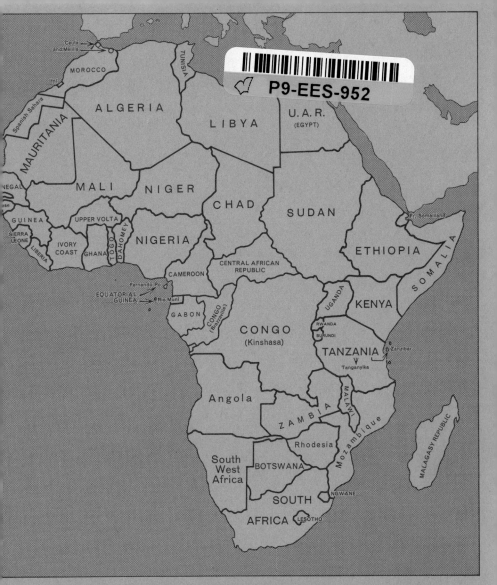

DEPENDENT AFRICAN TERRITORIES

Territory	Area (km²)	Est. Population (thousands)	Political Status
Angola	1,245,697	5,154	Overseas province of Portugal
Ceuta and Melilla	30	152	Parts of metropolitan Spain
French Somaliland	22,015	71	Overseas territory of France
Ifni	1,502	40	Overseas province of Spain
Mozambique	782,957	6,956	Overseas province of Portugal
Portuguese Guinea	36,001	525	Overseas province of Portugal
Rhodesia	390,966	4,260	British colony
South West Africa	822,843	574	Under de facto South African administration as a League of Nations mandate, declared lapsed by a U.N. General Assembly resolution in 1967.
Spanish Sahara	265,993	30	Overseas province of Spain

THE GREAT POWERS AND AFRICA

The
Great Powers
and
Africa

WALDEMAR A. NIELSEN

PUBLISHED FOR THE
COUNCIL ON FOREIGN RELATIONS
BY

PRAEGER PUBLISHERS
New York · Washington · London

PRAEGER PUBLISHERS
111 Fourth Avenue, New York, N. Y. 10003, U.S.A.
5, Cromwell Place, London S.W.7, England

Published in the United States of America in 1969
by Praeger Publishers, Inc.

Printed in the United States of America

To the memory of RFK
MLK
EM
TM

Contents

Part Four: A Future U.S. Policy Toward Africa

List of Tables

Preface

Africans say that "he who is carried does not realize how far the town is." Anyone who undertakes the long journey of writing a book such as this, dealing with the economic, cultural, military, and political policies toward Africa of a wide band of complex developed countries, must lean heavily upon the experience, guidance, and specialized knowledge of many others. I am well aware of the sore shoulders my trip has caused, and I have arrived at my destination even more grateful than most authors for the help I have received and the generous spirit in which it has been given.

Above all, I would like to acknowledge the assistance I have received from that extraordinary institution, the Council on Foreign Relations, and particularly from two discussion groups organized under its sponsorship—one on the evolution of the policies of the European and Communist powers toward Africa, which met through the winter and spring of 1966–67; and a second on the evolution of U.S. policy toward Africa, which met during 1968. Those who participated in the group on "Western European, Soviet, and Chinese Policy Toward Africa" were: Robert E. Asher, Col. Sidney Berry, USA, Rep. Jonathan B. Bingham, John A. Davis, William Diebold, W. D. Eberle, J. Wayne Fredericks, Rep. Peter H. B. Frelinghuysen, Gen. Andrew J. Goodpaster, USA, Robert Graff, Edward K. Hamilton, William A. Hance, James T. Harris, Jr., Louis Henkin, Graham Hovey, Andrew M. Kamarck, Ernest W. Lefever, Robert Lubar, David W. Mac-Eachron, Robert J. Manning, Robert Murphy, Philip Quigg, Rep. Ogden R. Reid, Zelia Ruebhausen, Jo W. Saxe, R. Peter Straus, Francis X. Sutton, Willard L. Thorp, Carroll L. Wilson, I. William Zartman.

Those who participated in the group on "The Evolution of U.S. Policy Toward Africa" were Harry Boardman, Joseph E. Black, Richard A. Falk, Ernest A. Gross, Ambassador Fred L. Hadsel, Edward K. Hamilton, Ulric Haynes, Jr., Roger Hilsman, Helen Kitchen, Dan B. Lacy, William E. Lang, George N. Lindsay, Ian K. MacGregor, John A. Marcum, Ruth Schachter Morgenthau, Herman J. Nissenbaum, George T. Piercy, Philip Quigg, Rep. Ogden R. Reid, Arnold Rivkin, Oscar Schachter, Immanuel Wallerstein, Adam Yarmolinsky.

From the long afternoons and evenings of discussion and debate with these distinguished persons from government, business, academic, and professional life, I have derived immeasurable benefit to my own thinking. In this regard I wish to commend Jane W. Jacqz for her clear and cogent reports of these meetings.

To a number of additional persons whose helpfulness went far beyond the call of friendship or professional obligation, I would like to express special thanks: Willard L. Thorp for his conscientious review of all the economic sections; Ambassador Charles W. Yost for his counsel on issues relating to the United Nations; Robert Legvold for his research and guidance in the preparation of the Soviet and Chinese chapters; Jo W. Saxe and the late Arnold Rivkin for their generous cooperation in the analysis of European Common Market relations with Africa; Ambassador Fred L. Hadsel for assistance in documenting the evolution of U.S. policy toward Africa in the postwar period; Edward K. Hamilton for further background information and assistance in the interpretation of those developments; Gen. Andrew Goodpaster and William Lang for help in the analysis of military and strategic questions; William Diebold and Helena Stalson for their tireless assistance in the preparation of the analysis of economic relationships; Robert S. Smith and Herman J. Nissenbaum for their careful criticism of the discussion of U.S. foreign-assistance policy; and Leo Model for his wise counsel, which repeatedly saved me from the pitfalls of particularism and the loss of broader perspective.

To the Council on Foreign Relations and its whole staff, particularly to Robert Valkenier, Lorna Brennan, and Jan Farlow, I wish to say that their gracious cooperation in innumerable matters is deeply appreciated. Nor can I omit mention of the devoted and intelligent help of my secretary, Elaine Keeve, and the meticulous research assistance of Mary Lynne Bird.

Despite the oversights, simplifications, and errors which an analytical overview almost inevitably entails, and the danger, therefore, of being ambushed at many points along the way by scholarly critics, I have felt the task was worth undertaking, not only for what it might contribute to an understanding of the changing place of Africa in the plans and priorities of the great powers but also for two additional and compelling reasons: First, an examination of the impact on international relationships of the political re-emergence of Africa in recent years can throw illumination upon the problems of universal importance now taking shape between the developed nations and the Third World. Second, a review of United States policy toward Africa in recent years against the background of the evolving policies of the other great powers may make it possible to gain a new perspective on our own national behavior and interests in relation both to Africa specifically and to the Third World generally.

This book closes with the end of the Johnson administration. But nothing has occurred in the first months of the Nixon administration, during which this book has been in the process of publication, to change my judgment that U.S. policy toward Africa is in a phase of stagnation, if not deterioration, and that it can benefit from a broad reappraisal.

Being in Iran at the moment, I am reminded that a book is not only a long journey of discovery, but also a carpet made of many fibers and colors, some of which can be provided by others. But the final design is something for which the weaver alone must take responsibility.

WALDEMAR A. NIELSEN

Tehran, Iran
May 30, 1969

Part One

Europe and Africa

1

The Altered Configuration of Power

The past quarter-century has been one of those periods of historical haste when, the old order having become unhinged, fundamental changes have taken place with remarkable speed in every aspect of international affairs. The Second World War, a gigantic release of long-gathered tensions, produced such alteration in the con-figuration of power and set into motion such profound new forces that the nations of the world are still in the process of adapting themselves and their policies to its consequences. Two new super-powers, the United States and the Soviet Union, emerged in the course of the war, and their subsequent competition has been the central division in world affairs ever since. The nations of Western Europe, after centuries of pre-eminence, were reduced to secondary rank and are still attempting, slowly and gropingly, to define new relationships with one another and to find a new role for themselves in the world.

Among the war's most massive and dramatic consequences were the disintegration of the old European empires and the appearance of a multitude of new, fragile, unstable, and impoverished nations. On the great continent of Africa, nearly four times the area of the United States, thirty-seven new states have become independent,*

* Given the rapidity of change, even such a simple statement of fact must be explained. Included in this number are only those states which have gained their independence since the Second World War. Not included are Rhodesia, which declared its independence unilaterally in 1965 but over which Britain continues to assert legal authority and responsibility, and Biafra, the seces-sionist eastern region of Nigeria. Zanzibar and Tanganyika, which, after their independence, joined to form the new state of Tanzania, are counted as one country.

3

a change which, in turn, has accelerated internal political, economic, and social evolution and has injected into the already complex equation of international relations many unfamiliar and further unsettling factors.

These changes, both within Africa and in the policies and attitudes of the various powers toward the new Africa, provide an unexpectedly revealing optic through which to view the contemporary world scene. Within Africa, given the relative transparency of its new political and economic structures, the processes of change and the underlying forces at work can be seen with unusual clarity. And, because Africa is an area of secondary rather than primary interest to all the great powers, observing their policies and conduct from that angle reveals facets not usually seen, somewhat in the fashion that a polar map exposes important geographic and strategic relationships obscured by the more familiar Mercator projection. Thus, important in itself, Africa is even more important for what it enables us to understand.

There, to a unique degree, are clustered the new dimensions, subtleties, and creative challenges to foreign policy which the so-called Third World presents to all the great powers. It is the embodiment of the predicament of poverty, expectation, and restlessness in which two-thirds of humanity now finds itself and which casts its great shadow on the face of the future. All the problems reflecting and exacerbating that predicament are present: painfully slow improvement in abysmally low material standards of life, compounded by extremely rapid population growth; steadily worsening terms of trade for the primary products it exports; the continuous and disturbing impact of modern communications and other new technology on stagnated social structures and attitudes; the spread of nationalism and other militant doctrines of discontent; and, not least important, racial tension—which, as a breeder of international conflict, could become in the years ahead what ideology and religion have sometimes been in the past.

For the foreign ministries of the great powers, one of the baffling aspects of the new Africa has been the fact that few of the orthodox concepts and rituals which have governed the dealings among sovereign nations since the Congress of Vienna 150 years ago seem to be relevant. A good proportion of the new states imperfectly fulfill even the minimum requirements of national sovereignty; some would promptly go bankrupt were it not for the continuation of foreign subsidies; some regimes have had to depend for their survival on military intervention and protection by

external forces; a number are not in effective physical or administrative control over considerable areas within their boundaries;
and, in many, the loyalty of the population is to tribal sub-units
rather than to the nation as a whole. The political institutions
bequeathed them at the time of independence have generally
proved unacceptable and unworkable and are increasingly giving
way to experimental structures blending older political traditions
with newer African concepts and requirements. Thus, the national
units themselves are in formation and flux.

But, if older concepts of diplomacy seem to have limited applicability in such a context, the newer ones seem to have found in
Africa their natural field of action. Agencies of multilateral diplomacy are fully engaged—the United Nations, the Commonwealth,
the European Common Market, and African regional and sub-
regional groupings of many types; and the newer instrumentalities
of diplomacy as well—foreign economic and technical assistance,
programs of educational and cultural relations, quasi-govern-
mental volunteer efforts such as the Peace Corps, and propaganda,
covert activities, and political warfare.

The problems of diplomatic method are merely symptomatic
of deeper dilemmas posed to the great powers by Africa and the
Third World. Previously, such economically and militarily power-
less regions had been of interest to the powerful only as opportunities for conquest and exploitation. But now they must be dealt
with on a new basis and cannot be ignored. It is sensed that they
present both opportunities and dangers which, though unfamiliar
and even intangible, could be important and might be crucial.
They constitute in a sense the ghettos of the world and, like the
ghettos within a modern nation, have, if nothing else, the capacity
to pollute the atmosphere with bitterness, lawlessness, and unpredictability. Where once their discontents and disorders could
simply be dismissed as unimportant or summarily suppressed if
necessary, it is now being recognized that in an increasingly intricate and delicately balanced social, economic, and political structure even the least potent elements can produce disruption and
danger to the workability of the entire system.

More than that, the festering problems of the international
ghettos feed back into other parts of the world, with powerful
impact upon the conscience and political conduct of those groups
—especially the youth—who share the idealistic conviction that a
nation's international behavior must be consonant with the ethics

of its national existence and whose influence in many of the industrialized nations, already significant, is on the rise.

In sum, Africa presents in provocative and insistent fashion questions of the very definition of national interest and international responsibility in the modern world. For the United States, given the special characteristics of its own society, such questions have special bite.

In the nuclear era, when mankind for the first time has the capacity to extinguish life on the planet, the gnawing insecurity of the great powers must be eased mainly by the stabilization of relationships among themselves. In this sense, the prospects for peace do not turn primarily on the pivot of such areas as Africa and the Third World. But they nonetheless have a bearing upon, and are an unavoidable element of, the total problem. In ways not yet clearly understood they represent, despite their lack of armies and industries, a kind of power and influence. Their problems and viewpoints must somehow be included in the economic, political, and strategic calculations of the more powerful states. They trouble the quest for stability and order in a dangerous age by adding immense uncertainties. But they also make it necessary to deal with the problem of peace in a context of progress toward a decent and civilized existence for the mass of mankind. Thus, they present not only risks and dangers of a new kind but also a hopeful challenge.

The Sweeping but Incomplete Political Transformation of Africa

Since the end of the Second World War, the structure of European political control over the African continent, which was largely built in the latter part of the nineteenth century, has crumbled. For ten years, from 1945 through 1955, the façade of the undermined structure continued to stand. The coming of independence to Libya in 1951, however, gave a hint of things to come, and, not long thereafter, large segments began rapidly to collapse. In 1956, three new African states were born; in 1957, Ghana broke free, followed by Guinea in 1958. Then, in 1960, seventeen new states swept into independence. Since then, fourteen more have taken their place on the world scene under their own flags. Some four-fifths of the African continent and three-fifths of its population have become independent since 1945. As of 1969, therefore, virtually all of North and tropical Africa, except for a few fragments of territory under Spanish or Portuguese control, has been decolonized. All of the former British colonies north of the Zambezi River have achieved independence, as have all of the former French colonies and the former possessions of Belgium and Italy. Spain's scattered territories are progressively changing their relationship to the metropole; Equatorial Guinea, which became independent on October 12, 1968, was the first to complete the process.

Great though it has been, the transformation is not yet complete. At the southern tip of Africa, below a horseshoe-shaped line south of the sixth parallel, lie areas which remain under foreign domination or the control of internal white minorities: the large Portuguese colonies of Angola and Mozambique, the British colony of Rhodesia, and South Africa with its adjacent dependency, South West Africa. In some respects the five component areas differ markedly. In legal status, the first two are colonies, although Portugal insists on calling them "overseas provinces"; Rhodesia, legally a colony of Britain, was largely self-governing for more than forty years before it rebelled and unilaterally declared its independence in 1965. South West Africa, originally a League of Nations mandated territory, is now in an ambiguous status, being *de facto* under the control and administration of South Africa but *de jure* an international responsibility of the United Nations, which in 1966 formally declared the original South African mandate to have lapsed. South Africa, in contrast to the others, is an independent, fully sovereign republic.

Other differences are equally apparent: South West Africa is a thinly populated, backward, desolate area; South Africa is powerful, rich, and highly developed; socially, economically, and militarily, Angola, Mozambique, and Rhodesia are somewhere between. Likewise, the actual conditions of the blacks in the several areas differ in degree: In the Portuguese areas the forms of social and legal discrimination are less absolute, but poverty and illiteracy are extreme. In South Africa all human rights for nonwhites have been obliterated, but their economic and educational level relative at least to that of Africans in other parts of the White Redoubt is rather higher. In ideology, Portugal describes its policy in the colonies as multiracial and nondiscriminatory; South Africa asserts the doctrine of *apartheid*, or "separate development" of the races, and applies it in South West Africa as well; and Rhodesia, once multiracial in doctrine, appears to be moving toward the South African position.

Such differences, however, do not alter the essential uniformity of the region in matters of political importance: The vast majority of the population is black, ranging from two-thirds in South Africa to 98 per cent in Mozambique.* The white minority in every case holds complete political and economic power; the blacks are subordinated and exploited; and the whites are adamant in their determination to maintain their position. These are the decisive realities that have created the international problem: To the many newly emergent nations formerly under colonial control, to the nonwhite majority of the world's population, and to many persons in the developed countries the situation is politically, morally, and emotionally intolerable.

But the problem has been and is what to do about it. The blacks within the areas themselves, impoverished and backward, have been no match for the control apparatus ranged against them, and their political efforts have been ineffectual. Those outside concerned with the situation have therefore been obliged to use such means of indirect influence as have been available—to a very large extent, the United Nations, including both its political organs and its judicial arm. Unremittingly since 1945 at the Trusteeship Council, the Committee of 17 (later 24), the General Assembly, and the Security Council, the siege has been maintained in the form of literally dozens of condemnatory resolutions and declarations and demands for collective action.

By 1961 it seemed that the steady effort might be achieving some slow success: The major world powers had been brought to the point of support of a call for the end of colonialism; Portugal, in the wake of disorders in Angola, had felt it necessary to introduce limited economic and social reforms in its colonies; Britain, in Rhodesia, was at work on a new constitution which

* Approximate recent population figures follow:

	Whites	%	Nonwhites
Angola	172,529	3.6	4,657,920
Mozambique	65,798	1.1	5,698,564
Rhodesia	221,490	5.1	3,538,510
South Africa	3,088,492	19.3	12,914,305
South West Africa	73,464	14.0	452,540

SOURCE: United Nations Statistical Office and *United Nations Demographic Yearbook*, 1963 (New York: 1964). The figures for Mozambique have been revised according to more recent information. African population statistics are frequently unreliable, and widely varying estimates are published. Those shown here should therefore be interpreted only as giving orders of magnitude.

would provide a ladder of political development for the Africans to climb; South Africa's policies and authority in South West Africa were being challenged by a formal proceeding before the World Court; and, even within South Africa, the reverberations of the Sharpeville massacre of March 1960 had caused a hesitation in the economic boom and disturbed the sense of security of the controlling group. The swelling number of newly independent African states, especially after 1960, added to the mood of optimism and sense of forward movement. Nationalist organizations committed to liberate the southern areas sprang into existence, and there was a general expectation in Africa and elsewhere, almost a sense of historical inevitability, that the momentum of the independence drive would carry it to the southernmost extremity of the continent within a few years, bringing about basic polical change in Angola, Mozambique, and Rhodesia. There were even those who anticipated that, once these areas had given way to African majority control, the great citadel of white supremacy itself, South Africa, would be compelled by some combination of internal and external pressures to abandon the detested policy of *apartheid* and begin a process of political concessions to its non-white majority.

In the event, however, the sweep of independence has been brought to an abrupt and what increasingly appears to be a protracted halt at the twisting frontier—the Battleline—dividing independent Black Africa from the southern White Redoubt. In a number of remaining British areas of responsibility in East and Central Africa and in the former High Commission Territories, the processes leading to independence that were under way in 1961 have been completed. In the five hard-core cases, white control not only has remained but has hardened. Hopes which once seemed reasonable that Portugal would concede the principle of self-determination to its colonies, that Rhodesia would peacefully evolve into some kind of constitutional multiracial state, that South African policies and control over South West Africa would be modified, and that the ruthlessness of *apartheid* in South Africa itself might be tempered have all, one by one, expired.

Portugal, small, poor and politically rigid though it is, has managed by a combination of skillful diplomatic maneuvers and limited measures of reform and development (sometimes called Portugal's Second Five Hundred Year Plan in Africa) to fend off the pressures upon it. More important, it has mounted a major and relatively effective military campaign to stop the spreading revolt in the colonies—an effort that has required it to maintain an army of 120,000 men in Africa, increase the term of military service for its citizens to four years, impose a crushing burden of taxes, and devote 50 per cent of the national budget to the cause. Whether it can continue such an effort, especially after the removal of the strong controlling hand of dictator Salazar, remains to be seen, but his successor, Premier Marcelo Caetano, apparently intends to try.

In Rhodesia, the small white settler group in power took the gamble in November 1965 of unilaterally declaring the colony's independence from Britain. The rebel regime under Ian Smith has thus far managed to survive the consequences. It has broken the strength of African political activity by tightening restrictions and by imprisoning or sequestering thousands of nationalist leaders. It has nullified British diplomatic efforts to re-establish control. It has set up a counterfire to offset official British and American criticism by launching a well-financed and effective propaganda effort in both countries (by mid-1967 some 121 Friends of Rhodesia groups had been formed and were operating in the United States). And, with South African financial and other assistance, it has blunted the economic effects of an international sanctions effort intended to bring the regime to heel. Whether or when Britain will agree to a compromise settlement in order to extricate itself from a humiliating situation of gross disparity between its responsibilities to the black population and its effective authority is now the question.

In South West Africa, a legal challenge to South African control over the former League of Nations mandate was removed by a decision of the World Court in July 1966. According to the plaintiffs, Ethiopia and Liberia, South Africa had contravened its obligation under the original mandate "to ensure the welfare and progress of the inhabitants of the territory" by its application of discriminatory racial laws. But the decision of the Court, handed down after six years of litigation, unexpectedly side-stepped the substantive issues and in effect favored South Africa. Legal efforts having failed, the independent African states thereupon turned to the political organs of the United Nations for remedy. In October 1966 the General Assembly voided South Africa's authority over the territory and took preliminary steps to establish international administration over the territory. To date, however, in the face of South African resistance, these actions have not been of practical effect. In South Africa itself, the power center and keystone of the Redoubt, an increasingly severe and effective program of political engineering—of comprehensive legal, police, economic, and other measures—has pulverized nationalist political activity and benumbed the nonwhite population. Its economy, nourished by its massive gold output, has continued to thrive, providing ample resources for a full apparatus of repression. All in all, the government is more firmly in control than ever before and racial oppression has become worse, not better.

Throughout the Redoubt, not only have the individual white minority governments strengthened their positions but there are growing indications of developing coordination and joint action among them. The flow of South African assistance to Portugal and Rhodesia in the form of equipment and advisory personnel has increased. Diplomatic and economic consultations are more frequent, meetings to exchange information and coordinate police and military actions are regularly held, and exploratory discussions have been undertaken on the possible creation of a permanent Southern Africa Economic Community.

Nor, it would appear, have even the stars been neutral. An international monetary crisis and gold shortage, an immobilizing economic crisis in Britain, a major oil discovery off the coast of the Portuguese enclave of Cabinda, the growing preoccupation of the United States with Asian and domestic problems and a consequent mood of withdrawal from further foreign commitments, the preoccupation of China with its "cultural revolution" and of the Soviet Union with fractiousness in Eastern Europe, the spreading preoccupation of the new African states with their own internal problems—all these and other coincidences have choked off or deflected many pressures for change with which the regimes of the Redoubt might otherwise have had to contend.

Under the impact of these events, the African nationalist movements have tended to splinter, and the morale of many supporters of their cause has begun to wilt. In contrast, the hopes and self-confidence of the white regimes, especially that of South Africa, have soared. In a radical policy shift from the defensive, it has now begun to offer diplomatic courtesies, trade agreements, investment, and economic and technical assistance to the nearby states of Botswana, Lesotho, Swaziland, and Malawi—aid which they in their extreme need and lack of alternatives have accepted. Zambia, the Congo, and perhaps others farther north are not beyond South Africa's possible range of targets.

One could find in such developments between the Redoubt and

the adjacent black states grounds for hope for some kind of accommodation, some easing of tensions and lessening of the likelihood of upheaval, if it were part of an evolutionary political adjustment within the states of the Redoubt itself. But it is a tactical shift, a counteroffensive to insulate and preserve the existing oppression. Hence it offers no prospect of stabilizing the area. Indeed, if South African power begins to penetrate more widely throughout Central and Southern Africa, it will only create further tensions, fear, and disequilibrium.

As a result of all that has happened in recent years, a crucial change in attitudes on both sides of the color line has now occurred. The whites, partly in fear and partly in overconfidence as a result of the apparent effectiveness of their recent measures, have turned away from compromise and internal political concessions and have put their hopes in intransigence, in the reenforcement of their capacity to maintain control. The blacks, on the other hand, have been driven to abandon hope that constructive political action can improve their condition. What little political contact and communication formerly existed have been broken; both sides have now come essentially to rely on physical force. Within the Redoubt, measures of white repression have been intensified to the point where open black opposition has meanwhile become almost impossible. But, around the borders, where blacks can obtain some outside help and can operate from sanctuaries in black-governed territory, the evidence of the turn to violence is clear. Angolan and Mozambican nationalist forces, though heavily opposed, are expanding their efforts, improving their tactics, equipment, and discipline, and imposing progressively heavier costs on Portugal to suppress their activities. Border incursions into Rhodesia are increasingly frequent, and the guerrilla groups are slowly becoming better organized. Casualty rates, though still small, are creeping upward. To cope with the incursions, Rhodesia has had to employ the most modern equipment, from trained dogs to helicopters and highly mobile armored vehicles, and has had to call on South Africa not only for financing and matériel but also for personnel to strengthen its border forces. As the defensive forces improve, so do the weapons and training of Rhodesian nationalist guerrillas—now provided variously by the Soviet Union, China, Algeria, and in limited degree Cuba and North Viet Nam. As the fire of violence burns ever more brightly, it consumes more and more of the few remaining possibilities of any political dialogue.

Southern Africa is a tragic commentary on the inability of the world in the late twentieth century to reconcile political ideals with political practices, and to reconcile the sovereign rights of individual nation-states with international goals and responsibilities. It is also testimony to the inability of the present international system to bring about evolutionary political change in a situation of impending conflict.

The situation remains inherently unstable and constitutes one of the great latent crises of the world. The seeming solidification of white resistance to black political advance in recent years has merely altered the timetable of coming political change. It has not dissipated the relentless and explosive underlying forces. If and when the explosion occurs, which could be soon or late, the emotions of people throughout the world will be aroused and many nations, including the great powers, will almost certainly become involved.

The Tempo of Change in Independent Black Africa

Conditions in newly independent Africa north of the Battleline are no less unstable and tense—though for totally different reasons—than in the white-controlled areas of the south. In the late 1950s and early 1960s, the new-born African states took their place in the world in an atmosphere of excitement and exuberance. For both the brown and the black people of the huge continent the ending of colonial status after decades and in some cases centuries of subjugation was an event of profoundly felt emotional and spiritual importance. A large part of a vast continent had been reborn, and it began as the young fortunately do, not in cynicism, despair, or hostility but in hope and idealism. Yet, within a decade, a striking reversal of expectations and mood has occurred.

Once Africans began to cope with their own tasks of development after independence, illusions of instant progress vanished. The intractability of age-old factors such as poor soil, obsolete forms of production, unskilled labor, inadequate infrastructure, and lack of capital quickly came to be understood in all its sobering reality. Lifting the heavy hand of colonial political control did not of itself release any new surge of productive energy or transform the inert elements in the unproductive African economic formula. Nor did expectations that new technology and new economic doctrines of development would enable Africa to leapfrog the intermediate stages of development prove to have much substance.

Under the pressure of necessity, an important sorting out of priorities and a refinement of ideas for development have consequently occurred. Earlier objectives of large-scale industrial development have been subordinated to stressing the development of agriculture and the improvement of rural community life. In education, earlier emphasis on university development and on mass literacy programs has shifted to greater recognition of the need for selective technical training and improvement of skills relevant to economic production.

Far more than they were just a few years ago, Africans are now also aware of the relatively limited aid they can expect from abroad and the tremendous impediment to their development imposed by the working of the international trading system. The so-called Decade of Development launched by the United Nations in 1961 has turned into a Decade of Disappointment. Economic progress is lagging while public expectations are still running far ahead of anything governments can reasonably hope to provide. As a result, the reactions of the new African governments to the aid and trade policies of the great powers have begun to shift and split. Some of these governments have begun to cling with a new tenacity to their principal sources of external assistance. Some have come to demand increased foreign aid with a new urgency. All attach greater importance than before to changes in the international trading system to improve and stabilize the prices of their products and to expand their export markets. And some, believing that hopes for trade reforms and adequate and sustained foreign assistance are vain, have come to place new emphasis on policies of belt-tightening and self-reliance. Concern and confusion have replaced the earlier bright hopes for development.

The political changes that have taken place since independence are equally striking. A decade ago, there was general awareness of linguistic, religious, and ethnic divisions within the new states, as well as recognition that the bizarre boundary lines colonialism bequeathed to Africa could breed trouble: Some states were so tiny they might never be viable, and others were so huge, diverse, and invertebrate that they might never be manageable as single entities. Nevertheless, it was optimistically assumed that, once alien hegemony was broken, methods and institutions for ensuring the unity and political viability of the new states could readily be devised. The leaders, most of whom had been imbued through education and experience with Western political concepts, were predisposed to seek political development within the familiar framework of democracy and parliamentary government.

But the unworkability of Western political institutions as they had been grafted on the new African states became quickly apparent. The interplay of political forces tended to follow older tribal lines rather than the new political frameworks, and the political methods employed by opposition forces commonly reflected the habits of negativism and violence developed in the course of the struggle against colonial authority. In a number of instances, secessionist tendencies came to the surface, and, in many others, factionalism grievously interfered with the unity necessary for development. As a consequence, the one-party state soon emerged as a typical African political pattern, replacing the inherited Western European constitutional forms. To a great extent it was a pragmatic response to urgent needs for stability and development. It was also a manifestation of the ongoing search for new, indigenous political forms which could accomodate the values and habits of African culture and tradition and at the same time satisfy the principles of legitimate and representative government.

However, the one-party state in Africa has increasingly been unable to fulfill the multiple tasks imposed upon it. Problems of inflation, unemployment, youthful discontent, and swelling public demands for immediate material improvement in conditions of life have proved overwhelming in a growing number of cases. In the face of such pressures, military elements as the single best organized and most powerful factor have tended to move in—or be drawn in—to deal with crisis conditions in country after country. These new regimes have often represented an improvement in competence, honesty, and patriotism over those they displaced. But, like the one-party governments they succeeded, the military regimes represent little more than a desperate effort to deal with a desperate problem. They are at best an interim and stop-gap arrangement; they are not a solution.

Thus, throughout Africa the quest for new political as well as economic concepts and forms goes on. In this respect, Africa has become one of the most fascinating of the world's laboratories experimenting with the new problems of nation-building. If not too many test-tubes explode, great discoveries may yet be made, but the prospect is not one of tranquility.

Similarly, in their relations among themselves, the new African states have, in the brief span of a decade, passed through a rapid evolution from romanticism to quarrelsomeness to the first stages of practical cooperation. Through the years of agitation against colonialism, the many nationalist movements shared a feeling of fraternity, of racial brotherhood, of a common history of oppression and exploitation, and of attachment to Mother Africa. With independence, however, the new states quickly began to behave in the usual fashion of sovereign entities, and the misty dream of African unity began to dissipate. The past decade has revealed to Africans the great range of their own differences and the practical difficulties of achieving common action. In principle, all subscribe to Pan-Africanism, but, in the first years after independence, the term quickly came to be a focus of organized and intense division rather than of cooperation. Some saw it as a mass movement, a revolutionary force directed to the creation of a centralized, unitary, continental political structure and a radical transformation of African society and political and economic relationships. Others saw it simply as an instrument for cooperation among sovereign states and for the coordination of efforts on behalf of commonly adopted objectives. The emotions aroused by the Algerian war and the successive Congo crises after 1960 intensified divisions between the so-called radical and moderate groups of African states and created the impression that Africa had generally become a scene of ideological confrontation in the cold war.

By 1963, however, it was possible for the clashing elements to join in creating an Organization of African Unity (OAU), founded on the principle of noninterference in each other's affairs and dedicated to modest and practical goals of interstate cooperation. Slowly the scars of the earlier disputes have healed, and the new organization has gradually begun to increase its effectiveness. It has been able to act as mediator in some intra-African disputes and, to a limited extent, as a vehicle for common action in dealing with problems of liberation in the south, for example. Reflecting the growing spirit of cooperation, a number of carefully planned and solidly grounded projects in functional areas have been launched, such as the African Development Bank and the Organization of Senegal River States. Moderation and practicality seem to have prevailed, even though to some Africans the evolution of Pan-Africanism in these directions signifies the decline or demise of a great revolutionary hope of continental and world transformation.

But one fact is unmistakably clear: Although immense changes of many kinds have already occurred in Africa, they are only the beginning. In the south, the center and the north, the continent is filled with strains, tensions, and problems, many of which are by-products of progress but some of which are potentially ugly and dangerous. This is the new Africa with which the great powers must cope and to which they are called upon to respond.

THE IMPACT OF AFRICAN EMERGENCE UPON THE WORLD POWERS

For the great powers, events in Africa to date have already required many adjustments of policies and attitudes. In the future, further and probably continuous adaptation to changing African realities will be necessary. An intricate and ongoing process of action and reaction is under way, the full implications of which are only beginning to be realized.

The immediate impact of African independence on the major external powers varied greatly, of course, depending largely on the nature and extent of their pre-independence relationships. For the Communist nations, the change, although it opened tempting political possibilities, did not disrupt old economic or other ties of any consequence since they had not been part of Africa's colonial past. Until well after the Second World War, Africa was virtually unknown to the Communist powers, and their perceptions of Africa were not only obscured by ignorance, but also distorted by a set of outdated doctrinal concepts that required time and considerable experience to break down. The revisions of policy necessary to cope with changed circumstances in Africa have come during a period when many other great issues have had to be dealt with: a deepening and dangerous rift between the Soviet Union and China; developing polycentrism throughout the former Soviet bloc; rapid and costly changes in military and strategic requirements; growing internal problems in all the Communist countries; and a shifting configuration of relationships with Western Europe.

For the United States as well, the new Africa has presented baffling problems of adapting policies, priorities, and methods to the new circumstances. Africa was only slightly known and indifferently regarded by Americans until the 1950s. Since then, the United States attempted to accommodate Africa directly into its international policies while preoccupied with relations with Western and Eastern Europe, Latin America, and above all Asia; with reshaping both strategic doctrine and foreign policies to fit the vast implications of nuclear weapons and advancing military technology; and with grave domestic issues of economic policy, urban development, and race relations.

Under the circumstances, the Soviet Union and the United States have moved to a certain extent along parallel courses: Both discovered Africa at about the same time; both developed their diplomatic apparatus there in step with advancing independence; both entered this new area of foreign activity with initial enthusiasm and stimulated in part by anxiety about the conduct of the other; both have had somewhat disappointing experience with the results of their initial policies and programs. After major confrontations in the Congo, both have adopted a somewhat more reserved and restrained posture; and for the future the probable course of action of both, as well as the degree of their involvement on the African continent, remains uncertain. Not only is it unclear whether the cold war may again make Africa one of its active arenas of conflict but also whether, quite apart from American involvement, the Soviet Union and China may find in Africa an area of particularly active competition, if not confrontation.

Still, for both the United States and the Communist powers, adjustment to the new circumstances of Africa has been one of their lesser concerns and preoccupations. For the major nations of Western Europe, by contrast, the changes have constituted a major upheaval. The African empires of Britain, France, and Belgium had become entwined over the years in national habits, viewpoints, and institutions, and occupied an important place in all policies and plans. Whatever practical military or economic significance the colonies may have had for the metropoles at various times, they also had important political and psychological consequences; and the task of disentangling these accumulated and interconnected ties has been difficult and painful. Moreover, old relationships have had to be severed and new ones created at a time when the European nations themselves were experiencing great difficulty in their own domestic, economic, and political life and a revolution in their relationships with one another and with the world at large.

This most recent exit or retirement of Western Europe from Africa is not the first such occasion in history. The amazing irrigation systems and fortifications still to be found throughout the desert regions of North Africa, for example, testify to the antiquity and the persistence of the European presence there. Over the centuries, however, that presence had generally been limited to certain portions of the periphery. Only in the last hundred years had Europe undertaken to cover the totality of the huge continent with its political control. Consequently, decolonization and withdrawal this time involved disruptions of unprecedented magnitude.

Why the nations of Western Europe were led to establish such sweeping hegemony is likely to remain a matter of mystery and debate. For centuries they regarded Africa as a region of secondary trading interest, and their colonizing efforts were focused on the Americas and the East, not Africa. As late as the mid-nineteenth century, the European mood toward African colonies in particular was one of skepticism, if not indifference. True, the Portuguese had laid claim to large but indistinct regions in the south of the continent; the Dutch settlers had begun to push inland from their trading station at the southern tip, Capetown; and the French had occupied areas on the Mediterranean shore. But the predominant European view was that African colonies in both economic and strategic terms were not likely to be worth their cost.

Yet strangely enough, in the latter part of the nineteenth century these same nations engaged in a frenzied effort to lay claim to all of Africa. On the plausible theory that colonialism must have been in someone's interest else it would not have occurred, a succession of scholars have attempted to explain the European expansion on grounds of economic gain or strategic needs. Economists have argued that Europe required African colonies to provide an outlet for surplus investment funds, to assure markets for manufactured goods, and to control sources of low-priced raw materials. A generation of European naval and military theorists argued the high strategic value to Europe of such regions as the North African Mediterranean shore and the Horn, as well as the sea passages around the Cape and through the Suez Canal. Another line of argument has held that humanitarian and religious considerations—the desire to suppress the slave trade and to bring Christianity and education to the natives—played a powerful role, especially in the case of Britain. But it remains highly questionable whether objective economic or strategic reasons or humanitarian impulses were in fact decisive at the time in precipitating the "scramble for Africa." More probably the phenomenon was the resultant of a great many components linked to the deepest and oldest characteristics of Western civilization. The European countries long manifested an unrivaled vitality and dynamism, as well as a deadly competitiveness. From antiquity, they were locked in struggle with one another; and by the

fifteenth century, these conflicts began to be projected beyond
Europe itself to new areas of the earth then being discovered and
explored by their daring sea captains and soldiers. Vast areas were
seized and colonized and the indigenous populations subjected to
European political authority.

Thereafter, having displaced the local rulers, the Europeans
turned to the game of displacing one another. The English and
the French thus took over great portions of the Spanish claims in
the Americas. The Dutch displaced the Portuguese from most of
their possessions in the Far East in the late sixteenth century. The
British and the French followed the Dutch to that part of the
world, Britain with more perseverance and determination than the
French, as a result of which it won India, the greatest prize of all.
When the quest for colonies went out of fashion for a time in
the early nineteenth century, partly as a result of the revolutions
which had shaken Europe and given impetus to new social and
political ideas, a very old habit of thinking was interrupted; and
it was not too surprising therefore that after 1870 a wave of
Western imperialism surged out once again upon the world. Africa,
its new object, suddenly and dramatically became the theater of
the resurgent European suspicions of one another and their deadly
competition.

Each found in the situation its own reasons to enter the fray.
Britain had been content not to try to extend its colonial holdings
as long as its general commercial and strategic position was considered to be secure. But once its virtual monopoly of trade in
Africa was threatened by other Europeans (and when these traders
sometimes became settlers and investors), Britain became fero-
ciously imperialist once again. In France, especially after the
Franco-Prussian War, it came to be considered essential to French
honor and status as a world power that France lay claim to vast
tracts of Africa, however valueless from a purely economic point
of view those territories might be. In Germany, despite the initial
clarity of Bismark's European priorities in the inter-European
struggle for power, growing pressures of public opinion encouraged
and inflamed by the ambitions of Wilhelm II drew it into the
strange and costly contest. Belgium got in almost by accident, as
a result of the personal ambitions of an energetic and headstrong
monarch. Italy, because its energies were largely consumed in the
struggle for national unification, entered late; but it too managed
to snatch a few last unclaimed crumbs from the African table.

A passage from the biography of Lord Salisbury, British Prime

Minister during the time of the partition of Africa, describes well
some of the noneconomic and nonmilitary elements which were
involved:

> The closing years of the nineteenth century were marked by an
> advance of the white races upon the continent of Africa which, in
> its circumstance, was a unique phenomenon in history. . . . This
> invasion was the product of forces over which Governments have
> little control and which it is not easy to identify. . . . Two phe-
> nomena . . . may be suggested. . . . One was the passion for adven-
> ture [which] expressed itself in the cosmopolitan stream . . . which
> . . . flowed continuously into and through Africa—a flow in which
> scores of men . . . risked, and in the majority of instances, ulti-
> mately sacrificed their lives to the ardour of discovery. . . . The other
> phenomenon was the slave-raiding horror which the reports of
> Livingstone and his contemporaries in the '60s and '70s first made
> vivid to the Christian public. Cynical commentators have doubted
> the genuineness and extent of the revolt of conscience which was
> roused by this revelation of preventable human agony on a vast
> scale. But its reality was witnessed to by the stubbornness of resolve
> which it engendered. . . . A multiplicity of individual motives,
> mingled of every shade of selfishness and altruism, were combined
> in the culminating initiation of the onrush;—the urge of trade, the
> ardour of evangelization, the love of gain, the pride of empire, the
> conscious trusteeship of civilization, the jealousies of patriotism.[1]

It is to be expected that after the event, scholars should seek
to factor out the rational elements underlying colonial expansion.
But the irrational aspects are quite possibly of equal importance:
romantic visions of grandeur and national glory, the intoxication
of vast projects to ambitious or visionary leaders, and not least
the psychological dynamics of the competitive process itself—the
impulse to enter a competition simply because others have entered
and because of the fear of unknown consequences if one does not.
Because it was believed that prestige and world position were
essential to national power, it came to be believed in Europe, at
least for a time, that colonies were an essential ingredient of a
nation's vital interest. Each nation then rationalized and justified
its conduct in its own terms, erected its own mythology of empire,
adorned it with its own particular vanities and baubles (usually
military), and manufactured its own pantheon of heroes. Like
some other phenomena of history, it may have been basically an
enormous "happening" in the sense that it was born of illusion,
misinformation, emotional impulse, or simply the fear of not

doing it, thereby setting in motion a process which the sluggish and imperfect machinery of politics was subsequently unable to check before it had run its headlong course.

The first years of the twentieth century, in John Strachey's arresting phrase, "glittered with the apparent splendor of colonial empires and clanked with their accoutrements." Superficially, in those years, and even until the Second World War, it might have appeared that imperialism was still in its heyday. When after the First World War the Austro-Hungarian and the Ottoman empires were demolished, foreign control over the pieces located in what is now called the Third World did not end, but only changed hands. Britain took over most of the colonies which Germany had formerly controlled, plus a major part of the Arabian domains of the Ottoman Empire. France, too, collected additional holdings. Later, before and during the Second World War, imperialism seemed to regain momentum with the expansionist drives of Germany and Japan, which seized control over great areas of Europe, most of China, and much of Southeast Asia.

But there is other and important evidence to suggest that by the turn of the century the passion and enthusiasm for empire in general and African empires in particular had subsided and that it thereafter steadily declined. In part this may have been merely a consequence of the fact that after the Conference of Berlin in 1885 not much remained in Africa to be acquired. More important, the new African colonies, which had been taken in great excitement and expectation, increasingly demonstrated that either their profitability had been overestimated or the benefits could be obtained only after long effort and heavy investment.

At the same time, less visible but more important changes were occurring, in the metropoles, that in the longer run would undermine the substructure of colonialism, including its domestic base of political support. At the conclusion of World War I the peacemaking process itself and President Wilson's Fourteen Points gave circulation to a new political vocabulary which both reflected changing social forces and political concepts in Europe and added impetus to forces of colonial resistance to imperialism just beginning to appear in the various parts of the world, particularly India. The Russian Revolution of 1917 resulted in the first major anticapitalist regime to appear on the world scene, which nationalists in the colonial areas viewed also as an anti-imperialist factor. The establishment of the League of Nations and its mandate system embodied for the first time the idea of international responsibility for the well-being of subject peoples. Anticolonial democratic pressures grew, and the heady dreams of empire that had had such appeal to Europeans in the late nineteenth century came to seem in the postwar atmosphere not only unreal but increasingly sordid.

During the 1920s and 1930s these various forces were at work both in the European metropoles and in the overseas territories. The economic distress of the times strengthened the political forces of labor and the Left and their spokesmen, both in Britain and in France, called for increased economic and social development of the colonies and greater concern for the well-being of their inhabitants. During this same period the world Communist movement began its first probings, largely through the Western European parties, into Africa and began to develop rudimentary ties with African nationalist groups and individual leaders.

Yet, as always, the tendencies were inconsistent and contradictory. Thus, when in 1929 Britain promised India eventual dominion status, fundamental stimulus was given to the hopes of nationalist elements throughout the colonial world. But during the same years, Mussolini's Italy was still pursuing the florid dreams of empire and grandeur which had been the fashion in Europe forty years before. In the invasion and conquest of Ethiopia in 1935 Italy avenged its "national honor" for the defeat inflicted by the Ethiopians in 1896 at Adowa and achieved a shoddy military triumph of the same sort that other European nations had gained elsewhere in Africa in the previous century. The measure of the change in political outlook was the fact that much of Europe looked upon the Italian action not with envy or admiration but with contempt.

By the outbreak of the Second World War, the forces in Europe opposed to colonialism, though growing, had not nearly reached the point where the metropoles would be prepared voluntarily to relinquish their control. But, by war's end, opposition to the system had become markedly more powerful. Socialist and labor elements with their anticolonialist convictions took power in Britain and exercised a major political influence in France. The United Nations, born in a spirit of dedication to human rights and international equality, adopted a trusteeship concept that went far beyond the old mandates system of the League of Nations. Within the colonial areas, nationalist sentiment, which had been scattered and weak, became vocal and well organized, particularly in South Asia, the Middle East, and North Africa. The Soviet Union, which had been little more than a vague anti-imperialist presence in

world affairs after the First World War, emerged greatly strengthened after the Second, and its encouragement of nationalist
elements in the Western European colonial territories thereby
became far more influential.

The factor of decisive importance, however, was that Europe
found itself after the Second World War so exhausted both
physically and spiritually that its own capacity to maintain control
was finally destroyed. The end of colonialism had irrevocably
begun. The patterns by which the European metropoles relinquished their imperial position were varied, just as their attitudes
toward, and concepts of, administration in their colonies had always
varied. Since independence, they have followed their own distinctive policies—in the extent to which they have attempted to
maintain political influence over the former colonies, their willingness to contribute to economic development, and their sense of
responsibility for African military security. Today, these varied
European attitudes and policies have produced contrasting results
and rather different prospects for British, French, and Belgian
relationships in the African continent, being in some respects far
better and in others far worse than might have been expected at
the time colonial control was removed.

The pattern of these differences now must be traced in greater
detail as a basis for understanding the likely future relationship
between Western Europe and Africa, two areas condemned or
privileged by geographical contiguity and much shared history
to be permanently of special importance to one another.

2

Britain's Decolonization and Post-Independence Relations

The transformation of Great Britain's colonial relationships in the years since 1945 has been but one aspect of the agony of that once pre-eminent imperial power to adjust to the consequences of the Second World War. The simple arithmetic of the changes in Africa alone suggests the scale of what has taken place: All its former territories with only one exception have achieved sovereign status, becoming fifteen new nations embracing three million square miles of land and 127 million inhabitants.

Not only have these changes had radical impact on the African areas themselves, but Africa's place in Britain's priorities and policies is now substantially altered. In the last quarter-century, Britain has been a besieged nation, confronted on every hand with the need for a fundamental revision of both its domestic and foreign policies. It would be difficult even at this point to say whether Britain has yet succeeded in finding a new basis on which to rebuild its domestic economic strength or in defining a new international role for itself compatible with the realities of its present capacities and interests. Given these formidable problems, perhaps the most remarkable quality of the changing relationship with Africa has been that Britain has responded to the necessities imposed upon it with a certain grace and decency and has, in the face of repeated disappointments and growing handicaps, attempted to fulfill its responsibilities to ease the difficult transition of the former colonies to independence and self-sufficiency. And yet, despite the bloodless, almost amicable process of British decolonization and the constructive cast of post-colonial policy, the general weakness of Britain's position plus some unfortunate blunders have resulted in an undue decline of its prestige and influence in Africa.

Superficially, Britain emerged from the Second World War apparently still one of the world's great powers, with its far-flung empire intact, and confident of the future. But beneath the appearances lay some ominous economic facts. Britain had had to dispose of a quarter of its overseas assets to finance the war effort. It had lost much of its merchant shipping fleet. Exports had dropped to about half of their prewar level. A vast debt had accumulated. The industrial plant had become obsolescent and inefficient. After years of wartime sacrifice and shortages, the population was both fatigued and discontented.

The first manifestation of the deep changes which war had wrought took abrupt political form. With the defeat of Germany in the spring of 1945, a general election was called. To the disbelief of Churchill himself and to the amazement of many in the United States, Labor won a clear victory by taking 390 seats in the Commons to 195 for the Conservatives, and a Socialist government was given power.

The new Labor government under Prime Minister Clement Attlee then undertook the ambitious task of trying simultaneously to rehabilitate the economy, extend the benefits of a welfare state, and fulfill the economic and strategic responsibilities of a global power. But within a year, by a combination of the consequences of its own actions and a series of unfortunate circumstances, Britain was faced with a major financial crisis from which it extricated itself only with the help of a large American credit. The winter of 1947 was the coldest in forty years and, partly as a result, 1948 was a crucial year of industrial paralysis and economic distress. To shore up the economy strict austerity was imposed, which the British public endured but not without grumbling, especially in view of substantial outlays for the Berlin airlift and for British troops stationed abroad.

With the advent of the Marshall Plan in 1948, Britain, along with the rest of Europe, received a major infusion of financial resources which not only relieved the foreign exchange position and assisted economic recovery but also enabled Britain to maintain the appurtenances of a contemporary world power—namely, a major aircraft industry, nuclear armament, and a network of strategic bases in Europe and in the Middle and Far East. Amidst all the difficulties, the horizons of British policy and outlook still encircled the world. The involvement with the Commonwealth was still considered a primary responsibility, and, even in the early 1950s, the idea of British entry into the Common Market still seemed to most Britons an unwise and unacceptable retreat from a world-wide to a regional framework of policy.

But economic pressures increased inexorably. In September of 1949, Britain was driven to a major devaluation of 30.5 per cent of the pound. In 1951 Britain faced another sterling crisis. By 1955, because exports and imports continued in serious imbalance, rumors began to spread once again of a new devaluation. Speculative movements again endangered sterling in 1957. Four years later, the British balance-of-payments situation provoked another crisis of confidence. In 1964 the British trade deficit reached new record levels. Repeatedly, Britain was obliged to borrow heavily from the International Monetary Fund, the U.S. Export-Import Bank, Swiss banks, and other central banks to stave off disaster. Steadily Britain fell further and further behind the dynamic development of Germany, France, and later Italy; for the decade 1950-60 the annual growth of British output averaged only 2.6 per cent, the lowest of any of the developed Western nations.[1] In the face of persistent economic distress, Britain became preoccupied with internal problems of productivity and poverty and, in turn, the managerial and structural weaknesses of the economy. Indeed, as the 1960s wore on, many Englishmen began to sense that their country was becoming the "poor man of Europe" and felt the economy to be in such a precarious state that it had to be spared every possible shock and strain. Finally in 1967 the second postwar devaluation of the pound occurred. Following that action, Mr. Harold Wilson's government, as part of a drastic effort to restore world confidence in British prospects, made changes in defense policy and imposed restrictive domestic economic measures of a kind which would have been unthinkable even a few years before.

These brutal economic facts and their internal political consequences form the context of the general evolution of British foreign policy in the post-World War II period. As regards decolonization specifically, economic weakness was one of the significant factors contributing to Britain's willingness to withdraw control from Africa, but other, equally influential forces were also involved.

Within the African colonies, the experiences and events of the

Second World War reinforced tendencies already moving them toward demands for independence. Nationalist movements became stronger and better organized, and their programs found greater interest and response on the part of the African populations. Along with the other European colonial powers, Britain became aware of a marked change of opinion regarding colonialism in many parts of the world. Britain's closest ally, the United States, was clearly opposed to the kind of colonialism then prevalent, a view which President Roosevelt had repeatedly expressed to British representatives even in the course of close wartime cooperation. The Soviet Union likewise took advantage of public and private opportunities to object to the colonial position of Britain and other Western countries. The signing of the Atlantic Charter, and after the war the birth of the United Nations and the glowing feeling with which delegates in 1945 at San Francisco supported its Declaration of Human Rights, gave clear warning to the Colonial Office of the anticolonial storms to come. Later in the 1950s, as the membership of the United Nations itself came to include a growing number of Afro-Asian states, the world organization became an additional source of anticolonial pressure.

Nor was the British public by any measure a solid bastion of support for colonialism. Powerful and vocal elements were actively opposed and Britain's capacity, even will, to withstand external anticolonial pressures was therefore weak and divided from the start. Although the wartime experience had not shattered and indeed in some respects had strengthened belief in the strategic importance of the colonies, conviction as to their economic value had largely disappeared. Statistical evidence did not support the argument that Britain through its colonies was able to obtain raw materials at advantageous prices or especially remunerative markets for manufactured goods. Although the colonial relationship produced benefits to particular British firms and investors, the over-all cost of the colonies to the Treasury had steadily risen over the years. Moreover, in the postwar years the old Hobsonian argument that Britain needed colonies as an outlet for excess capital lost all plausibility in the face of the huge needs of Britain itself for new social and economic investment. In brief, the economic rationale and underpinnings of the case for the colonies had been eaten away.

Similarly, the basis of political support within Britain for retention of the colonies, influenced in part by such economic facts, had been undercut. Labor came to power in 1945, bringing its long tradition of opposition to the idea of empire and of sympathy with the indigenous colonial populations. In its election manifesto, the party had called for self-government in the colonies; and a central aim of its policy was defined in 1948 by Arthur Creech-Jones, Secretary of State for the Colonies, as being "to guide the colonial territories to self-government within the Commonwealth and in conditions that insure to the people concerned both a fair standard of living and freedom from oppression from any quarter." The policies of the various postwar governments were also influenced in the direction of decolonization by the activities of an energetic and dedicated pro-African lobby in Britain with close connections among the Fabians and Labor party elements as well as among some of the younger Conservatives.

During these years, strong conviction in favor of maintaining the empire was limited to those with direct economic interests in the colonies, a few who had been connected with the military or the colonial civil service, and to some of the older and more right-wing Conservatives. However, Conservative-Labor differences on colonial questions, even in those years after the war when sharp clashes erupted in Parliament and in public discussions on many political issues, never reached the point of intransigence where workable compromises were impossible. Over time, the Conservative party fully accepted the inevitability if not the desirability of decolonization, and it was a Conservative Prime Minister, Macmillan, who in 1960 publicly recognized and implicitly sanctioned the "wind of change" in Africa. In fact, most of the British African territories which have achieved independence, have done so under Conservative governments.[2]

Thus, the fundamental fact about Britain's political attitude toward the colonies after World War II was that it was on the whole ready to get on with the task of cutting them loose. There were some dissenters and some determined defenders of empire, and traces of the imperialist mentality were still to be found as late as 1956, when a convulsive effort to turn back the tide of history led Britain to join France in an effort to reimpose control over Suez. But the record indicates that the evolution of India toward independence had been accepted even before the war; and afterward, as African nationalism grew, there was no real readiness to resist its pressure by serious military or other repressive effort.

This remarkable state of affairs was partly explainable perhaps by the fact that Britain had not been defeated or occupied in the

Second World War, and therefore the great adjustment of outlook required to dismantle the empire was not made additionally painful by general feelings of national humiliation. Neither were the forces in Britain receptive to decolonization sabotaged by resistance on the part of the military or the civil service. Unlike their counterparts in some other Western European countries, the military remained faithful to their national tradition and did not attempt to play a political role. Nor were British civil servants responsible for colonial administration obstructionism during the period of the transfer of power to the Africans. Indeed, some of the most prominent civil servants shared the views of African nationalists on the ends to be achieved and joined with them in effective cooperation on questions of means and timing.

Two other important aspects of the British colonial tradition facilitated evolutionary change in Africa: There were precedents for decolonization in the British experience; and the process was not handicapped by the existence of obstructive legal or constitutional conceptions.

The great diversity of the British Empire in this regard is worth recalling. As the empire grew after the seventeenth century and well into the twentieth, Britain's holdings were not only the most extensive in the world but by far the most diverse, ranging from Australia, Canada, and New Zealand on the one hand, to Tobago and Zanzibar on the other. At various times the empire included colonies, dominions, protectorates, protected states, trust territories, condominiums, and leased territories. Through the centuries and indeed until after the Second World War, Britain continued to acquire colonies and dependencies while at the same time relinquishing some, trading off others, and—after the early part of the nineteenth century—progressively granting autonomy, internal self-government, international status, and, in the end, full independence and sovereignty to its major dominions.

Britain's experience in decolonization began in 1776, in a well-known incident. As one repercussion of the successful American rebellion, unrest developed in Canada; and in 1837, Lord Durham, who had been sent from England to investigate the disturbances, reported that the only possible solution was to grant internal self-government. By 1859 Canada had been allowed to set up protective tariffs not only against foreign goods but against British manufactures. By 1911 the principle of decentralization of power within the British Empire had already been firmly established, when Prime Minister H. H. Asquith declared to the representatives of the dominions, "We each of us are, and we each of us intend to remain, masters in our own house." After the First World War the independent role of the dominions in international and foreign policy matters was increasingly accepted, and in 1931 the Statute of Westminster gave formal parliamentary ratification to the equal status of the dominions with Britain in the Commonwealth.

While the major colonies were thus progressing to full sovereignty, Britain, after the First World War, both acquired some new dependencies and divested itself of others. Egypt, which had been occupied since 1882 and had been a protectorate since 1914, was declared an independent kingdom in 1922; the mandate over Iraq was terminated in 1932; and in the Far East and elsewhere, Britain relinquished a number of smaller holdings. Thus, well before the Second World War, Britain was already an experienced practitioner of decolonization.

Moreover, the fundamental conception of the relationship between Britain and the colonies made disengagement when it had to be faced something less than an operation of amputation on the British body politic itself. Britain never contemplated the immediate or even the eventual incorporation of the colonies into the constitutional structure and political life of the British Isles themselves. The residents of the colonies were not conceded full British citizenship or political rights in Britain. From the beginning, the colonies were regarded as separate entities—and by implication, separable. Over the decades British policy made explicit the assumption of eventual separability either by permitting the incorporation of some colonies into other states or by granting their full independence in some instances. Thus, structural impediments and rigid legalism did not, as in the case of France, block the interplay of political forces in reaching compromises and flexible settlements in modifying constitutional arrangements.

In addition, the British tradition of political pragmatism helped assure that decolonization in Africa would be a process rather than a disjointed sequence of ruptures. Although Britain repeatedly resisted specific nationalist demands and persisted vigorously in all negotiations to protect its interests, the fact of essential importance was that these were incidents along the road of progress toward autonomy for the colonies.

THE PACE AND STYLE OF DECOLONIZATION

Almost as soon as the Second World War ended, the dismantling of the empire began in earnest. The mandates over Transjordan and Palestine in the Middle East were terminated in 1946 and 1948. In 1947 the colony which had been the centerpiece of the empire itself, India, became the independent states of India and Pakistan. In 1948 Ceylon achieved dominion status. India, though a republic, was able to remain in the fold of the Commonwealth by acknowledging the British sovereign as head of the association —thereby opening the way to eventual transformation of the Commonwealth from a small group of Dominions largely British and almost wholly European in origin and outlook to a multiracial collection of states with varying traditions and cultural back-grounds. Particularly with the change in India's status, every factor in the British colonial equation changed—political, strategic, and economic. Once begun, this new phase of decolonization further aroused the forces of nationalism throughout British Africa.

Even before the war began, the Colonial Office recognized that the African peoples would eventually participate in the affairs of government. But no one gave serious thought to any timetable. Nor was there any clarity as to what "political participation" might involve. It tended to be defined as cooperation or consulta-tion. Almost everyone assumed that the prospects for African self-rule were remote and that control would remain in British hands for a long period to come. But once India, Pakistan, and Ceylon became independent, British administrators urgently be-gan to consider guidelines for the decolonization of Africa and methods for controlling its pace.

In general they had in mind norms derived from the Asian experience. It was felt important that any area given independence have sufficient size, population, and resources to become econom-ically viable. There was consequently a desire to avoid casting im-poverished scraps of territory such as Zanzibar and the Gambia into sovereign status without affiliation to some larger unit. In the case of somewhat larger colonies, such as Kenya and Tanganyika, Britain hoped they could remain associated in economic groupings and arrangements for common administrative services. For similar reasons it favored the federation of the three major tribal regions of Nigeria—Yoruba, Hausa-Fulani, and Ibo—into a single entity, and federative arrangements in Somalia and in Central Africa.*

Politically, the intention was to gradually turn over power to qualified African politicians and administrators and to leave be-

* Some critics of British policy, especially the French, have called this tendency the "federalist subterfuge," seeing it simply as a device to strengthen British post-independence influence and control.

hind functioning institutions of representative government. There was also concern and consideration for the position of minority groups in the governmental structures created, including special concern for the rights and status of British white settlers.

The achievement of these rational and tidy objectives was to be accomplished through a sequence of steps toward self-government guided and controlled by the British Colonial Office. These stages would provide democratic experience in a series of carefully regulated doses for the indigenous populations and would develop the competence of African leaders in the actual procedures and responsibilities of governing. In general, constitutional progress was to pass through three stages:

First, direct rule by a Governor appointed by and responsible to the British Secretary of State for the Colonies. The Governor at some point would create a Legislative Council initially composed of a majority of civil servants and Europeans. Later it would be made up of persons elected rather than nominated. Still later, some Africans would be appointed or chosen on a basis other than popular election.

The second crucial step was the granting of what was called "representative government." At this stage, a majority of the members of the Legislative Council would be elected rather than appointed. The Africans could form political parties, and members of the Executive Council would be chosen from the ranks of the winning party. In time there would be elected majorities in both the executive and legislative councils and a Chief Minister in charge of government business. However, the three most important civil servants—the Chief Secretary, Finance Secretary, and Attorney General—would still be appointed. Fully responsible government was obtained only when these three posts were filled by native ministers.

The third and final phase would be independence itself. For this, the British Parliament would pass an enabling act, and the Crown would issue an Order-in-Council granting sovereignty.[3]

The system, in theory, gave the British government power to steer the process to its conclusion and had the practical advantage of providing an almost infinite number of devices with which to accelerate or retard the rate of political advance. It led to independence on a piecemeal basis, offered as a response to specific situations and as a means of solving particular problems.

However laudable the intentions of Britain may have been, the assumption on which the policy was founded proved to be faulty, namely, that Britain could or had the determination to control the new political forces which had been set in motion. By the late 1950s their momentum had already reached a point that compelled the British government to accept the futility of trying to check the onrush of events. It did not have money, men, or time enough to produce the requisite number of well-trained Africans to administer government and economic affairs. Nor did it have the will to use the force which would have been required to delay the final outcome. A succession of colonial secretaries accepted a more and more limited notion of the responsibilities of the British government in "preparing" the territories for self-government, and they readily gave way to the pressures for increased speed of decolonization. By the late 1960s, in granting independence to Basutoland, Bechuanaland, and the Gambia, Britain seemed very much like a government disposing almost gladly of some minor and rather pestiferous problems.

Speaking of the headlong quality of the final phase of the decolonizing process, one British critic has observed, perhaps too harshly: "Colonial policy in the 1960s has been a series of tactical maneuvers carried on in the absence of the necessary strategic framework. In short, Britain, in the rush to divest herself (rightly and properly) of empire, has sometimes seemed to abandon policy altogether."[4] The following is the actual timetable for decolonization which resulted in Africa:

	Date of Independence
Sudan	January 1, 1956
Ghana	March 6, 1957
Somalia (British section)	June 26, 1960
Nigeria	October 1, 1960
Sierra Leone	April 27, 1961
Cameroon (British section)	October 1, 1961
Tanzania	[April 26, 1964]
Tanganyika	December 9, 1961
Zanzibar	December 10, 1963
Uganda	October 9, 1962
Kenya	December 12, 1963
Malawi	July 6, 1964
Zambia	October 24, 1964
Gambia	February 18, 1965
Botswana (Bechuanaland)	September 30, 1966
Lesotho (Basutoland)	October 4, 1966
Ngwane (Swaziland)	September 6, 1968

By the end of 1968, all of Britain's former African territories had been decolonized except one, Rhodesia, which has unilaterally declared its independence but over which Britain still claims legal authority and responsibility.

Were it not for Rhodesia, one could speak of a virtually unique historical experience in the intelligent and orderly transfer of power by a strong nation to a group of its weaker possessions. Rhodesia, however, spoils the record. Before examining that distressing situation and its dark implications, it will be useful to review the evolution of post-colonial British relationships with the fifteen former African colonies that have, with Britain's assent, become independent.

Some Continuities

The achievement of independence by a former colony implies more of an abrupt separation from the metropole than in fact tends to be the case. A new constitutional framework as well as new symbols of nationhood are created. The design of its flag changes as well as the words of the national anthem and the name of the head of government. But a great deal does not change—at least not immediately. Perhaps nothing exemplifies more clearly this quality of continuity than the ties which still remain between Britain and its former colonies. Although its control in Africa endured for only a relatively brief period, the experience marked both parties in many ways, both subtle and profound, which continue to exercise their influence long after the formalities of political separation have been accomplished.

Among the most important continuing bonds is the English language, which remains the *lingua franca* of the former British colonies and their essential communications bridge in dealing with one another and the outside world. Since independence there has been perhaps some decline in the quality of spoken and written English in the African areas; and in Tanzania, Swahili has been elevated to equal status with English as the vehicle of instruction. But English remains largely the instrument and influence it was before.

Compared to France, Britain has been less active in promoting the use of English and in strengthening cultural relations in general with Africa. But British educational ties are still extensive: thousands of Africans continue to receive their higher education in the U.K. Most English-speaking African lawyers, doctors, professors, and military officers—the normal sources from which politicians are recruited—are still British-trained. Many British institutional forms and ways of doing things persist with only gradual modification. Administrative procedures in government offices, curricula and teaching methods in schools, legal procedures in many African courts, and most business and banking practices continue to reflect British tradition. Likewise, British influence over the flow of information to the former colonies remains strong, an important element of continuity in itself which also conditions the atmosphere within which other post-independence relationships—economic, military, and political—have functioned. The BBC provides extensive news materials and other services, including training for the personnel of the African broadcasting systems. British wire services are the source of much of the news printed in the daily papers. The book trade, including textbooks, is largely in British hands, and British periodicals circulate widely.

The continued presence of thousands of British citizens operating business firms throughout Africa, occupying key technical positions as expatriate employees in government services or teaching in secondary schools and universities is likewise a factor of great importance. Relationships between expatriates and Africans are not uniformly cordial, but on the whole a multitude of friendly ties still exists between individual Englishmen and the numerous British-trained Africans who have shared educational experiences or worked together in the past.

Monetary, Commercial, and Investment Relations

Another general area in which British ties have been relatively unaffected by the shift from colonialism to independence has been the economic. Like the other European metropoles, Britain brought into being a series of dependent economies in its African empire. In each colony the core of the modern sector was primary production for export, and British enterprises controlled the sources both of mineral output and, to a somewhat lesser degree, of agricultural products. British traders and investors enjoyed important privileges, and the trade linkage to metropole was reinforced by the establishment of British commercial firms throughout the colonies. The end result was that Britain absorbed a large proportion of their exports and was the dominant supplier of their imports. Trade and financial flows occurred within a framework of imperial and, later, Commonwealth tariff preferences and of monetary arrangements known as the Sterling Area, which was brought into being after Britain left the gold standard in 1931. The economic circuit thus created was not as closed and impregnable as that of the French empire, but it was sufficiently so in Africa as to have the practical effect of discouraging all but a few non-British traders and investors from entering the territories.

After the first decade of independence in Africa, the pattern of economic flows and the general framework of economic relationships between Britain and its former colonies are to a large extent still intact. But some changes have begun to occur which have important implications for the future.

The Sterling Area

The financial and monetary connection of the former African colonies with Britain is maintained through their cooperation with the Sterling Area and as a consequence of their continued reliance on British banking and financial institutions operating in Africa. In both aspects, however, the ties are loosening.

Upon becoming independent, all the English-speaking African states chose to remain within the Sterling Area, a kind of unstructured international financial club whose members believe it offers certain privileges but feel free to leave when their interests dictate. Although there is no written constitution, membership originally implied adherence to an explicit code of behavior. Its obligations included linking the external value of a member state's currency to sterling, maintaining balances in London for settling international transactions, and adhering to rules imposed by the United Kingdom on its own nationals for controlling transactions with other areas. In addition an important part of private assets were held in London, and foreign exchange transactions with countries outside the area were normally carried out through London.

Prior to 1939, the system did not constitute a menace to Great Britain's own currency reserves, which seemed more than ample by the standards of the time. After World War II, however, the weakness of the British balance-of-payments situation and successive devaluations of the British pound greatly weakened the internal discipline of the Sterling Area. The African member countries now tend to hold an even smaller proportion of their balances for settling international transactions in London. They adhere, but only selectively, to United Kingdom controls over transactions with other areas; and in November 1967, in response to the second postwar British devaluation, most of them took independent action in adjusting the value of their own currencies to sterling. In consequence, the obligations of membership in the system as it exists at present are becoming more diffuse as sterling declines in significance as an international currency.

The increasingly independent conduct of the former colonies in monetary matters is facilitated by the fact that in the post-independence period Britain has not attempted to retain decisive influence over their internal monetary and fiscal policies. All have their own currencies, which are controlled by their own central banks. Yet British financial influence continues to be felt since commercial banking tends to be concentrated in the hands of a small number of large British institutions operating an extensive system of branches. Such banking arrangements have served to anchor and perpetuate financial and commercial ties with Britain and also to reinforce the position of British commercial firms operating in Africa. However, the influence of the British banks is also in process of dilution partly because of the growing presence of American and other non-British financial institutions, partly because of increasingly stringent restrictions upon all foreign banks imposed by the new African states and in one case at least, Tanzania, by the nationalization of foreign banks.

It is possible that the Sterling Area may be greatly modified in the future as the entire structure of international monetary arrangements is adjusted to new requirements. So long as it endures on its present basis, the African members, for want of a better alternative, are likely to remain within it though they may follow increasingly separate courses of action. Similarly, the influence of British financial institutions will not end abruptly but will probably continue to decline as non-British banks extend their activities and as African financial institutions themselves slowly grow in strength and number. A further factor contributory to a dilution of dependence on Britain are the activities of the International Monetary Fund and the World Bank, which provide both resources and advice formerly provided by the United Kingdom. In time, the monetary and financial relationships inherited from the colonial period are destined to disappear or to evolve into some quite different system. But as of now, a decade after independence, much of the earlier structure persists although important changes are beginning to be visible.

Trade

Trade relations between Britain and the former African colonies at the end of the first post-independence decade are also largely

unaltered. The former colonies remain within the Commonwealth, with its structure of tariff preferences. The list of products
they export is largely unchanged as is the pattern of their imports.
Added to the continuity of these fundamental factors has been
the influence of commercial and financial habit: Transactions continue to move in accustomed channels, and buyers and sellers as
well as borrowers and lenders continue to deal with familiar firms.

The significance of the African market to Britain and also some
of the emergent problems are suggested by Table 1, which indicates the totals of British exports and imports with the various
areas since 1963. Africa over-all, excluding the U.A.R. and South

TABLE 1. United Kingdom Trade, Total and with Africa, 1963–67

(In millions of U.S. dollars)

	1963	1964	1965	1966	1967
Exports					
World total	11,855	12,342	16,711	14,662	14,390
To Africa[a]	852	873	941	899	866
Algeria	8	19	20	9	9
Libya	44	50	62	82	64
Morocco	15	15	13	15	19
Rhodesia	114	114	89	8	3
Sudan	80	57	47	46	49
Tunisia	8	10	11	8	5
Tropical Africa[b]	583	608	699	731	717
South Africa	560.4	637.3	749.2	694.2	726
Imports					
World total	13,497	15,437	16,138	16,672	17,744
From Africa[a]	1,059	1,140	1,417	1,328	1,216
Algeria	21	24	50	64	42
Libya	119	178	207	171	182
Morocco	29	29	32	32	34
Rhodesia	274	282	84	13	—
Sudan	34	24	22	14	18
Tunisia	8	8	9	11	7
Tropical Africa[b]	574	595	1,007	1,023	933
South Africa	376.4	421.5	584.2	634.2	693

[a] Excluding U.A.R. and South Africa.
[b] Including Malawi and Zambia.

SOURCE: IMF/IBRD, *Direction of Trade*, various issues.

Africa, absorbs 6 per cent of Britain's exports and is the source of 8 per cent of its imports. The continent thus constitutes a secondary but still significant trading area for a nation which is in economic difficulty, which lives by trade, and for which it is vital to hold all present markets while it fights severe international competition for new ones.

British trade with Africa has grown in recent years but not as rapidly as that with the industrialized countries, which, of course, is consistent with world-wide trends of trade among developed and underdeveloped areas. For example, British trade between 1958 and 1966 with other developed countries rose 75 per cent in volume, but its trade with the less developed areas in the same period increased only 9 per cent. Three of the trends of trade with Africa reflected in Table 1 deserve special note:

1. Trade with South Africa has grown vigorously in recent years. That country alone now constitutes a market for British exports as large as all of Tropical Africa, and preliminary figures for 1967 indicate that it had become Britain's second largest export market for the period.
2. Direct trade with Rhodesia, once quite significant in volume, has been almost entirely choked off as a result of the sanctions program imposed in an attempt to bring the colony's rebellious regime to heel.
3. Trade with Tropical Africa has not been stagnant. The rate of increase of British exports has been moderately strong and that of imports from Tropical Africa somewhat more so.

These trends have rather contradictory implications for the difficult political and economic choices Britain must make relating to or affecting Africa in the period ahead. In Southern Africa sanctions against Rhodesia as well as the arms embargo imposed on South Africa because of its racial policies have recently come under strong attack within Britain as general economic difficulties have mounted. Opponents of the sanctions against Rhodesia have argued that they have proven ineffective in accomplishing their political purpose and have mainly had the effect of destroying a small but lucrative export market which Britain once dominated. Critics of the arms embargo on South Africa similarly contend that Britain is failing to accomplish any political result while jeopardizing an extremely important and remunerative outlet for British goods. Those in Britain who have felt that political considerations should take precedence over economic in these two situations have so far prevailed; but the opposition to their views remains strong and, if the position of the British pound does not improve, could become even stronger.

With respect to the maintenance of the Commonwealth trading system, Britain likewise faces difficult choices. As members of the Commonwealth, the former African colonies have a privileged position of access to the British market where their exports enjoy tariff preferences. Nor has Britain to any degree resorted to quantitative restrictions to discriminate against the products of principal interest to the African members. The Commonwealth therefore, even though the value of its preferences has been somewhat reduced in recent years, still has economic meaning and involves British commitments. Out of respect for these, Britain, in the negotiations for entry into the European Common Market, has insisted that they be taken into consideration and appropriate adjustments made. If and when the point is reached where British membership is agreed to by the Six, some compromise will have to be made between the divergent requirements of the Commonwealth and of the Common Market. To what extent Britain will then find it in its interest to attempt to protect various Commonwealth trade arrangements remains to be seen. The proportion of Britain's total trade with the Commonwealth in recent years has been in steady decline while trade with the Common Market countries and with those of the European Free Trade Association (EFTA) has been rising, and trade with the latter two groups now exceeds that with the Commonwealth. At the same time, the older countries in the Commonwealth, such as Canada, Australia, and New Zealand, are taking an increasingly practical view of their commercial relationships with Britain. In Canada, antidumping duties and surcharges have discouraged British exporters. In Australia, increased tariff levels have had the same effect. All around there has been an erosion of special tariff and trade advantages because of multilateral agreements under GATT, as well as because of policy shifts by individual Commonwealth members.

Both Britain and its African trading partners are in the economic doldrums and would therefore like to maintain whatever benefits can be realized from existing trade relationships, but both are beginning to direct most of their marketing initiatives to new areas, especially to the thriving industrialized countries of Western

Europe. Forces of inertia in the present trading relationship between Britain and Africa will tend to perpetuate it. At the same time not much more than inertia is holding it together. There is the likelihood therefore that the old colonial linkages will continue but tend to become weaker. At some point in the future, however, they could be abruptly affected by such developments as possible British entry into the Common Market or the possible supervention of a new system under UNCTAD of universal nonreciprocal preferences between the less developed countries on the one hand and the industrialized nations on the other.

Private Investment

In comparison to monetary and trade relations, however, the pattern and flow of British private investment have been affected more by independence in Africa. The United Kingdom has been a substantial exporter of private capital to less developed countries for generations. In Africa during the colonial period, British-owned enterprises came to dominate the modernized sector of the economies, including mining, manufacturing, construction, distribution, transport and communications, shipping, and commercial agriculture. Perhaps half of all British private investment in Africa was centered in one country, South Africa. In West Africa, Nigeria followed by Ghana and Sierra Leone were the principal areas of investment interest. In East Africa, Kenya was the focus; and in Central Africa, Rhodesia and Zambia.

With the coming of independence, however, three immediate and important issues were posed: What would be the view of the new African states toward British investments within their boundaries; what would be the view of British private investors toward maintaining or increasing their holdings in Africa; and what would be the view of the British government in encouraging or restricting the flow of private investment toward Africa? In the decade since, answers—or indications of answers—to all these issues have appeared.

The new African governments upon taking power held a common conviction that their territories and peoples had been victimized and exploited by colonialism. They shared a concern about the domination of their economies by British and other non-African firms and investors. President Nkrumah of Ghana was an ardent and outspoken opponent of capitalistic intrusion; but most of the leaders of the other former British territories were more circumspect. On the one hand, they were careful not to discourage or drive out foreign investment by extreme statements or actions; but on the other, they proceeded to re-examine critically the concessions and privileges which had been accorded to British and other foreign investors. Most of them have begun to take measures to impose heavier burdens and restrictions upon foreign investments. The basic terms of concessions in some cases have been revised; new taxes have been levied; labor costs have been increased; and miscellaneous privileges have been cut back. In Kenya the extensive land holdings of white settlers were the principal point of attack; in Tanzania, foreign banks; and in Zambia, the rich copper-mining enterprises.

Although some nationalization has now occurred, the direction of movement is not consistent: Ghana, for example, following the deposition of Nkrumah, has begun to de-nationalize certain state-owned enterprises, and a number of states have formulated programs to attract capital from abroad. But evidence to date suggests that despite recognition by most of the former British colonies of their continuing need for private investment, they will continue to whittle away the special advantages formerly enjoyed by investors. It is probable too that the general atmosphere of political and social instability in the former colonies will serve as an additional deterrent to British and other investors. In sum, as a result both of their own actions and of their various other difficulties the former British territories have lost much of their glitter as opportunities for profitable investment, and the flow from Britain has begun to dry up. The precise changes in the volume and pattern of movement, however, are exceptionally difficult to measure accurately, because of technical difficulties. The methods by which such investments are valued permit wide variation; information on petroleum investments, an item of importance in Africa, is not made public by the companies concerned; and private investment can take many forms, ranging from direct investment to portfolio investment to long-term export credits, not all of which are regularly included in the several statistical series that are available. Nevertheless, the broad outline, at least, of the response of British private investment to the new circumstances in Africa in the post-independence period can be discerned.

In recent years British private investment has continued to move to all parts of the world: in 1960 the total value of direct British investment abroad was estimated at some £2,950 million ($7 billion) and in 1965 it was estimated at £4,215 million ($10.1

billion.)[5] The volume of such investment increased more rapidly in the developed than in the less developed countries. In Africa the increase of British investment in South Africa was quite vigorous throughout the period 1960–65. In Commonwealth Africa, the volume grew moderately from 1960 through 1962, but since then some disinvestment has occurred. Table 2 gives an indication of the movements. However, the table does not reflect the fact that during the period since 1960 a significant amount of private investment in petroleum has gone to Nigeria, Libya, and Algeria. Because of this and other inadequacies in the data of British overseas investment, the table should be interpreted as presenting only an approximate picture.

On the whole, it would seem that British private investors no longer consider the former colonies in Africa a particularly advantageous area for current investment. Their difficulties with investments already in place are increasing; their alternative opportunities in the more developed countries of the world, including South Africa, are more remunerative;* and there is no indication that they have great confidence that the situation is likely to change soon for the better. It can be surmised therefore that new private investment will not be available except in the case of exceptional opportunities, probably in the extractive industries. Even there, much will depend on the terms, conditions, and inducements offered by the African states in the future.

The official attitude toward private investment in the former African colonies has become steadily less encouraging as Britain's own economic difficulties have intensified. Basically, after independence the government attempted to protect the position of

---

* Note, for example, the contrasting rates of return reported on direct investment in South Africa and Commonwealth Africa in the post-independence period. For Commonwealth Africa the average rates of return on direct British investments appear to have been significantly lower than in South Africa, as follows:

	South Africa	Commonwealth Africa
1960	10.3%	11.0%
1961	10.4	9.2
1962	12.1	7.9
1963	12.9	9.5
1964	14.8	12.1
1965	12.1	8.5

SOURCE: *Board of Trade Journal,* January 26, 1968.

TABLE 2. United Kingdom Private Direct Investment in Africa, 1960–65

(In millions of pounds sterling)

	1960	1961	1962	1963	1964	1965
Commonwealth Africa:	280.3	315.5	327.3	323.4	300.9	309.5
Central Africa	78.4	95.1	103.2	97.7	82.5	78.2
Malawi					8.4	8.4
Rhodesia					66.1	62.0
Zambia					8.0	7.8
East Africa	56.9	59.9	60.5	59.4	59.1	60.5
Kenya	43.8	46.3	47.0	46.2	46.3	43.2
Tanzania	8.0	8.2	7.7	7.3	6.8	9.3
Uganda	5.1	5.4	5.8	5.9	6.0	8.0
West Africa	145.0	160.5	163.5	166.3	159.3	170.8
Gambia	0.9	1.2	1.0	0.8	0.6	0.6
Ghana	47.8	50.2	53.2	49.9	47.9	53.4
Nigeria	88.0	98.6	94.8	99.8	92.4	96.7
Sierra Leone	8.3	10.5	14.5	15.8	18.4	20.1
Other Africa:						
Libya	3.3	3.6	3.2	3.9	2.4	2.2
Mozambique	8.9	8.9	8.9	9.2	9.4	10.4
Sudan	4.6	4.9	5.4	5.4	6.0	6.1
North Africa, n.s.d.	0.6	0.9	1.0	1.1	1.2	1.9
Africa, Other, n.s.d.	65.1	67.1	70.8	73.1	75.1	78.2
South Africa	258.3	270.6	290.0	319.4	352.9	391.7
Total, Africa	621.1	671.5	706.6	735.5	747.9	800.0

NOTES: Book values of net assets attributable to the United Kingdom at year-ends. The figures cover British direct overseas investment in all industrial and commercial enterprises, except oil, banking, and insurance. Book values are based on net assets (i.e., fixed assets, less accumulated depreciation provisions, plus current assets, less current liabilities). Current assets and liabilities will approximate present-day values, but fixed assets acquired some time ago are likely to be considerably below market value (particularly in the case of rubber, tea, and other plantation and mining companies).

SYMBOLS: n.s.d. means "not separately distinguished." Returns which distinguished areas but not countries are also included.

SOURCE: *Board of Trade Journal*, January 26, 1968.

British investors in the former colonies and to interpose no obstructions to a continued flow of British private funds to those
areas. But in more recent years Britain has enacted various
measures to protect its balance of payments and to institute reforms in domestic taxation, all of which tend to accentuate the
declining flow of private investment to Africa. The corporation
tax announced in the 1965 budget, which became operational in
1966–67, alters the balance of advantage between home and overseas investment by British companies in favor of the former. A
White Paper on investment incentives issued in January 1966
announced new measures to encourage investment in British
industry, the net effect of which is also likely to further discourage
overseas investment. In the 1966 budget a program of voluntary
restraint on foreign investment was introduced, but so far as the
Sterling Area was concerned, investment in less developed countries was exempted. Even so, as Britain's balance-of-payments
situation has worsened, the impact both of official regulations and
the policy of private banks has been to further discourage overseas
investment. The time therefore is one of ambiguity and hesitancy
on the part of all parties, both British and African, as regards the
position and future of British private investment. Under the
circumstances, the behavior of investors has been immobility or
withdrawal—and in any case the opposite of thrusting economic
neo-colonialism, the erstwhile fear of the former colonies. Partly
because of this, they have come to depend heavily upon Britain
for the external aid their development programs must have.

British Aid to African Development

British economic and technical assistance to Africa has remained
substantial and steady in the post-independence period. The aid
programs and policies have gone through great evolution, particularly in the last decade, but the course that changes have taken
exemplifies Britain's responsiveness to the special needs of the
former colonies as well as an admirable sense of responsibility for
their development despite its own severe domestic requirements.

During the colonial period the English-speaking areas fared
somewhat better economically than most of the others in Africa.
The portions Britain colonized were generally those of greater
economic resources and potentiality; and, with certain exceptions,
they were carved into states of more viable size. The flow of private
capital to the colonial economies was sufficient to produce a

moderate degree of growth in the commercialized sectors even though the life and well-being of the average African inhabitant was little affected. A number of Africans, however, especially in West Africa, acquired technical and managerial skills and formed the beginnings of an indigenous bourgeoisie.

It was long-standing British policy that development capital for the colonies should be provided by the private sector and that the colonies should meet their ordinary budgetary expenses out of locally raised revenue. The latter policy at least had the virtue of not saddling them with extravagant administrative structures at the time of independence. Even though the thrifty hand of the British Treasury firmly restrained any impulse there might have been to lavish assistance upon the colonies, official concern about their economic development began relatively early. Before the First World War, various institutes and other organizations had been set up to study the economic and social problems of the colonies; and after the war, efforts were made to find and expand markets for their products in Britain by providing tariff preferences.

The first major departure from the policy of opposition to regular, official development finance for the colonies was the Colonial Development Act of 1929. By its terms, loans or grants could be made on a government-to-government basis to aid and develop agriculture and industry in the dependent territories. In the following eleven years more than £7 million was provided to improve transport, power, water supplies, and other facilities; about half of the sum went to Africa.

In 1939, at the outbreak of the Second World War, a reappraisal of policy toward colonial development was formulated in an important "Statement of Policy on Colonial Development and Welfare." Whereas the 1929 Act had recognized only the need for official assistance for capital financing, it was now proposed that external grants toward recurrent expenditures on health and social welfare be provided. As a result, the Colonial Development and Welfare (CD & W) Act was passed in 1940 which provided for annual expenditures of some £5 million. At the end of the war in 1945, the Act was enlarged to make £120 million available for a ten-year period to be spent on projects organized into a development program in each colony. Subsequent acts raised the ceiling of expenditures up to £220 million for the 1946–60 period.

To supplement and stimulate the flow of private investment into the colonies, the Colonial Development Corporation was established in 1948 with power to borrow from the British Treasury for investment in industry, agriculture, and commerce. This creative innovation, subsequently renamed the Commonwealth Development Corporation (CDC), encourages the expansion of a wide range of economic enterprises through the making of loans and equity investments that are expected to attain commercial standards of profitability. Its sphere of activity thus lies between the purely governmental sector and the wholly commercial. By the end of 1966 its total investments had an outstanding value of more than £100 million, of which 70 per cent was in Africa.

Through the 1950s British economic aid to the colonies continued on this enlarged, if still limited, scale. Grants were made for administrative and special purposes; CD & W funds were provided for development; and CDC funds were available for investment. In addition, the colonial governments were empowered to borrow funds directly from the London market.* As the date of independence of the African colonies approached, Britain gave greater recognition to their varied needs for aid and development in a succession of measures and made increased resources available. But as late as 1957, regular financial aid to independent countries was still considered contrary to policy. In a White Paper of that year it was stated that government-to-government loans were not envisioned as a "normal way of assisting" independent ex-colonies. "Their interests can better be served if they build up their own credit and . . . raise money in London and elsewhere."† But in the following months it became clear that a threatening economic situation existed in India and Pakistan, that they and other former colonies could not borrow on the London market nor qualify for World Bank credit, and that there was need to provide them with a new source of loan funds. The turning point came at the Commonwealth Economic Conference in Montreal in 1958, following which a policy of large-scale loan

* An important aspect of British colonial securities was that they were classified as trustee investments in the United Kingdom, which meant that trustees could invest in them just as they could in British government securities. This provision opened up a large market for them. Coincident with independence, British laws governing trustee investments were further liberalized, allowing substantial investment in equities as well as bonds.

† This policy for a number of the colonies approaching independence was reasonable in view of the build-up of their reserves which had taken place after World War II and during and after the Korean War. But not for all. And after independence, the reserves of most of the former colonies, primarily because of declining primary product prices, began to run down rapidly.

assistance for both independent and other Commonwealth territories was announced.

After Ghana's independence, British aid policies in the late 1950s
were further modified to make it possible to provide other areas
about to change their status with substantial "independence
settlements" consisting of the following elements:

1. Loans or grants for a period of several years to support the
   new country's first development program
2. Unexpended balances of CD & W funds allocated to the
   country prior to independence
3. Loans to finance the country's half-share of the cost of
   financial compensation to civil servants whose careers were
   interrupted as a result of independence, and of the cost of
   commutation of their pension rights
4. Long-run technical assistance agreements

In consequence a number of African countries received a sharp
increase in aid immediately after independence, notably, Nigeria,
Kenya, Uganda, Tanzania, Malawi, and Zambia.

However, in according such independence settlements, Britain
by no means threw off all the restraints which had previously
governed its aid policies. In a White Paper of 1960[6] Britain
recognized the responsibility of the industrially advanced countries to provide financing for the social and economic progress of
the poorer countries. But at the time Britain was still careful not
to become heavily involved in long-term development commitments. Partly to avoid criticism on grounds of neo-colonialism
and of intervention in internal affairs, it claimed to operate on the
principle that independence had to mean complete responsibility
on the part of the new states in proposing and requesting assistance. Moreover, British policy in the early years of the 1960s
continued to be guided by the principle that aid to independent
countries should be "hard" in its terms and tied to British procurement.

Since 1963, however, the terms of British aid have "softened"
extraordinarily, beginning with the introduction at that time of
interest-waiver periods as long as seven years. Still more important
was the decision taken in mid-1965 to extend interest-free loans on
a large scale. Under present policy, countries with incomes of less
than $100 per capita are normally qualified to receive such loans;
countries with incomes between $100 and $250 per capita may

qualify either for interest-free loans or for waivers of interest. As a result, the United Kingdom loan program is now the "softest" of any of the Western countries. By such measures Britain has constructively recognized the increasingly difficult financial predicament of the former colonies and particularly their threatening external debt position. The United Kingdom has also made, despite a difficult balance-of-payments situation, an effort to extend untied financial aid; but in this it has done neither much better nor much worse than the other industrialized donor nations.

Until 1964, British economic and technical assistance consisted of a considerable number of uncoordinated programs administered by various branches of the government: the Foreign Office, the Commonwealth Relations Office, the Colonial Office, the Treasury, the Department of Technical Cooperation, the Export Credit Guarantee Department, the British Council, the Ministry of Education, and others. Much of this administrative complexity was removed in 1964 when a new Labor government under Harold Wilson created the Overseas Development Ministry (ODM), whose head—for the first two years—sat as a member of the British Cabinet. The new Ministry promptly set forth its philosophy in a White Paper of 1965 that was markedly different in tone from those which previous British governments had issued on the subject of economic assistance.[7] In it, warm recognition was given to "the need to make our full contribution in the cooperative effort to promote the development of the poorer countries and the expansion of the world economy." As the Overseas Development Institute, a private organization in London, commented, "Previous White Papers on aid were produced by the Treasury . . . and it is therefore perhaps not so surprising that this White Paper displays signs of enthusiasm for the task of helping developing countries that had previously been hard to discern."[8]

Even in this brave document, however, some reservations were apparent. Though a long-term commitment to aid was expressed, there was no indication of the amounts that Britain might provide in the future, and it was emphasized that British balance-of-payments difficulties imposed severe restriction on the assistance which might be given. Then, within a month, the White Paper was noticeably undercut by the government's publication of a National Plan covering the years up to 1970. The Plan stated that "aid to developing countries will be restrained and the effectiveness of each pound of aid increased," and it expected that British private investment abroad would be curtailed. It exuded none of

the generous spirit toward the developing world that had characterized the White Paper on development published a short time
earlier.

Despite the contradictory climate in which it was formed, the
new Ministry introduced some important new measures in the
following years. The terms and conditions of British aid were
much broadened, and steps were taken to increase its operational
effectiveness. In addition to improving the coordination and
quality of aid administration, the ODM also gave intelligent and
effective voice to those elements in Britain favorable to greater
concern for the underdeveloped and impoverished parts of the
world. The caliber of British representatives of the new Ministry
was such that they were accorded a respected leadership role in
the international fraternity of aid administrators—a not inconsiderable army. When in 1966 the head of the new Ministry was
dropped from the British Cabinet, however, concern was felt in
Africa and elsewhere that the influence of the supporters of a
widened British role in international development might be
weakening. But two years later, despite the battering of a continuing trade deficit and a devaluation, the level of British
aid remained remarkably stable.

The Flow of Bilateral Economic Assistance

Table 3 summarizes the volume and pattern of British economic
and technical assistance to all developing countries over the ten
years following the independence of Ghana in 1957. From these
figures, the over-all characteristics of British assistance during the
past decade can be identified: The volume has more than tripled
from a total of £65 million in 1957-58 to £205 million in 1965-
66. Grants for economic development have increased relatively
little. Loans, on the other hand, have expanded greatly, as have
expenditures for technical assistance. The strong support of Britain
for multilateral assistance is reflected in the fact that contributions
to such programs have grown from £3 million at the beginning
of the decade to £19 million at the end, increasing from 5 per
cent to 10 per cent of the annual totals.

British aid is heavily concentrated—87 per cent of the total—
on the colonies and the Commonwealth, partly because of a
special sense of responsibility, and partly, as spokesmen have
explained, because other donor countries expect Britain to carry
the bulk of the burden of assistance to the former colonies. Although Britain provides assistance to more countries than does

TABLE 3. United Kingdom Economic Aid to Developing Countries; Summary of Government Disbursements, 1957/58–1966/67

(In millions of pounds sterling; financial years)

	1957–58	1958–59	1959–60	1960–61	1961–62	1962–63	1963–64	1964–65	1965–66	1966–67[c]
Bilateral aid:										
Grants for economic development[a]	46	44	47	52	62	53	47	64	59	56
Loans for economic development[b]	12	38	56	70	74	68	87	83	94	104
Technical assistance	4	4	7	8	20	21	24	28	34	31
Total	62	86	110	130	155	142	158	175	187	191
Contributions to multilateral agencies:[a]										
International Development Association	—	—	—	11	9	9	9	9	12	12
Technical assistance	1	1	1	3	3	3	4	4	4	4
UNRWA (Palestine refugees)	2	2	2	2	2	2	1	2	2	2
Congo civil assistance	—	—	—	1	—	—	1	1	1	—
World food program	—	—	—	—	—	—	1	1	1	—
Total	3	3	3	17	14	14	15	16	19	19
Total, British government economic aid:	65	88	113	147	170	156	173	191	205	211

NOTES: Columns may not add exactly due to rounding. Symbol [—] indicates nil or less than the unit used. Economic aid includes Exchequer advances to the Commonwealth Development Corporation but not total CDC overseas investment; development countries as classified by the OECD. [a] Includes contributions to the Indus Basin Development Fund, which are now reported as bilateral and not multilateral as in previous White Papers. [b] Loans are reported gross. [c] Provisional figures.

SOURCE: Ministry of Overseas Development, *Overseas Development: The Work in Hand* (London: H.M.S.O., Cmnd. 3180, 1967), p. 30, and *Annual Abstract of Statistics* (London: Central Statistical Office, 1967), p. 250.

any other donor except the United States, over half the aid goes to Africa. Table 4 indicates the distribution of bilateral British economic aid in Africa since 1960.

The level of aid in 1961–62 was easily the highest for any single year up to that time and reflected the new and expanded aid policies announced in 1958. After a dip in 1962–63, the level has since risen slowly but steadily. In early 1968 the British government announced that its assistance to less developed countries would be maintained for the next three years essentially at the level of the period 1964–67.*

Technical Assistance

Technical assistance has always been given a high priority in the United Kingdom's aid program. One-third of the assistance provided Africa is in this form, which reflects the large-scale need for administrative personnel, advisers, and teachers.

Under the Overseas Service Aid Scheme (OSAS) started in 1961, Britain pays most of the difference between the cost of employing British staff over and above the cost of employing local staff. Some 10,000 out of the total of 16,000 British personnel serving in less developed countries are financed under this scheme, many of them in Africa.† In addition, the British Expatriate Supplementation Scheme (BESS) to help supply personnel to universities and public corporations outside the civil service is in operation in West, East, and Central Africa. The British technical assistance effort also includes a substantial volunteer effort comparable to the American Peace Corps, under which more than 1,300 young teachers and other specialists are serving abroad each year, mainly in Africa.

Britain is also an important supplier both of teaching personnel and capital financing for universities in Africa as well as of places for students and trainees in the United Kingdom. Several thousand young Africans with such financial aid are in industrial and

* The British devaluation in November 1967 has resulted in some diminution of the real total of aid, even though the level in sterling terms is being maintained. But since a considerable portion of British aid is tied, the impact of devaluation is thereby lessened, or at least delayed.

† On January 1, 1966, according to British official estimates, there were about 8,000 OSAS staff in Africa. Britain was also "topping up" the salaries of some 1,300 officers and teachers serving in African Commonwealth countries, as well as of an additional number serving in non-Commonwealth African areas.

TABLE 4. United Kingdom Bilateral Economic Aid to Africa; Disbursements, 1960/61–1966/67

(In millions of pounds sterling, years ending March 31)

	1960–61	1961–62	1962–63	1963–64	1964–65	1965–66	1966–67[c]
Grants, all developing countries	59.8	81.4	73.7	71.7	91.6	92.6	87.6
Africa total[a]	25.2	45.3	40.1	38.5	52.0	47.3	40.2
Rhodesia	0.6	0.2	0.4	0.2	1.1	—	0.3
Libya	3.2	3.3	3.3	3.3	3.3	—	—
Swaziland, Basutoland, Bechuanaland	2.0	4.6	4.8	5.2	7.9	10.5	13.1
Tropical Africa[b]	19.4	37.2	31.6	29.8	39.7	36.8	26.8
Loans, all developing countries	70.4	74.0	67.8	86.6	83.4	93.7	104.2
Africa total[a]	31.5	40.0	23.2	34.3	29.8	34.7	29.3
Rhodesia	—	12.1	0.8	2.2	—	—	—
Swaziland, Basutoland,	3.0	2.8	2.3	0.4	0.9	1.8	3.8
Tropical Africa[b]	28.5	25.1	20.1	31.7	28.9	32.9	25.5

[a] Excluding South Africa and U.A.R.
[b] Including Malawi, Zambia.
[c] Commitments.

SOURCE: United Kingdom, *Annual Abstract of Statistics, 1967.*

university training in Britain. In 1966 the OECD reported that 4,115 students from underdeveloped countries were studying in Britain under government grants, plus 4,906 technical trainees.[9]

Even more than trade or investment, the volume and quality of the economic and technical assistance programs are of decisive importance to the British position in Africa. Many recipient countries, faced with ominous economic difficulties, are heavily reliant on British help. Without it all their plans for growth and stability would be jeopardized, a fact of which they are fully aware. From the British viewpoint, these programs are the most prominent evidence of Britain's friendship with Africa and its sense of responsibility as a world power. In purely practical terms, aid is the anchor which holds most of the other elements of British influence in Africa in place. In its educational and technical assistance aspects, British aid is a powerful reinforcement to the British presence in education, governmental administration, and cultural affairs throughout English-speaking Africa. It is the price, the *quid pro quo*, with which Britain has been able to ease some of its most trying political problems in Africa, as in the case of relations with Zambia. Even more fundamentally, as Mr. David J. Murray has emphasized, "External aid provides a necessary prop for the established economic and social order in many African countries and for the British influence that remains from the colonial period as part of that order. Without such support, developments internal to African countries could well undermine Britain's position."[10]

As to the future, there is some anxiety whether Britain will be able or will wish to sustain the level which its economic assistance to Africa has now reached. Public opinion in Britain, as reflected in the large number of private, nonprofit bodies active in the aid field, seems to remain favorable to a substantial assistance effort. Nevertheless, a degree of uncertainty over the future of the aid program could be noted in the statements of high British officials, particularly after the devaluation crisis in late 1967.

British Military Policies in Evolution

In contrast to the considerable continuity of cultural and economic ties between Britain and Africa in the post-independence period, military relationships have changed greatly. Indeed, Britain's military presence in Africa has now virtually disappeared.

British strategy for Africa, though now radically altered,

evolved rather slowly in the first two decades after the Second World War. Britain continued to think of itself as a world power, conceiving its interests and responsibilities in global terms. So great was the accumulation of military commitments—to some thirty islands and other territorial remnants of empire scattered throughout the world, to miscellaneous areas such as the Arab states bordering the Persian Gulf and the south coast of Arabia, and to various regional defense groupings such as NATO, CENTO, and SEATO—and so deeply had the habits acquired during the centuries when Britain was the world's greatest imperial power sunk into its institutions and attitudes that neither the Conservatives nor Labor was prepared to see the United Kingdom as a "regional power." Even though his party had frequently attacked the Conservatives for their "delusions of grandeur," Harold Wilson in his first speech on foreign affairs as Prime Minister said in 1964: "The problem we are facing in defense matters derives from the fact that alone in the world—apart from the United States and the U.S.S.R.—we are trying to maintain three roles. There is the strategic nuclear role. There is our conventional role within NATO . . . and there is our world role, one which no one in this House, or indeed in the country, will want us to give up or call in question."[11] But, in fact, from the mid-1950s onward, many British leaders, including Wilson himself, had been calling in question every element of the "triple role." The controversies over the *Blue Streak* and *Skybolt* missiles, over the size and cost of the British army of the Rhine, over the TSR-2 aircraft, and over the desirability of an independent British nuclear deterrent dominated the debates on defense prior to 1964. Thereafter, the issue of Britain's military role "East of Suez" acquired new prominence, an essential element of which related to its facilities and responsibilities in Africa.

During the colonial years Britain's military presence and policies in Africa derived from two separate but related objectives: the defense of world-wide strategic interests; and protection of the colonies both from internal disorder and from external threat. The principal British strategic interests in Africa related less to the area itself than to its location along major supply and communications routes with the East—to India and later to the oil-rich kingdoms of the Persian Gulf. Hence Britain placed great importance on freedom of passage through the Suez, maintenance of British influence in the adjacent African and Arabian territories, and protection of the alternate sea route to the East around the

Cape of Good Hope. To this end, the British have long maintained strategic naval facilities in South Africa, notably the important repair and refueling station at Simonstown.

World War II emphasized in British eyes the strategic importance of the Mediterranean littoral of Africa and the essentiality of airbases in the area. Britain established a naval mission and training facilities in Libya, stationed infantry units at Benghazi and Tobruk, and operated an airbase at Idris. Their function related to the defense of all Africa, the Middle East, South Asia, the Far East, and Australasia. Britain was also assisted and encouraged to maintain these and other African forces and facilities by the United States, which considered them to be not only a stabilizing factor within Africa but an important element in world-wide arrangements for the containment of Communist expansion.

British strategic interests in Africa, however, were basically modified with the independence of India and Pakistan in 1947. Because of its size and economic value India was the centerpiece of the prewar empire, and of great military importance as well. In the Second World War, more than two million Indians had done military service, Indian production had been put at the service of the Allied forces in the whole Asian area, while Indian geography had been of major significance in Allied plans and operations. Indian independence together with the strong neutralist policies of Premier Nehru necessarily altered British strategic calculations concerning the subcontinent as well as the importance of related African strategic facilities.

Moreover, the political feasibility of maintaining such facilities in Africa and eastward came increasingly in question. Following the Arab-Israeli conflict in 1949, the British military position throughout the Arab world generally underwent a rapid deterioration. Nasser's take-over of political power in Egypt in 1954 was followed by the elimination of direct British control over the operation of the Suez Canal and the abrogation of British military rights in the area. Britain's participation in the ill-starred Suez operation of 1956 caused a final rupture of military cooperation and produced shocks and strains in its relationship with the rest of the Arab world, including Libya. There in mid-1967, after the recrudescence of the Arab-Israeli war in June, Britain was obliged to relinquish the last of its strategic facilities in northern Africa. On August 3, 1967, a spokesman for the Libyan Foreign Ministry announced that agreement had been reached with the United

Kingdom for the evacuation of all British military units stationed in the country and the surrender of their installations to the Libyan government within a maximum period of six months.

British relationships with South Africa, where military and naval cooperation has been of long standing, have likewise steadily deteriorated over recent years but for quite special reasons. Generations of British admirals have stressed the importance of South Africa's command of the sea route to the East. South African troops in large numbers fought alongside British forces in two world wars, and the South African army, navy, and air forces were created with British help and patterned to British models. South Africa's military and naval equipment traditionally was almost entirely of British origin.

But as early as 1955 strains in the relationship began to appear. In that year, the British Minister of Defense in signing a renewal of the agreement on British use of the Simonstown naval base, insisted that explicit distinction be made between arms provided by Britain for external and for domestic use within South Africa, to the great displeasure of his South African counterpart. By the early 1960s when the enforcement of *apartheid* became more severe and after the newly independent African members of the Commonwealth had begun to exert pressure on Britain directly and at the United Nations to change its military policies toward South Africa, Britain responded by repeatedly expressing sharp criticism of South African racial policies.

Voices in Britain, particularly from the Labor side, began to call for an embargo on the sale of all forms of weapons to South Africa, and when the embargo was subsequently imposed, the South African government began to look for alternative sources and to press domestic manufacture of small arms and army vehicles. There was of course no lack of alternative suppliers from among the Western group of countries. West Germany in late 1960 agreed to sell South Africa troop carriers; and France in the following year sold Mirage III-C jet fighters and Alouette helicopters; the United States began to sell military transport aircraft; Canada sold Sabre jets as well as helicopters and bombers; and Belgium sold small arms.

By 1967 close military collaboration between the two countries had been greatly weakened although not entirely eroded. South Africa had substantially freed itself from dependence upon Britain for essential military supplies. By tacit agreement Britain was still able to make limited use of the Simonstown facilities, but the

South African Prime Minister, Mr. Vorster, warned that, in view of Britain's refusal to lift its arms embargo he might have to reconsider the Simonstown Agreement. Within Britain, opponents of the embargo began to find a larger audience. After the closing of the Suez Canal in consequence of the six-day war between Israel and Egypt in mid-1967, the diversion of shipping to the alternate route around the southern tip of Africa gave rise to a renewed awareness of the strategic and economic importance of South African repair and refueling facilities. Coincidentally, the intensification of British balance-of-payments problems also enabled domestic critics of the arms embargo to make more persuasive use of economic arguments against it. But, even if such criticism should bring about modification of specific aspects of British policy toward South Africa in the future, there is no visible prospect that the general decline in British strategic interests and engagements in Africa would be altered.

The shrinkage in Britain's role and responsibilities for the maintenance of internal order and stability in Africa has been equally great in recent years. Upon becoming independent, the former colonies took immediate control of the local military forces and subsequently entered into military arrangements of a sort, under which Britain has given various kinds of military assistance including financial aid, funds for the purchase of arms and equipment, technicians and crews to operate certain facilities, and training personnel for their armed forces. In addition, Britain has provided places in its own military establishments for trainees from Africa.[12] Such assistance has been limited in amount, however, and Britain on the whole has been reluctant to give hardware except when compelled by special needs, as in the Sudan and Libya, where important overflight and base rights were at stake, or when the country concerned inherited a serious security problem upon independence, as in the case of Kenya on its northern border.

Because the former colonies are now members of the Commonwealth, they are blanketed with Britain's general obligation to help, "by all appropriate action," any fellow member which is the victim of aggression. But the actual meaning of Britain's present commitments for the defense and security of the African members is murky as a result both of the vagueness of the Commonwealth concept itself and the obscurity as well as the contradictions of the security needs and foreign policy positions of the new African states.

From both the British and the African sides, there has been a tentativeness in the military understandings that have developed. Only Kenya, among Britain's former colonies, has undertaken military commitments of a genuinely reciprocal character upon independence. That decision of President Kenyatta to provide Britain with overflight and staging facilities for the Royal Air Force in return for military assistance has been roundly criticized by several other Commonwealth members, all of whom have asserted their adherence to the doctrine of nonalignment in international affairs. On the whole, the former colonies have preferred to avoid comprehensive arrangements or long-term commitments, and they have been careful to avoid even the appearance of a military alliance with Britain. This attitude was expressed by President Nkrumah of Ghana in 1962 after Britain has granted military aid to the Indian government to repulse a Chinese invasion: "The Commonwealth is not a military alliance and it would be most detrimental to its progress if the impression were created that Commonwealth members did not judge each issue independently on its merits but instead automatically sided with a fellow Commonwealth country when that country was engaged in a dispute with an outside power."

Despite such reservations, however, a number of the former colonies have called on Britain for military assistance in dealing with crises—and Britain has responded. In January 1964, the troops of President Nyerere in Tanzania mutinied, and he immediately issued an urgent call for British military assistance, which was promptly supplied. Within days a similar instance occurred in Uganda and shortly thereafter another in Kenya. In all three, British forces dispatched from nearby naval units in the Indian Ocean made it possible to put down the danger.

But the countries which had called for help were embarrassed by their predicament and felt obliged to apologize to their African colleagues. President Nyerere of Tanzania said to the Organization of African Unity shortly afterward that he hoped British forces would be replaced as promptly as possible by other African forces since "the success of the policy of nonalignment may depend not only on remaining outside such [East-West] conflicts but also on being seen to remain outside them."[13] Clearly, the heads of the East African governments would have preferred to be able to call on other African or inter-African forces had they been available.

British reaction to the incidents was also an ambivalent, even fluctuating, one. Following the East African interventions, Conservative Sir Alec Douglas-Home in a speech to the House of Commons on February 6, 1964, said, "When we gave independence to our Colonial Territories, we meant them to keep it and we mean them to keep it and to be given a fair chance to preserve their independence, their own identity and their own way of life." With some pride, he added:

We have responded five times in the past two weeks to appeals from Commonwealth partners whose life and independence have been threatened. In Malaysia we are there to prevent a Commonwealth country being dismembered by subversion and by force. In Cyprus, we are there to prevent a very unhappy people suffering from civil war in the island and to try to prevent Greece and Turkey from being drawn into a war. In Kenya, Uganda and Tanganyika we are there in response to requests from their Governments to prevent illegal take-overs by mutinous elements who would overthrow the elected Governments who are only a few months, or, indeed, a few weeks, old. . . . I hope, therefore, that the Commonwealth countries understand that when the chips are down, the Commonwealth can rely on Britain.

Subsequently, however, Britain has maintained strict limits upon the magnitude and nature of its military assistance and has not offered to intervene militarily in troubled situations even where major economic interests were at stake. The case of Nigeria, where civil war broke out after June 1967, gives recent indication both of the reservations of the former colonies in calling on Britain for military assistance and intervention and of British reservations in responding. Britain permitted the federal government in Lagos to purchase certain categories of arms (but not aircraft or bombs) and facilitated their delivery while at the same time blocking efforts of the secessionist regime in Biafra to obtain British supplies. But Britain made no offer of troops or flying personnel, nor was any encouragement given of the possibility of direct military involvement. Likewise, the government in Lagos at no time requested Britain to intervene militarily. However, as the struggle between the federal government and the Biafrans approached its climax, Britain became increasingly involved in attempts to bring about a negotiated settlement and to this end offered to participate in a Commonwealth peace-keeping force.

By 1968 it had become clear that military cooperation or commitments between Britain and the former colonies were minimal. As independent states they were responsible for their own defense and security. Britain was prepared to continue to provide limited amounts of training and equipment, and also to sell them arms. But this appeared to be as much for reasons of economic self-interest as out of a sense of commitment or responsibility for the maintenance of their internal order and stability.

The Decision to Dismantle

By late 1965, the visible tendencies in British policy to reduce strategic facilities in Africa and to step back from responsibility for internal stability in the new states were given formal and sweeping confirmation in new budgetary decisions and statements of defense doctrine. In announcing major cuts in defense expenditures at the time, the government made reference to reductions "in the scale of Britain's overseas commitments," while at the same time reaffirming a general interest of the United Kingdom in the stability of the Third World.

In February 1966, the government set forth in its "Defence Review"[14] the view that Britain should retain a military capability outside Europe but that it should not undertake major operations of war except in cooperation with allies; military assistance would be provided to other countries only on condition that they were prepared to provide promptly the facilities necessary to make such assistance effective; and there would be no attempt to maintain defense facilities in any independent country against its will. The statement also announced the government's decision not to begin construction of new aircraft carriers to replace those then in service, which meant that by the mid-1970s the Royal Navy would no longer have carriers operational and the Fleet Air Arm would no longer exist. Carrier-based air power would thus no longer be available to deal with situations such as those which erupted in East Africa in 1964.

In a subsequent White Paper of July 18, 1967, the government made explicit what had already become evident, namely, that in Africa and elsewhere Britain was withdrawing from a world strategic role and was giving up any remaining responsibility for the defense and stability of the former colonies. Under the imperatives of economic necessity, the "triple role" was abandoned; instead, Britain's defense horizons were essentially reduced to the circumference of its immediate region. Britain declared that its security depended above all on the prevention of war in Europe, an area that would become even more important as Britain developed closer political and economic ties with its continental neighbors. The aim of policy outside Europe was stated to be "to foster developments, which will enable the local peoples to live at peace without the presence of external forces" and thus allow British forces to withdraw from their stations in the Middle East and the Far East.

In its statement on "Public Expenditures in 1968–69 and 1969–70" on January 16, 1968[15] and its "Supplementary Statement on Defense Policy 1968," in July of that year,[16] the government established an accelerated calendar for the cutbacks of its forces and facilities. The total number of men in the services would be reduced by 20 per cent and units would be withdrawn from bases in the Persian Gulf and Southeast Asia by the end of 1971. Though Britain would concentrate the remaining forces in the NATO area, the White Paper had the following to say regarding military obligations outside Europe:

So long as Britain is responsible for dependent territories, she will have certain military obligations which will require her to station small elements of all three Services overseas—for example in Hong Kong—and to reinforce them if necessary. She may also wish to cooperate in keeping the peace under United Nations' auspices or to support her friends. Thus, although the Government has decided to retain no special capability for major operations overseas, Britain must preserve some of the special military skills which might be needed there and must keep the ability to send her forces outside Europe if she judges it her duty or interest to do so; thus we plan to keep the use of Gan and Masirah in order to maintain a number of route options. . . .

Such forces could include a substantial number of naval ships, an amphibious force, several squadrons of combat aircraft of various types, and a land force of at least brigade group size. Deployment timings would obviously depend upon the precise circumstances, but we could expect naval and air forces and lightly-armed ground troops to be quickly on the scene, although it would take longer to build up the support facilities and supplies required for a major operation. In general, we do not propose to maintain stockpiles of operational equipment and supplies outside Europe, though we may find it economical, as we do at present, to hold small stocks of equipment for training and exercises in areas regularly used for these purposes.

It will be a necessary part of our policy that our forces should train overseas in peacetime. Such training is already undertaken on a considerable scale in many parts of the world. It will be even more important to continue this for the following reasons. Our forces must remain experienced and efficient. We must overcome the limitations of, and familiarity with, the training areas in this country.

We must preserve our present operational techniques and skill in different climates and terrains and our ability to assist in peace-keeping.

These arrangements conveyed an impression of British intent to continue to play a significant military role in the world beyond the European area. But insofar as this might be true, it would seem to relate essentially to the Far East and possibly the Persian Gulf. Elsewhere as in black Africa, direct unilateral British action is difficult to envision. With almost no formal military oligations to the new states, it is most unlikely that Britain would be called on for military intervention, except under the most desperate circumstances. And to judge from its most recent policy statements and behavior, Britain, even if called, would be unlikely to respond as readily in the future as it did in 1964 in East Africa.

In Rhodesia, where the black African states have repeatedly urged Britain to take military measures, it seems equally unlikely that Britain would do so. It is inconceivable that Britain would take military initative to depose the Ian Smith regime and bring about political change, especially in view of the increasing number of South African police and security personnel now in the country. Nor is it likely it would do so even in the event of a complete breakdown of internal order—though some Africans suspect that under those circumstances Britain would feel impelled to do so to protect white "kith and kin."

It can be concluded, therefore, that the former British colonies in Africa by their own desire and by the terms of British policy are now militarily on their own. For better or worse, whatever value the British military presence in Africa may have had in terms of internal stability, it is now removed. The second major conclusion to be drawn from the evolution of British military policy is that Britain no longer accepts responsibility for maintaining in Africa facilities of general strategic value to the Western countries or in behalf of world stability.

From the viewpoint of the independent African states at the present time, the removal of the British military presence in Africa and Britain's abandonment of strategic responsibilities is not a matter of immediate concern. Consistent with the doctrine of African nonalignment, they have steadily opposed such great-power military presence on the continent. Britain has claimed, in defending its shift in defense policy, that the loss of bases and the withdrawal of military forces from Africa and elsewhere will make little difference in the general power balance or to Western strategic positions because of new developments in military technology. Nevertheless, a set of facilities, an access, and some alternatives have been cut off or lost. Because of the inherent imponderability of defense requirements in an insecure world, this naturally tends to make military authorities in the other Western countries uneasy. But even though it is not clear what the removal of the British strategic umbrella and its influence on internal stability in Africa may be, or what if anything may have to replace that presence, for Britain at least the costs and responsibility of military links with Africa have now essentially been eliminated.

POST-INDEPENDENCE POLITICAL RELATIONSHIPS

If Britain had in mind some general conception of long-term ties with Africa in the post-colonial period, it most probably related to political relationships. It was assumed that cultural and linguistic links would remain. It was intended that commercial and investment relationships should be preserved. Later at least it became clear that military linkages would be allowed to wither. But it was in the political sphere that expectations for continued association with the new African states were highest and where intentions were most discernible.

It has long been a matter of pride for Britain that its own political institutions have become a symbol of law, order, and responsibility in the world. Many in Britain believed that the most important bequest to the colonies was in the form of the structures of administration and government introduced there. Many believed too that in the post-independence period this common fabric of constitutional concepts and institutions would provide an enduring foundation of friendship and cooperation. The Commonwealth, under British leadership, was seen as the vehicle of such consultation and collaboration with the new states.

Ironically, however, it has been in the political sphere—both in the preparation of the African areas for self-government and in the development of the Commonwealth—that Britain's plans and efforts have gone most awry. In the closing years of colonialism, British administrators gave considerable attention to preparing Africans to carry new political and administrative responsibilities and to devising a variety of structures to improve the chances for successful self-government by the new states, ranging from interlinking African judicial systems with those of Britain to grouping some of the colonies into federations or organizations for common services.

On the whole, however, the British contribution to political development has been exaggerated and overestimated; and British constitutional innovations in Africa have largely failed. In training Africans for administration, in fact, Britain only partially met its self-imposed obligations. Programs were begun relatively late and only after much pressure, and the ex-colonies at the time of independence usually had only a fraction of the qualified administrators and senior civil servants they required. As a result they were, and to a considerable degree still are, heavily dependent on expatriates to staff their vital services. There is, moreover, little evidence to suggest that the political leadership which has arisen in the former British colonies has been superior in any respect to that which has emerged elsewhere in Africa. In some of the new Anglophone states, extraordinarily capable and admirable individuals have come to power; but in others there have been some of the worst examples of corruption, incompetence, irresponsibility, and dictatorial tendencies to be found anywhere.

Likewise, Britain's efforts to implant Westminster-type parliamentary government and the experiments with federation have all come to nought in the space of relatively few years or fallen into serious difficulty. Everywhere in former British Africa, the forms of parliamentary democracy have failed to survive the test of independence and have been replaced by one-party states or military regimes. In a good number of instances this outcome has not been deplorable either in terms of African development or stability, or even human rights. But it is markedly different from what the British intended or anticipated.

In Central Africa, the Federation of the Rhodesias and Nyasaland, established with much fanfare—and for mixed motives—in 1953, proved unworkable and disintegrated by 1963. In East Africa, the Common Services Organization that had been structured for Kenya, Tanganyika, and Uganda encountered serious problems after their independence and has had to be reconstituted on a new and more limited basis. The great Federation of Nigeria never functioned effectively after independence and has finally exploded in a succession of military coups and civil war.

These political disruptions and disappointments are not unique to British Africa, nor has British action or policy been the principal cause in bringing them about. But they throw serious doubt upon the durability and relevance of the British legacy to the former colonies of political concepts and of constitutional forms and procedures. Perhaps all that can be said is that it was quite understandable and appropriate for Britain to have tried to create political institutions in Africa in the image of its own national experience and principles. It is equally understandable and appropriate that the Africans, once independent, should proceed to overhaul those initial structures according to their own needs, conceptions, and traditions.

The idea of a new and multiracial Commonwealth was both a noble aspiration and a comfortable narcotic for many Britishers and for many Africans as well during the period of transition to independence. For many Englishmen it gave the feeling that Britain was not so much losing an empire as acquiring a family of diverse new nations linked to the proud old mother in permanent relationships of friendship and mutual interest; that through the Commonwealth Britain would still be able to play an important role in the world stage; and that in the expansion and development of the Commonwealth, Britain was advancing bold new concepts, not merely rationalizing a retreat. It also had a practical political value in Britain in facilitating decolonization itself. As *The Economist* once put it, "The liquidation of the old British Empire that has proceeded since 1947 might have dangerously inflamed quite a large section of right wing opinion in this country if many nostalgic ex-imperialists had not comforted themselves with the quite erroneous belief that the newly independent nations had, by remaining within the Commonwealth, accepted a sort of maternal British authority."[17]

For many Africans the Commonwealth idea was equally tranquilizing: it eased anxieties of setting forth on the road to independent statehood all alone and without special sources of assistance and support if need should arise. It gave a sense to these new nations of being engaged in an enterprise of major international proportions and helped feed their hope of being part of the larger world scene. Moreover, the principles on which it was organized aroused their positive enthusiasm, at least for a time. Speaking of the Commonwealth in 1962, Julius Nyerere of Tanzania said:

> Stronger than treaties, less selfish than alliances, less restrictive than any other association, the Commonwealth seems to my colleagues and myself to offer the best hope in the world today of lasting peace and friendship among the peoples of the world. More than any other group of nations in the world today, the Commonwealth binds together in friendship and in likemindedness an astonishing

variety of nations, great and small without distinction between them and without discrimination amongst them.[18]

The Commonwealth, which has evoked so much high-flown rhetoric over the years, is an institution even more difficult than other British constitutional structures to describe. It is a loose, formless set of arrangements, agreements, procedures, and traditions among the twenty-six nations that now compose it. The African members at present are: Ghana, Nigeria, Sierra Leone, Tanzania, Uganda, Kenya, Malawi, Zambia, Gambia, Lesotho (Basutoland), Botswana (Bechuanaland), and Swaziland.* The British monarch is acknowledged to be the symbol and head of the association; each member has joined of its own volition and enjoys complete control over its own domestic and foreign policies. There is no central government or constitution; there is no defense force or judiciary; and there are no rigid obligations or commitments.

Membership in the Commonwealth carries some concrete benefits for the African and other members. There are long-standing trade advantages. In the field of educational cooperation, scholarship exchange programs have been established, periodic meetings are held among university representatives, and extensive exchanges of teachers are arranged. In the field of scientific cooperation, periodic conferences are held, specialized scientific institutions are maintained, particularly for agriculture, and programs for the interchange of scientists among member countries are supported. In the sphere of communications, extensive cooperative arrangements exist regarding merchant shipping, air communications, telecommunications, and postal services. The United Kingdom has agreements with particular members of the Commonwealth regarding social security reciprocity and health services, and some members by agreement utilize the Judicial Committee of the British Privy Council as their final court of appeal on certain legal issues.

If indefiniteness and adaptability are among the prime characteristics of the Commonwealth system, consultation is its essential operating procedure. The system of consultation includes not only official correspondence from government to government, but also meetings of prime ministers and ministers and innumerable official and personal contacts between representatives of governments. High Commissioners represent the governments of the

* South Africa withdrew from the Commonwealth in 1961.

Commonwealth member-countries in the capitals of other members, and they usually have special access to the highest officials of the government to which they are posted.

Although the Commonwealth has no centralized governing institutions, it has established a variety of consultative councils and committees; and in 1966 a permanent Secretariat was established in London—the nearest approach to anything resembling a central administrative mechanism.

In theory, all Commonwealth members take no independent action in a matter of common concern until every effort has been made through consultation to achieve a common view. But even Britain has at times failed to fulfill this requirement, as in 1956 when it attacked Egypt—following which a majority of Commonwealth members either remained aloof or joined in condemning the British action. By 1965 internal diversity and divisions had reached a point unprecedented even in Commonwealth history. In 1964 two of the largest members, India and Pakistan, demonstrated their "community of interest" by going to war against one another. The only effective mediator in the situation turned out to be not Britain or any other Commonwealth member but the Soviet Union. And in numerous other instances, at the United Nations and elsewhere, disagreements among Commonwealth members in various parts of the world and even among African members themselves, have been manifested. Not only has a reasonable degree of unified action not been achieved, but even the assumption of British leadership of the association is no longer necessarily true. Not merely has British influence been greatly reduced, but the Commonwealth has become in many respects a pressure group, the main intent of which is to reshape British policy along the lines desired by the outlying members. In this sense one can now speak of the Commonwealth being "turned upside down," in the phrase of Professor Denis Austin of the University of Manchester, and under the circumstances both Britain and the African states have found new reasons to complain about its functioning. As a result the Commonwealth has been subjected to a long series of "agonizing reappraisals" and melancholy predictions of its demise. But it has survived, perhaps because of its indescribability and elasticity. And simply because of its existence and availability, it has proven more useful in some crises than its critics would have expected, as in the Nigerian civil war in 1968 when through its Secretary-General, Mr. Arnold Smith, it played a valuable role in the effort to reopen negotiations between the antagonists. Despite its constant changes and transformations, the Commonwealth seems to have all the durability that the frankly improbable so often acquires in human affairs.

If there remains meaning in the Commonwealth idea, however, it no longer turns on its once-imagined economic or military advantages, nor on its significance as a group of like-minded nations operating within a common general framework of foreign policy. Its potentiality for the future lies essentially in its quality as an association of diverse states, large and small, industrialized and poor, white and nonwhite. In a world increasingly confronted by a widening gulf between the developed and the underdeveloped nations, and haunted by the specter of spreading racial hostility, the Commonwealth represents one of the precious few available channels of contact and communication across the breach of race and poverty.

Lord Caradon has heavily stressed the interracial aspect:

> If there is no participation of freedom, if the Commonwealth is not a free association of peoples of different races, it is nothing. If the Commonwealth does not stand against race discrimination and race domination, it is worthless. If the division of the world between the Africans and the Asians on the one hand, and the White West on the other continues, the first casualty will be the Commonwealth. The trial and the test approach. Soon we shall discover whether the Commonwealth with all its great potentiality for good can survive.[19]

If this is to be the test not only of the Commonwealth but of the British position and influence in Africa, then the prospects are not encouraging—essentially because of the issue of Rhodesia. There, in coping with a treasonable action by some 200,000 white settlers, Britain muddled itself into a position where its responsibility to protect the interest and welfare of the African majority became far greater than its real authority and capacity to do so. As the situation skidded out of control, it dragged Britain's prestige in the mud behind it. Since illegally declaring its independence in late 1965, the rebel regime under Ian Smith has repeatedly flouted the authority of the British Crown, humiliated British official representatives, and made Britain appear in the eyes of Africa as "a toothless old bulldog," in the words of a Zambian diplomat. Throughout, Britain has displayed not only a lack of firmness but also a remarkable degree of diplomatic ineptitude by first letting the situation drift beyond the point of retrieval, then incorrectly assessing the problem and the probable effectiveness of the measures taken to deal with it, and finally, in desperation, asking the United Nations to attempt to cope with the situation in the face of the ineffectiveness of its own policy.

Had any one of the new African states carried out such a contradictory, vacillating, and simply imprudent sequence of diplomatic and political actions, it would have been taken by many Britons and others as proof of African immaturity and incompetence. That Britain should have made of itself such a graceless spectacle can be explained only by the brutal conflict between British principles and responsibilities on the one hand and a sense of abject weakness on the other. The sense of weakness, however, was greater than the fact, in the judgment of Africans. In their view, after the crisis began to emerge nearly a decade ago, Britain on several occasions could have exerted far greater influence than it did, but was incapacitated from taking a firm hand by what they are persuaded is the powerful undercurrent of racism in British life. Though its colonial policy was less harsh in many respects than that of some Western countries, Britain's conduct in Africa traditionally was distinctive by its insistence on social segregation between the races and by the absence of assimilationist objectives, as in the case of the French and the Portuguese. These suspicions of racism were greatly reinforced by the argument unfortunately used by some pro-Rhodesian elements in Britain in defending the government's policy; namely, that British troops could not in principle be used against "kith and kin."

Black Rhodesians and other Africans, however, have not distinguished themselves by their own performance in working against the political deterioration which has taken place. Partly perhaps because of frustration with their own splits, confusion, and general ineffectiveness as well as their resentment of racial slights, African hostility to British policy in 1966 and 1967 became very intense. During that time, respect for Britain and for British assertions of support for democratic principles and human rights took a nose dive, and several African Commonwealth members went so far as to break diplomatic relations. They have one by one re-established them since, suggesting that, despite continuing emotional resentment, they have realistically begun to fit Rhodesia back into the total perspective of their various international interests and objectives. But the situation remains a dangerous irritant to British-African relations. At best, it is unlikely to diminish in the near future as a source of friction; and it could become a new catastrophe if Britain should decide to reach an accord with the Smith regime on terms which the Africans would regard as a "sell-out" of the political rights of the blacks.

In consequence, acceptance of British leadership of the Commonwealth has greatly diminished, and anything resembling a bloc or even common front among its members has dissolved. This is quite possibly as it should be, but it is not what Britain originally expected or intended. The future of political relationships between Britain and Africa is likewise unpromising and uncertain. Not only are there many and severe sources of strain, but it is unclear what value Britain now attaches to the maintenance of its African links and of the Commonwealth itself. Britain is a society that has been badly wounded. In dramatic and drastic fashion it has begun to take belated measures to reduce its world commitments and responsibilities to correspond with its capacities. The needs of the society are urgent and, trading nation that Britain is, commercial relationships with all parts of the world—including South Africa—have to be maintained almost at all costs. Governments in such cruel distress cannot be expected to show excessive concern for the sensibilities and demands of others. Fundamentally, Britain has decided to give priority to its own domestic requirements and to its association with the industrialized nations of Western Europe. If and when a choice should have to be made between Commonwealth interests and responsibilities on the one hand and the requirements of British entry into the European Common Market on the other, it is difficult to predict what course might be taken, but the former will not likely be controlling. For the English-speaking African states as well, given the weakness of the British economic position and the objectionable quality of some aspects of British policy in Africa, particularly in Rhodesia, it is uncertain how far they would go—if an alternative were available—in attempting to maintain the diminishing advantages of their special relationship with Britain. Given the multitude of cultural, economic, and other links between Britain and Africa during the historical period of colonialism, Britain can never be simply another outside power. But it seems equally unlikely that Britain now or in the years ahead will exert any great degree of political influence over its former colonies.

IN CONCLUSION

The British exit from Africa since the Second World War, except for the case of Rhodesia, has been one of the most reasonable and amicable end-processes in the recorded history of imperialism. As nationalist pressures for independence in Africa mounted, and as difficulties at home intensified, Britain at first somewhat hesitantly and later almost gladly relinquished its colonial holdings. It could be argued that the course Britain took in Africa was not one so much of nobility as of simple objectivity. The African colonies had not in fact proven to be of great economic value. Their strategic consequence, once India became independent, was hardly more than incidental. And the cost of trying to maintain control—had that been attempted—would have rapidly become unmanageable in financial, military, and political terms given Britain's painful task of finding a new and considerably reduced role for itself in the world.

But whether or not decolonization made good sense in terms of Britain's self-interest, the fact remains that for most imperial countries in times past, the persuasiveness of a rational course of policy was often outweighed by considerations of national pride, delusions of national glory, and the inflexibility of habits and structures inherited from the colonial past. There would have been ample precedent had Britain attempted desperately and blindly to hold on.

Once the time for decolonization had arrived, Britain was prepared and willing to accord meaningful independence to the African territories. In doing so, there was no grand design but only a hope for orderliness, gradualism, and a desire for the maintenance of economic and commercial ties as well as of friendly and cooperative political relationships. The method, as it were, by which Britain pursued its somewhat amorphous goals was expediency and pragmatism. Not only was such an approach considered a positive virtue in the British tradition, but, given the wide variety of situations to be dealt with in West, East, and Central Africa, it seemed to have particular applicability. The result of such diversity of conditions, issues, and political atmospheres led to an unwillingness to set specific timetables, to an abhorrence of generalized policies and principles, and a consequent tendency to deal with problems as they arose on a case-by-case, piecemeal, and practical basis. The method adopted was therefore less a method than a tactic; and as a tactic, it was essentially responsive to external forces and premised upon an acceptance of gradual African take-over.

The means which Britain was prepared to employ in support of its objectives were both mild and limited. Although British diplomacy resisted strenuously any U.N. involvement or intrusion of other international pressures in its problems of decolonization, it was not prepared to employ major military force to suppress or even significantly delay the process of charge that was under way. As the second postwar decade advanced, Britain's willingness and capacity to employ military measures to repress nationalist elements virtually disappeared. Nor was Britain prepared to employ police or legal measures of any scope or severity to try to impose its will. Individual riots were quelled, and a certain number of African leaders were imprisoned. However, in comparison not only to the repressive practices of imperialism in the nineteenth century but even to those of other colonial powers in the twentieth, Britain's approach was moderate and humane—which of course has not prevented critics, especially in Britain, from calling it rubbery and weak.

Since independence was granted, Britain has given the former colonies substantial economic and technical assistance, and the total of such help has steadily grown over the years. The objective of such assistance has been to make them self-sufficient; developmental objectives have not been subordinated to antithetical political objectives. Economic grants and favors have not been employed as mere devices to reward the former colonies for compliance with British policy or to keep then generally in a state of continued dependence. Most recently, although Birtain has been confronted with acute economic and budgetary problems at home, the level of economic assistance has not been cut as drastically as the military budget, for example, or even certain domestic expenditures.

A good many of the original objectives and hopes of British policy have not been realized: The new governments have tended in the direction both of instability and the abandonment of parliamentary democracy; and the Commonwealth has not functioned in the manner originally intended. To some, the obstreperousness of the former colonies in their relations with Britain and the lack of influence over them is a sign of "failure" in British policy. But from another point of view, particularly that of the Africans themselves, their achievement of real independence is the ultimate proof of its success.

It is ironic, therefore, that Britain's generally decent and re-sponsible policies both before and since independence in Africa should have left it, by 1968, in a position of deteriorating reputa-tion and declining influence. But, as a white nation, it was trapped in the racial tensions of southern Africa, where it has attempted to resolve its dilemma by compromises which are no longer ade-quate to satisfy the demands of the nonwhites of the world. Britain is trapped, too, by its own fundamental economic weakness —and history shows little pity for weakness.

Given its present mood, Britain is not able to make the most even of the limited possibilities its predicament permits. After twenty-five years of severe overstrain, following an exhausting war, there seems to be a droop in national spirit; and not only a lack of national power but a feeling of powerlessness and a consequent facelessness in British policy. As Peter Calvocoressi wrote in *The Times* of August 10, 1967:

> In the past Britain has stood for the Imperial Idea or the Rule of Law or the defense of small peoples or anti-slavery or the parlia-mentary system. You might approve or disapprove of these things and you could point out that they were imperfectly applied—the Irish, for example, were excepted from most of them—but they meant something all the same and they gave Britain an identity. . . .
>
> Granted that Britain is no longer top power, are we standing up for ourselves in a way befitting our still very considerable station in the world? Every country has its grade. Nobody can fairly expect to compete outside its grade, but it must perform worthily within it.

But, for all the present troubles, Britain remains a redoubtable nation that, although it may for the time be down, is not out. If, in Rhodesia, it can resist the powerful temptation to close the present gap between responsibility and authority by an agreement conceding legitimacy to the Smith regime on its terms, the poor situation in southern Africa may at least not get worse. If Britain can maintain, in the face of urgent claims of domestic programs, the impressive and admirable level of its aid to independent Africa, the foundations of Britain's general influence should remain intact. Then, in time, with a revival of strength and self-confidence, Britain could yet realize its enormous potential influence in Africa for constructive relations between that continent and the rest of the world.

3

France: From Colonialism to Community to Independence

France at the end of the Second World War was no less battered and drained than Britain and far more deeply divided. Great physical and economic damage was manifest, while beneath the surface was still greater social, psychological, and political destruction. The ignominious defeat of the French forces in the first months of the war, the wartime collaboration between important elements of the French Right and the German occupiers, and the prominent role of the French Left in the Resistance intensified internal strains and divisions that had already been a crucial political problem long before the war began. In a mood of humiliation, anxiety, and factionalism France had to face the tasks of economic reconstruction, the development of a new constitutional framework, and the re-establishment of its position in a radically changed world of power relationships.

To these new tasks all the contradictory elements of French life addressed themselves in distinctively French fashion—logical and passionate, idealistic and materialistic, humane and violent. To the new undertaking, likewise, were brought all the assets, as well as the liabilities, of French history, tradition, and social, economic, and political concepts.

In the obscurity and uncertainty of the French predicament as the fighting ended, one of the few clear points of consensus was a belief in the importance and urgency of reconstructing the French empire. General de Gaulle, in whose hands political power was provisionally placed, favored the objective for a complex of political, strategic, and sentimental reasons; the rightist elements in French life, including the military, strongly supported it for their own political, strategic, and sentimental reasons; the French Left, including the Communists, were also, as a result of their own patterns of political reasoning, favorable to the full integration of the colonies with France.

In the years following 1945 France devoted massive energies and resources to that task. It employed major and bloody programs of repression as well as astonishingly large expenditures for economic and social development. But in the end, France like the other imperial powers had to give way to the forces of contemporary nationalism. Yet in the French fashion, that retreat was not simply the gradual, formless degeneration of an empire. France has consistently tried to shape the course of events, and for the first fifteen years of the postwar period it attempted to adjust to the changing forces by progressively modifying—but not abandoning—a basically imperial structure, that is, by granting steadily greater autonomy to the colonies but with institutionalized and centralized links to France.

Although France worked hard, spent heavily, and took serious political risks to rebuild the empire on a new basis, by 1960 the whole effort had failed. Or apparently failed. For in this as in so many aspects of the enigma called France, appearance can be too easily confused with reality. In a deeper sense, however, it can be said that French policy, up to the present at least, has succeeded: French influence in Africa has been substantially maintained; French prestige in many parts of Africa is high, and even those Africans who dislike France respect it; and a large number of African states regard France as their friend and supporter and in many matters follow its leadership.

What France has obtained, however, has been purchased at heavy cost. But how long will it be prepared to bear the burdens of maintaining its position in Africa? How long will the present African view of France survive? To speculate intelligently about the answers to these crucial questions, it is necessary to return briefly to the history of French colonialism, so tightly is the present interwoven with the past.

FRENCH COLONIALISM

In regard to all questions of empire, France has historically been divided, inconsistent, and self-contradictory. Those largely associated with the French Right have seen the French colonial tradition as one of the nation's greatest glories—from Cartier and Père Marquette in North America to French colonial officers bringing civilization to the heathens of the desert and the jungle, to the Legionnaires hunting Communists in Indochina, to *"les paras"* heroically defending Western civilization in Algeria. The empire in their view expressed the very essence of French character and honor and formed the core of French power and prestige in the world. Reinforcing the political influence of those who favored colonialism on geopolitical and romantic grounds has been a long and mongrel train of camp followers whose self-interests have been linked to the empire: economic adventurers who formed chartered companies to exploit the imagined riches of the conquered territories; segments in the Church who found in the colonies an enlarged area for influence as well as missionary activity; the more conservative service families who found careers in the colonial army and administration; and numerous settlers, traders, and investors whose lives and fortunes increasingly were tied to the maintenance of French colonial control.

On the other hand, from the time of the Revolution there were whole classes of French society that associated colonialism with kings, Bonapartism, and reaction and steadily opposed it. On those intermittent occasions when revolutionary or republican sentiment was in political ascendancy in France, sympathetic concern for the indigenous populations in the colonies quickly sprouted in the interstices of policy.

These continuing differences of viewpoint in French political debate took highly conceptualized form. One doctrine was called "assimilation" and derives from the egalitarian ideas of Descartes and Rousseau. It held that the peoples of the colonies should have the same rights and duties and the same institutions and opportunities as Frenchmen in France itself. Thus immediately after the Revolution in 1789, the inhabitants of the areas then controlled by France became French citizens and elected deputies to the French parliament. In the following decades, assimilationist principles contributed to the abolition of slavery after 1815 and to various other improvements in the condition of the colonial populations. But assimilation, which was based not only on idealism but also on unquestioned belief in the absolute and universal superiority of French culture, made its own contribution to the destruction of native traditions and institutions. The doctrine that people in the colonies should be given the same rights and institutions as Frenchmen at home led to liberalized policies in certain matters but it also provided the rationale for centralizing all power in Paris and for the Procrustean imposition of rigid administrative uniformity on the colonies.*

The alternative formula through which prewar colonial policy was expressed was "association." Its roots were not in idealism but in the conservative concern increasingly felt in the late nineteenth century that the rapid expansion of French territories in Africa threatened to impose dangerous economic and financial burdens on the metropole. It was also realized that literal application of the principle of equal rights for all French subjects might produce a vast electoral bloc of Africans in the French parliament and that France might become, as Herriot said at a later time, a "colony of her colonies." Thus association was not so much a doctrine as a shorthand term for a paternalistic and practical program to give France the benefit of its colonies at minimum political and financial cost. As in the case of assimilation, it produced contradictory consequences. On the one hand, it led to legislation, which was in force until 1940, severely restricting French contribution to colonial development and exacting from the territories to the extent possible the revenues necessary for their support. On the other hand, the same impulse to encourage self-sufficiency in the colonies permitted a useful degree of decentralization and a lessening of the rigidities of assimilationist concepts as applied to administration.

Although the French Left and Right split sharply on assimilation versus association, there were fundamental points of agreement, including a common belief in the superiority of French civilization, the desirability of a uniform structure for the colonies, and repudiation of any notion of their immediate or eventual self-government. These elements of agreement and disagreement among the contending political elements had important practical effects on the actual course of French policy in the colonies during the nineteenth and early twentieth centuries.

The first was that although political opposition to colonialism

---

* As Deschamps, a colonial governor, wrote in 1953: "Cartesian ideology ruined in advance any idea of 'self-government.' . . . A system of government which is based on universal reason is valid for all climates, for Frenchmen and for Hurons. They are the same humanity and it would be unreasonable to treat them differently merely because some of them wear three-cornered hats and some of them wear feathers." Quoted in *French Aid* by Teresa Hayter (London: Overseas Development Institute, 1966), p. 19.

in France was inadequate to prevent colonial expansion in Africa in the latter half of the nineteenth century, it did prevent single-minded devotion to the strengthening and development of the empire. Led by the military, France proceeded within the space of a few years to acquire vast tracts of relatively worthless real estate through its participation in the European scramble for Africa. French colonial officers and administrators always felt handicapped by the "politicians" in Paris and were obliged to get along with a lesser degree of home support than, for example, their British counterparts.

The second practical consequence of the division of opinion in France was wide fluctuation in colonial policy as domestic political control alternated between one group and another. Thus slavery was abolished during the Revolution; re-established during the Napoleonic period; suppressed again after 1815. In 1848, with the advent of the Second Republic, revolutionary principles were re-affirmed; in 1860, Napoleon III disavowed them; and in 1870, they were reasserted by the Third Republic. From idealistic liberalism the pendulum has swung to extreme conservatism and back again repeatedly. As a consequence, policy changes on colonial issues have again and again been introduced suddenly, without adequate preparation and often with disregard for their long-term consequences.

Third, because conservative elements were generally predominant in French political life through most of the nineteenth century until after the Second World War, French colonial policy during that long period was on the whole repressive and exploitive. Rightist governments consistently denied the application in the colonies of democratic political, economic, and social principles accepted within France. In black Africa the concept of assimilation had such limited actual effect that less than one hundred thousand Africans had been accorded citizen status by 1939; all others were French "subjects" with no rights of political representation either in France or Africa and no access to higher posts in the civil or military service or to universities. They lived under an authoritarian system governed not by legislation but executive decree. They were liable to forced labor and involuntary conscription for military service. They were subject to a legal system known as the *indigénat* by which administrative officers could try and punish suspects summarily without the possibility of appeal or judicial review.

Nor were their economic conditions much better. Traditionally,

France preferred to leave economic exploitation and development to private groups rather than provide funds from the treasury. Such groups and enterprises were almost exclusively French, because it was virtually impossible for non-French investors to enter the territories. In granting concessions and monopolies the government stipulated, usually in rather general terms, that the company should provide for the welfare of the native populations and carry out certain limited programs of public works. However, these obligations, limited as they were, were not enforced. Paris intervened little, and the commercial companies in full complicity with local military commanders and administrative officials often misused their freedom. Flamboyant abuses occurred, and opinion in France was repeatedly aroused by revelations of colonial scandals in parliament and in the press. Nevertheless, the colonies in Africa continued to be administered to a great extent by local officials without serious supervision from the metropole and without a tradition of responsibility to the native population.*

By the 1920s and 1930s limited programs of public health and medical services had been instituted and a few scattered educational institutions created. But few Africans in Western or Equatorial Africa were able to enter primary school, only a small percentage of these reached secondary school, and a minuscule number went on to universities in France.

* The French possessions in Africa which are here, for the sake of brevity, called "colonies" were in fact of differing size, state of development, ethnic composition, and legal status. They consequently proceeded to independence at different rates and by different routes. Two which were protectorates, namely Tunisia and Morocco, achieved independence earliest. Last to achieve independence and with greatest difficulty was Algeria, which had been considered an integral part of France and was designated an "overseas department." The other territories which are referred to variously as sub-Saharan, tropical, or black African were the least advanced and juridically the most subordinate. Much of the following discussion of the process of French decolonization relates to them more than to the special situations in North Africa. They constituted two colonial federations in French West Africa and French Equatorial Africa called "Overseas Territories," consisting of Niger, Dahomey, Upper Volta, Ivory Coast, Soudan, French Guinea, Mauritania, and Senegal (French West Africa) and of Chad, Gabon, Middle Congo, and Ubangi-Shari (French Equatorial Africa) plus two territories originally mandated by the League of Nations, Togo and Cameroon, called "Associated Territories." In addition, there were the two colonies of Somaliland on the horn of Africa and the great island of Madagascar in the Indian Ocean. For purposes of this summary review most of these technical but important distinctions of status will be ignored. For a more detailed description see *Statesman's Yearbook*, 1958 or 1959.

Until the outbreak of the Second World War, therefore, a severe verdict must be passed on the practices of French colonialism in Africa. Among its most harsh critics were prominent French leaders, usually religious or of the Left, who repeatedly demanded more humane and generous colonial policies, and intellectuals who constantly reiterated assimilationist ideas. But the influence of the humanitarians and the intellectuals seldom prevailed. The colonies were subordinated to the metropole and exploited in a fashion comparable only to that in the Portuguese African territories.

This being so, it is a remarkable paradox that Francophone African leaders generally respected France, took pride in their French culture, and profoundly admired the nonracial feelings of the French intellectual and political elite. Such feelings help explain the phenomenon of African colonial support for France during World War II. In the earlier years, most of the French colonial governors remained loyal to the Vichy regime. But when, in the name of the Free French, de Gaulle appealed for support, the governor of the equatorial territory of Chad promptly declared for him and was followed soon afterward by other governors in French Equatorial Africa and by some in French West Africa. Africa then became the territorial base for the Free French movement, and thousands of Africans rallied to its cause. At one time nearly half of de Gaulle's forces were Africans from the colonies, and black African troops took part in General Le Clerc's historic desert crossing and in the liberation of France itself. Such demonstrations of fidelity in a time of desperate need added an important sentimental factor to the complex of forces which were to shape French policy and colonial relationships in the postwar period.

Evolving Political Relations After World War II

France entered the Second World War as an imperial nation proud of its position as a world power, an indispensable element of which (in the French view) was its colonies. Nor did France at the time sense an urgent threat to its position, although there had been manifestations against French rule in Indochina and the Middle East and, to a lesser degree, in North Africa, where nationalist movements had gained some strength. But in Tropical Africa such discontent, though occasionally apparent, was feeble and unorganized.

By the end of the war, however, almost everything had changed for France except its illusory conception of itself. In the United Kingdom, the task of postwar reeonstruction and adaptation, though formidable, could be undertaken with constitutional structures intact and with the various elements of the nation still able and willing to function in effective political relationship with one another. In France, the same tasks of adjustment had to be undertaken in a society haunted by defeat, torn into irreconcilable factions, and unequipped with a workable set of basic governing institutions. The story of the years since has been that of the troubled transformation of every aspect of French society, politics, and foreign policy—one element of which has been the transformation of the relationship with the former empire.

But, whereas Britain was prepared and able to respond flexibly to the growing demands for independence in its colonies, France took a precisely opposite stance. The injured pride of Frenchmen after the experiences of the war made it emotionally impossible to consider relinquishing any symbol of French prestige and world position as potent as the empire. As the war drew to an end, the provisional government of General de Gaulle was aware of the necessity to overhaul its anachronistic structure and was motivated by a sympathetic interest in the welfare of the African territories. Nevertheless, it was bound by the assumption that whatever changes might be made, the essence of imperial control had to be maintained. Initially the intention was to introduce radical new reforms that would maintain the integrity of the system but begin to give substance to the long ignored goals of equality, justice, and material progress for the people of the colonies. In the following fifteen years, in a series of wrenching crises, these initial plans and intentions were twisted into unrecognizable forms under the impact of forces within France, the colonies, and the world at large, and in the end they had to be abandoned completely. The main stages in that difficult process by which France moved from the hope of unqualified restoration of empire to final granting of independence have been analyzed in detail by a number of scholars and need not be recounted here.[1] Four principal milestones along the road to decolonization should, however, be noted:

1. In January 1944 the provisional government called a conference at Brazzaville in Equatorial Africa to consider the problems of the colonies and protectorates. The participants consisted mainly of the governors and administrators of black Africa and Madagascar as well as representatives from Morocco and Tunisia.

The spirit of the occasion was one of generosity and gratitude toward the African colonies, which had loyally and importantly supported the Free French forces.

The conference, in the presence of General de Gaulle, agreed on a series of steps intended to strengthen and make more equitable the French empire but not dissolve it. Administrative and economic decentralization was recommended as well as the encouragement of traditional African institutions. A comprehensive program of economic and social reforms was sketched out: Medical services were to be extended, for example, and the higher ranks of the administrative services were to be opened to Africans for the first time.

These major changes were to be carried out within the old political framework, however. Any idea of self-government, immediate or eventual, was ruled out. In the opening paragraph of the Final Resolutions of the meeting it was stated: "The aims of the civilizing work accomplished by France in the colonies exclude any thought of autonomy, any thought of evolution outside the framework of the French Empire; the idea of establishing, even in the distant future, 'self-government' in the colonies must be discarded."

2. In 1946, when postwar France organized to draft a new Constitution for the Fourth Republic, the goal of rebuilding the empire on a flexibly interpreted assimilationist basis was built into the new structure with the full cooperation of African leaders themselves. The colonies and protectorates were represented in the Constituent Assemblies; sixty-three of the six hundred seats were reserved for them. The African delegates together with representatives of the Left-wing metropolitan parties, including the Communists, campaigned for assimilation mainly in the form of parliamentary representation and full French citizenship.

Under the Constitution as finally adopted the black African colonies and Madagascar became Overseas Territories of an "indivisible" Fourth Republic. The Constitution conferred citizenship on all subjects of the empire, which for the great majority of the inhabitants of the colonies formerly in "subject" status meant the ending of forced labor and the *indigénat* system of arbitrary administrative justice. Political participation by the inhabitants of the colonies was provided for in both local and metropolitan affairs. They elected representatives to a sovereign legislature, the French National Assembly, and to a Consultative Assembly of the French Union, which was the name given to the reconstituted empire. Elective assemblies were set up in each territory with limited powers, and some wording even suggested the possibility of their eventual evolution toward a greater degree of autonomy if not self-government.

Subsequently, a plan for economic and social development of the French Union as a whole was adopted with generous provision for metropolitan financing. The contrast with prewar policy was striking, and hopes were high both in the colonies and in certain sectors of France that the old dream of assimilation might at last become reality.

One of the main consequences of the new arrangement was a general stimulation of political activity at all levels on the part of Africans. Political parties were formed, usually affiliated to metropolitan parties, principally the Communist and the Socialist. African leaders participated in French politics and were active in the French Assembly where their allegiance, particularly in the latter years of the Fourth Republic, could make or break governments in the delicate maneuvering for parliamentary majorities.

3. In the following ten years from 1946 to 1956, however, the French Union encountered increasing difficulties because of developments within France and the colonies and in the world at large.

During that period, the general overseas position of France was under heavy pressure. In the Near East, France's attempt to hold its mandates over Syria and Lebanon by force failed, and, by 1946, it had been obliged to give them up and to withdraw its remaining troops. In the Far East, immediately after the war, violent resistance to French authority broke out, culminating in 1954 with a stinging defeat of French forces at Dien Bien Phu, which led to the independence of the component states of Indochina. Nationalist movements in Morocco and Tunisia became rapidly stronger, and France relinquished its protectorates over them in 1955 and 1956, respectively. In Algeria, nationalist opposition had broken out into active rebellion by the mid-1950s.

Over these same years India and Pakistan achieved independence, while political evolution was visibly under way throughout English-speaking Africa. These developments only sharpened the awareness of African leaders in the French-speaking sub-Saharan territories of the fact that despite the structural reforms in the 1946 Constitution, the French colonies were still effectively restricted politically by such devices as a double electoral system, which limited their political representation and subordinated them to permanent control by metropolitan France.

In France itself, the parliamentary regime created by the Constitution proved unworkable in the face of the continuing fragmentation of national political life. A chronic condition of instability and *immobilisme* in government resulted, which the Africans saw as greatly retarding their progress toward assimilation and perpetuating their unequal political status. In the absence of new legislative and policy directives from France, old habits and the natural tendencies of the French system toward centralization reasserted themselves. Educational reforms were blocked; the Africanization of the local administrative machinery barely got under way; and the economic assistance and development programs that had been launched were increasingly turned to the profit of French firms and expatriates rather than to the benefit of the African populations.

Under the circumstances the demands of the black African states for greater political concessions and reforms became more and more insistent. Finally, in 1956 a Socialist government under Guy Mollet managed to survive long enough to pass an important *loi cadre* embracing a number of important and seriously overdue reforms. The new legislation redefined and restructured political relationships with the territories and constituted in effect, if not by intent, a considerable move toward self-government.

It instituted universal direct suffrage, abolished the dual electoral colleges, and gave more powers to the territorial assemblies. A French-appointed governor still headed each territorial executive, but an African normally became his principal deputy and acquired the status of a prime minister. The visibility and political influence of certain African leaders were accentuated, and African political activity was further stimulated. Although the intricate political compromise represented by the *loi cadre* was a major advance, it still left the territories locked within a framework of French control. It was followed by a series of major decrees which gave substance to its provisions and intentions—but the gains represented were rapidly overtaken and overwhelmed by other African events, notably the war in Algeria.

4. By 1957 the Algerian rebellion had not only developed into a major and costly war (with more than 400,000 French troops engaged) but had degenerated into ugly forms of torture and terrorism that shook opinion within France and aroused protest throughout the world, including that of a young American senator

from Massachusetts, John F. Kennedy. *La sale guerre* had become the most divisive factor in French life since the German occupation.

Given the intensity of their own discontents and the evident contradictions and inadequacies of French policy, a group of the most important sub-Saharan African leaders convened a conference in Bamako, in Soudan (now Mali), in September 1957, to clarify their own views on the future of their territories. Ghana had obtained its independence six months before, but few of the Africans present at Bamako were as yet prepared to seek complete independence from France. It was on this occasion, under the leadership of Houphouët-Boigny of Ivory Coast, that the idea of a French African Community as a coherent federal system rather than a loose commonwealth was first put forth.

By 1958, the Algerian violence had produced a *crise de régime* for France. There the French army and its European settler allies rejected the authority of the Fourth Republic, sponsored a subversive rightist revolutionary movement in France, and finally deposed the government in Paris. In the midst of this vast calamity, General de Gaulle emerged for the second time to help save France from itself.

The failures of the Fourth Republic necessitated a basic overhauling of the French political system. The draft Constitution for the Fifth Republic, prepared under de Gaulle's direction, left the way open for the sub-Saharan African territories, whose continued political support was important to the General's effort to settle the Algerian problem, to take another step toward political self-determination. The 1958 Referendum on the Constitution of the Fifth Republic offered the African territories the choice of becoming Departments of France or autonomous republics within a newly conceived French Community; or they could opt for independence. Since Mr. Houphouët-Boigny was one of the group which prepared the new plan, it was not surprising that the idea of the Community should reappear as one of the alternatives. In effect, the choice offered was open but not free, for de Gaulle made it clear on a tour of tropical Africa before the Referendum that continued association with France and the new Community would bring substantial benefits, whereas a vote for independence would mean a total break and the loss of all economic assistance.

Throughout French-speaking territories there was serious talk for the first time about "immediate independence." But, in the Referendum of 1958, with the dice loaded in favor of a "yes" vote for the Community, only Guinea, under the leadership of Sekou Touré, voted "no." None of the other black African leaders were ready to face a rupture with France, partly because of the dependence of their territories on French financial and technical support and partly because a number of them genuinely believed in continuing Franco-African association.

France thereafter fulfilled both its pledges and its threats. Guinea suffered in full the consequences of its vote for independence: Financial assistance was discontinued as well as trade support; the Guinean account in the French Treasury was blocked; and even the pensions of Guinea war veterans were eliminated. In contrast, those territories which had voted for continued association with France and membership in the Community were offered generous economic aid.

Under the Gaullist conception of the Community the new African states would be completely self-governing internally; but in affairs that concerned them all they would agree "to a diminution of sovereignty by sharing it with France." The Community would have common organs and institutions, including a President and Executive Council, a Senate and a High Court of Arbitration.

However, the contrived and semi-involuntary agreement reflected in the vote on the Referendum was of only temporary significance in checking the movement of the African territories toward independence. The Federation of Mali in 1960 was the first to ask for it. After long negotiations and with great reluctance, France conceded that Mali might become independent and yet remain associated with the Community. France thereby agreed also to continue its aid—which shattered the conception of a Community whose political linkage with France was the price of economic privileges.

Thereafter in the course of that single year, 1960, all thirteen remaining territories became independent, either inside or outside the Community; and all signed "cooperation agreements" with France simultaneously or soon after. They thereby achieved what de Gaulle considered as "international sovereignty" with separate membership in the United Nations.

The signing of the cooperation agreements represented a fundamental change in the relationship of the tropical African territories to France. They marked the abandonment of the French effort to maintain centralized and institutional links with the territories—the institutional aspects of the Community essentially became a dead letter—and the beginning of contractual arrangements on a basis of sovereign equality. Table 5 indicates the number and complexity of the contractual ties which were established.

In the various agreements signed there are numerous minor differences, but in practice relationships have tended toward uniformity. Generally, the six states which chose to remain within the Community (Senegal, Madagascar, Gabon, Chad, the Central African Republic, and Congo-Brazzaville) were accorded greater intimacy of relationships with France than those which remained outside.

In subsequent years France has included three additional states to a limited degree in the system of cooperation agreements—Burundi, Rwanda, and Congo-Léopoldville (now Congo-Kinshasa)—which were formerly under Belgian control and never part of the French empire. Their inclusion signals France's desire to widen its sphere of influence in Africa, but particularly reflects its special interest in the French language and therefore in all French-speaking states.*

In a certain sense the achievement of independence by all the former states of the empire in Africa might be thought to represent the final failure of postwar French policy on that continent. It could be argued that in the end France lost on all fronts: It lost in the political confrontations with the Arab nationalists of North Africa as well as with Madagascar and the black Africans south of the Sahara. It lost the war in Algeria. Every halfway constitutional house it attempted to erect was eventually and often quickly demolished: the renovated assimilationist empire, the ill-fated French Union, and the short-lived French Community. Moreover, from a purely legal point of view it might seem that although France and Britain traveled by different routes, they in the end arrived at the same destination—namely, contractual rather than institutional links to their former African territories and acceptance of their full independence. It could be contended that the main difference was merely in style and method: Britain in its pragmatic fashion through a multitude of small adjustments to growing pressures oozed out of Africa, while France moving from

---

* Conversely, the association of the Francophone areas with the European Common Market, which was accomplished at French insistence, exposed them to a degree of political as well as economic intrusion by the other European members. But this slight risk was a price France was evidently ready to pay in exchange for trade and aid benefits to the territories.

TABLE 5. Dates of Principal Cooperation Agreements Between France and the African States

	POLITICAL			ECONOMIC AND FINANCE			
	Foreign Policy	Defense	Strategic Raw Materials	Monetary, Economic, Financial	Postal and Tele-communication	Civil Aviation	Merchant Marine
Central African Republic	18 VIII 60	13 VIII 60	13 VIII 60	11 VIII 60	—	—	—
Congo-Brazzaville	15 VIII 60	15 VIII 60	15 VIII 60	13 VIII 60	—	—	—
Gabon	17 VIII 60	17 VIII 60	17 VIII 60	7 VIII 60	—	17 VIII 60	17 VIII 60
Chad	11 VIII 60	15 VIII 60	15 VIII 60	15 VIII 60	—	60	60
Madagascar	27 VI 60	27 VI 60	27 VI 60	27 VI 60	27 VI 60	27 VI 60	27 VI 60
Senegal	22 VI 60	22 VI 60	22 VI 60	22 VI 60	—	22 VI 60	22 VI 60
Ivory Coast	—	24 IV 61	—	24 IV 61	24 IV 61	24 IV 61	24 IV 61
Dahomey	—	24 IV 61	—	24 IV 61	24 IV 61	24 IV 61	24 IV 61
Upper Volta	—	24 IV 61[a]	—	24 IV 61	24 IV 61	24 IV 61	24 IV 61
Niger	—	24 IV 61	—	24 IV 61	24 IV 61	24 IV 61	24 IV 61
Cameroon	—	13 XI 60[a]	—	13 XI 60	—	13 XI 60	—
Togo	—	10 VII 63	—	10 VII 63	—	—	—
Mauritania	—	19 VI 61	—	19 VI 61	19 VI 61	19 VI 61	19 VI 61
Mali	—	—	—	9 III 62	—	—	—
Guinea	—	—	—	22 V 63	—	—	—
Rwanda	—	—	—	4 XII 62	—	—	—
Burundi	—	—	—	11 XII 62	—	—	—
Congo-Kinshasa	—	—	—	—	—	—	—

[a] Technical Assistance Agreements in military matters only.

TABLE 5. Dates of Principal Cooperation Agreements Between France and the African States (cont.)

	LEGAL			SOCIAL AND CULTURAL		
	Judiciary	"Establish-ment" Conventions	Consular Conventions	Cultural Cooperation	Higher Education	Technical Cooperation
Central African Republic	12 VII 60	13 VIII 60	13 VIII 60	13 VIII 60	15 VIII 60	17 VII 59
Congo-Brazzaville	18 V 62	15 VIII 60	—	15 VIII 60	15 VIII 60	23 VII 59
Gabon	31 XII 59	17 VIII 60	—	18 XI 59	17 VIII 60	18 XI 59
Chad	12 VII 60	11 VIII 60	—	16 VIII 60	15 VIII 60	29 XI 59
Madagascar	27 VI 60	27 VI 60	25 IV 63	22 VII 59	27 VI 60 / 5 IV 62	7 VII 59
Senegal	14 VI 62	22 VI 60	—	4 II 60	22 VI 60 / 5 VIII 61	14 IX 59
Ivory Coast	24 IV 61	—	—	24 IV 61	24 IV 61	24 IV 61
Dahomey	24 IV 61	—	—	24 IV 61	24 IV 61	24 IV 61
Upper Volta	24 IV 61	—	—	24 IV 61	24 IV 61	24 IV 61
Niger	24 IV 61	—	—	24 IV 61	24 IV 61	24 IV 61
Cameroon	13 XI 60	—	13 XI 60	13 XI 60	8 VIII 62	13 XI 60
Togo	10 VII 63	—	—	10 VI 63	—	10 VII 63
Mauritania	19 VI 61	—	—	19 VI 61		19 VI 61
Mali	9 III 62	—	9 III 62	9 III 62	9 III 62	9 III 62
Guinea	—	—	—	22 V 63		22 V 63
Rwanda	—	—	—	4 XII 62	4 XII 62	—
Burundi	—	—	—	11 II 63	11 II 63	—
Congo-Kinshasa	—	—	—	17 VII 63	—	—

SOURCE: Notes et Etudes Documentaires, Secretariat General du Gouvernement, Paris, October 25, 1966.

one splendidly logical but unrealistic constitutional scheme to another relinquished control in a series of grand lurches.

It would be a mistake, however, to draw too close a parallel between the results of the two processes. Indeed, it probably would be a mistake to call the outcome of French policy a failure, for it has to a considerable degree achieved the continuation of French influence and control. For this, France has been prepared to invest considerable resources. It has taken political risks and made bold demands. When independence had to be conceded, it sought to insert into the subsequent agreements of cooperation provisions which Britain would not have attempted and which in any event the former British colonies would not have accepted. And France succeeded. It is quite remarkable that in the political agreements a number of the Francophone states were prepared to concede, even in a period of intense nationalism, that their foreign policies and those of France are "inspired by the same ideals and based on the same principles." Moreover, in carrying out the various agreements signed in 1960, France has done so in a spirit of active concern to maintain close relationships with the new countries, to exercise leadership, and to maintain discipline among them. Specific French policies toward Africa in the following years have undergone repeated modification, but there has been little change in the existence of a special French interest in Africa and in the militancy of France's policy to maintain its influence there.

More recently, however, the first signs can perhaps be detected of a narrowing of the scope of French goals in Africa, of a greater degree of selectivity in the making of commitments, and possibly, as French internal problems multiply, of a lessened priority for Africa in French policy generally. If these early indications prove accurate, a major additional element of unpredictability will have been added to the evolving European-African relationship.

POSTWAR ECONOMIC RELATIONS

If France experienced a special degree of anguish in accepting the severance of political and constitutional ties to the former colonies, it has had equal difficulty in modifying its economic relationships—and for essentially the same reasons. For France, the colonies were not mere appendages loosely related to the metropole; they had been incorporated into a tight trade and monetary system, the Franc Zone, built into the life of France itself. To cut them loose even partially meant therefore the risk of trauma to both severed parts, France as well as the colonies.

Immediately upon the ending of the Second World War, French economic authorities gave urgent attention to the state of the economy, which was in a gravely weakened condition. France's productive establishment had been dislocated by wartime requirements; plant and facilities were deteriorated and inefficient; the country was in the grip of serious internal inflationary pressures; and its trading accounts, particularly with the dollar area, were badly in deficit. Given the stringency of France's position, it was considered a matter of the highest importance to strengthen the defenses of the economy by tightening the system of trade and financial relations with the colonies and by increasing its protectionist features, including import licensing, quantitative restrictions, and exchange controls. France thereby maintained guaranteed markets for a significant proportion of its exports and obtained assured supplies of essential raw materials. Its exports did not have to be competitive in price in world markets, and it obtained supplies without having to use foreign exchange which in those years was exceedingly scarce.

From the French point of view the system functioned satisfactorily through the first postwar decade. Although, under the trading arrangements, France paid more than world prices (called *surprix*) for certain primary products from the overseas territories (just as the territories paid above world prices for their imports from France), the balance of advantage, at least through 1954, was still markedly in France's favor, though declining as time went on.*

In addition to the imposition of measures to maintain the Franc Zone as a closed trading and monetary system, however,

* An incidental advantage of the system from a French perspective was the right of French individuals living and working in the territories to make unlimited transfers to France at a favorable rate of exchange. These included many thousands of French administrators, army officers, and private investors and managers. Because of their specific self-interest and because of their key positions of leverage within or upon the French bureaucracy, which in the parliamentary paralysis of postwar years was even more important than it normally is in the functioning of the French government, their influence on economic policy and its implementation was considerable. For them, questions of convertibility rates between currencies of the overseas territories and the metropolitan franc and arrangements for the repatriation of profits or salaries directly affected their real incomes and the size of their savings accounts. They were never lax in making sure that their own privileges were not injured by the policies or procedures established.

French authorities after the war for the first time began to give major attention to the economic development of the colonies. Previously, beginning as early as the 1920s, a number of projects related to development had been supported, such as mineral surveys, tropical disease control, and the establishment of a few agricultural experiment stations; but these were of limited scope. At the Brazzaville conference in 1944 the call had been issued for a new emphasis on development and the primacy of African welfare had been laid down as a cardinal principle. In the spring of 1946, after the Fourth Republic had begun to function, a ten-year development plan was drawn up for the dependencies, and integrated with the Monnet Plan for the reconstruction and modernization of the metropole. In part the motivation for this sharp break with the colonial tradition was a sense of gratitude for the loyalty and cooperation of the African territories with the Free French forces during the war. In addition, there were those who accepted the new plan less out of regard for the native populations than out of recognition that something had to be done to reduce the great disparity in economic level between the metropole and the territories if the empire were to be rebuilt and if a stable base were to be created for broader French strategic and political ambitions.

The plan, though economic in character, was conceived so as to serve the overriding political goal of interlocking the overseas part of the Union with metropolitan France. Its main operative concern was with equality and uniformity; it was specifically not aimed at developing the economic viability or the administrative self-sufficiency of the separate territories. Its integrationist objectives were re-enforced by the monetary aspects of the Franc Zone, which also served to encourage the interdependence of the parts and their subordination to Paris. But in time, larger forces tore apart the political unity the plan was intended to create. Before that occurred, severe administrative and financial problems had already blunted the impact of the plan in purely developmental terms.

Despite the hopeful departure from previous economic patterns which the plan represented, it was launched in adverse circumstances. Both capital and consumer goods were in shortage in France. There was no money in the treasury with which to purchase needed equipment and materials outside the Franc Zone. It began operations without benefit of adequate preliminary scientific and economic studies.

The bulk of the funds provided were given in the form of out-right subsidies annually allocated from the metropolitan budget. These were of considerable scale although the precise totals are difficult to establish because of the characteristics of French statistics at the time. According to one estimate, French West Africa alone between 1947 and 1952 received infusions of capital amounting to some 270 billion francs (more than $500 million) of which more than 55 per cent was supplied from the French treasury, 25 per cent by French West Africans, and 20 per cent by private investors.[2] According to an official American estimate, French investments for the development of the colonies during 1951 alone reached approximately $320 million.[3] After 1948, a significant portion of the funds allocated to the development of the African territories by the French budget derived directly or indirectly from the Marshall Plan, which specifically provided for such use of American aid.

In the first few years, heavy emphasis was given to credits for ports, railroads, waterways, roads, airports, and other costly infra-structure projects, while the share assigned to increasing local production and for social development was kept to a minimum. In the execution of these large-scale programs, however, serious difficulties developed. Progress was delayed by bureaucratic quar-rels and power struggles; and metropolitan economic interests were increasingly able to deflect the plan from its declared pur-poses to their own benefit, giving rise to repeated charges of favoritism and the mishandling of funds.

By 1952 the French public had become throughly discouraged by reports of waste, mismanagement, and corruption. The view was also widely held that the burden imposed by the program on the French budget had become disproportionate since private capital and the Africans themselves were not contributing to development costs to the extent originally hoped. The prospect that large-scale Marshall Plan credits to France would no longer be available after 1952 added to the belief that the colonial development effort had been conceived in overly ambitious terms.

Basic policy changes in the program were consequently intro-duced: The emphasis on large infrastructure projects was cut back, while projects to increase production in all fields were to be given stress. But these and other changes did little to improve the over-all situation, and discontent with the plan and its results continued on both the French and African sides.

There was widespread criticism among Africans that industrial development had been not only neglected, but also suppressed, and that too little emphasis had been given in expenditure patterns to improving the well-being of the black populations. Outlays for high-cost administrative personnel—largely French—had ballooned and were absorbing 60 per cent of their territorial budgets, as compared to 40 per cent before the war. One point on which much criticism focused was the charge that only a small fraction of the sums expended remained in Africa, the remainder being repatriated to France in the form of savings and profits.

By 1956, what had begun as a bold and hopeful new approach to development in Africa ten years before had degenerated into disillusionment on all sides. The heavy outlays to improve infrastructure of the territories had been converted into a bonanza for French contractors and entrepreneurs. The assistance given, though of long-run value, had done little in the short term to alter basic production patterns or to increase productivity in the recipient areas. Conditions of life for the inhabitants had changed little, and except for a few isolated situations, it was difficult to detect anywhere even the beginnings of dynamic or self-sustaining development. Expenditures on education had served principally to expand a system ill-adapted to the development requirements of the African territories, and the technical assistance given encouraged the maintenance of an extravagant number of expensive expatriate administrators. This had the double disadvantage of blocking the development of qualified Africans and also of burdening the budgets of the overseas areas with heavy salary and personnel costs. The error of having created excessively costly administrative structures was multiplied when the federations in both West and Equatorial Africa broke up in 1956 and 1958, with the result that each state had to set up the full range of political and administrative institutions.

The whole great colonial development effort had been conceived and executed to serve a political objective that by the end of the first postwar decade had become unrealizable—namely, the maintenance of an imperial structure between France and the colonies. As a consequence, the economic program that was to have integrated them as component parts of a new French Union instead left them a collection of dependent and fragmentary states.

From Loi Cadre to Community to Independence

In the brief period from the passage of the *loi cadre* in 1956—the first major French response to the growing pressures of African dissatisfaction—until the advent of General de Gaulle to power in 1958, the energies and attention of France were focused on the climactic military and political events in Algeria, not on economic relationships with the tropical African territories. In that interval, trends in international trade further increased the dependence of the tropical areas on France, and their need for economic assistance was, therefore, a powerful influence on their response to the 1958 Referendum on the Constitution of the Fifth Republic. Following the referendum, although the political outcome was clear, a confused malaise both in France and in Africa with respect to trade, monetary, and economic assistance relationships persisted until 1960, without fundamental new decisions being taken. In that year when independence was finally conceded to the sub-Saharan territories, economic and other relationships were then established on a bilateral contractual basis in the cooperation agreements that were signed.

So formidably complex and interrelated had been French economic and other ties with the colonies that no single element could be understood or evaluated except in relation to the whole. And in the agreements signed after independence, the same complexity and interrelationship of the parts persisted. There was an umbrella agreement to cooperate in economic, financial, and other matters of mutual interest, under which separate agreements on trade, fiscal and monetary matters, aid, education, strategic materials, and military cooperation were made. The package of agreements and commitments was interlinked, and no one part could stand alone. Commercial as well as financial ties were maintained under the monetary and fiscal arrangements. In return for its aid and technical assistance, France obtained priority access to strategic materials, including uranium. Under the aid agreements, French trade benefitted since commodities had to be of French origin and delivered by French transport. Under the education agreements, France eased the budgetary strain on the recipient states and at the same time contributed to their economic development by providing a growing number of technicians and teachers. The military agreements contributed not only to the stability but also to the economies of the tropical states as a result of stationing large numbers of French forces there whose local expenditures were sizable. Thus each of the agreements fitted into and to some extent served the purposes of the others, and there was a careful balancing of interest and obligations on a *quid pro quo* basis between France and its tropical African partners. Sometimes economic commitment was balanced by economic commitment; more often the counterpart of economic or educational assistance was military or cultural privilege. In analyzing separately the economic agreements, therefore, it will be found that the willingness of France to perpetuate certain apparently disadvantageous arrangements in trade and aid is explainable only by reference to trade-offs in other noneconomic areas of the total system of cooperation.

The Franc Zone and Trade

In effect the new contractual economic agreements meant that the links of the sub-Saharan states with the trade and monetary aspects of the Franc Zone remained intact—including habitual trade preferences, a degree of French guarantee of the currencies, and French control over monetary and fiscal policies. The latter was accomplished primarily by French membership on the governing boards of the African central banks.

In subsequent years the Franc Zone, like other monetary systems, has become liberalized and more flexible, and "grades" of membership have developed. It has even become difficult in some cases to tell whether a state is or is not a member. So loose are the links with some of the North African states, for example, that their relationship is but slightly different from that of any outside government. But for the sub-Saharan states, the advantages of membership remain important in terms of trade and aid as well as the stability and convertibility of their currencies. They have, therefore, willingly chosen to remain both within the Zone's diminishing but still significant confinement and its shelter.

In trade relations the historical pattern of preferential ties to France was preserved in principle in the agreements signed after independence. But new forces were already at work to compel modification. France's trade position by 1960 was such that many of the advantages it had derived in the immediate postwar period from its special relationship with the African territories had disappeared. Shortly after de Gaulle took power in 1958 the French franc was devalued and exports of manufactures became more competitive in relation to world prices. The subsequent resurgence of the French economy, the increased convertibility and stability of the franc, the growth in currency reserves, and the steadily growing impact of the trading provisions of the European Common Market all encouraged a liberalization and diversification in France's trade patterns.

With Africa, some loosening did occur, but the major elements remained unchanged—quotas, reciprocal tariff preferences, and price subsidies on certain tropical products paid by France. Within this framework, trade flows have continued as much as before. Table 6 indicates the trend of French exports and imports with Africa in recent years, as compared with the total movement of trade.

In absolute terms, French exports to and imports from Africa have increased in recent years, but only moderately. On the other hand, French world trade has expanded rapidly, with the result that, between 1962 and 1967, exports to Africa decreased from 20.3 per cent of total exports to 14.4 per cent. In the same period French imports from Africa declined from 21.6 per cent of the world total to 14.9 per cent.

Within Africa there are also some significant regional differences in the movement of French imports and exports, as shown in Table 7. In the pattern of French exports the most rapid increase in percentage terms has been to Anglophone Tropical Africa and Southern Africa, particularly the latter. Exports to Francophone Tropical Africa have increased, but those to North Africa, formerly the more important market, have decreased. On the other hand, French imports from North Africa have grown to some extent, largely because of oil and gas from Algeria.

Narrowly viewed, the trade arrangements established nearly a decade ago now appear anachronistic and disadvantageous, and it can be asked why France continues in the face of all economic logic to bear their heavy cost. In terms of France's immediate economic self-interest, Africa is not an area of dynamic trade development and, though of continuing significance, has become relatively less important than France's rapidly increasing commerce with other developed countries of the world, particularly in Europe. The imports which France has been obtaining from the Franc Zone in the form of food and raw materials can be found equally well and often more cheaply in other areas.* French

* It has been estimated that in 1961, for example, the net cost to France of arrangements to maintain the prices of tropical products from Africa approximated 350 million francs, or $70 million. See Teresa Hayter, cited, p. 75.

TABLE 6. French Trade, Total and with Africa, 1960–67
(In millions of U.S. dollars; and as percentages)

	1960	1961	1962	1963	1964	1965	1966	1967
French exports								
Total	$6,864	$7,222	$7,365	$8,087	$8,997	$10,055	$10,907	$11,836
To Africa[a]	2,024	1,856	1,498	1,606	1,644	1,660	1,600	1,647
Percentage to Africa	29.5%	25.7%	20.3%	19.9%	18.3%	16.5%	14.7%	14.4%
French imports								
Total	$6,281	$6,679	$7,522	$8,732	$10,073	$10,345	$11,888	$12,409
From Africa[a]	1,418	1,504	1,621	1,671	1,808	1,769	1,909	1,849
Percentage from Africa	22.6%	22.5%	21.6%	19.1%	17.9%	17.1%	16.1%	14.9%

[a] Excluding U.A.R.
For coverage, see Table 7 on French trade with Africa.
SOURCE: International Monetary Fund, *Direction of Trade*, various issues.

TABLE 7. French Trade with Africa, 1962–67

(In millions of U.S. dollars)

	1962	1963	1964	1965	1966	1967
French exports to:						
North Africa[a]	832	846	806	799	736	710
Francophone Tropical Africa[b]	549	596	651	640	651	708
Anglophone Tropical Africa[c]	52	81	94	102	88	86
Southern Africa[d]	52	71	79	104	102	120
Other Africa	14	13	15	16	24	23
Total, Africa	1,498	1,606	1,644	1,660	1,600	1,647
French imports from:						
North Africa[a]	918	885	956	953	982	942
Francophone Tropical Africa[b]	560	587	649	585	649	651
Anglophone Tropical Africa[c]	40	82	73	137	185	168
Southern Africa[d]	98	106	119	83	84	78
Other Africa	6	11	11	12	9	9
Total, Africa	1,621	1,671	1,808	1,769	1,909	1,849

[a] Excluding U.A.R.

[b] Of which:	1962	1963	1964	1965	1966	1967
French exports to Congo (Kinshasa)	11	11	14	18	17	22
French imports from Congo (Kinshasa)	34	31	35	34	55	58

[c] Before 1965, Malawi and Zambia included with Rhodesia in Southern Africa.

[d] The apparent decline in imports from Southern Africa and the sharp increase of imports from Anglophone Tropical Africa is largely a result of the reclassification of copper-producing Zambia after its independence in 1964 from the Southern African region to Anglophone Tropical Africa.

CLASSIFICATION: *North Africa*—Algeria, Libya, Morocco, Tunisia. *Francophone Tropical Africa*—Cameroon, C.A.R., Chad, Congo (B.), Congo (K.), Dahomey, Gabon, Guinea Rep., Ivory Coast, Madagascar, Mali, Mauritania, Niger, Reunion, Senegal, Somaliland (Fr.), Togo, Upper Volta. *Anglophone Tropical Africa*—Burundi, Ethiopia, Gambia, Ghana, Kenya, Liberia, Malawi, Mauritius, Nigeria, Rwanda, Sierra Leone, Somali Rep., Sudan, Tanzania, Uganda, Zambia. *Southern Africa*—Angola, Mozambique, Rhodesia, South Africa. *Other Africa*—Guinea (Port.), Guinea (Span.), other Spanish Africa, other Africa, n.e.s.

SOURCE: International Monetary Fund, *Direction of Trade*, various issues.

exports to other parts of the world have grown on a competitive basis, whereas, given the economic condition of its former territories in Africa, France will probably be able to increase exports to them only to the extent that it is prepared to subsidize their purchases directly or indirectly. The system has the additional disadvantage of permitting uncompetitive and backward industries in France to delay necessary adaptation and modernization because of protected markets in Africa.

But certain countervailing gains to France must be considered. France benefits from access to agricultural commodities and raw materials (including petroleum from Algeria and uranium from Gabon) payable in French francs, which represent a savings in foreign exchange equivalent to several hundred million dollars a year. The aid contributions to Tropical Africa from the other five EEC members of the European Development Fund (EDF) in the form of lira, Deutsche marks, etc., provide additional foreign exchange to France. Moreover, the African members of the Franc Zone now make a substantial annual contribution to French currency reserves as a result of their trade surplus with non-Franc areas. Immediately after the war, these territories ran deficits ranging up to $200 million per year, which had to be covered by France. But in recent years their trade has in effect contributed $200 million to $300 million per year to French currency reserves. Thus, in balance-of-payment terms, France is turning a rather handsome profit in Tropical Africa.

With the passage of time, France has loosened the Franc Zone structure and to reduce some of the cost to itself: It has sought to scale down and eventually eliminate certain of the *surprix* paid for African products or to transfer the burden of some of these payments to the Common Market. It has sought to diversify its overseas trade and has encouraged the French-speaking African states to do likewise, particularly with the Dollar Area. But after taking into account all such adjustments, the fact remains that France continues to impose upon its own consumers and taxpayers a considerable price in order to maintain these special economic links.

In part the explanation may lie simply in the fact that France and many elements of French business have been addicted to closed and noncompetitive trading arrangements for so long that it takes time to break the habit. Another reason may be the sense of continuing obligation on the part of France to assist the former colonies in surviving an extremely difficult period of economic

adjustment and distress. Inherently poor, their productivity was
not improved by French economic policies of the past; and now
that world economic conditions have conspired to make the predicament of most of the primary agricultural product producers
quite desperate, France may feel it cannot in good conscience
abandon them. To expose them nakedly at this time to the rigors
of international commercial competition would produce disaster
for many and in turn would destroy the position of those indigenous elements on which present relationships with France are
based. So long as France remains determined to maintain general
influence over its former colonies, the net disadvantages of the
present trading system probably have to be considered a necessary
incidental cost.

French Private Investment

During the colonial period French private companies in Africa
enjoyed strong protection and were permitted a free hand in their
quest for profits. Their many advantages tended to become even
greater because they exerted a powerful influence not only upon
the local French administrators but also upon the general cast
of colonial policy set in Paris. As in the other European colonies
in Africa, private interests from the metropole came to dominate
banking and every aspect of the modernized sector in commerce,
manufacturing, and agriculture. Since independence their position
in most of the Francophone states has been only slightly preju-
diced, but in a few it has been considerably changed. In Algeria,
for example, at the end of that bitter struggle, French properties
were seized, French business firms were nationalized or their
privileges removed, and some 90 per cent of nearly one million
French residents were driven out or left. In Guinea, which refused
to join the French Community, a number of French commercial
firms subsequently encountered severe difficulties, although the
position of some large French investors was unchanged. In Mali,
which later withdraw from the Franc Zone, many French business
interests also were adversely affected.

But elsewhere the position of French private business and
investors was protected by special "establishment" agreements,
and the new governments have since hesitated to interfere with
their activity because of heavy dependence on France in most
economic matters. These firms in turn have not only been unin-
hibited in insisting upon their own privileges but, with the full
support and collaboration of French officials, have exerted them-

selves to keep other foreign firms, particularly American ones, from entering what they regard as their preserve.

In the initial years after independence, considerable withdrawal of French capital and disinvestment from certain parts of Africa occurred. An exodus of private capital from Morocco and Tunisia began in 1956, followed by massive removals from Algeria, which reached their peak in 1962–63. According to some estimates, this movement totaled more than $1 billion in 1962 alone. The withdrawal of private capital from the tropical Francophone states after 1960 was less dramatic and of lesser magnitude. It appears, however, that there has been a steady repatriation of capital by many French investors in these areas too.

In attempting to trace these movements, special complications exist: Private transactions within the Franc Zone are not fully recorded, nor until 1966 did regular balance-of-payments figures exist of the kind which are available for transactions between France and non–Franc Zone countries. The figures compiled by the *Comité Monétaire de la Zone Franc* for the previous years are illuminating, however, and a reasonably clear picture can be discerned from them. The persuasiveness of these data is the greater because they confirm the observations of many economists and businessmen who have traveled regularly in the Francophone African territories. Table 8, based on *Comité Monétaire* data relating to the general balance of payments between France and the overseas countries of the Franc Zone from 1957 to 1966, gives a measure of private flows to France.[4] It is to be noted that the annual outflow from Africa in recent years has decreased markedly since its peak in 1962.

The category of "invisible operations" in the table includes both private capital transfers and remittances. The remittances consist in part of savings by technical assistance and other French personnel stationed overseas. But the more important element, probably through 1964, was the repatriation of capital by French firms and individuals. The volume of these private flows toward France in the period 1961–64 was sufficiently large as to generally offset the net balance of official French transfers of resources to the overseas territories.

Although the emergence of the African territories to independence has stimulated recurrent waves of disinvestment by private French interests, this has been offset (to what degree cannot be established precisely) by new investment flows into particular industries and to particular African countries. Private investors

TABLE 8. Balance of Payments Between France and the Overseas
Countries of the Franc Zone, 1957–66

(In millions of French francs)

	1957	1958	1959	1960	1961	1962	1963	1964	1965	1966
(1) Public transfers (balance)	5,975	6,237	6,710	7,557	8,902	9,141	4,571	3,008	2,640	2,516
(2) Private transfers (balance)	4,884	5,758	6,823	8,103	9,139	9,988	5,290	4,840	3,918	3,187
of which:										
Trade balance with the overseas countries	2,492	2,963	4,080	4,224	2,992	935	1,621	1,379	2,288	1,797
Invisible operations	1,879	2,394	3,039	3,662	6,465	9,053	3,669	3,461	1,630	1,390
(3) Counterpart of foreign exchange transactions on the Paris Market	513	401	296	257	318	742	651	1,289	1,328	1,247
(4) General balance	1,091	479	113	546	237	105	68	543	50	576

NOTE: Figures in *italics* indicate an outflow from France, figures in roman type are inflows to France.

SOURCE: *Comité Monétaire de la Zone Franc*, annual reports.

have continued to be attracted to Ivory Coast, Gabon, and, to a lesser extent, Senegal. By sectors, the major investment has been in the mining of iron ore, copper, uranium, and, above all, the exploitation of petroleum and gas discoveries in the Sahara, often through the device of "mixed" enterprises combining private funds with those of the French government. The recent discovery of uranium in Niger and Chad is expected to lead to substantial increases in French private and public investment in those countries. According to figures of the Development Assistance Committee of the OECD taken from information provided from French official sources, the total movement of French private capital to the newly independent countries of Africa, including direct investments and net increases in private export credits of more than five years' duration, totaled $224.7 million in 1965 and $246.8 million in 1966, of which nearly half was concentrated in Algeria. Direct investment declined, but was more than offset by a marked increase in export credits.[5]

The conclusions to be drawn from these several and somewhat contradictory trends include the following: One general result of French post-independence policy in Africa has been to preserve and protect the position of French business and investors in most of the former dependencies; nevertheless, the political changes have undermined the confidence of many French investors and a substantial withdrawal of capital has occurred; new investment is taking place, but on a spotty and limited basis. Over-all therefore, although the position of French private business in Africa has been reduced, its influence has by no means been eliminated. French governmental as well as private investment interests are coming to be powerfully focused in certain extractive operations located in a few of the former colonies. These new configurations may be of great significance in estimating the probable evolution of French ties with different areas of Africa in the future.

ECONOMIC AND TECHNICAL ASSISTANCE

For more than a decade before their independence in 1960, France had provided the overseas African territories with substantial economic and technical assistance including budgetary subsidies, and this large flow of French aid continued under the new cooperation agreements. In the years immediately after 1960 the total of French private and official assistance to the less developed countries averaged more than 2 per cent per year of national income, a spectacular proportion almost double that of any other donor country. Three-quarters of the total has gone to Africa, making France by a considerable margin the largest single source of aid to that continent. This huge effort of what France calls "cooperation" has been the principal instrument in the attempt to maintain the cohesion of a Franco-African ensemble, to maintain France's presence and political influence, to preserve linguistic and cultural links, to build a showcase for its *oeuvre décolonisatrice*, and to augment French prestige throughout the Third World.

This ambitious undertaking had to be launched in 1960 out of the debris of the costly effort to promote African development after World War II within the framework of the French Union. Most of the fourteen tropical African states which signed cooperation agreements were extremely needy clients, being not only poor, unproductive, and uncompetitive economically, but also saddled with excessively heavy administrative costs. The initial agreements, perhaps because they had to be formulated in haste, provided a general framework rather than detailed aid plans. With uncharacteristic pragmatism, the French authorities took advantage of the latitude provided to deal with the immediate danger of administrative and economic disintegration in the new states, leaving until later the elaboration of a "doctrine" for development. French commitments to the sub-Saharan areas in the years immediately following independence averaged more than $300 million annually. A substantial proportion consisted of support to the operating budgets of the new states in the form of French personnel. Direct grants were also given to make up annual budgetary deficits.

As Algeria's independence approached in 1961, France was faced with another major assistance emergency and provided more than $400 million both to ease the acute transitional problems of that war-shattered country and to help protect the position of hundreds of thousands of French settlers and the rights of French investors. In that year French assistance to all of Africa reached an extraordinary total of nearly $700 million from official sources alone.

The outlays aroused concern among French economists and financial experts not only because of their magnitude, but also because a great proportion of the funds was being used for salvage and holding operations, not development, and for political purposes. By 1963 the incoherence of the situation necessitated a fresh review of the rationale of all French economic assistance to Africa, and indeed to the entire Third World. This assessment was done in the so-called Jeanneney Report.[6] Looking back over the evolution of French assistance in the postwar period, the Jeanneney Committee, though it tactfully avoided some of the more drastic criticisms of the wastefulness of French aid programs then current, nevertheless called attention to some major weaknesses. In considering the future, it made specific recommendations for changing French aid objectives, patterns of aid distribution, and terms and conditions of future aid arrangements, most of which were in line with new policies the government had already begun to put into effect. Specifically, it urged that a still greater emphasis be given to technical assistance and that infrastructure projects be increasingly de-emphasized in favor of greater stimulation of agricultural and light industrial production. It recommended also that assistance be expanded to include non-Franc areas, and that a larger portion of aid funds be channelled to multilateral programs. Concurrently, the Report went to great lengths to try to prove to Africans and other foreign skeptics that the motivation of French assistance was benign and not contrary to the aspirations of the recipient states for genuine independence; and it took care to document in detail that the net cost of Franc Zone trading arrangements and overseas aid programs were an extremely heavy burden on the French taxpayer.*

---

* The French government has given much stress in its official publicity to the high volume of French assistance to the less developed countries, which has provoked a somewhat defensive reaction on the part of some economic assistance experts in other countries to the effect that French figures are inflated and include major items not properly considered "aid." It has been charged, for example, that French totals at one time included sums which could more accurately be described as military expenditures. Other accusations have been that much of France's aid is spent on paying its own civil servants, that French services and goods financed with aid are overvalued, and that the projects selected have sometimes been of more benefit to French construction firms and exporters than to the recipient countries in Africa. It is charged likewise that the French count, as part of their official assistance, expenditures which by American practice would be part of the budget of the U.S. Information Agency and the Voice of America, for example. At one time or another there has been a degree of truth in all of these charges. At the same time it has to be recognized that "aid" is not only an elusive term to define, but that all donor countries include in their definitions items which other countries do not. Most in fact tend to include some items which provide ample basis for skeptics to accuse them of inflating the figures. U.S. aid in the form of surplus agricultural commodities would be in this category. On the whole, French practice in computing assistance totals is probably no more vulnerable than that of other donors to the accusation of purposeful exaggeration.

In the years since the Report, French assistance programs have passed through a considerable evolution, though not necessarily because of or in the direction of the Jeanneney Committee's recommendations.

Table 9A summarizes the flow of official French bilateral aid to Africa in the years 1960 through 1966. The total of grants and net official loans (gross loans less amortization) reached its peak in 1961 and has declined steadily thereafter. If price levels were to be taken into account, the decline would be appreciably greater.

TABLE 9A. Official French Bilateral Aid to Africa, Grants and Official Loans (net), 1960–66

(In millions of U.S. dollars)

	1960	1961	1962	1963	1964	1965	1966
North Africa							
Algeria	$354.1	$435.9	$357.6	$239.4	$182.4	$135.1	$ 94.9
Other North Africa[a]	29.1	28.3	45.4	71.7	79.9	60.5	45.9
Total	383.2	464.2	403.0	311.1	262.3	195.6	140.8
South of Sahara (Franc Zone Countries)							
Total	307.5	304.0	325.9	337.3	345.6	319.2	317.7
Total, Africa	690.7	768.2	728.9	648.4	607.9	514.8	465.3[b]

[a] Excluding U.A.R.
[b] Includes $6.8 million for *"organismes inter états."*

SOURCE: *Geographical Distribution fo Financial Flows for Less Developed Countries—1960–64* and *1965* (Paris: OECD, 1966, 1967).

The year-by-year reduction through 1965, however, is explainable essentially by the sharp drop in assistance to Algeria, which decreased by some $300 million between 1961 and 1965. Otherwise, apart from Algeria, French aid to other countries of Africa has remained relatively stable and at an unusually high level. Information for the years after 1966 suggests that the tendency of a gradual decline in French assistance has continued, and, because

French national income has continued to grow, French aid as a percentage of national income has steadily decreased:[7]

	1962	1963	1964	1965	1966	1967
Official aid	1.76%	1.39%	1.24%	1.06%	.95%	1.02%
Private aid	.76	.68	.82	.80	.75	.63
Total aid	2.51	2.06	2.07	1.87	1.70	1.64

Within the totals of French assistance, certain elements have remained relatively constant; others have changed. France continues to place heavy emphasis on bilateral aid, while contributions to multilateral programs other than those of the European Common Market have been and remain rather small. Similarly, the extension of aid to additional countries outside the Franc Zone has progressed, but very slowly.

Grants comprise more than one-half of French official assistance, and their proportion in the total has been rising, as Table 9B indicates. Whereas at one time grants were used for economic and social capital investments in the development plans of the recipient countries, France has recently attempted to shift the financing of such projects to other donors, including the European Development Fund and other international organizations.

Geographically, the emphasis in French aid in recent years has shifted from North Africa to the Franc Zone countries south of the Sahara. At the same time, important modifications in aid consistent with the Jeanneney recommendations have been intro-

TABLE 9B. Official French Bilateral Aid to Africa, 1964 and 1966

(In millions of French francs)

	Technical		Loans		Grants		Total	
	1964	1966	1964	1966	1964	1966	1964	1966
North Africa	347.5	318.0	343.9	91.4	622.8	334.2	1,314.2	743.6
Algeria	183.2	182.2	115.3	23.0	602.0	309.6	900.5	514.8
Morocco	81.4	79.2	209.4	66.9	4.0	8.9	294.8	154.0
Tunisia	82.9	56.6	19.2	1.5	16.8	16.7	118.9	74.8
Other Africa	734.7	215.1	79.9	26.6	553.1	544.2	1,367.7	785.9
Total	1,082.2	533.1	423.8	118.0	1,175.9	878.4	2,681.9	1,529.5

SOURCE: *L'Usine Nouvelle*, February 15, 1968.

duced, all with the objective of assisting and encouraging the sub-Saharan countries to become somewhat more self-sufficient and economically competitive.

Similarly, the character of French administrative assistance has been modified. At the time of independence in many of the recipient states, French specialists not only served in advisory capacities, but also in numerous instances exercised general administrative authority. Since then, the effort has been pressed to train qualified Africans to replace French expatriates in such functions and to limit French personnel to advisory roles. According to government statistics, more than 3,000 French administrative officers were employed in the newly independent African states in 1960; by June 1966 this number had been reduced to 1,267, and it has decreased further since. To support this effort of Africanization, Institutes of Public Administration have been created in several sub-Saharan countries with French financial assistance.

Another major trend observable in French aid programs is the intention to reduce progressively the over-all total of aid but to continue to give top priority to the provision of French technical personnel and to educational and cultural programs. This is being accomplished in part by reducing certain costs—for example, by substituting low-paid French military draftees for more highly paid French teachers.[8]

From the beginning, French aid has stressed technical and educational assistance; and with the changes recently introduced, the proportion of this activity in the total program is increasing. Twenty-one per cent of French aid in Africa was earmarked for this purpose in 1961; by 1966 the proportion had risen to nearly 35 per cent. The French Ministry of Foreign Affairs reported in 1967 that the number of technical assistants made available to the sub-Saharan African governments had remained relatively stable over the years since independence, increasing from 12,000 in 1960 to 13,000 in 1966. The number of Volunteers for Progress, a French counterpart to the Peace Corps, had grown to a total of 400 in 1967. French teachers and training personnel in sub-Saharan Africa had increased from 2,844 in 1960 to nearly 6,000 in 1966. Some 10,000 students and trainees from sub-Saharan Africa were in France in 1967 under French government scholarships. An additional 9,000 students, many of them supported by French government scholarships, were in attendance in the five universities and centers of higher education established in French-speaking black Africa with French government assistance. In North Africa an equivalent effort is being made. There, some 10,000 French teachers are at work, and thousands of students are being supported by French scholarships for study both in local institutions and in French universities.

In cultural relations, a wide range and high volume of activity are also being financed. Libraries and film centers are maintained; great quantities of educational materials—books, periodicals, radio and television programs, and audio-visual displays—are subsidized; and intensive efforts are made to assist in the training of African specialists who plan careers either in teaching or in the mass media.

Finally, there has been a sharp reduction in budgetary subventions. Immediately after independence, France gave funds to cover budgetary deficits for a number of the former colonies, but, in more recent years, it has provided both encouragement and inducements to reduce needless administrative expenditures and eliminate this form of "palliative" aid. Three states (Upper Volta, Dahomey, and Congo-Brazzaville) received budgetary assistance in 1964; by 1966 only Dahomey remained on the list. The total of such subventions, which amounted to some $36 million in 1961, had dropped to less than $7 million in 1966. As a result, a number of the African states have had to begin the painful process of cutting back their bureaucracies, reducing the privileges of civil servants, such as automobiles and luxurious housing, and lowering some inflated salaries.

To appraise the impact of a program as huge, complex, and changing as that of French "cooperation" with Africa is particularly difficult. Prior to independence, the French territories in Africa received far less developmental benefit from French assistance than its considerable volume would suggest. In the years since, French aid has become somewhat more coherent and better related to the development needs of the recipient states and to long-term French objectives. Whether or not the program seriously aims at making the former colonies self-sufficient, it has at least now eliminated the worst of its uneconomic aspects and is serving to encourage tendencies toward budgetary economy and improved export earnings. Measures have also been introduced to remove some of the specific irritants that troubled Franco-African relations in the past, such as the presence of French officials in high administrative posts in the new governments. But in analyzing French aid, as in appraising the system of trade relations between France and Africa, the principal meanings and motivations are to be found in the sphere beyond the economic.

Since 1960 France has replaced the dream of reconstructing its former empire with the goal of maintaining a distinctive degree of prestige and influence in Africa and in the Third World generally. Its aid programs have been shaped and honed increasingly as instruments in the service of France's unique belief in the power of language, culture, and education in building a durable and effective foundation of cooperation between a highly developed nation and newly emergent areas.

Though now very much below its peak level, France's aid in Africa continues to be unusually high. In the Fifth Plan of Economic and Social Development for the period 1966–70, the government declared its intention to increase foreign aid in proportion to the growth of the French economy—and to redeploy its aid on a world-wide basis, which would mean a relative decline in the privileged position of the Franc Zone countries.[9] But whether this document can be taken as a reliable guide to future French action is a debatable question. For as long as the French economy does not founder, it would seem likely that any future changes in aid levels to Africa would be gradual and in the direction of present trends. The French aspiration for prestige and influence in these areas goes far back in history and reaches deeply into French psychology. In the budgetary recommendations made to the National Assembly in late 1968, following the student and labor demonstrations of the preceding May, a new emphasis on domestic programs was apparent, as well as a lower priority for foreign aid. But no drastic cut in the latter was proposed.

On the other hand, powerful forces of social and political unrest are becoming apparent in France. The economy is in trouble. The burdens of the nuclear program on the French taxpayer have become oppressive. And the semi-authoritarian methods of the government under the Fifth Republic, which have hindered the expression of political discontents, have led to periodic violent eruptions. It is impossible to say, therefore, whether French assistance and economic relationships with Africa will continue to evolve along their present course or may be abruptly transformed in consequence of a political upheaval in France. At best, the African states probably have to resign themselves to a decreasing volume of increasingly useful French assistance for their economic development. At worst, it is not inconceivable that they will have to face a rather sudden drop-off. If the latter should occur, one of the consequences for France might well be the liquidation of a large portion of the good will and hoped-for future influence in which it has been investing so heavily.

THE EVOLUTION OF FRENCH MILITARY RELATIONS

As France has transformed its imperial ambitions and shifted its policy to the pursuit of influence through cooperation, French military relationships in Africa have necessarily been subjected to radical modification. But as the end of the first decade of independence approaches, the French military presence, though in decline, remains an instrument of discipline and intervention highly useful in special situations. The strategic facilities to which France still has access, coupled with new, highly mobile conventional forces based in France, also reinforces to some degree the semblance of a global military posture that France has sought to create primarily through its nuclear force.

Africa and the other parts of the empire long had a distinctive place in the French military tradition. The army was intimately involved both in the acquisition and the administration of the colonies. The defense of the empire was considered an aspect of the defense of France itself; and because most of the colonies were in Africa, its defense formed an important element in strategic plans. France, therefore, developed major naval and military installations along the south Mediterranean coast and maintained troops throughout the area. The Second World War emphasized the strategic importance of both North and sub-Saharan Africa. North Africa was both a major theater of action and the springboard for the invasion of southern Europe by the Allied forces and the eventual liberation of France, and, by their loyalty and support, the black African territories gave vital sustenance to the Free French movement.

After the war, French strategists were convinced that only by organizing defense plans on a Eurafrican basis, making full use of African manpower, materials, and bases, could France reestablish itself as a major power. Thus after 1946, as the new Fourth Republic set about to rebuild national strength and reestablish the empire, the military pressed forward to re-equip and extend its garrisons and bases in Africa. Simultaneously, French forces were called upon to fight a costly war to try to repress nationalist revolt in Indochina.

These costly efforts both in the Far East and in Africa were supported in principle by the United States and heavily financed out of American aid. When NATO was formed in 1950, France succeeded in extending its mutual security obligations to include Algeria, thereby making the United States and the other alliance partners responsible for the defense of a major piece of African territory. Thereafter France received more than 40 per cent of the total of U.S. bilateral assistance to the NATO countries as well as hundreds of millions of dollars of NATO infrastructure, including airfields and pipelines, which was constructed in France. "Offshore procurement" arrangements for military equipment manufactured in France provided additional large-scale assistance to the French balance of payments.

By 1956 the Indochinese War had been lost, and the focus of French military operations had shifted to Algeria, where another violent rebellion was developing. For the French military establishment after its undistinguished performance in World War II and its stunning defeat in the Far East, the Algerian War came to represent a last-ditch stand against all the forces and tendencies which endangered it and to which it was opposed: the influence of the liberals and the Left in France, heightened nationalism in the colonies, and the general deterioration of the French position and prestige in the world. Eventually in trying to cope with a determined and elusive enemy they could not defeat, French military leaders sanctioned the most discreditable practices, and in their frustration with the paralyzed parliamentary system in the metropole, they finally resorted to violence and treasonable actions to bring it down. When defeat finally came in Algeria, its consequences were momentous: It ended the Fourth Republic, led to the creation of the Fifth, and installed General de Gaulle in power; it reopened all the old wounds of the body politic in France; it led to constitutional changes in Africa which resulted in independence; it led in time to a complete reorientation of French military priorities and strategic plans as well as a purging of the French officer corps; and, as one of its side effects, it altered the basis and character of the French military presence throughout Africa.

Even while the Algerian catastrophe was building to its climax, political developments elsewhere in North Africa had already begun to require the dismantling of some French military facilities. Morocco and Tunisia had achieved independence by 1956 and negotiated new military agreements with France. In the case of Morocco, France made a major gift of military equipment and thereafter continued to provide technical assistance. But the historic French bases at Fez, Agadir, Marrakesh, Meknes, and Khouribga had to be relinquished by 1961. Similarly, after Tunisia's independence, France provided most of the initial equipment and training for the small Tunisian army, in return for which it was to be permitted to retain occupancy of the major naval base at Bizerte "temporarily"—an imprecise stipulation which resulted in a dramatic military clash between French and Tunisian forces in July 1961. France finally was compelled to evacuate the base except for a handful of French advisers.

Reforms had been gradually introduced in the practices of the colonial army in sub-Saharan Africa in the same period to provide for more equal treatment of Africans and open greater training opportunities and possibilities of advancement to the higher grades. But, as the 1950s drew to a close, French military thinking remained fixed in a colonial pattern and was quite unprepared for the political crises impending.

The Evian agreements were finally signed in March 1962, conceding independence to Algeria and bringing that conflict to an end. By the terms of the negotiations, French forces were to be reduced to 80,000 by 1963 and to be completely evacuated by 1964. France was to be permitted to use its nuclear and missile test sites in the Sahara until 1967, to retain the use of the naval base at Mers-el-Kabir for fifteen years; and to continue to use Algerian air communications facilities.

With the signing of the Algerian accords, French access to the strategic facilities it had developed in North Africa in the course of decades was further restricted and was scheduled to end within a brief period. These changes, together with the consequences of independence in sub-Saharan Africa in 1960, washed out the political foundations of French Eurafrican strategic concepts and necessitated both a reformulation of plans and a restructuring of military arrangements with the newly sovereign states, which took the form of a web of interconnected bilateral and multilateral military cooperation agreements.

Military Aspects of the Cooperation Agreements

By these agreements France undertook military assistance of various kinds to its former territories and was accorded certain military rights in exchange. All except Guinea and Mali signed military technical assistance agreements providing for French assistance in the organization, equipment, and training of their national armies and police forces. Eleven of the sixteen signed bilateral defense pacts: Senegal, Mauritania, Madagascar, Togo, Central African Republic, Congo (Brazzaville), Chad, Gabon, Ivory Coast, Niger, and Dahomey. These agreements stipulated that each state was to be responsible for its own internal and external defense but that in certain circumstances it could call on France for military support. Each country committed itself to coordinate defense matters by consultation with French authorities, and French forces were accorded bases and facilities to permit France to fulfill its military obligations.[10]

In the years since, France has given millions of dollars worth of arms, vehicles, and other equipment to the new African armies, and has provided large numbers of technical and training personnel. It has trained hundreds of African officers and NCO's in French military institutions. It has also given extensive assistance to gendarmeries and mobile police forces.

At the same time France has attempted to maintain its capacity to intervene in behalf of the maintenance of stability in the new states. This has had to be done during a time of changing military technology and of evolving strategic doctrines and military priorities in France. The result has been a succession of major changes in policy on troop deployment and the maintenance of bases in Africa—sometimes the result of deliberate planning, but more often the outgrowth of budgetary imperatives or unexpected political requirements.

Between 1962 and 1964, France proceeded to strip down its forces and facilities in Africa primarily because of a redirection of military priorities toward European defense and the development of a nuclear force. Nearly 300,000 French troops were withdrawn and an additional 20,000 Africans serving with French forces were demobilized to take service in African national armies. Most of the major military facilities were closed down. Only four were left: at Dakar in Senegal, the principal French naval base in the South Atlantic; at Abidjan in Ivory Coast; at Fort Lamy in Chad; and at Diego Suarez in the Malagasy Republic, France's naval base and future missile-firing submarine base for the East. In addition, several small guard and service detachments are maintained elsewhere.

Then in late 1964 further major changes were instituted. French troops stationed in Africa were to be reduced from 27,800 to 6,600, and an estimated additional 10,500 African troops serving with the French army were to be demobilized. At about the same time it was announced that a special mobile *force d'intervention* stationed in metropolitan France had been created to be available on short notice to support the remaining units in Africa in responding to emergencies. The force consists of the Eleventh Airborne Division and includes one paratroop brigade and two brigades (one marine and the other air portable) equipped with recoilless rifles, light artillery, and armored vehicles. These army forces are backed up by amphibious forces and seaborne commandos, plus some 200 aircraft.

The reasons for abruptly scrapping divisional forces stationed in Africa and shifting emphasis to a French-based mobile reserve are complex and somewhat unclear. New military technology making it possible, in case of need, to move troops armed with effective firepower from France as quickly as from African bases was unquestionably an underlying factor. The more compelling considerations were probably budgetary stringency resulting from the heavy cost of developing the nuclear force and the political repercussions that followed the controversial Gabon intervention in 1964 to restore friendly President M'ba to power after he had been removed by a military coup.

According to official French definition and the cooperation agreements, the new mobile intervention force can engage in two types of missions: (1) as reinforcements to assist an overseas department or territory, an isolated garrison, or a friendly country in difficulty and (2) in offensive actions to protect French interests or those of allied countries in a hostile country or a country plunged into anarchy.[11]

The commitments and rights to intervene militarily in Africa, which are a basic element of the defense accords signed after 1960, have confronted France with a succession of difficult decisions that have produced major political repercussions. France has been called upon repeatedly to intervene—more often to protect endangered regimes from internal threats than to defend the new states from external threats—and has done so.

The French Minister of Information, Alain Peyrefitte, in early 1964 made public a partial list of such interventions up to that time. The occasion of his revelation was a press conference to defend the Gabonese action in February of that year. Peyrefitte stated that the intervention had been "at the request of the legitimate government" and required under the terms of the 1961 defense agreement. He noted that it was precisely because of the danger of military coups to the stability of new African states that they had "signed accords with France to guard against such

risks." Among the other similar interventions after 1960 which
he mentioned were: (1) in Cameroon, 1960 and 1961, to help
re-establish order; (2) in Congo-Brazzaville, 1960, to help the
government quell intertribal warfare; (3) in Congo-Brazzaville
and Gabon, September 1962, when a disputed soccer game resulted
in ill treatment of each other's nationals; (4) in Chad, "several
interventions" between 1960 and 1963; (5) in Niger in December
1963, "a show of force" to discourage a military uprising against
President Hamani Diori; and (6) in Mauritania in 1961, once to
assist the government in dealing with tribal agitation and later
(for reasons not given) in Nouakchott and Port Etienne. On the
other hand, the Minister explained that France did not intervene
after the assassination of President Sylvanus Olympio of Togo
in January 1963 because Togo had no mutual defense agreement
with France at the time, and that in any case President Olympio
was killed before counteraction could have been taken. In Congo-
Brazzaville in August 1963, he said France offered help but
President Fulbert Youlou decided to resign. In Dahomey in
October 1963, French troops did not intervene because President
Hubert Maga gave up his presidency voluntarily.

Following the Minister's statement to the press, some of the
named African governments reacted vigorously, categorically denying that the French had ever intervened in their countries under
the defense agreements. On the other hand, the heads of several
Francophone states spoke in the most complimentary terms about
the French intervention in Gabon and the willingness of France
to "respect its engagements."

The Gabonese case is interesting not only because of the strong
reactions provoked, but also because of the variety of French
motives apparently involved: to fulfill a commitment to a cooperative leader; to make clear to other good friends they could count
on French support in case of need; and to help create a "climate
of order" in the face of an epidemic of coups in French Africa
engineered by the new armies France had helped create, equip, and
train. After 1963, following President Olympio's assassination in
Togo, two other heads of state had been overthrown in Congo-
Brazzaville and Dahomey and plots were unearthed in Ivory Coast
and Chad.

Because of the tide of opposition which the Gabonese intervention aroused, France felt obliged thereafter not only to reduce the
visibility of its military presence in Africa, but also to begin to
follow a more selective course in responding to appeals for military

help. Official statements have come to emphasize that military action will be taken "only exceptionally and in accordance with signed agreement. . . . No African government can oblige France to send in her troops." In short, intervention is neither "a right for Africans nor a duty for France." In practice, France has declined to intervene in recent years in Dahomey and Upper Volta when called. But it dispatched forces to deal with threatened disorders in the Central African Republic in November 1967, and authorized troops stationed in Chad to join with local forces to put down rebel raids and establish order in the northern part of that country in August 1968. Clearly France is now disposed to judge each case on its own merits.*

Moreover, wherever possible, France seems inclined to employ measures other than military force to protect the internal stability of the former colonies and to punish regimes which take over in the face of French disapproval. Thus, following military coups in the Central African Republic and in Upper Volta in early 1966, a member of President de Gaulle's cabinet, Mr. Jean Charbonnel, said that France was concerned by the coups and added that these events were "of a nature to affect French aid and cooperation policy which can only be efficiently carried out in order and legality." This was understood in Africa as a warning that even where France may not intervene militarily it may employ economic deterrents to check the contagion of disorder.

However, if the direction of movement in French military relations in tropical Africa is toward restraint and a degree of mutual withdrawal, broader military relationships with the strategically important North African states, which have been limited to technical assistance and the supply of hardware in recent years, may be at the point of reappearing. President Bourguiba has made clear that he does not exclude the possibility of Tunisian military cooperation with one or more of the great powers—including France—if Tunisian security should so require. A discreet expansion of military cooperation between France and Algeria was reported in the spring of 1968. According to the influential French newspaper, Le Monde, a small program of military technical assistance began between the two countries as early as 1963. Subse-

* The great and puzzling exception to the policy of cutting down its military involvement in Africa has been the movement of French arms into Biafra, beginning in August 1968. However, the complexity of the possible motives in supporting this secession, from anti-Anglo-Saxonism to oil concessions, would require separate analysis.

quently, in 1964, an agreement was signed by which the French government agreed to provide training and other assistance to the Algerian national police. Algerian military doctors have been trained, and French instructors have been assigned to certain Algerian military schools. Several hundred Algerian military personnel have been brought to France for short-term courses. Because of the success of these several tentative efforts of cooperation, it is believed that a general agreement for military cooperation may have been signed between the two countries in December 1967.

In reviewing the evolution of French military relationships with Africa in recent years, the first and most obvious fact is that whereas little more than a decade ago France had bases and strategic installation throughout West, Equatorial and North Africa and hundreds of thousands of troops stationed there, it has today left or been displaced from all but a few and has cut its forces to hardly more than a handful. Where Africa was once central to French conceptions of strategy and defense, it is now peripheral.

For the new states of Tropical Africa, however, French military presence, though reduced, has not been removed, and some of them count heavily upon it for protection and maintenance of internal order. Despite the shift of military attention to Europe and to the development of a nuclear force, France has equipped itself to respond to calls for help in accordance with its commitments; but there is visible tendency to respond more selectively, and to utilize economic and other measures short of force wherever possible.

In North Africa, the situation remains obscure and in flux. But it is difficult to imagine that France—apart from any interest it might have in the maintenance of order within the North African states—is not interested in the re-establishment of some pattern of military cooperation that will help protect its southern flank. In this regard, French military journals have begun to devote considerable attention to the implications of growing Soviet naval activity in the Mediterranean.

French military presence and policy in Africa in the first years after independence helped make possible an orderly transfer of authority and contributed to general stability. But that physical presence has now been reduced to a shadow of its former scale. In the future, much will depend on the actual effectiveness of the *force d'intervention* which has been created. By the equipment of such a force and by special training measures and joint operations with African forces, as in Ivory Coast in 1967, France has given concrete evidence of its intention to fulfill its security commitments and maintain its capability for military action in specific situations. Nevertheless, even though these airborne troops are to be available "in a matter of hours," it remains to be seen whether they can provide to a shaky African government either the psychological or the substantive equivalent of French forces actually stationed in the locality.

Regardless of how extensively or effectively French commitments for military help to the new Francophone states are fulfilled, it is manifest that Africa has been dropped on the list of priorities. Precisely where it now fits in the new French strategic conceptions is unclear. As long as he held power, General de Gaulle was primarily concerned with "decolonizing" the army and modernizing and nuclearizing it in order to enable France to play a role not of policeman for the Third World but of leader in Europe and of catalyst and mediator, if not inspiration, in relations among the superpowers. But, with his resignation from office, one can summarize France's present position regarding Africa by saying that it means to fulfill commitments and maintain a military presence as long as it does not cost too much, does not cause too much trouble, and does not distract France from its major strategic interests and objectives.

EVALUATION AND PROSPECTS

Within the brief span of two years, from 1958 until 1960, General de Gaulle took a series of decisive measures to put relations with the African territories on a new basis. In the 1958 Referendum on the Constitution of the Fifth Republic, they were offered a substantial degree of autonomy within a new French community; and that measure proving inadequate, they were accorded formal sovereignty and independence two years later. These dramatic changes, significant as they were, did not, however, mean that France was prepared to set the former colonies genuinely free. In sharp contrast to the attitude of Britain in according independence to its African colonies, France was determined to maintain predominant influence even after independence. To this end, it entered into a web of contractual agreements embracing every subject from postal services to the coordination of foreign policy. In more recent years, the predominance of French influence in most of these areas, especially in administration and in aid and military relations, has been reduced. But the French presence in education, culture, business, the media, as well as in general political, economic, and military matters remains very great.

The result after nearly a decade—almost incredible, given the rampant nationalism prevailing in Africa—is that French policy, measured by the test of its own objectives, has proven a considerable success. It has been consistently denounced by elements in Africa and elsewhere as "neo-colonialist," as a cynical exploitation of the Africans and a denial of their rights. It has been repeatedly predicted that the system was so flagrantly contrary to the mood of world opinion and sentiment within Africa itself that it could not last, that a new group of younger radical African leaders would sweep it away at any moment.

Nevertheless, the system remains standing. The governments of the Francophone African states are no more unstable than others in Africa, and among them are some of the most stable. Despite their special handicaps, they have not made a worse record of economic development than others, and among them are several whose economic prospects seem to be exceptionally promising. In their official attitudes toward France, some of their leaders have begun to be more openly critical on specific issues, but on the whole they have remained friendly and cooperative. Moreover, Mali and particularly Guinea, which took antagonistic positions toward France, have, after experiencing many difficulties, come round to a markedly more friendly view. Relations with Tunisia, which at one time had broken into open violence, have become cordial, and President Bourguiba has been among those who have proposed the formation of a new international grouping of French-speaking states. Algeria, despite the horrors of its struggles with France only a few years ago, has continued to cooperate economically with France, and this has more recently extended to military and political matters in limited degree.

Throughout Africa, France is held if not in general affection at least in respect; and at international gatherings it has been frequently noted that France alone among the Western powers has been exempted from African political attack despite its flagrant refusal, for example, to join in the international arms embargo against South Africa. At the United Nations, the French-speaking African states infrequently oppose and often conform to French leadership on many issues. Moreover, because of widespread anti-Americanism, France's practice of regularly plucking feathers from the eagle's tail has resulted throughout much of the Third World in its being considered, if not a friend, at least a kind of comrade-in-arms.

History is full of surprising outcomes but the present standing of France in Africa, given the situation only a decade ago, is something that few would have predicted. Two tantalizing questions are raised: How did it come about, and how long can it last?

As to the first, one element of the answer has to do with power and weakness. Especially since 1962, with the resurgence of the French economy and the removal of the incubus of the Algerian War, France has been able to move with greater authority and self-confidence. At the same time, most of the Tropical African states, trapped in a deteriorating spiral of world prices for their products, became even more dependent upon French subsidies, French aid, and the protection and advantages of the Franc Zone trading system. Moreover, because France had the will and determination to maintain its influence in Africa, it has utilized its power firmly, occasionally ruthlessly, in behalf of its goals. The obedience of the former colonies in following France's leadership on a number of international questions and their unwillingness publicly to attack it unquestionably derives from the certain knowledge that such conduct will bring prompt and painful retribution. Because the French-speaking countries of Africa neither criticize France nor permit it to be criticized, the other African states in the interests of African cooperation have also tended to withhold their fire.

The French position, however, consists of more than the mere absence of open unfriendliness on the part of the Francophone states. There are many intangible, yet powerful personal and emotional links between their present leaders and France. Many were educated in French schools, often in France; and long before independence, some sat as elected members of the French National Assembly, in the course of which they developed close working relationships and friendships with their French colleagues. Many of them hold General de Gaulle in high personal regard, both because of common wartime experiences and because of his role in bringing about political and economic advancement for the colonies immediately after the war and again in 1958.

The many personal ties have been strengthened and multiplied by French administrative methods in Africa in the post-independence period. French aid missions in Africa as well as French economic authorities in Paris are in constant contact with their African counterparts on development questions. Political consultations of great intimacy take place between French and African representatives in Africa, at the United Nations in New York, and in Paris. Among the most important of these were the regular private conversations between General de Gaulle and the various black African heads of state. The French method of executing policies, because it has involved such extensive communication and close consultation, has helped create a genuine sense of Community, even though the formal structure of that concept has remained moribund.

But beyond power, discipline, and friendships—and even beyond French determination and willingness to employ major resources and take considerable political and even military risks to maintain its influence in Africa—lies a more mysterious and influential factor: namely, the respect and admiration among French-speaking Africans for French culture, language, and civilization. How this feeling has been transmitted is difficult to say, but that it exists cannot be denied. In all likelihood, one of its essential elements is African awareness of and appreciation for the absence of the most offensive forms of racialism in the French outlook. Even though French colonial practices were harsh and although France has pressed with heavy weight on the fragile new African states, it did not maintain an official color bar in the colonies and long before the era of independence was prepared to accept African leaders in Paris on a basis of full social and intellectual equality.* It is not in fashion among geopolitical thinkers to consider that such sentimental and spiritual factors can play a great role. But the evolution of French-African relationships in recent years throw some question on such a widely held conclusion.

Apart, however, from the apparent success of French policy until this time and the reasons which may explain it, there remains the problem of how long it may last. How prepared are the African states to see the present degree of French influence continue? How durable is the French determination to maintain that influence, and, as a matter of policy, how long is it likely to be willing to invest in the task the energies and considerable resources required?

* In Africa itself, French nonracialism requires some qualification. In the principal cities, for example, there were areas where Africans were not expected to be seen after dark, except on duty; and other more subtle social barriers existed as well. Similarly, in the French colonial army both social and professional distinctions were maintained until 1956.

The evidence which can be adduced is contradictory. On the one hand, the sub-Saharan Francophone states in some ways seem even more dependent on France than before, more determined to retain the advantages of their present association, even to the point of trying to keep other African states out of the charmed circle, and more prepared if France will increase its economic concessions to reciprocate with political and cultural collaboration.* On the other hand, dissident anti-French elements exist in all of them, and in the political changes that inevitably will come in the future, some elements may take control. On balance, however, it appears at this time that, with few exceptions, the Francophone states are not likely to seek to drive French political influence out of Africa if, as is probable, the cost would be to deprive themselves of the present economic and other benefits of their association.

Yet, with the passage of time, some of the threads and present ties must inevitably be broken. General de Gaulle has left office, and the African leaders with whom he has been closely associated are aging and will eventually pass from the scene. Because of the special circumstances and experiences which have bound that group together, their successors cannot have the same sense of fraternity.

On the part of the French public, there is accumulating evidence that although the desire to maintain influence in Africa remains strong, willingness to devote large resources and energies to the task is waning. Slowly but unmistakably, a long process of evolution seems to be under way not toward a French withdrawal from Africa but toward a lesser and more limited kind of involvement. As more attention and energies are devoted to new tasks at home and in Europe, France appears to be ready to accord an increasing degree of genuine independence rather than the mere formality of sovereignty to the former colonies and is experiencing a "decolonization" of its own mentality.

One reason to believe that these trends will not be reversed is that the political and economic base within France of the colonial fixation has begun to dwindle. Decolonization was a singular agony

---

* The launching of plans for *Francophonie*, a kind of world-wide French-speaking commonwealth, in December 1966 by a number of the former French colonies in Africa, was received with mixed feelings in Paris. Satisfaction with this gesture of spiritual solidarity would have been greater if it had not so obviously been an attempt to trade cultural allegiance for new assurances of continued French aid.

for France because it was an aspect of the nation's political and spiritual struggle within itself. Historically, French colonialism has been intimately associated with the French Right, that miscellaneous grouping of reactionaries, monarchists, fascists, militarists, and economic extremists. The determination—and on some occasions the ferocity—of efforts to hold on to empire are explainable essentially by the fanaticism and the special influence of these groups in French political life. But Algeria was the great climax and defeat. Since then, settlers in large numbers have come back to France from North Africa, and many investors have repatriated their capital. Not only has the bulk of the French army been withdrawn from the former colonial areas, but, in consequence of the Gaullist policy of transforming the French army into a modern nuclear force, a large proportion of the old French officer corps, with its imperial habits of mind, has been retired from active service. Thus, the very core and root of the political basis for the French commitment to empire has been cut. Those elements, once so hardened and absolute in their defense of the French presence overseas, are now likely not only to lose interest in the former colonies, but to be among those who press for a policy of French indifference to their post-independence predicament.

Thus a quarter of a century after the Second World War and a decade after the advent of independence for the colonies, France remains a factor of great influence in Africa.

Many—but not all—of the pillars supporting that influence are beginning to crumble. How much France will be prepared to invest in shoring up those foundations to maintain its position in Africa —and for how long—remains to be seen.

4

Other Western European Bilateral Relations

At the zenith of their imperial power, Britain and France controlled more than half the area of the continent and its population, and hence in the recent evolution of the policies of these two countries, much of the story of the changing relationship between Western Europe and Africa since World War II is told. But not all. This chapter reviews various other smaller but significant European presences in Africa and attempts to put the evolving British and French relationships with the continent into a larger Western European perspective.

Several other European countries have been involved in African colonialism, either recently or in time past, and in their own fashion they have likewise had to accommodate to the new circumstances of the independence era. For Germany, which lost its African colonies half a century ago, this has taken one form; for Italy, which lost its colonies more recently, it has taken another; for Spain, with a few scattered possessions, it has provided occasion for a careful, intelligent retreat from control; for Portugal, the challenge has resulted in a determined and costly resistance effort. Even nations such as Sweden and Austria, which were never colonial powers, have had to make some alteration in their policies.

Although much has changed, much remains unaltered. And Africa today is still in many respects an appendage of Europe—a "sphere of influence" not so much in political terms as in the reality of an important European presence in the governmental structures, the economic life, the educational institutions, the flow of information, and the habits and outlook of the modernized sector of every African society. Western Europe continues to be by far the most important external element in the affairs of the new Africa—which is perhaps only to note that powerful factors of continuity accompany all phenomena of change in the complex evolution of human affairs.

Nevertheless, the political changes that have occurred, even if they mark only the beginning of decolonization rather than its end, have set in motion a process tending toward a loosening and dilution of all relationships between the former colonies and their metropoles. Politically, economically, culturally, educationally, and militarily the new African states are moving, even though slowly, toward a diversification of their external linkages and a reduction of their dependence on Europe. For the former metropoles the logic of the process now under way produces a steady diminution of public and official interest in the former colonies and a redirection of energies and resources toward newer domestic and international objectives.

This evolving separation has been accelerated by events both in Africa and in Europe. Impelled by their own problems, the new African states have repeatedly taken actions which by intent or otherwise have discouraged or driven out the European presence; similarly, the growing preoccupation of the countries of Western Europe with their own immediate problems of development and security has tended to encourage a withdrawal from African responsibilities. This immense evolutionary current proceeds at different rates in different sectors; and although the general direction can be discerned, there are eddys, cross-currents, and backflows.

The Special Case of Belgium

Belgium's importance in Africa derives from the central significance of its former great colony, the Congo. Relationships between the two constitute one of the most bizarre episodes in the recent history of European colonialism.

Belgium entered the competition for African colonies in the late nineteenth century largely because of the initiative of an energetic king, Leopold II, who saw in the huge territory of the Congo basin not only an important opportunity for enterprise and empire-building, but also the possibility of inventing for his small country a "frontier" that could widen its horizons, challenge its youth, and involve it in the great affairs of the world. Having been accorded what was called the Congo Free State by the Conference of Berlin in 1885 as a private fiefdom, Leopold made the mistake of permitting commercial concessionaires to exploit the territory and its population with such rapacity that even the blunted conscience of the Victorian world was shocked, forcing him to turn over administration of his giant domain to the Belgian government in 1908.

Thereafter Belgium devised a system for the control and development of the colony resting on a close working alliance between government administrators, the Catholic Church, and a few large private enterprises. The state—that is, Belgium—was responsible for roads, transport, public services, and internal order, which was maintained through the tightly disciplined *Force publique* manned by Africans and officered by Belgians. The Church, with governmental subsidy, was responsible for the development of an extensive system of mission schools; and the evangelization of the African population was regarded as one of the integral and higher objectives of Belgian control. The corporations were responsible for economic development, and in this they were actively supported by the colonial administration. In addition, because of their highly concentrated economic power and their political connections, they were able to exercise great influence on governmental policy-making in Brussels.

The system produced what was regarded as a model colony. Industry and agriculture prospered, and by 1950 the living standard of the Congolese was probably higher than that of any other black people in Africa. Extensive social and welfare services were provided, and a large-scale housing program virtually eliminated slums in the cities. By the late 1950s some 40 per cent of the Congolese were literate, an extremely high figure for Tropical Africa, although educational opportunities beyond the primary level were severely restricted. Until well after the Second World War there were few visible signs of political discontent, and the population displayed little interest in pressing for political rights, largely, it was thought, because of the enlightened labor and welfare policies which had been followed.

Thus Belgian paternalism seemed to be paying off. And Belgium, confident that it had almost unlimited time before steps needed to be taken in the direction of decolonization, repeatedly delayed the preparation of Africans for higher education and responsible posts in administration, postponed their political participation, and took careful measures to insulate them from outside political contact. In these decisions the Belgian colonial administration, in contrast to its British and French counterparts, was seldom exposed to criticism from political, academic, or journalistic quarters at home. The colonies somehow did not engage public interest or arouse the passions in Belgium that empire and its connotations did in the other European metropoles.

The situation continued to appear as tranquil as a millpond even after nationalist upheavals had begun in many other parts of Africa. The factors necessary to insure the maintenance of colonial control for a considerable period were assumed to be present: a passive population whose political discontents had been calmed by the material benefits of a generous economic and welfare policy; an elaborate system of administrative control reinforced by well-organized and internal security forces; and, in the background, rich industrial and commercial corporations determined to protect their interests and ready to take whatever measures and to devote whatever resources might be needed for the task.

Insofar as Belgians thought about decolonization at all, it was in the context of a long time span—perhaps a century—during which Belgium could set the pace and guide its evolution by the employment of various legal and other devices. Ideally, an African middle class would slowly arise, and local governmental institutions would be developed to provide political training for the population. What would finally result would not be a sovereign and independent Congo but, rather, a Eurafrican society administered jointly by Belgians and Congolese and integrally linked to the mother country and the royal family. These comfortable self-deceptions were no more sordid or self-centered than those of the other European colonial powers at the time. The main difference was that Belgium persisted in them longer and, well into the 1950s, continued to imagine that history would permit plans formulated in the privacy of business and bureaucratic circles to control the future of the colony.

But events were to sweep away the assumptions on which Belgian policy had been erected and to do so with such abruptness that the situation soon raced ahead largely out of anyone's control. Over the four years prior to Congolese independence the Belgians, without benefit of plan or timetable, shifted from almost total resistance to demands for independence to virtually total surrender. Up to that time, occasional reference had been made by Belgian leaders to the possibility of political change. As early as 1952 a Belgian governor-general in the Congo had declared the time appropriate to begin preparing for eventual "emancipation."

In 1954 a Socialist government in Brussels used the word "independence" but in an ambiguous fashion; and in May 1955 Belgium's young king, Baudouin, in the course of a visit to the Congo, hinted at a shift in official attitude by saying with elaborate qualification, "When White and Black give proof of the greatest possible understanding of one another . . . the moment will have come—though the exact date of its advent cannot yet be stated—for giving to our African territories a statute which . . . will insure the perpetuity of a genuine Belgo-Congolese community guaranteeing to all, Black and White, the share due to them in the government of their country."[1] But when a leading Belgian scholar in 1956 published a plan envisioning Congolese independence in thirty years, Belgian officialdom and most Belgians in the Congo regarded his ideas as wildly premature.

In 1957, however, after the Congolese themselves had begun to assert demands for independence, Belgian officials became aware of the need to present statements of greater specificity about the colony's political future. Part of the pressure upon them derived from the situation in adjacent Rwanda-Urundi, two small kingdoms formerly under German control which had been acquired by Belgium as a League of Nations mandate after the First World War and which subsequently had been placed under U.N. trusteeship. As an outcome of debates at the United Nations in New York, Belgium was obliged to establish a deadline for their independence, an action which inevitably had repercussions in the Congo itself.

Thereafter, the government quickly began to institute limited reforms: more freedom of speech for the Africans, the outlawing of racial discrimination, and authorization of a degree of African participation in governmental affairs. Then in January 1959 the government, to the astonishment of many, proposed a five-year plan for independence. One year later at a round-table conference in Brussels with Congolese leaders, Belgium readily accepted a demand for independence within six months, or by June 30, 1960.

In the course of these final climactic months Belgium gave up, one after another, the conditions it had stipulated: that the Congo could achieve sovereignty only within the framework of a Belgo-Congolese community; that the whites in the Congo would share political control on some basis with the blacks; and that the King would continue to be sovereign of the Congo as well as of Belgium. In the end, the tide of nationalism swept them all aside.

In retrospect, it is difficult to comprehend why the Belgians reacted in the panicky and erratic fashion in which they did. Sharp differences of opinion on Congolese developments existed in Belgium, which apparently contributed to a paralysis of decision on the part of a characteristically weak government and to rapid alternation of policy as successive changes were made in the leadership charged with the management of colonial affairs.

But whatever the causes, Belgium hurriedly granted independence to a territory that was not a nation in any real sense, and within two weeks after the flag-raising ceremonies, the country was hit by quadruple disaster: breakdown of civil order, army revolt, secession, and external military intervention. Ever since, the huge and invertebrate political creature has had to struggle desperately simply to survive.

If the Congo was unprepared to receive and handle independence, the Belgians were equally unprepared genuinely to accord it. Deep-seated colonialist attitudes toward the Congo and the Congolese, which had been formed over decades, were not suddenly changed or dissipated by the change in political arrangements. And given the suddenness with which independence came and the carry-over of such attitudes, it would have been most unlikely under any circumstances that there would not have been many transgressions after independence on Congolese sensibilities and the Congo's sovereignty. Events, however, conspired to make the worst happen almost immediately; and thereafter the Belgians, encouraged by some provocation on the part of the Congolese, succeeded in turning a situation of bad relationships into an almost hopeless one.

In the weeks just prior to June 30, one of the most unfortunate consequences of the final stampede to independence was the fear and bitterness engendered between Belgians and Congolese. As the day approached, there were increasing acts of violence against whites in many parts of the country. What should have been a day of national rejoicing was instead a time of fear and hostility. Terrible prophecies circulated—that white estates were to be plundered, white women raped, and white men massacred. Europeans were in such a state of psychological tension that general panic was feared at the first incident.

In the following week, disorders in fact broke out. There was revolt in the *Force publique*, resulting in the ouster of its Belgian officers, and thousands of Europeans began to flee in terror to the airports and the frontiers. Thereupon, Belgian forces without invitation re-entered the capital to restore order and Belgian paratroopers were dropped at other points throughout the country. Almost at the same time, in copper-rich Katanga Province, Belgian mining interests encouraged. Moïse Tshombé, the Premier of the province, to declare its secession on grounds that the central government was trying to establish a "ruinous and Communist state." With the active and direct help of Belgian advisers and Belgian financial backing, Katangan armed forces were organized and a political and propaganda assault on the central government was set into motion.

When the young Congolese Premier, Patrice Lumumba, called upon the United Nations for assistance in putting down the secession and in forcing the Belgians to remove their troops, the Belgian reaction was one of acute resentment. In the following months, after U.N. experts had arrived in considerable numbers to assist in the pacification and administration of the country, the Belgians considered them not only as incompetent and inexperienced but as "intruders." Endless friction between the two groups developed, and, in the view of most U.N. officials the Belgians not only were uncooperative in restoring unity and order but were bent on re-establishing their colonial presence.

By June 1964 the U.N. forces had brought an end to the Katangese secession; but, because of a shortage of funds, the United Nations was able to maintain only a skeleton corps of civilian technicians in the country. The Congo quickly began to fall apart once again—and Belgian intervention quickly recurred. In November of that year, when Belgian paratroopers transported in American military aircraft were dropped on Stanleyville to rescue some 1,700 white hostages, the Congolese and Africans generally were violently critical because of the general background of Belgian meddling and manipulation in the country. Since then, and until quite recently, charges and countercharges between the Belgians and the Congolese have filled the air. Belgian mining and commercial interests have wrangled with the new government on many questions of taxation, political interference, and nationalization. Belgian and other white mercenaries, even when employed by the central government of the Congo, have repeatedly aroused suspicion; and when a group of them rebelled in mid-1967 and made an attempt at secession in the eastern portion of the country, the specter of Belgian neo-colonialism—or recolonialism—was raised again.

From the Congolese point of view, the evidence added up to an ironclad case of Belgian subversion, chicanery, and neo-colonial intent. Virtually all trust and confidence in Brussels was shattered as a result. The Belgian list of grievances was also impressive. Crimes against Belgian property had been numerous, as had been instances of ill-treatment of Belgian citizens. The Congolese were considered to have consistently violated or ignored solemn agreements, to have carried out provocative acts, and generally to have behaved incompetently and irresponsibly, necessitating intervention on occasion to protect Belgium's rights and to fulfill its responsibilities toward its own citizens. The downward spiral of friction and misunderstanding continued through 1967, to the point of obscuring and undermining Belgium's constructive actions of assistance to the new country—which have not been inconsiderable.

In the years since independence, the Belgian government has made moderately large bilateral contributions in support of the Congolese economy, quite apart from its contributions to the Development Fund of the European Common Market. Contributions to the Congo, Burundi, and Rwanda represent 90 per cent of all Belgian bilateral assistance, about two-thirds of which is earmarked for financing the Congo public debt and the payment of pensions and allowances to Belgian civil servants formerly stationed in the Congo.* About one-third is given in the form of bilateral grants for technical assistance and capital projects. Capital projects, however, represent a small proportion of the total (less than 7 per cent in 1966). Technical assistance expenditures have been much larger: in 1965 they totaled $23.7 million and rose to $27.1 million in 1966. From these funds some 1,500 teachers, 300 advisers, and 800 operational personnel were provided. The specialists financed out of such aid have helped maintain the effectiveness of the judicial system of the Congo and have carried important responsibilities in the departments of public works, finance, agriculture, and communications. The teachers have formed the backbone of the instructional staffs of the universities and secondary schools throughout the country.

In mid-1967, however, Belgian technical assistance, the principal remaining thread holding the metropole and its former colony

* To put the matter of Belgian aid in perspective, Belgian bilateral disbursements to the Congo from 1960 through 1967 totaled slightly more than $200 million, of which less than $100 million represented resources directly available to the Congolese government for rehabilitation or developmental purposes. During the same period, U.S. bilateral aid in all forms available for such purposes approached $400 million.

together, became badly frayed. Following outbreaks of violence against Belgian residents resulting from the rebellion of mercenary troops in the Eastern Congo, Belgium decided to hold up most of its technical assistance until it was able to obtain what it considered adequate guarantees of safety for its citizens. Its aid program for the Congolese judiciary was interrupted, gravely affecting the administration of justice in the country. In the fall of the year the universities had to be closed because of the withdrawal of Belgian teachers, and the effectiveness of public services throughout the country, already poor, further deteriorated with the decline of Belgian technical assistance. Matters had reached a very low point.

Belgium's once model colony, of which it had been so proud, had become the saddest example in Africa of unpreparedness for independence, followed by tangled, destructive relationships between a former colony and its metropole. The resentments on both sides had produced a situation in which Belgium interests seemed on the way to being liquidated and any remaining sense of metropolitan responsibility for the fate of the former colony extinguished. Almost nothing wholesome or promising for the future seemed to remain in the relationship. For Belgium, the old colonial illusions had been demolished, and its image both in Africa and in the world had been tarnished. Belgian opinion, notoriously subject to great swings of mood toward the Congo, had become first disenchanted and then angry. Complaints were commonly expressed about the "ingratitude" of the authorities in Kinshasa; individual incidents of violence against Belgians were heavily and emotionally played in the Belgian press. Periodically the impulse to "punish" the Congolese found expression both in private and official statements. A Belgian form of "Cartierism" had developed, and there was a serious question of how long the flow of Belgian aid would continue.

For the Congolese, it seemed by 1967, the rough, intrusive hand of Belgian neo-colonialism had been forced to draw back, but under circumstances which left their country damaged and weakened. For all of Africa, the aftermath was that a huge, stagnant, and unstable country appeared on the verge of being abandoned by its former metropole. But the unpredictable history of the Congo was to contain yet another surprise. In late 1967, once the mercenary-led rebellion in the eastern part of the country had been suppressed, calm returned and Congolese President Mobutu —partly in response to consistent prodding by American officials—

took a series of sensible initiatives to check the deterioration of relations with Belgium and to reopen communications. In June 1968 he paid a visit to Brussels as a guest of the King, which opened the way to further and more specific discussions. In August the Congolese Foreign Minister Justin Bomboko went to Belgium for long conversations to re-examine the entire relationship between the two countries, the outcome of which was a series of new understandings by which Belgium agreed to increase its assistance in exchange for Congolese guarantees against the nationalization of Belgian investments, the indemnification of Belgian victims of earlier disorders, the unblocking of Belgian accounts, and the settlement by compromise of various other points in dispute.

Bomboko subsequently called the discussions the "end of Belgian paternalism in the Congo and the re-establishment of trust in the relationship between the two countries." In explaining earlier difficulties, he said that neither Belgium nor the Congo had had any previous experience in the decolonization process. It had therefore become necessary to "rethink and re-orientate the policy of cooperation between the two countries in the light of what had happened in the eight years since independence."[2]

Thereafter Belgian firms began once again to receive contracts, Belgian technicians to return, and the tone of day-to-day relationships between the Congolese and Belgians working in the Congo to improve. By the end of 1968 it began to appear as though the two parties, after a hard and tumultuous experience, had concluded that, on balance, maintaining a familiar relationship with all its difficulties was preferable to the alternative of a complete rupture. If the new rapport persists, the story of Belgian colonialism may yet have a creditable ending. If it does not and bitter conflict again occurs, the long-term implications for the territorial integrity, stability, and development of the former colony could be disquieting indeed, for the question remains whether the afflicted Congo can survive without the concern and steady support of some special sponsor such as Belgium among the wealthy, developed nations.

The Special Case of West Germany

West Germany, whose colonial links with Africa were broken a half century ago, has now, following its strong economic revival since the end of World War II, begun slowly to rebuild its relationships, utilizing economic assistance as its principal instrumentality. Imperial Germany was one of the last of the European powers to acquire African colonies in the late nineteenth century and, as a result of defeat in the First World War, among the first to lose them. As its share of the original spoils in Africa, Germany took control of territories embracing more than a million square miles and a population of nearly 14 million, only a few thousand of whom were white. The territories were South West Africa, Tanganyika, Rwanda-Burundi, Togo, and Cameroon. In the early years, while attempting to establish control over the new acquisitions, German administration was particularly brutal. But after 1907, with the establishment of a colonial ministry in Berlin following a series of native uprisings that had been bloodily repressed, increased emphasis was placed on improvements in education and medical services and on general economic development.

After the First World War, France, Britain, and Belgium took over all of Germany's African territories as League of Nations mandates. During the interwar period there was some evidence of continuing German interest in Africa, and on a few occasions Adolf Hitler demanded the return of the former colonies; but the issue never reached major proportions. In the first decade after the Second World War, West German energies were devoted to rebuilding a shattered and divided economy and generally to recovering psychologically and politically from the shock of defeat. As the economy and self-confidence revived, West Germany at first cautiously and later more vigorously moved to re-establish its world-wide relationships, including the development of ties with the new African states. Since then it has moved on many fronts: diplomatic representation has been established; agreements intended to increase German trade and secure private investment throughout Africa have been signed; and cultural and educational programs have been rapidly extended, along with propaganda activities. The West German overseas broadcasting service, for example, now beams more hours of programs to Africa than does the Voice of America and roughly matches the scale of activity of BBC and *Radio Diffusion Française*. A West German equivalent of the U.S. Peace Corps has been organized on a modest scale; and private organizations of many kinds, including trade unions, church groups, and cooperative societies, have been encouraged to develop collaboration with their counterparts in Africa.

By far the most important method employed in this African thrust has been economic and technical assistance. In the late 1950s when the economy was experiencing a remarkable upsurge

and Germany was seeking a new and acceptable international outlet for its energies and ambitions, economic aid given through
multilateral agencies won widespread domestic support, even enthusiasm. During those years the German contribution to the
United Nations and investment in bonds of the World Bank
markedly increased. With the establishment of the European
Common Market in 1957, Germany matched France's substantial
contribution to its Development Fund for the associated countries
and territories. German bilateral assistance programs, however,
remained very limited.

By 1960 the United States was beginning to suffer from a heavy
balance-of-payments deficit and increasingly urged West Germany,
then enjoying a considerable surplus, to assume a bigger share of
the task of Western aid to the underdeveloped countries. President
Kennedy, after his election, persisted in these efforts which had
been initiated under President Eisenhower. Somewhat grudgingly
at first, Germany stepped up its contributions by combining funds
from individual German states and industry with leftover Marshall
Plan funds and direct budgetary allocations. In 1961 the world-wide
total of German official assistance jumped to nearly $250 million;
in 1962 it exceeded $275 million; in 1963 it approached $330
million, and West Germany had edged past the United Kingdom
and ranked third after the United States and France in its contributions to the development of the emerging nations.[3]

Initially, German bilateral assistance in Africa was concentrated
on those countries with which there had once been a colonial
relationship, such as Togo and Cameroon, and on a few of the
more developed areas, notably Nigeria, Tunisia, and Morocco.
For some years, Germany also attempted to tie political strings
to its assistance by threatening to cut off help to any state which
violated the so-called Hallstein Doctrine; that is, which recognized
the East German government. Subsequently, however, this impulse diminished; and later, even when Germany broke relations
with certain African countries on this issue, it did not terminate
economic assistance. More recently the total of German aid has
risen further, and both the proportion devoted to Africa and the
number of African states receiving it have increased. Africa is unmistakably on the rise in West German foreign policy priorities
and long-term objectives.

Official grants and loans to Africa since 1960 have grown from
$5.5 million in 1960 to more than $80 million in 1965. Unofficial
figures for the period since suggest that the increase has continued

and that by 1967 German assistance in Africa exceeded $100 million. Available information on German intentions for future years indicates that still higher totals may be reached.

By 1965 Africa was receiving one-third of total German aid commitments to the less developed countries, including 27 per cent of the loans and 57 per cent of technical assistance grants. By comparison, Africa received less than 5 per cent in the 1950s and less than one-quarter in the early 1960s.[4]

Although German assistance is now distributed largely without discrimination as regards the political orientation of the recipient states, it has, nevertheless, a distinctive ideological quality in its strong insistence on support for principles of private enterprise. Because of its own successful experience in applying that philosophy in its postwar economic recovery, the special meaning of private-enterprise concepts in a nation divided into capitalistic and Communistic halves, and the unusual domestic political power of private industry and finance, West Germany to a greater extent than other donors has linked aid to domestic business interests and to the support of their efforts to open up trade and investment opportunities. When discussing foreign aid, prominent spokesmen of the Bonn government continue to make flat demands for the developing countries to revise their attitude toward private capital, to overhaul their business practices, and generally to offer greater economic concessions to investors as a condition for continuing German assistance.

The case of German aid in Africa therefore is of special interest on a number of grounds: In magnitude it is becoming the fourth most important source of outside assistance, after France, Britain, and the United States; and the volume has been increasing rapidly at a time when the other major European aid programs have begun to taper off. In fact, the increase in German aid has to a considerable degree offset the decline in other European aid programs thus far.

Apart from its volume and growth, however, the German effort reflects an approach to Africa in sharp contrast to that of the other former colonial powers. Germany has broken away from an exclusive concentration on assistance to those areas with which it had historical ties. Nor is its aid any longer focused on the preservation of a few specific or local interests or on the achievement of short-term political objectives. It has now become all-African in scope: In 1965 thirty-one independent African states received grants from West Germany, ranging in amount from $50,000 to more than $3 million. In the same year, sixteen African states received loans from West Germany, ranging in amount from $50,000 to more than $13 million. It would appear that the decision has been taken to utilize economic and technical assistance as a means of developing a West German presence throughout Africa in order to develop a general climate of friendly relations in support of long-term commercial objectives and to some degree perhaps of general cultural and political goals. The policy supplements and extends the wider access in Africa that Germany has acquired through the trade arrangements of the Common Market and the fact that European Development Fund expenditures are tied to the Six. From the African viewpoint, the scale of German assistance in any specific country is sufficient to support a particular project but not to provide resources for a development program. From a German viewpoint, although the level of assistance has been increasing, particularly in Africa, the over-all total has been kept under strict control and represents a decreasing burden on the prospering German economy: whereas official aid approached 1 per cent of national income in 1961 (including IBRD bond purchases), it had declined to 0.69 in 1962 and to 0.54 in 1966.

In certain respects, therefore, Germany has both decolonized and normalized relationships in Africa to a degree unique for a European power. As a middle-sized industrial nation, it is pursuing national economic and political interests through the usual methods of diplomacy but with special emphasis on widespread dispersal of limited amounts of assistance. The West German approach thus represents the antithesis of the old ambitions of the era of imperialism. Pragmatic, detached, and eclectic, it implies the fullest respect for African sovereignty and the unqualified assumption that Africa is competent to deal with outside nations on the basis of equality. It also represents something less than a sense of deep involvement and continuing commitment to the growth and stability of the new African nations.* If such tendencies—the opposite of feared neo-colonialist intrusion—should come to characterize French and British policy, or American, then the new states of Africa may be spared one kind of danger. But they will be left to travel a hard road of self-reliance

* As distinct from the United States and France, West Germany does not maintain in the less developed countries a presence in the form of special staffs concerned with economic development, but operates through its embassies, plus visiting representatives from Bonn.

in their efforts to achieve development and stability. In essence, the West German case raises the question of whether such an approach to emergent Africa—a policy of objectivity and "business as usual" on the part of wealthy and industrialized nations—is quite enough.

EUROPEAN MONETARY RELATIONS, TRADE AND INVESTMENT IN AFRICA

In the economic sphere, factors of continuity between the two areas are particularly evident. The two European monetary systems, the Sterling and the Franc areas, have preserved most of their African membership. But these two important economic groupings, which have divided and to a considerable extent still divide Africa into separate commercial systems, are beginning to erode. The trade preferences associated with membership in the Commonwealth are being diluted, and the continuing difficulties of the British economy have undermined the strength of the pound and the discipline of the Sterling Area. The erosion of the Franc Zone varies from region to region, the North African states now maintaining only limited links. But the tropical Francophone states, many of which are in serious financial straits, find themselves heavily dependent on French subsidies and trade arrangements and generally incapable of taking independent courses of action. They remain closely tied to the system, though their discontents are increasingly audible.

Trade patterns have on the whole remained intact. Europe continues to be the most important outlet for African products and the principal source of supply for African imports although some diversification in sources and markets has occurred. One of the most immediate and visible effects of decolonization was to stimulate various lesser European nations to explore the possibilities of developing new markets and investment opportunities in the African territories formerly walled off by colonial arrangements. Literally hundreds of European missions in quest of trade and investment have traveled through Africa in the last decade. In the search for new markets the West Germans and the Italians have shown the greatest persistence and ingenuity.* Both equipped their exporters with special credit arrangements in order to offer African buyers attractive terms which, in some cases, have been

---

* Among the European nations, that is. The Japanese, however, have been far more enterprising and effective than either.

so irresistible that African governments have been induced to buy unwisely and excessively. The West Germans have sometimes supplemented easy credit with technical assistance grants to train Africans to operate the equipment purchased. By creating imaginative consortia of some of their major engineering and manufacturing companies, the Italians have made an especially effective effort to obtain public works contracts in Africa. In Tanzania and Zambia, for example, after political tensions with Rhodesia became acute, they devised a timely plan to establish and operate a wholly new transport system by truck and pipeline between the two countries that would help Zambia escape its previous dependence on routes across Rhodesian territory. With the help of substantial credits provided by the Italian government, the participating companies thereby created a market for several millions of dollars of equipment. Over-all, however, these various European initiatives, though they have produced some diversification in trade patterns, have had only a limited effect on the total volume, which has remained anchored by the generally slow rate of African economic development. The exception of course has been South Africa, whose booming economy has presented the most enticing marketing opportunities.

Although African trade represents a decreasing proportion of total European trade, this in itself does not signify declining European interest in the maintenance of its present African markets. Likewise, from an African point of view, Europe has been a market of slow growth but still of great importance. For the foreseeable future, therefore, important commercial ties between Africa and Europe are certain to continue for reasons of mutual self-interest and for want of better alternatives.

After the British and French colonies gained independence, European private investors—particularly West Germans—showed new interest in exploring African possibilities. To encourage such efforts the Bonn government signed investment agreements with a number of African countries providing security against nationalization for a term of years and formalizing rights for the transfer of profits. In addition, Bonn offered German investors guarantees against expropriation and other political risks and even assured them a reasonable profit. Despite these and other measures, however, German private investors, with few exceptions, have not been attracted to Africa. Over-all, a limited amount of new European investment has entered Africa—not only German, but also Italian, Dutch, and Scandinavian—but the flow fluctuates widely from year to year and tends to be concentrated on a few selected areas and largely in extractive enterprises.

The African states themselves seem to have an ambivalent view of the advantages of foreign private investment, many of them asserting their desire for capital from abroad, while at the same time taking measures that discourage and drive it off. From the standpoint of European investors, Africa has lost much of its attractiveness not only because of the passing of colonial political control, but also because of the relatively greater prospects in other parts of the world. New direct investment in Africa (north of the white-minority-controlled areas in the south) has been largely off-set if not exceeded since independence by withdrawals of capital by earlier colonial investors. Such withdrawal is not exceptional since it has also been taking place in recent years from Latin America, Asia, and the Middle East. Nevertheless, the disinvestment from Africa appears to have been greater than that from some of the other less developed regions. Despite statistical complications, however, one point at least is clear: Africa is in no danger of being inundated by private European capital. On the contrary, it cannot count on the general availability of such resources for the implementation of its development plans.

EUROPEAN ECONOMIC, TECHNICAL, AND EDUCATIONAL ASSISTANCE

Because African economic development is indispensable to any prospect for stability on the continent, the extent of continuing European responsibility for providing capital and technical assistance is a crucially important matter to appraise. In the post-colonial period, the most commendable single aspect of the policy of the former metropoles has been their willingness to provide technical and economic assistance in considerable volume to their former colonies. In addition, a number of the smaller European nations have now joined in. These increasingly numerous European sources of aid to Africa are, in turn, part of a world-wide flow which must be reviewed briefly to put the matter in full perspective.

Broadly, the Communist nations of Eastern Europe, the Soviet Union, and China provide very little aid to Africa. (Their assistance programs are reviewed in Part II.) The so-called Free World countries are the source of nine-tenths of the help which Africa obtains.[5] Table 10 summarizes their commitments of economic assistance to Africa for the period 1959 through 1967.

TABLE 10. Free World Economic Assistance to Africa,[a] 1959–67

(Estimated commitments, millions of U.S. dollars)

	Former Metropoles (Belgium, France, Italy, U.K.) and EEC	International Organizations (IBRD, IDA, IFC, and U.N. Agencies)	Other Bilateral Donors, especially Federal Republic of Germany	Total United States (AID, P.L. 480, Export-Import Bank, and other Economic)	Total
1959	791	80	40	185	1,096
1960	862	198	26	211	1,297
1961	1,003	64	169	460	1,697
1962	1,016	94	163	488	1,761
1963	890	95	155	490	1,630
1964	791	179	138	359	1,467
1965	818	258	218	330	1,624
1966	895	274	216	384	1,769
1967	729	271	223	388	1,611

[a] Excludes South Africa and U.A.R.

SOURCE: Agency for International Development, Washington, 1968.

Africa has been accorded more than $1.5 billion of Free World assistance annually from official sources since 1961, a sum that has remained relatively steady. This assistance represents a large fraction of all aid to the less developed areas. In 1966 Africa received about 26 per cent of the world total ($1.7 billion out of a total of $6.6 billion) and approximately 23 per cent in 1967 ($1.6 billion out of a total of $6.8 billion). Such assistance has been provided by a large number of bilateral donors, including some twenty-five European and non-European nations. Some countries whose aid has been relatively modest in the past have more recently been increasing their programs in Africa: Canada, for example, now provides five times as much as it did in 1965. Also, the growth in assistance from international organizations has partially offset the recent trend toward a shrinkage of assistance from the former metropoles.

In per capita terms, Africa's receipts of assistance for both 1965 and 1966 were higher than those of any other underdeveloped region except Oceania. In 1966 it averaged $5.35 as compared with an average of $4.23 for all the less developed countries; by comparison, Latin America received $4.78 per capita and Asia, $3.26. Whether or not Africa's higher per capita average means that it received a disproportionate amount of aid is a moot question among economists. Some feel that the large number of African countries, their small population in many instances, and their low level of income make crude per capita averages of little meaning in terms of actual needs for development assistance.

Africa receives by far the largest proportion of its assistance from Europe ($1 billion out of $1.6 billion in 1967) and is the main focus of European foreign aid. Table 11 indicates the contributions to this flow of assistance by the principal European donor nations.

TABLE 11. Total Official Western European Bilateral Assistance to Independent Africa,[a] Grants and Net Loans, 1960–66

(Disbursements, millions of U.S. dollars)

	1960	1961	1962	1963	1964	1965	1966[d]
France	690.70	768.20	728.90	648.40	607.90	514.80	464.80
United Kingdom	132.71	237.12	181.56	172.76	220.45	212.38	170.68
Belgium[b]	86.00	70.50	63.40	75.79	76.46	96.10	61.91
West Germany	5.52	13.43	60.88	55.53	44.33	83.36	115.62
Other Western Europe[c]	17.07	22.45	14.65	41.14	24.24	44.77	53.23
Total	932.00	1,111.70	1,049.39	993.62	973.38	951.41	866.24

[a] Excludes U.A.R. and white-minority controlled southern areas.

[b] Belgian assistance, following OECD practice, includes service payments on Congo public debt and pensions and other payments to Belgian civil servants formerly stationed in the Congo.

[c] Includes Austria, Denmark, Italy, Netherlands, Norway, Sweden, and Switzerland.

[d] Preliminary figures.

SOURCE: Geographical Distribution of Financial Flows to Less Developed Countries—1960–64 and 1965 (Paris: OECD, 1966 and 1967).

The predominance of the assistance programs of France and Great Britain is clearly reflected in these figures; yet the lesser but significant programs of Belgium and West Germany are also to be noted.

After Britain and France, the two European nations of most importance in Africa are Belgium and West Germany. Each presents a case of special interest. That of Belgium illustrates the extraordinary volatility of post-independence relationships when neither party—metropole or colony—was prepared for the event. West Germany, on the other hand, presents an intriguing and important example of the attitudes and approach of a major Western European country toward Africa long after the severance of its colonial links.

Qualitatively, European bilateral aid to Africa in recent years including that of the lesser or more recent donors such as Sweden and Italy, has generally improved. Initially, the donor countries began their programs with inadequate concepts and poor administrative machinery. But within the last five years many of these initial weaknesses have been corrected. More realistic and sophisticated concepts have been introduced, and separate new aid ministries have been established or existing agencies reorganized. The terms of aid legislation have been improved and administrative practices revamped; as a result, the effectiveness of each country's program has been significantly increased in terms of African requirements.

Since bilateral programs are the channels for the bulk of their assistance to Africa, the European nations have on the whole operated competitively, not cooperatively. A formidable number of programs are in existence, which in itself is encouraging. In 1965, for example, Kenya and Tanzania each had eleven Western European sources providing technical assistance. Many others were receiving assistance simultaneously from four to six European countries. But the problems of coordination resulting from a multiplicity of donors, each with its own approach and varied concepts, can be severe for the African recipients with their meager resources of staff and experience. Through the OECD and its Development Assistance Committee (DAC) in Paris, efforts have been made to improve the coordination of assistance, but the results achieved have not been spectacular. There are, however, small signs of progress. The continuing efforts of the DAC are producing at least a greater exchange of information among donors as well as a few positive examples of collaborative action. The European Development Fund of the Common Market, which is discussed in the next chapter, is now a major coordinating mechanism for one portion of European assistance in Africa. The development of consultative groups by the World Bank as vehicles for assistance in Africa, the growing interest of European donors in African regional organizations, and the work of the United

Nations and its various specialized agencies all contribute additionally to a gradual reduction in the excessive degree of proliferation which was characteristic of Western aid programs until quite recently.

Quantitatively, European aid to Africa has to be appraised according to several criteria. In absolute terms, the over-all total of European assistance to Africa, bilateral and multilateral, has been in slow decline for the past few years. The over-all reduction is more than accounted for by the drop in French assistance to Algeria alone, which fell from $358 million in 1962, according to DAC figures, to $135 million in 1965 and $95 million in 1966. In effect, therefore, the level of assistance to the other independent areas of Africa has been sustained. At the same time the "mix" of European assistance has been altered: The aid programs of France, Britain, and Belgium were all in decline as of 1967. Other donors, notably West Germany, have increased their contributions. And there are signs that some of the smaller European nations, such as Denmark, Sweden, and Norway, which had an unimpressive record of generosity in the past, have taken steps to try to bring their contributions up to the 1 per cent of gross national product that is commonly considered the desirable norm for the aid programs of an industrialized nation.[6] Thus there is a basis for the view that Western Europe has shown a sustained and commendably high level of concern for the development of the new African states and that, although some programs may be falling off, others are growing and the total has not yet been seriously affected. Before reaching a final judgment, however, it is also relevant to examine the amount of European assistance to Africa in relation to the growth of European prosperity. By this measure the flow is rather less impressive.

Western Europe generally has been in a period of marked economic growth and prosperity in recent years, but the assistance provided to the less developed countries as a percentage of national income of the various donor nations has steadily declined on the whole. Table 12 summarizes these tendencies. The figures suggest that European preoccupation with internal needs and problems is growing, an interpretation supported by political and social developments in the major European countries. Britain, of course, is in grave balance-of-payments distress; in France, accumulated internal problems, which have been masked by Gaullist prestidigitation for a number of years, are beginning to break into view and are likely to lead to significant policy changes in the direction of

TABLE 12. Net Western European Official Aid to Less Developed
Countries, as Percentage of National Income, 1962–67

	1962	1963	1964	1965	1966	1967
Austria	0.25	.04	0.22	.48	0.49	.48
Belgium	0.77	.81	0.66	.84	0.64	.65
Denmark	0.12	.16	0.15	.16	0.30	.30
France	1.76	1.39	1.24	1.06	0.95	1.02
West Germany	0.69	.60	0.53	.55	0.54	.61
Italy	0.33	.28	0.13	.20	0.24	.38
Netherlands	0.59	.32	0.35	.44	0.55	.62
Norway	0.17	.47	0.35	.22	0.23	.25
Sweden	0.16	.18	0.23	.25	0.34	.35
United Kingdom	0.64	.60	0.66	.61	0.60	.57

SOURCE: *Development Assistance Efforts and Policies, 1967* (Paris: OECD, 1967), p. 104.

a further de-emphasis on foreign activities. Public support in Belgium for continued assistance to the Congo and Africa has sagged. Even in Germany, where the level of assistance has been growing, a continuing current of parliamentary and popular skepticism about foreign aid is evident.

MILITARY RELATIONS

Military relations between Africa and Europe have been affected far more than economic or cultural relations by the impact of independence. At least 90 per cent of former European forces and facilities have been removed in the past decade. The departing metropoles left the new African states with the rudiments of national armies and militia, for the development of which they have since provided both arms and training in limited amounts. Although the former colonial powers have remained the principal suppliers of armaments to their ex-colonies, other Western European countries now participate in the traffic. Some, such as Sweden and Norway, have been involved only in a small way in specific training projects and sales of equipment. But two, Italy and Germany, seem interested in obtaining a larger share of the African arms market, and they are increasingly able to offer a certain range of weapons as well as relevant training in effective competition with the traditional metropolitan suppliers. The African states themselves have been eager to diversify their sources

TABLE 13. Western European Suppliers of Military Services
and Equipment to Africa

Recipient Countries	Supplier Countries				
	U.K.	France	Belgium	Germany	Italy
Algeria	E	ACD	—	—	—
Burundi	—	—	AD	—	—
Cameroon	A	ABC	—	—	—
Central African Rep.	—	ACD	—	A	—
Chad	—	ACDH	—	A	—
Congo (B.)	—	ACD	—	—	—
Congo (L.)	CE	—	BCDE	—	BDE
Dahomey	—	AC	—	—	—
Ethiopia	E	—	—	C	A
Gabon	—	BCDEG	—	—	—
Gambia	ACE	—	—	—	—
Ghana	ACDE	—	—	—	—
Guinea	—	—	—	AD	—
Ivory Coast	—	CDEH	—	—	—
Kenya	BCEFG	—	—	—	—
Liberia	—	- -	—	—	—
Libya	AED	—	—	AE	E
Malagasy Rep.	—	ABCEH	—	?CE	—
Malawi	ACEG	—	—	—	—
Mali	—	A	—	—	—
Mauritania	—	ABCDG	—	—	—
Morocco	C	ACDEF	—	—	—
Niger	—	ACDE	—	—	—
Nigeria	ADE	—	—	CDEF	A
Rhodesia	CE[a]	—	—	—	—
Rwanda	—	—	AD	—	—
Senegal	—	ACDH	—	—	—
Sierre Leone	CDE	—	—	—	—
Somali Rep.	—	—	—	—	A
South Africa	CE[a]	CE	—	—	—
Sudan	CDE	—	—	AE	—
Tanzania	AE	—	—	—	—
Togo	—	BDG	—	A	—
Tunisia	—	DE	—	—	E
Uganda	E	—	—	—	—
Upper Volta	—	ABC	—	—	—
Zambia	CEG	—	—	—	—

[a] British army supplies to both Rhodesia and South Africa have in recent years been cut off, in Rhodesia because of UDI and in South Africa as result of an arms embargo established in 1964.

SOURCES: The Pattern of Miltiary Assistance (David Wood, The Armed Forces of African States, Institute for Strategic Studies, Adelphi Papers No. 27, London, April 1966), p. 30; Africa Research Bulletin, various issues.

of military equipment and training, for reasons explained by President Nyerere of Tanzania in 1965 just after his army had mutinied:

> Ideally I would have preferred to see our Army trained by a joint Commonwealth mission. . . . If the Commonwealth and the small powers are unwilling or otherwise unable to help, my duty was to insure that I would not put my country under the hands of any single major power for military assistance. The need, therefore, was to secure some kind of balance.[7]

Table 13 indicates the types and distribution of military assistance and other activities by the principal Western European nations now supplying Africa.

Clearly, Britain and France are the principal providers in both the volume and dispersion of their assistance. Italy's interest has been centered in Ethiopia, Libya, and Somalia, all areas at one time under Italian control, plus the ex-Belgian Congo where Italy participated in a multinational military aid effort organized in 1963, and Tunisia, to which it has sold jet trainers and provided pilot and mechanic training.

West Germany is increasingly active in the provision of military assistance although detailed information is difficult to obtain because of the reluctance of the Ministry of Defense in Bonn to discuss such matters. In a number of instances the recipient country pays part or all of the cost of assistance provided, which can therefore hardly be classified as "aid." As of 1965, according to various unofficial reports, Germany was giving the following military assistance to Africa:

1. Arms and equipment had been delivered to Ethiopia and an expanded agreement was being negotiated.
2. A $10 million program of equipping and training the air force in Tanzania was being completed.

KEY:

A—Supplying financial aid

B—Supplying funds for military purposes

C—Delivering arms and equipment (whether against payment or not)

D—Supplying training missions for armed forces in local country

E—Providing military training facilities in home country

F—Supplying crews and 'technicians' to operate armaments

G—Providing officers and NCO's on secondment for local troops

H—Maintaining bases in local country

3. $20 million had been allocated for equipping (and possibly training) Sudan's frontier forces.
4. $7.5 million had been committed for Guinea's military engineering unit.
5. $6 million was being provided for the Malagasy Republic's navy.
6. $2 million had been offered for training Somalia's police and internal security forces.
7. In Nigeria, until the January 1966 military coup, Germany helped organize, equip, and train the air force with a 75-man advisory group headed by Colonel Wolfgang Thiming, a World War II *Luftwaffe* pilot.

On the whole, however, such German military assistance to Africa is still small in volume, averaging about $10 million a year, including assistance for public safety and police functions.

Belgium has concentrated its military activities exclusively on the three areas formerly under its control, Rwanda, Burundi, and the Congo, especially the last, where, since 1963, it has supported a bilateral program of military assistance to provide support of various kinds. At one time this was done through a cadre system under which Belgium officers and NCO's virtually administered the Congolese army, this having been made necessary because of the dismissal of the 1,100-man Belgian officer corps in the Congo by Prime Minister Lumumba in 1960. In mid-1966, however, after new tensions developed between Brussels and the Mobutu regime, the cadre system was replaced by one of "logistical and administrative advisers." Since then, the number of such advisers has dropped from 300 in 1966 to less than 100 in 1968. In addition, Belgian military personnel who formerly piloted and maintained transport aircraft of the Congolese army were withdrawn in 1967. Just as in the case of Britain and France, which had assumed major military responsibilities in Africa before independence, Belgium has now been forced greatly to reduce its military presence and involvement.

The Western European nations other than the former metropoles, though somewhat active in the supply of arms and in training activities in certain instances, do not, however, represent a significant military factor in independent Africa. Their arms sales and military assistance have been limited in scale and, in comparison with the activities of the Soviet Union and to a lesser extent the United States and China, cannot be considered to have made a noticeable contribution to an arms race or to military instability in Africa.

Far more complex and difficult than the provision of military training and equipment, however, have been two other issues which the major European powers have had to face since African independence—namely, the problem of military intervention and that of Africa's shifting place in their strategic plans. European military intervention in post-colonial Africa must be considered in two quite different aspects: that of the major metropoles, which, partly because they have repeatedly been invited by their former colonies to give military help, have had to formulate some general doctrine on intervention in those areas, and that of other European governments and private groups that have on occasion intervened, or meddled, in serious trouble spots on an *ad hoc* basis and for special reasons of immediate self-interest.

The variety of the latter cases has been considerable, the incidence is not decreasing, and the effect has been to add another inflammatory element to European-African relations. In the Congo the recurrent intervention of Belgian forces was impelled primarily by a desire to protect Belgian lives and property, but the consequence was to render serious damage to all relations between the metropole and the former colony. Equally if not more damaging was the action of private Belgian financial groups in aiding and abetting the Katanga secession; and still later, the periodic involvement of white Belgian mercenary troops in outbreaks of violence kept suspicions of Belgian intervention alive. The participation of white mercenaries in various African conflicts since independence—most of whom have come either from the white minority-dominated countries of Southern Africa or from the former metropoles, particularly France and Belgium—has been a far more troublesome element in European-African relations than their small number would suggest because of the racial and neo-colonialist implications of their presence. More recently, the involvement of Portugal and France in supplying and transporting arms to the secessionist state of Biafra, as well as the presence of white mercenary officers in charge of some Biafran units, has once again fanned the flames of African feeling about European intervention. As long as conflicts continue to erupt in Africa and as long as European governments and private freebooters attempt by military means of one kind or another to exploit for their own interests the opportunities such conflict provides, the consequences both for political developments in Africa and for the climate of European-African relations will continue to be extremely negative.

Formal military interventions by Britain and France have been of a quite different character, and the results in terms of African stability and European-African relations have been more mixed. In dealing with the question of intervention, each nation has followed a distinctive approach. Britain was particularly careful to avoid giving basis to charges of neo-colonialism after the independence of its colonies, although it was invited on several occasions in the early 1960s to provide military help to an ex-colony in trouble and did so. Britain's willingness and military capacity to respond to such calls have greatly declined. Following recent changes in defense policy, it has taken steps to create special forces capable of interventions overseas—but how effective such forces will be and under what political circumstances, if any, they might be employed in Africa remains to be seen. France has also been invited repeatedly to send military assistance to beleaguered governments and has done so in many cases. It is, moreover, prepared both by policy and the existence of special forces to intervene again in the future, either in response to calls for assistance or to protect French interests, economic or military. In actual application, however, it would appear that France is applying the doctrine of intervention with somewhat greater selectivity and restraint.

Africa's place in the strategic plans of the major European powers has changed radically in recent years, partly because of the political transformation of their empires, partly because of changes in the technology of warfare, and partly because of the growing pressures of domestic and European regional concerns. Africa once had an important relationship to Britain's world-wide role and interests in India and the East, but Britain has now essentially abandoned its traditional strategic role and responsibilities. The former importance of the continent deriving from its location along the major comunications routes to the East has thus become almost irrelevant.

The transformation in French strategic thinking has been nearly as complete. Whereas French possessions in Africa, particularly Algeria, once constituted a primary focus of French military and defense policy priorities, France since the advent of General de Gaulle has shifted its strategic concerns to Europe and to the development of an independent nuclear force. Consistent with their decreasing strategic interest in Africa, Britain and France have drastically reduced the troops and facilities formerly maintained on African soil.

On the whole, therefore, it would appear that the countries of Western Europe are prepared to sell arms to the new African states, to give limited amounts of training and equipment, and, to a minimal extent, to provide external military assistance to cope with internal disorders. But as far as Europe is concerned, Africa must now largely rely on its own resources and capabilities to cope with internal threats and disorders—which is in accord with the desires of most of the new African regimes. Strategically, Africa is no longer sheltered by European commitments or forces—again a condition consonant with African aspiration—but the relationship of Africa, especially of the northern Mediterranean littoral, to European strategic interests remains in a state of flux and obscurity. For all practical purposes, Africa has now been stripped of European strategic protection. Does it therefore necessarily represent a "power vacuum" in the traditional sense, an unstable element in the equation of world peace? Whatever the answer, the usual assumption that stability in such a situation can only be provided by some other great power moving in to replace the departed protector is open to serious question.

Political Relations

The evolution of general political relationships between the European powers and their former African colonies in the post-independence period have varied greatly, in part because of markedly different conceptions of their imperial objectives in the pre-independence period. For Britain, the colonies were more than a business enterprise, but not very much more. In addition to economic interest they represented certain strategic values and moral and political responsibilities. They accumulated much sentimental and ceremonial encrustation. But they were external entities, not integral parts of the mother country herself. In the case of Belgium, the Congo was of great interest to limited financial groups but commanded little general public emotion or sense of attachment. Relationships between the metropole and the colony developed without benefit of a coherent political conception, the Belgians having followed neither the British notion of separateness nor the French theory of assimilation. Instead a pragmatic patchwork of administrative and economic control interspersed with paternalism became the operative philosophy. For

France, on the other hand, the African territories were not merely points of economic and strategic interest; they were interconnected in the minds of many with the soul and destiny of France and to some extent were part of the fabric of French political institutions.

Out of these differing traditions and points of view, the three nations came to different stages of readiness to concede independence in Africa when that necessity had to be faced. But in one respect at least, all shared the common hope of retaining some special links and influence with the former colonies after independence was granted. Their excessive confidence that such hope would be realized suggested that the metropoles had drunk too deeply of their own intoxicating myths to the point where they believed strong emotional ties to the "motherland" were actually felt by the populations of the colonies. But the hope was also a practical intention, for there were important economic interests to protect and political objectives to be served.

Belgium dreamt a small dream of a continuing Belgo-Congolese community, which momentarily at least seemed to have some possibility of realization. Patrice Lumumba in 1957, while being held by the Belgians in jail, wrote:

> We must get it into our heads that in the Congo, without the Blacks, the Whites are of no value, and without the Whites, the Blacks have no value either. This economic interdependence makes union necessary for us. Our dearest wish—perhaps some may find it Utopian—is to found in the Congo a Nation in which differences in races and religion will melt away, a homogeneous society composed of Belgians and Congolese, who with a single impulse will link their hearts to the destinies of the country.[8]

But by the occasion of the independence celebrations in Léopold-ville in mid-1960 in the presence of the Belgian king the same Patrice Lumumba said: "Our lot was eighty years of colonial rule; our wounds are still too fresh and painful to be driven from our memory. . . . We have known ironies, insults, blows which we had to endure morning, noon, and night, because we were 'Negroes'. . . . From today we are no longer your Makak (monkeys)."[9]

In the succeeding years, bitterness grew as calamity followed calamity. Relations degenerated into endless quarrels and bickering at the official level and into all manner of escapades, plots, and machinations by Belgian economic interests, Belgian private citizens, and Congolese. Belgium no longer enjoys any special feelings of good will nor any persuasive influence over the policies of the Congolese government. The Congolese have long since outgrown the habit of considering Brussels to be the center of their outside world or even as a source of guidance or leadership. Only within recent months has a glimmer of hope for some repair of cooperative relations reappeared.

Thus the former metropoles approached the problem of post-independence political relationships in different ways with different objectives and with markedly different results. France continues to have some influence; Belgium and Britain have relatively little.* To the extent that they continue to exercise political influence in Africa, however, it is not only contradictory but, on balance, probably negative. It more often adds to various tensions and frictions than contributes a constructive or stabilizing tendency. Belgium remains the object of much suspicion and dislike in the Congo and throughout Africa. France, however respected by the present elites in the Francophone states, is bitterly resented by the younger and more radical elements and is distrusted in most of the English-speaking countries. The constructive effect of its aid must be weighed against the impact of its involvements in the Algerian War, in selling arms to South Africa, in obstructionism in the United Nations, and in its interventionist actions in Biafra. Britain has provided a valuable stabilizing influence at times in a number of African situations, but because of its implication in Rhodesia and South Africa and because of racialist tendencies in domestic affairs it has now fallen greatly in prestige. The political impact of the various other nations of Western Europe in Africa is likewise mixed. Germany, Italy, Switzerland, and the Scandinavian countries are not disliked, but neither are they factors of great influence. Portugal, on the other hand, is an object of hostility on the part of most Africans, who oppose its colonial presence and exploitive practices.

Politically, therefore, Europe is a complicating but also a slowly fading factor in Africa. To a substantial and growing extent, the

* But Africans and others sharply disagree on the extent of continuing European political influence. As late as November 1966 after a meeting of the Organization for African Unity in Addis Ababa, President Julius Nyerere of Tanzania angrily declared: "What this conference demonstrates more than anything else is that France and Britain have more power in the OAU than the whole of Africa put together and it is really up to Africa to be truly independent or to remain colonies of France and Britain." See *Africa Report*, January 1967, p. 27.

new states are shaping their own policies and conducting their relationships with one another and with other nations in terms of their own conceptions and their own interests as they see them. The European states are having difficulty reconciling themselves to that fact, but in time they must.

In Conclusion

By the fact of geographical proximity and all its economic, military, and cultural consequences, Western Europe and Africa have had a special relationship over many centuries. Beginning with the outward thrust of its power in the fifteenth century, Western European civilization—dynamic, aggressive, and with growing technological, economic, and military strength—came to enjoy world pre-eminence. One result was the establishment of colonial dominion over Africa, which, though limited to the coastal areas at first, became almost total in the past century.

The period of European colonialism in Africa not only was relatively brief but was a troubled time for the nations of Europe, marked by two world wars, several lesser ones, and periodic economic crises. The second of the great wars finally broke their world primacy and led to the collapse of their control over Africa, roughly a decade ago.

On the whole, the European response to the changes in Africa in the last decade has been true to the old European tradition of separateness and competitiveness. The major colonial powers gave up their holdings in ways as diverse as those by which they acquired them. Since African independence, the various European nations, large and small, have responded to the new circumstances in a piecemeal, diverse, and even random fashion. They have reacted to specific pressures or taken advantage of specific opportunities without coordination, consistency, or the benefit of common guiding concepts. Their behavior gives the impression of that of small nations in an age dominated by superpowers pursuing their own interests separately and often selfishly, while avoiding involvement in larger issues, commitments, or responsibilities. They have been alert to search the new African states for marketing possibilities, for example. But they have been much less interested in working individually or collectively with the developing nations in Africa and elsewhere to find larger solutions to the problems of the international trading system that are causing such difficulties for primary-product producers. In their programs of economic assistance for Africa, some have shown a sustained interest and responsibility, but to a large extent they all have conducted their bilateral programs individualistically and competitively.

In military matters they have been prepared to offer limited amounts of training and equipment, but, for many, particularly the smaller European states, such arms sales reflect little more than a desire to recover military research and development costs, dispose of equipment that has become surplus or obsolete, provide diversified tropical experience for some of their personnel, and earn foreign exchange. The interest of the former metropoles in problems of internal security and stability and their willingness to intervene when requested have in the case of France begun to decline and in the case of Britain have almost vanished. The place of Africa in the general strategic priorities of both has fallen abruptly. Neither any longer feels a strong sense of responsibility for the continent's strategic protection. Moreover, the major European powers as well as many of the lesser ones have taken little positive interest in the initiatives launched through the United Nations to provide multilateral peace-keeping forces available for disturbances in Third World areas such as Africa.

Thus, militarily and economically, the new African states are in serious danger of being thrust into self-reliance before they can provide adequate resources for their own growth and development and before new international peace-keeping structures are devised to protect Africa from intra- and extracontinental military hazards. Whereas Africans generally have feared a neo-colonialist drive by Western Europe after independence (and with some justification in the case of certain countries at certain moments), the emerging reality and prospect now seem to be that of European withdrawal, if not a kind of abandonment.

The same qualities of opportunism and smallness of perspective evident in other spheres have characterized Europe's conduct in its political relationships with independent Africa. The large as well as the smaller European states have established diplomatic relations and posted diplomatic representatives. They have made their contribution to the flood of officially sponsored and subsidized foreign publications, radio broadcasts, and cultural activities in which Africa is currently drowned. But with few exceptions, the intent has been to maintain communications and to develop generally cordial relations without becoming implicated in the major political questions of broad concern in Africa, primarily the issues of race relations and liberation in the south. There have been some exceptions: The Scandinavians, for example, particularly Sweden and Norway, have repeatedly expressed their sympathy for the suppressed black majorities and have given some material help. But most of the European nations have tried to stand aloof, developing their commercial and other relationships both with independent Africa and with the states of the south as opportunity offered. They have consistently declined to provide financial or military assistance to the liberation movements and guerrilla forces from the southern areas; and at the United Nations—again with the exception of some of the Scandinavians —they have shown notably little enthusiasm for the efforts of that organization in respect to the issues presented in Southern Africa. On the whole, therefore, in their commercial, military, diplomatic, and political policies the countries of Western Europe have been careful not to involve themselves deeply in matters felt to be beyond their influence and capacity; and they appear to share the view that responsibility for security, order, and the resolution of major issues in Africa reposes elsewhere. As a group they lack any generally formulated or accepted conception of long-term European interest and responsibility in Africa or the desirable form which general economic, strategic, and political relationships should take in the new context of African sovereignty. Indeed, it appears that there is less clarity and less agreement in Europe today on these matters than even a short time ago. At present, the nations of Europe—not unlike most other affluent states—are obsessed by their immediate material objectives and are still groping to find new roles for themselves in the world. In this atmosphere, the position of Africa has become a matter of limited and diminishing concern.

It would be quite unrealistic to expect the nations of Europe to reverse these tendencies and assume any new or costly responsibilities toward Africa in the near future. Over the longer term, however, it is possible that the present mood and situation will be seen to have been an interval and an interim. New perspectives and new relationships of a more coherent, adequate, and durable nature may appear. The earlier emphasis on One World, typified by the establishment of the United Nations, implied a global community over-riding narrower groupings and relationships. More recently, there has been increasing emphasis on regions as bases for special cooperative arrangements. One of the forms this newer impulse may take may be a revival of the grand design of Eurafrica, that is, of the building of a comprehensive multilateral structure embracing most or all of the countries of the two continents—which, regardless of the present cross-currents and conflicts, share a great deal of common history and cannot escape the fact of contiguity and a considerable degree of interpenetration and interdependence. Of these regional conceptions, the great existing example is the European Economic Community, usually known as the Common Market, with its extensive African aspect.

5

Multilateral Relations Through the Common Market

In their bilateral relationships with Africa, the nations of Western Europe are, on the whole, apparently tending to draw back and to behave competitively in pursuit of purely short-term objectives. But such an interpretation confronts a towering paradox and contradiction: namely, the existence of a highly developed structure of multilateral relationships between the European Six and the Eighteen Associated African states of the European Economic Community (EEC), plus several other African states with which special status is being negotiated. Through its trade and aid arrangements with the associated states, the Common Market is of far greater importance in Africa than is generally realized; and there are some who continue to see in these arrangements the beginnings of Eurafrica—that durable old vision of an integral linkage between the two great, interrelated, and in some respects complementary regions of the world. But realistically, what promise does the Eurafrica concept offer as a means of insuring future cooperation between the nations of the two continents in the interests of both? 1969 will be the year of decision.

How did this institution, so contrary to the European habit of nationalism, come into existence? How did it come to have a major African aspect? The great originator and animator of the Common Market, Jean Monnet of France, has ascribed the birth of the EEC to the realization by the nations of Western Europe after the Second World War that if they were to survive they had somehow to escape from the pattern of their long history of conflict and begin to build a new basis of cooperation. In his words:

> They had to change. Five years after the War, they began to find the way. If they could not directly solve the problem, they could at least transform the conditions which gave rise to it. They did not set out to solve—directly—the problem of Franco-German enmity. They did not attempt to create a community of nations over night. Instead, they began slowly, and painstakingly, with something unspectacular in a limited area. Six nations started off by identifying a common interest, by pooling their resources of coal and steel under common institutions. Later they extended this principle to the whole of their economies. By doing so, they have begun to create a real solidarity of material interests among themselves. Equally important, they have learned to apply to their dealings with each other in the economic field, a system of common rules, maintained by common, democratic institutions. In time they will extend these principles into other areas of policy and action. Europe is thus gradually acquiring a new identity. It is becoming a great power.[1]

Some might feel that Mr. Monnet is overoptimistic in his evaluation of the strength of the European impulse for cooperation at the present time. One point, however, is indisputable: The EEC was a creative response by the nations of Western Europe to the central problem of their own survival. It was not conceived as a device for the preservation of the European empires, nor as a framework for European-African relations. Yet almost by accident and coincidence it acquired from the beginning a major African aspect.

THE TREATY OF ROME AND THE ASSOCIATED AREAS

The movement which had begun with the establishment of the European Coal and Steel Community gained momentum and by March 1957 culminated in a treaty signed in Rome setting up the European Economic Community. The idea of including the colonial territories of the European members in the structure, though rumored earlier, did not enter the negotiations until the eleventh hour. When France in February of 1957 injected it, press reports at the time stated that it "landed like a stick of dynamite" and produced great annoyance among the other European participants at what was regarded as pressure to force them to finance the development of France's colonial territories as the price for getting it into the Common Market. The problem of tariffs and the anticipation of political changes in Africa, however, were also deeply involved in the French initiative. The colonies had free access to the French market. If they became independent states and were not associated with the EEC, they would suddenly be foreign states outside its tariff wall, unable in many cases to survive economically. A week of intense negotiations culminating in a last-minute summit meeting between the French Premier, Guy Mollet, and the German·Chancellor, Konrad Adenauer, settled the matter largely on French terms. On February 20, the Six accepted a modified version of the French proposals, which would include in the new institution the French, Belgian, and Italian territories in Africa, as well as the Dutch territories of New Guinea in the Pacific, and Surinam in South America.

Political and strategic as well as economic motives may also have been present. At that time the French Union, after ten years of difficult existence, was in grievous trouble; and France, under heavy pressure as a result of the fighting in Algeria and of increasing discontent in its other African colonies, saw in the Common Market a means of reducing the tensions and the likelihood of disruption in the transition of these territories to independence. The French Premier argued, for example, that the new structure was necessary to blunt the force of growing Soviet penetration in Africa. France, somewhat equivocally backed by Belgium, also considered association of the colonial territories as a starting point for a broader future cooperation between Africa and Europe. Germany, Italy, Holland, and Luxembourg, however, saw it as a not very satisfactory way of overcoming a French threat to the frail beginnings of European unity. Other European observers, such as the London *Times*, recognized the plan as a "startling departure in colonial policy" but viewed it with reservations both as a threat to continental markets for products from British and Portuguese colonial territories and as a trap which could enmesh Germany and other European members in French colonial intrigues.

Whatever the complex and contradictory motivation of the European members, the arrangements relating to the colonial territories finally included in the Treaty of Rome were of sweeping significance. Article 31 of the original Treaty in 1957 defined them in the following terms:

The member states [the European Six] hereby agree to bring into association with the Community the non-European countries and territories which have special relations with Belgium, France, Italy, and The Netherlands.

The purpose of this Association shall be to promote the economic and social development of the countries and territories and to establish close economic relations between them and the Community as a whole.

As a result of this provision, the classic colonial pattern of exclusive relationship between the metropole and its dependent territories was, for a large part of Africa, transformed into a new multilateral relationship. In its most immediate effects, Italy, Germany, the Netherlands, and Luxembourg—in principle at least—were to be admitted to trade, investment, and commerial relations with the French and Belgian territories in Africa on a basis increasingly equivalent to that of the "mother countries" themselves.

The Treaty of Rome set forth three general objectives regarding the associated areas, which can be sumarized as follows:[2]

Trade Expansion. The European market of the Six for the tropical products of the associated states was to be enlarged through tariff preferences provided under a common external tariff. Conversely, the African territories would reduce tariffs and enlarge quotas on imports from the Six.

During a transitional period of 12 to 15 years, the African territories were obliged to abolish their tariffs on commodities from the Six and from each other according to an agreed timetable. This, however, was subject to the important proviso that they could continue to levy duties on trade within the area "in accordance with their development needs and the requirements of their industrialization or those which, being of a fiscal nature, have the object of contributing to their budgets."

Economic and Social Development. A second aspect and major innovation of the Treaty was the creation of a new institution, the Development Fund, for the overseas countries and territories (commonly referred to as the European Development Fund or FED, after its French initials). The FED was given the sum of $581.25 million for the first five years, 1958–62. Assistance from the Fund was to be in addition to the bilateral aid of the metropolitan countries to their overseas territories. The greater share was destined for French overseas territories and departments—in effect, its possessions in Africa.

The funds were to be contributed and spent roughly as follows:

	Contributions to the Development Fund
France	$200 million
Italy	40 million
Belgium	70 million
Holland	70 million
Luxembourg	1.25 million
Germany	200 million

In the allocation of these funds, nearly two-thirds of which was to be contributed by France's partners, the French territories obtained the bulk:

	Initial Allotments	Actual Commitments
	(In millions of dollars)	
France—Mainly the 14 dependent territories in Tropical Africa, plus Algeria	$511	$506
Netherlands—New Guinea, Surinam, and Netherlands Antilles	35	35
Belgium—Congo (Kinshasa), Burundi, and Rwanda	30	30
Italy—trust territory of Somalia	5	10

All assistance from the Development Fund was to be in the form of nonrepayable grants. The Six abandoned exclusive control over their national contributions, and expenditures were to be made on the basis of tenders open equally to enterprises in the six member countries and the associated territories. Because of the inevitable problems of setting up an aid staff and of getting agreement on projects from the associated states, the actual commitment of funds lagged well behind the planned schedule. It was not until some two years beyond the original five-year period that the first five-year fund had been fully allocated.

Private Investment. The third aim of the Treaty of Rome was to define a nondiscriminatory "right of establishment" for the Six in the overseas territories. Essentially this meant that nationals of all EEC members and overseas territories could make investments, found business enterprises, and conduct commercial activities in each territory on the same basis as nationals of the territory itself or those of the metropolitan country with which the territory formerly had had special relations.

THE CONVENTION OF YAOUNDÉ

It was originally contemplated in 1957 that at the end of five years, relations between the associated states and the Six would be re-examined and renegotiated. By 1962, the date of the first renegotiation, however, a revolution had taken place in the status of the associated African areas, all of which had in the interval since 1957 become independent. The discussions nevertheless proceeded. Aid became one of the major issues, the associated states demanding a larger development fund. A second issue related to the export subsidies (*surprix*) which the former French states received from France. At the particular insistence of Holland and Germany, it was finally agreed that these subsidies would be reduced in stages so that within five years the associates would have to sell their exports at prevailing world prices. To make this easier, part of the Development Fund as replenished would be used for "aids to production" to compensate for the loss of export subsidies. The third major issue was trade preferences, which the associated states hoped markedly to increase. But in this their aims were largely frustrated.

Finally on December 20, 1962, a new Convention of Association was agreed upon to run for five years ending May 31, 1969. Ratification of the new Convention was expected to be completed in 1963; but, partly as a consequence of France's veto of the United Kingdom's application for membership in the EEC, Germany, the Netherlands, and Italy delayed signature of the document nearly eighteen months. This second five-year agreement, called the Convention of Yaoundé from the African city in which it was initialed by representatives of the twenty-four countries participating, continued certain provisions of the earlier agreement but included some major innovations.

The trade provisions of the Treaty of Rome were in effect maintained. The Development Fund likewise was continued and was endowed with $800 million for the period 1965–69, an increase of more than $200 million over the first five-year fund. Of this sum, only $70 million was destined for non-African areas. Of the $730 million for Africa, $500 million was earmarked for economic and social development and technical assistance; $230 million was earmarked for projects to improve the efficiency of production and to assist the diversification of the agriculture of the eighteen associated states.

The Yaoundé Convention also took cognizance of the problem

of unstable commodity prices and deteriorating terms of trade for the underdeveloped associated states. Up to $50 million of the Development Fund could be used as advances to commodity stabilization funds.

A second major innovation of the Convention was the creation of a number of new joint institutions offering widened consultation and participation by the newly sovereign African states in EEC affairs. These included a Council of Association, a Parliamentary Conference of the Association, and a Court of Arbitration. The Council of Association, which establishes the general lines of technical and financial cooperation, consists of members of the EEC Commission on the one hand and representatives of the associated states on the other. The Parliamentary Conference, a joint body, is composed on the basis of a parity of members of the Assembly and members of the Parliaments of the associated states. The Court of Arbitration consists of two African and two European judges to settle disputes on the interpretation or application of the Convention if the Council of Association fails to agree.

Another innovation of some importance was the direct representation and access of the Eighteen to the EEC organs in Brussels. The Eighteen can now speak for themselves through direct bilateral channels with EEC headquarters officials, as well as through representation in the new institutions created under the 1962 Convention.

Lastly, the Yaoundé Convention opened the door much more widely than had the Rome Treaty to other African states that might wish to become "associated." It was this "open door" policy which led to high expectations by the spring of 1967 that almost the whole of independent Africa would soon be linked institutionally with Europe through the Common Market. At that time it appeared that Algeria, Tunisia, and Morocco would be brought in as part of a package deal in which Spain would also be allowed special trade links with the Six.

An agreement reached with Nigeria, the largest African member of the Commonwealth, in July 1966, broke important new ground by opening up the possibility of a more limited type of relationship between the EEC and the nonassociated African states. Ever since achieving independence in October 1960, Nigeria had been interested in the possibility of a special new type of association with the Common Market. Until 1965 there were only the alternatives of institutional association or nonassociation. In July of 1965, however, agreement in principle was reached by which Nigeria would enjoy the same pattern of trade relations as are enjoyed by the other associated states but with a minimum of other involvements. Nigeria would not receive economic and social development assistance nor agricultural productivity and diversification assistance from the Development Fund or the European Investment Bank. Neither would it participate in the joint institutions created under the Yaoundé Convention. However, Nigeria was accorded "reduced reciprocity," meaning that whereas the eighteen associated African states are committed progressively to reduce their tariffs on all imports from the EEC member countries, Nigeria is required to reduce them on only twenty-six products, a small fraction of its total imports from the EEC area.

The Nigerian arrangement promptly led a number of African states to take advantage of the new and more limited pattern of association. Kenya, Tanzania, and Uganda began talks in Brussels, and by 1967 it appeared that the only parts of Africa not then thinking about association with the Six were Egypt, Ethiopia, the Portuguese colonies, and Rhodesia.

However, a series of unforeseen difficulties subsequently intervened. The Nigerian agreement, though of great importance as a precedent, has never come into effect because of a constitutional crisis and the outbreak of civil war in that country, and also because of French coolness and procrastination. The negotiations with Kenya, Tanzania, and Uganda were protracted because of disagreements on the question of reciprocity. Finally, on July 26, 1968, an agreement was signed by which tariffs and quantitative restrictions on trade between the two groupings were removed, but with the proviso that the East African states could, under certain conditions, preserve or establish tariff rates on products from the Six if necessary for their development and industrialization or for revenue purposes. The East African states would not receive development or other assistance from the European Development Fund.

Negotiations with the North African states made even slower progress because of some complex issues. North African exports of wine, olive oil, fruits, and vegetables are competitive with products of some of the Six, and pressure against their entry by European producers has been a major obstruction. Another is the demand of Morocco and Tunisia for some economic aid. In addition, there are political problems created by earlier actions of nationalization and expropriation of European properties by Algeria, restrictions on the transfer of capital and earnings by European investors, and the problem of migratory North African workers in France and the related issues of the repatriation of their earnings. Discussions proceeded through 1968, and agreements in principle on certain trade preferences were reached with both Morocco and Tunisia, which might in time lead to further negotiations for association.

RENEGOTIATING THE AGREEMENTS

By 1968, after ten years of operation, all parties to the EEC structure had begun to make fundamental re-examination and evaluation of its advantages and disadvantages. The outcome of these examinations would set the framework for the impending renegotiation of agreements in 1969 and in turn would determine the future evolution of the structure of cooperation between the European members and the African areas.

The criticisms and fears becoming manifest on the part of the European members, the African associates, and other African states are revealing not only in their implications for the future of the Common Market system itself, but also for eventual patterns and possibilities of broader European-African cooperation. The associated African states have both many complaints about the working of the system at present and deep fears about its possible dilution or dismemberment. Their complaints concern primarily trade, not aid. Instead of a growth in trade as originally hoped, they claim there has been stagnation while the exports of some nonassociated underdeveloped countries and areas have increased with Western Europe, in percentage terms at least, far more rapidly than have their own. They assert also that reductions in tariffs of EEC members against their products have been more than offset by new internal taxes of various kinds which have been levied.

On certain trade issues the Eighteen find themselves, if not in conflict with one another, at least disposed to place different emphasis on objectives. The countries with weaker economies, such as Chad, Dahomey, and Niger, are interested mainly in the export of primary materials and in subsidies. The more developed countries with more diversified economies, such as Gabon and Ivory Coast, are interested in exporting not only primary products, but also manufactured and semi-processed goods. There are also certain ideological and political differences between some of the associated states, which at times have introduced an additional note of discord into their deliberations.

On the other hand, they are unanimous in their feeling that they have a position to protect, and they are not inclined to look with favor on sharing their access to EEC markets and to FED development assistance with other African states. They have insisted that they be consulted "on any request for association with the Community made by a state which has an economic structure and production comparable to those of the associated states." The second UNCTAD Conference in New Delhi in 1968 provided further evidence during the general debate on preferences that the eighteen associated states stand apart from the rest of Africa on any questions threatening their privileged position within the Common Market structure. Whatever their complaints, most of the associates are probably too poor to do without the Common Market and are therefore in a weak position in the coming negotiations with the Six on renewal of the system. Many of them have unviable economies, and their general economic predicament is generally growing worse because of lagging development plans and deteriorating terms of trade. They are therefore increasingly dependent on their present affiliation, for which there is no available alternative.

The African states not affiliated at present also have mixed views. Most would like to share in the trade preferences of the Common Market system, and some have applied for association not with any optimism or expectation of great benefits but simply to "keep their hand in." In the case of Nigeria, the failure of the Six to put the agreement signed in 1966 into effect caused officials in Lagos on October 3, 1968, to declare rather bitterly that Nigeria no longer wished to be associated with the EEC, for it has a "neo-colonialist element and is no longer relevant to the Nigerian economy." They went on to say that no effort would be made to renew the agreement in 1969. In principle, most African states also would like to share in the flow of development aid, but not at the price of involving themselves in institutional linkages. Memories of colonialism are still too fresh and suspicions about French intentions toward Africa still too great for the political leaders of many of the new, English-speaking African nations to risk getting their countries trapped in what they have felt is a French-controlled net. If and when Britain should become a member of the Common Market, African fears of French dominance would of course be significantly reduced.

The attitudes of the European Six are at least as complex and divided as those of the Africans regarding the future of the system. A number of central issues, such as agricultural policy, have proved to be extremely difficult to resolve; and profound strains have been created by the strength and bluntness of General de Gaulle's determination to keep Britain out, largely it was felt, because of political and personal, not economic, reasons. The question of British entry remains of course the key issue for the future. Now that General de Gaulle is out of office, prospects for the enlargement of European membership seem brighter, although many technical problems remain.

The entire set of problems represented by the presence of the associated African states in the structure constitutes another important focus of disagreement among the European Six in the negotiations of 1969. Germany, Holland, and Italy had many reservations about the association of the overseas territories with the Market from the beginning, which have increased, not lessened, with the passage of time and the accumulation of operating experience. Holland and Germany in particular have felt that their contributions to the Development Fund have been disproportionate to the benefits they have gained in terms of African trade; and both have supported the Nigerian agreement, for example, on grounds that it would open the association system to markets more worthwhile from their point of view. Since their interests in Africa are not confined to the Francophone states, they would like to see both the trade and aid aspects of the Common Market system broadened to correspond with the continental scope of their interests.

Moreover, there is strong discontent with the way that the EEC aid program has been administered. The fourteen ex-French tropical African countries have received a disproportionate share of EEC funds (84 per cent of the $804 million obligated during the period 1959–67). The funds have been used, largely at French insistence, for infrastructure projects, which in turn have disproportionately benefited French contractors. (During the first five years, French firms received more than 80 per cent of all EEC contracts; by 1967 this had been reduced to approximately 65 per cent as a result of the persistent complaints of other EEC members.) Finally, there has long been unease because the French attitude on trade and aid has tended, in effect, to perpetuate high-cost, unviable economies in African areas. The others have therefore attempted though not with complete success, to reshape the policies of the Common Market with regard to the African associates in the direction of inducements toward competitiveness, diversification, and increased productivity.

Because the African extension of the Common Market system is largely the result of the original French initiative, and because it has been designed and utilized very largely for French objectives and benefit, it has produced deep division and growing resistance on the part of the other European members. Nothing less than an extraordinary degree of French pressure and leadership will suffice to prevent a major overhaul of present arrangements in the decisions to be taken in 1969. Given the recent internal difficulties and political changes in France, it is not clear that such determination and leadership will be forthcoming.

Due to the many outstanding issues to be dealt with and the many divisions of viewpoint both among the African states and the European members, it would be particularly inappropriate, even futile, to attempt to anticipate the outcome of the difficult and protracted negotiations now under way. But in broad terms certain likelihoods at least can be indicated.

First, it is unlikely that the system of association will be completely dismantled. The African associates would vigorously oppose such an outcome; and the European members, particularly France, would be unlikely to agree to such drastic and disruptive action. Some indication of their viewpoint was provided in April 1968 when the Common Market Executive Commission formally advocated renewal of the treaty linking African states to the Market.[3] The Commission declared in a memorandum concerning the forthcoming negotiations that the new treaty should provide both financial aid and continued preferential trading arrangements. It recommended measures to improve the position of the associated states' agricultural exports on the European Market by allowing the Eighteen "a certain level of preference," which would give them a price advantage but which "would not create real difficulties for other exporting countries." It advocated that the Six make separate renewal agreements with the eighteen associated African states, on the one hand, and with the new affiliates, Kenya, Uganda, and Tanzania, on the other.

But, if it is likely that the African aspects of the Common Market system will not be dismantled, it is equally likely that they will be considerably modified. The geographical scope of association in Africa will probably be extended through agreements of the

Nigerian type, which will involve diminished requirements of reciprocity. The insistence of the Six on tariff reciprocity in the negotiations with the East African states may well have been influenced by tactical considerations and a desire not to give ground on this fundamental issue in negotiations with new applicants for association before talks with the present associated states are completed.

Second, it is likely that a majority of the Six will insist on a continuing phasing-down of price subsidies on the products of the associated states and perhaps even greater emphasis on agricultural diversification and improved productivity in the distribution of Common Market economic aid.

Third, the administration of development assistance by the EEC will probably be improved to ensure that funds are distributed more equitably among the eighteen eligible African states, that they are employed for more productive developmental purposes than elaborate infrastructure, and that firms in all member states are enabled to participate equitably in equipment and service contracts. Until now the EEC, in its administration of development aid, has had a longer pipeline and implementation lag than other donors partly because its administrative structure lacked the policy mandates, staff, and field representation necessary to carry out aid projects effectively. It has taken a passive approach, which did little to stimulate realistic development plans or the formulation of adequate project criteria. It has therefore tended toward the random financing of projects and to considerable waste and inefficiency. Some remedial action can be anticipated.

Fourth, it is likely that European multilateral aid to Africa via the Common Market will trend downward in the future, perhaps markedly. France's willingness to sustain past levels of aid to Africa is beginning to decline, and there is little reason to suppose under present circumstances that it will be able to persuade its partners in the Six to provide continuing large funds to the FED to enable France to continue to shift the burden of aid to African development to that agency. Except for West Germany, their own level of bilateral assistance to Africa is beginning to decrease. And, given the inherent discrepancy between the geographical scope of the Common Market in Africa and Germany's economic, commercial, and political interests, it is questionable whether Germany will choose to channel any increased aid to Africa it might provide through the FED.

THE PROS AND CONS OF THE EXPERIMENT

If these speculations and estimations of the probable future course of European-African multilateral ties through the EEC prove substantially correct, the economic implications will be considerable. But there are other implications of even greater consequence. Since the Common Market linkage with Africa is a unique multilateral structure of collaboration between the two continents, its future development or modification can be of far-reaching importance, not only for the associated African states and their economic position, but also in much broader terms of political orientation, stability, and international responsibility. As one of the world's major postwar experiments in new patterns of relationship between developed and underdeveloped countries, the Common Market has attracted the most serious interest on the part of all those concerned with this great problem. It has acquired eminent critics as well as distinguished advocates.

There are critics who feel that on balance the Common Market arrangements with Africa have been negative, if not pernicious, in their impact. They should therefore be reduced and diluted, if not dismantled, in the interest of the long-term welfare and independence of the African states, as well as of all the less developed countries. The arguments given in support of this view cannot be dismissed lightly.

The trade arrangements of the Common Market system are seen by supporters of the most-favored-nation approach under GATT to be fundamentally wrong because they tend in the direction of a segmented and compartmentalized world economy of closed preferential systems, which can only lead to inefficient allocation of resources and obstructions to maximizing trade advantages and economic growth. The reciprocity aspects of the system are considered incompatible with the development of universal and multilateral trade to the advantage of both the underdeveloped and the developed nations.

The long-term economic effect on the so-called beneficiaries of the Common Market trading arrangements, including price subsidies on tropical products, it is argued, is to perpetuate unrealistic price levels and economic dependency. In turn, such conditions can lead only to exacerbation, not solution, of their internal social and economic problems. Critics likewise contend that the aid given through the Common Market system is discriminatory and unfair. Citizens of the associated African states receive two or three times as much aid per capita as citizens of other African states and ten times as much aid, for example, as citizens of India. To perpetuate such "privilege" is felt to be wrong, given the scope of the development problem throughout the Third World, and to justify it is condemned as a parochial view.

It is argued further that the political effects, quite apart from the economic, have been negative. The system of trade preferences and development aid has served essentially to prop up and prolong colonial-type relationships in Africa and more specifically to reinforce French efforts to maintain a kind of post-colonial hegemony over its former African territories. The effect of this anachronistic effort has been contrary to the interest of the African states in achieving genuine independence. Moreover, it is contended that the system has had divisive consequences within Africa, creating groups of privileged and unprivileged states and thereby impeding inter-African cooperation and continental unity. In global perspective, the desire of the associated African states to perpetuate their special relationship and advantages has undercut the unity of the less developed countries in their efforts to deal with the developed nations in the rectification of universal problems of trade and development.*

Those who share these general views feel it will be in the interest of all the Third World, and even of the associated states in the long run, if the African aspect of the Common Market structure is broadened and loosened as quickly as possible, if not dismantled.

But there are other thoughtful and knowledgeable students of the international scene—and not all of them with special interest in Africa—who take a different view. In their estimation, the Common Market system in its African ramifications may be theo-

* Dr. Raoul Prebisch, in a statement to the U.N. Trade and Development Board on August 16, 1967, warned of the political consequences of economic "sectionalizing" of the world in these terms: "I should like to point out that this concept of multilateralism is not only of economic import but also has a tremendous political significance which I could not pass by without mentioning. A series of events is about to take place which will determine the economic structure of the international world for many decades to come. Is the trend to be towards a multilateral system in which a developing country has open to it the market of all the developed countries, including the socialist countries? Or is the trend towards the sectionalizing of the economic world into vertical compartments, into spheres of influence of the northern countries of the south? I have been drawing the Board's attention to this point for some time. It has been said that these fears are imaginary, that there is no such danger. But there is such a danger. And the danger is growing."

retically objectionable, but on balance it has made a positive contribution. Therefore, tampering with its structure should be done with great care and with full realization of the practical consequences and repercussions. Their case also has a strong foundation.

As to the trade arrangements, they point out that the Common Market did not create the closed circuit of trade and monetary ties between France and most of the associated African states, but that these were inherent in any concept of empire and existed at the time the Treaty of Rome was signed. Since then the effect of the Common Market arrangements has been to break the old circuit and to dilute the worst aspects of the pre-existing pattern, not only by opening additional European markets to the associated African states, but also by progressively granting exceptions and concessions which have eased the reciprocity obligations on the part of the African associates.* Simultaneously, the European members have lowered their own tariff barriers to the entry of the products of the nonassociated states. The nonexclusive character of the trade patterns which have developed is documented by the considerable growth of exports from nonassociated African states to Western Europe and by the growth of Latin American exports to Europe in the years since the Treaty of Rome went into effect. Little by little, the Common Market system, it is argued, begins to approach the formula of nonreciprocal tariff preferences which all the underdeveloped countries pleaded for at the first and second UNCTAD meetings in 1964 and 1968. Because UNCTAD has not succeeded in bringing into existence a universal trading system on this basis, it would be foolish to destroy the beachhead

* The extent to which their exports are beginning to diversify in the EEC areas are reflected in the relative decline in French dominance and the relative increase in the share purchased by other members of the Six, as shown by the following tabulation:

Exports of the Associated States to the Six
(In millions of dollars)

	1964	1965	1966	1967
France	609.7	547.0	600.1	609.9
Belgium and Luxemburg	227.0	233.9	340.9	287.8
Netherlands	55.6	53.4	54.0	61.9
Germany	158.2	160.8	170.5	179.8
Italy	98.9	151.0	153.4	164.6

SOURCE: *Economist Intelligence Unit,* Annual Supplement, 1968.

and partial victory which the Common Market arrangements in Africa now represent.

It is further pointed out that the direction of movement in the trade policies and practices of the Common Market has been away from closed and colonial principles toward broader, more universal arrangements. If and when Britain and the other members of the European Free Trade Association gain entry to the Common Market, another major step would be taken both in broadening the European participation in the system and in giving a much wider scope to African association. Even if that does not occur, the Nigerian-type agreement offers a basis likely to result in broader African association on a basis of diminished reciprocity.

Furthermore, supporters of the Common Market idea emphasize that the evolution of the assistance policies of the FED has tended increasingly to stress improved productivity and agricultural diversification, which has helped correct the deformities in the African economies existing at the time the Common Market was created. According to its advocates, the EEC did not create the economic and trade problems of the associated African states, which were an inheritance from the colonial period; but it has provided a means for the constructive and progressive rectification of the worst features of the past. Again, it is contended that, if all the problems have not yet been resolved, the solution is not to dismantle the EEC arrangements but to strengthen them.

Regarding the political consequences of the Common Market arrangements in Africa, essentially the same defense is made: The political division of Africa is a legacy of the colonial era, and the EEC system has made an important contribution to the gradual bridging of the cleavage. It does not prevent the establishment or maintenance of customs unions, free trade areas, or Common Markets among associated states or between associated states and others. The Nigerian agreement, which as a precedent can have many benefits in reducing the distinction between the eighteen associated states and the rest of Africa, specifically incorporates the principle of noninterference with African efforts toward economic integration. At its signing, J. M. A. H. Luns, past President of the Council of the EEC, stated: "In no circumstances can the Agreement hinder African unification, the importance of which we fully realize. Several provisions either in the Preamble or in the Agreement itself, expressly encourage this unification."[4] In addition, if and when Britain's entry into the Common Market is agreed to, not only will any divisive effect of African association be greatly diluted, but a positive mechanism and structure for a coordinated European relationship to Africa, as well as broad African collaboration and cooperation, will then exist.

In regard to the continuing dependency of some of France's former territories on its aid and political leadership, it is argued that neither was this problem created nor has it been accentuated by the existence of Common Market arrangements. Rather, the inherent weakness of some of these economies, combined with the deleterious effect of recent trends in world trade, has tended to keep them in the French orbit.

To these arguments of the supporters of the Common Market regarding its impact on trade structures and political relations within Africa, two points can be added, one specific and practical, the other rather more broad and basic.

First, if the EEC and its trade and aid arrangements are prematurely dismantled, the consequences for at least twelve of the eighteen associated states could be disastrous. They are among the weakest and most fragile economies in the world. Without the preferential arrangements of the Common Market, they could not even maintain their exports to the Six. And without the assistance of the $230 million agricultural fund of the EEC, their problem of diversifying their exports and overcoming their low agricultural productivity could be insurmountable. If other measures and resources were in fact available to assist these extremely needy states, then it might make sense to abandon the existing EEC arrangements. But other bilateral assistance is not available and is not likely to be in the foreseeable future. World Bank and IDA loans to these states have been increasing, and this upward trend may continue, which offers some encouragement. However, such aid does not constitute an alternative to that of the EEC, which still provides them indispensable shelter and sustenance. It would be neither wise nor humane to destroy what now exists in behalf of some theoretically preferable but either nonexistent or inadequate alternatives.*

* The dimensions of the problem are illustrated in the following figures on the sources of so-called public and private investment in the 14 former French Tropical African states:

	1962	1963	1964	1965	1966 (preliminary)
Domestic	10.3%	12.0%	9.0%	12.2%	11.3%
Foreign:	89.7	88.0	91.0	87.8	88.7
Of which, EEC (FED) share:	8.5	9.3	12.9	14.5	15.9

SOURCE: La Zone Franc en 1966, p. 135.

Second, even though the Common Market structure is economic in its modalities, its significance touches the broadest issues of international stability, political relationships, and great-power responsibility. Perhaps the most disturbing tendency in Western European affairs at present is the quality of separatism, selfishness, and nonresponsibility in the actions of such wealthy, developed countries toward the underdeveloped areas and toward international affairs generally. In this perspective, the Common Market has done a great deal to coordinate the approach and policies of the Six toward Africa. It has certainly had the effect of causing them to accord to the associated states both greater trade advantages and more development assistance than would have been the case had the Common Market structure not existed. If the structure with Africa should now be dissolved, it is highly probable that the result in the proximate future would be a measurable net drop in the Western European contribution to economic development in Africa, with no offsetting increase in assistance to other underdeveloped areas. Beyond that, the very existence of the Common Market relationship with Africa has been an influence in behalf of a continuing sense of European concern and responsibility not only for Africa and its economic problems but in some degree—precious even if small—for the interrelated problems of the Third World.

The meaning of the Common Market system must of course not be overestimated. Its policies cannot rise above the level of their headwaters in the political understanding and economic capacity of its component European members. But it can give coherence and help maintain the momentum of the constructive measures they choose to undertake. It provides a basis and framework for cooperation and international concern at a time when the world is in particular danger of fragmentation and lack of concern on the part of the developed nations toward the underdeveloped. Thus, it represents an existing asset and a potentiality of great value which it would be imprudent, even reckless, deliberately to undermine.

A quarter of a century after the end of the Second World War the old pattern of European control over and concern for Africa has been shattered. African independence has strikingly altered political relationships but has by no means completely severed other ties. As of now, both parties to the former relationship are in a transitional period of searching for their own solutions to their problems and have as yet only a most unclear idea as to the lines along which future relationships between the two areas should evolve. It is a period of convalescence and confusion following colonialism. In time, conceivably, Africa might become for Europe just one more region of the world, and vice versa. But a far more likely outcome is that the influence of history and geography added to other factors will produce some pattern of special relationships on a new foundation of sovereign collaboration. As both Europe and Africa head into the uncertainties of the remainder of the twentieth century and the insecurity of the twenty-first, new and still unforeseen dangers may yet cause each to feel a special need of the other. In such a time, conservatism in its generic sense hopefully will prevail as decisions are taken in 1969 concerning the future of European-African cooperation through the EEC.

Part Two

The Communist World and Africa

6

Soviet Relations

With the emergence of the new African nations as sovereign entities, the Communist powers, like the major non-Communist states in Europe and elsewhere, moved to adjust their policies and relationships accordingly. But whereas for the European countries this required the modification of a tightly woven and long-established fabric of involvement in Africa, the Communist powers had to build their first direct relationships virtually from bare ground —with both the advantages and the disadvantages that that can mean. The Communist powers have now been at the task for just over a decade, and the record shows much awkwardness of style because of inexperience, repeated shifts of course, fluctuating enthusiasms and disappointment—and a famine of triumphs.

The task of interpreting Communist behavior in Africa, as elsewhere, is inherently exasperating for a number of familiar reasons. The extraordinary tactical flexibility of Communist policy obscures and confuses perception of its more steady strategic purposes. The Communist powers consciously conduct their foreign policy on two planes—that of normal interstate diplomacy and that of revolutionary action working through party machinery and front organizations, propaganda, and subversion. Activities taking place simultaneously on these separate planes in any given area can be utterly contradictory. Adding to the complexity is the fact that the Communist world has now not merely bifurcated but fragmented into several segments whose policies on many issues may be in disarray if not in conflict. Moreover, to decipher Soviet and Chinese purposes and policies one must necessarily rely to a considerable extent on official statistics and on the flood of official documents and semi-official ideological writings which flow from both sources. The statistics are often contrived to conceal more than they reveal even when they are complete and available, which is infrequently the case. Nor are more general written materials always consistent or clarifying. Because of frequent ideological disputes and occasional long periods of policy confusion, quotations can usually be found from one "authoritative" source or another, or from one point in time to another, to defend widely varying theses or interpretations. The opportunity is thus open to any analyst to treat Communist documentary material as if it were fruitcake, plucking out those morsels to his liking and leaving the uncongenial parts on the plate. Nevertheless, despite the murk and complexity, and even though the period since the Communist nations first became seriously involved in Africa is too brief to permit definitive assessment, some tentative description of general trends and patterns can be ventured.

Africa in Communist Doctrine

Russia and China have not been part of Africa's colonial past, nor has Africa and its special needs and characteristics been part of the doctrinal or revolutionary history of contemporary communism. Traditionally, and until well after the Second World War, the world Communist movement had little interest in Africa as such and almost no direct contact with it. Few, if any, Soviet scholars even traveled to the area. It was regarded as an appendage of Europe, and such Communist organizations as existed in Africa were insignificant offshoots of the parent European parties.

Born out of the social and economic conditions of Europe in the nineteenth and early twentieth centuries, the fundamental concepts of Communist ideology are Euro-centric in nature. Similarly, the classical Communist theory of history, which purports to explain the process of development of all countries and societies in terms of class structure and conflict, is based purely on the experience of Europe, thus denying an independent history to Africa or a distinctive character to African society and historical development. It condemns Africa to the role of follower in the wake of the most advanced class in those advanced nations that are the bearers of history's purpose. Although colonialism, imperialism, and the struggle of colored peoples in the world have long been of interest to Communist theoreticians, their interest has centered on the role which, it was believed, disorder in the colonies would play in bringing about the final victory of the Communist proletariat in the industrialized countries.

Through the Stalinist period until after the Second World War the logic of Communist doctrine, undisturbed by any serious understanding of African circumstances on the part of Communist theoreticians, led to a trim and tight series of propositions which were believed to predict the future course of events in that continent as well as in the other colonial areas: the imperialist powers would never voluntarily relinquish control; only violent struggle could accomplish their liberation; and the liberation struggles could not be victorious unless the proletariat with the Communist party in the vanguard played the leading role. In the case of Africa, given the infinitesimal size of its industrial proletariat and the lack of class consciousness and militancy on the part of both peasants and workers, it was further propounded that leadership in the struggle for independence could only come from the relevant European Communist parties.

Yet Africa and Africans have long been a considerable inconvenience and embarrassment for Communist doctrine. Their leaders have been determined to overturn the view that Africa's history is a mere derivative of European history, and they deeply believe that Africa has an identity as distinct as that of Europe, America, or Asia—that it is not, in the words of Kwame Nkrumah, "an extension of Europe or of any other continent." Their conviction has been dramatically borne out by the events of recent years, during which African history has taken its own distinctive course, powered by distinctive factors related to distinctive African circumstances. As Lenin once said, history in the end proves "more cunning than anyone," even Communist ideologists, and African history has been no exception.

One aspect of the inconvenience of Africa for communism had become manifest well before the wave of African independence, indeed even before the Russian Revolution, namely, the intellectual insubordination, from a Marxist viewpoint, of the black leaders who first began to give voice to the discontents of black people in Africa and elsewhere. One of these, Marcus Garvey, an American Negro, organized the first mass movement around the theme of black nationalism. He was the first to sense the possibilities of anticolonial solidarity, and his ideas stirred a response in many parts of Africa. He was considered by many, especially in Europe, as a dangerous radical. But throughout his flamboyant and creative career he regarded communism as an abomination and never ceased to denounce it.

Another early American leader in the English-speaking group of black intellectuals was W. E. B. DuBois, who from the turn of the century had spoken in behalf of the world-wide rights of black men and of Pan-Africanism. As a lifelong opponent of capitalism, his thinking was deeply influenced by Marxism. But during the long course of his active years, as he wavered uncertainly between democratic socialism and communism, he was regarded by the Communist hierarchy as ideologically unreliable, indeed frequently disobedient. Among other Communist concepts he openly challenged was the fundamental concept of the class struggle as applied to Negroes. In his view, white workers in the industrialized nations commonly have refused to regard Negroes as fellow members of the proletariat, whereas Negroes have generally manifested "widespread inter-class sympathy."[1]

After DuBois the mantle of leadership of Pan-Africanism fell on the West Indian, George Padmore, a professional revolutionary of penetrating intellect. He tried for a number of years to work for colonial liberation through the Comintern and at one time was the most trusted Negro leader in the Communist apparatus. He never forsook his principles as a socialist, but in the 1930s he broke with communism and thereafter inculcated a generation of African leaders in the British colonies with an awareness of the dangers of international entanglements and of the cynicism of Communist support for colonial liberation movements.

In French-speaking Africa, Pan-Africanist ideas took a different shape under other leadership, mainly literary, based principally in Paris. The *Négritude* movement which emerged was hostile to bourgeois capitalist society and racism and was permeated with both Marxist and Communist ideas. But in 1956 the movement broke with communism with a famous Open Letter written by its head, Aimé Césaire, the leading Negro Communist in France. Césaire's break was as great a shock for the Communists as Padmore's had been a quarter of a century earlier, for it was the culmination of a series of resignations of leading Negroes who had worked closely within the Communist International and had ended up disillusioned. They had joined in the hope of finding personal dignity and an opportunity to help the emancipation of colored peoples. They had left embittered by the experience of being forced to subordinate their primary objectives to party priorities and dogmatic rigidities. As Césaire wrote in his letter to

Maurice Thorez, the Secretary-General of the French Communist party: ". . . what I want is that Marxism and Communism be harnessed into the service of colored people, and not colored people into the service of Marxism and Communism."[2]

The continuity and strength of this thread of dissent on the part of leaders speaking for black people is a fact of some importance in interpreting the more recent record of communism in Africa and in appraising its future. The evidence continues to accumulate that the African nationalist and Pan-Africanist is more devoted to his own objectives and convictions than to those of international communism. When there is a conflict between the two, the Garvey-DuBois-Padmore-Césaire syndrome recurs.

The Stalinist Era

For a brief time in the early 1920s the leaders of international communism gave some thought to the scope and potential of the restlessness of the nonwhite people in the colonial areas for their world-wide revolutionary objectives, and they debated the best means of working with their movements and championing their cause. But by the late 1920s this transitory interest was subordinated to other more pressing concerns, and throughout the 1930s only the most tenuous and uneasy liaison was maintained with the spokesmen for black nationalism and Pan-Africanism. World communism in the Stalinist period had little confidence in their revolutionary capacity or in the prospects for African revolution. Their nationalism was considered inherently mischievous because it engendered exclusive loyalties, not international proletarian identification. Pan-Africanism was officially branded reactionary, and virtually all the leaders of the African independence movements that achieved success after the mid-1950s, including such persons as Nkrumah of Ghana and Azikiwe of Nigeria, had regularly been castigated in previous years by the Communists as imperialist stooges and supporters of colonialist reaction.

In the postwar period, an intensified effort was made, working through the Western European parties, to begin to build Communist organizations in Africa, but it met with little success. The Italian Communists achieved some limited results in organizing student groups and Communist cells in the trade unions in Somalia. The Belgian Communists did nothing in the Congo before 1958, and in the brief period from then until independence were able to do hardly more than formulate preliminary plans. The

Communist party of Great Britain, always small and weak, had an especially difficult task in attempting to work in the African colonies because there was no organic relationship between their political movements and the political parties of the metropole; and the English-speaking territories were far less exposed to and interested in the Marxist currents of thought then in vogue in Europe than were the French-speaking African areas. In contrast, however, the political efforts of the French party were relatively successful in Africa for a time, particularly the liaison established with the *Rassemblement Démocratique Africain* (RDA), the most important political party in French West Africa. But elimination of the Communists from the French government in May of 1947 greatly reduced the value of the alliance from the standpoint of the RDA. When over the next three years the cooperation proved no longer to be of value to his African objectives, the powerful leader of the RDA, Félix Houphoüet-Boigny, took the organization off on an independent course. Although it included some Marxists, they were too weak and few to take command and prevent the breakaway, and as a result the most noteworthy Communist political accomplishment in Africa in the pre-independence period came to an end.

Thus, when North and most of Tropical Africa achieved independence in the late 1950s and early 1960s—on the whole peacefully, under African leadership, proclaiming democratic and socialist doctrines, and not associated with communism—the Soviet Union and the world Communist movement were confounded. Suddenly they were confronted by a growing number of new African governments, many of which, among their first acts, outlawed Communist activity within their borders. Colin Legum has pointed out that the new governments were in fact much tougher and more competent than the colonial powers in this particular field, and he quotes A. Zusmanovich, a leading Communist writer, who in 1958 mournfully surveyed the landscape of newly independent Africa in these terms:

Anti-Communism, "Communist-phobia," the suppression of Marxism-Leninism as a system of thought, the attempt to crush Communist organizations—all this is not only a limitation on democracy in Africa. It is no less a limitation on national development, a weakening of the national cause, of the truest interests of the mass of the people. . . . It is regrettable that some African leaders have picked up this tattered mantle of the dictators and imperialists.[3]

The Khrushchev Period[4]

In the mid-1950s, after the advent of Khrushchev to power, a general shift in the traditionally indifferent Soviet attitude toward the less developed countries, including Africa, became visible. The policy changes which occurred reflected an awareness of changing world political relationships as well as growing pressures within the Soviet Union for new policy priorities. They also reflected the ebullient, even impetuous, quality of the new Soviet leadership and its willingness to undertake new experiments in policy, program, and even ideology. By 1955 a general drive was under way to relax tensions, both at home and abroad, to close some of the splits which had developed within the ranks of the Communist states, to find an accommodation with the West, and to strengthen Soviet influence among the new nations of Asia and Africa.

The Bandung Conference in 1955, to which the Soviet Union was not invited, spurred Khrushchev to intensify his efforts to develop relationships with the less developed countries, and to identify the Soviet Union with their anticolonial and anti-imperial grievances. Thereafter a new series of diplomatic initiatives was launched. Nehru was invited to Moscow and given a massive welcome. Late in 1955, Bulganin and Khrushchev visited India, Burma, and Afghanistan. In the Middle East, long an area of special strategic interest, Moscow offered President Nasser economic credits and a major arms deal.

The new tack in policy was facilitated by the decisions of the 20th Party Congress in February 1956, emphasizing the necessity of peaceful coexistence to avoid nuclear holocaust. The rigid Zhdanovist two-camp concept was dropped along with its corollary, that in a divided and hostile world neutrality was an illusion. Moscow was thereby free to try to make itself the champion of Third World neutralism.

Effective collaboration with the emergent states, however, presented major ideological as well as practical problems. Although they were strongly anti-Western, and were also non-Communist, acceptable theoretical grounds were needed to permit collaboration with their "nationalist-bourgeois" leadership. This Khrushchev was eager to do in order to weaken their ties with the West and win their general support to Soviet positions. He promptly muted the earlier Stalinist line, which had encouraged local Communists to try to seize power in these countries. He declared, ex cathedra, the African nationalists to be "essentially progressive" and proceeded to launch a program of economic and military assistance, even though it took the theoreticians almost four years to formulate the doctrine of "national democracy," legitimatizing the collaboration and enabling ideology to catch up with reality. In pursuit of its objective of cultivating increasingly close economic, political, and cultural ties with the new nations, the Soviet Union then made its first direct entry into Tropical Africa—but hesitantly at first and with obvious reservations.

Ghanaian independence in 1957 was greeted perfunctorily and politely, not as an opportunity for a vigorous extension of Soviet influence. Trade agreements, economic aid, and military assistance were not to be provided until much later. Nkrumah, despite his penchant for Marxist vocabulary, was regarded as an equivocal figure who had publicly proclaimed his loyalty to the Commonwealth, insinuated that Africans should liberate their continent without any external assistance or interference from East or West, and given other evidence of tainted thinking.

In late 1957, however, the image of himself as a man of peace advocating a policy of coexistence, which Khrushchev had attempted to develop, was shadowed by a significant new turn in Soviet policy. In August of that year the Soviet Union successfully fired its first intercontinental ballistic missile and in October launched its first Sputnik. The military implications of these achievements were self-evident and led Soviet leaders to believe that their careful exploitation could produce a decisive change in the international power balance to the benefit of the Soviet Union, without undue risk of nuclear war. A broad political offensive was thereupon undertaken. Its purpose, in effect, was to subject the United States and the Western powers to the pressures of a giant pincers movement: graduated nuclear blackmail on the one hand, and intensified support for colonial revolution on the other. The results over the following five years were the provocation of tension at key points, principally Berlin and ultimately Cuba, and more aggressive support for "wars of national liberation" in the underdeveloped world. In Africa the course of events by late 1958 fitted in with the new policy thrust and aroused visible Soviet enthusiasm for the political opportunities being presented.

The independence of Guinea marked the turning point. Sékou Touré in the 1958 referendum had led his country to reject membership in the French community. Thereafter the Soviets moved quickly to exploit the vacuum created by the abrupt withdrawal of France and the hesitancy of the Western powers to affront de

Gaulle by offering aid. Two days after the Guinean national assembly proclaimed independence, the Soviet Union extended diplomatic recognition. By December 1958 the Soviet leaders, through Czechoslovakia, had made an unconditional offer of arms; by February 1959 they had signed the first trade agreements; by August they had granted the first economic credit; by November they had persuaded Touré to visit Moscow and had secured his public support for the Soviet approach to international problems; and by January 1960 Khrushchev had received and accepted an invitation to visit Conakry. According to official U.S. estimates, Soviet credits for at least $116 million were extended, and as many as 1,500 Soviet and Eastern European technicians entered the country.[5]

In retrospect, it would appear that by its violently anti-Western orientation at the time and the radical course of its internal development policies Guinea reassured Soviet leaders that they had perhaps finally found in Africa a situation in which true Marxist-Leninist principles could be applied. Guinea, moreover, offered convenient access to revolutionary movements in Western and Equatorial Africa, a number of whose exiled leaders had taken refuge there. The closed horizons of the Stalin period had been broken open, revealing exciting prospects for new global endeavors.

The wave of African independence was then rushing forward, and Moscow's optimism about the promise of the situation swept forward with it. Under the buoyant Khrushchev, Communist analysts began to see the beginning of a new "world revolutionary process," with the emerging nations turning away from the capitalist path of development and grouping themselves behind the Soviet Union and the "progressive forces of the world." Some were so confident of the prospects of the new states that they were prepared to accord to them not leadership, of course, but almost shoulder-to-shoulder status with the advanced Communist countries in the process of historical advance. One such commentator in Moscow explained in 1961: "Even though the countries having achieved liberation continue in most instances to remain in the system of world capitalist economy, they no longer constitute the rear and reserve of imperialism, as they had in the past. Now these countries are an important ally of the socialist camp in the struggle for peace and international security, for the full liquidation of colonialism."[6] Confident they had found a promising and advantageous field in which to challenge the West, the Soviets, having secured their perch in Guinea, began to cast about for new African opportunities.

Under the circumstances, the strife and chaos in the Congo after July 1960 was irresistibly attractive. As civil order broke down, the Soviets believed they were presented with an opportunity to come dramatically to the aid of a popular leader and thereby be in a position not only to shape the internal development of a huge and rich country in the heart of Africa, but also to rally to the Soviet banner impatient nationalists throughout the continent. Their manner of attempting to seize the opportunity involved, however, some important tactical miscalculations and in the end may have dampened considerably the newly born enthusiasm of the policy makers in the Kremlin. Certainly it illuminated the state of Soviet policy at the time and the emerging direction of its African strategy.

The first miscalculation related to the willingness of the United Nations to intervene in the situation. In the days immediately following Congolese independence, disorder had spread, the army had mutinied, Katanga moved to secede, and Belgian military forces had re-entered the country to protect Belgian lives and property. Premier Lumumba and President Kasavubu ordered all Belgian troops to return to their camps—an order which was ignored—and on July 13, less than two weeks after the independence celebrations, they cabled the United Nations to dispatch a U.N. military force. Although in a press conference Khrushchev praised the Congolese government for having appealed to the Security Council for help, he made clear his expectation that it would be unable to act. "This body should be shown for what it is, so that the peoples may see that the Security Council has been turned by the U.S.A. into an instrument for suppressing the freedom-loving peoples and keeping the peoples in colonial bondage."[7] Yet, one day after receiving the Congo's appeal, the Security Council authorized the Secretary-General to organize a peace-keeping operation, and two days later the first U.N. troops arrived in the Congolese capital.

For Russia, the U.N. intervention was an extremely troublesome complication. Having taken a position favoring U.N. action it could not gracefully pull back. Soviet organs immediately complained that the Western powers were pursuing their imperialist ambitions under the U.N. flag and insisted that the United Nations take more effective measures to suppress the Belgian "aggression."[9] As they began to sense they had been outmaneuvered, the

Soviets warned that if the imperialists did not cease aggression against the Congolese people, "then the Soviet Union would not hesitate to take decisive measures."[10] Moscow simultaneously moved to strengthen the hand of Lumumba by dispatching Soviet trucks and transport aircraft to him.

As an incredible confusion developed in the following weeks, young Lumumba, who earlier had shown such powers of leadership, proved unable to cope with the multiplying problems. His behavior became more and more erratic and finally, in desperation, seeing the country disintegrate, he called for Soviet planes and tanks to come to his aid. Whereupon President Kasavubu removed Lumumba as Premier in early September, and called on the United Nations to take over full responsibility for law and order. Within days thereafter the Congolese armed forces under General Joseph Mobutu seized power, promptly ordering all Communist representatives out of the country, closing the Parliament, and arresting Lumumba. The hopes Moscow had placed in the colorful Congolese leader had suddenly collapsed, and the Soviet Union reacted by bitterly attacking the Secretary-General and by dissociating itself entirely from the United Nations-Congo enterprise. Lumumba was murdered in late September, and the Soviet Union tried to convert the resulting widespread indignation among African leaders into revulsion against the United Nations and its Western supporters.

The Russians, however, seriously underestimated the strength of African sentiment in favor of the United Nations. In September of 1960, the Soviets threw a Security Council debate on the Congo question into deadlock by using its veto, whereupon the General Assembly took up the matter over Soviet opposition. After heated debate, including vigorous discussion among the African representatives themselves, all the African states in the end voted to endorse the action of the Secretary-General in dealing with the Congo crisis, and only the Soviet bloc states abstained.[11]

Quite apart from the question of whether there was some merit in Soviet charges of biased conduct by the United Nations in the Congo operation, a matter on which there are sharp differences of view,[12] an important Soviet initiative in Africa had been rebuffed by a conjuncture of African and Western efforts. When the United Nations finally achieved an objective which Moscow had sought to champion, the ending of Katanga's secession, the Soviet Union was again caught in the awkward and unprofitable position of having supported a cause that had been won by forces which it had denounced, using measures it had vigorously opposed.

But if the Congo was a case of Soviet errors and misjudgments, it is important to note that the Soviet Union, despite the intemperateness, indeed almost the hysteria, of its various declarations and denunciations, was careful to avoid any major risks. It gave the Congolese cause at most a highly restricted and closely controlled commitment. It supplied Lumumba with limited funds and equipment, but it refrained even in the face of his final appeals to send arms or military aircraft. After Lumumba had been ousted, jailed, and finally killed, Moscow still failed to act. In entering the Congo initially, it intended to probe an apparent opportunity, not to undertake a direct confrontation with the United States. To avoid such a possibility, it was therefore careful not to commit its own forces. Later, it equivocated in its support of the Stanleyville regime of Antoine Gizenga, Lumumba's successor, and in the end restored diplomatic relations with Cyrille Adoula, the moderate and pro-Western Premier in Léopoldville. The Congo crisis exposed in graphic fashion the limited extent to which African nationalists could count on the backing of the Soviet Union—either because of its lack of commitment, or lack of bases available to its aircraft, or both.

If the Congo may have taught Soviet policy-makers a lesson about the unsuspected complexities of Africa, the Algerian War, which was heading toward its climax after 1960, forced it as a world power to make a visible choice between its African and non-African priorities, thus revealing to Africans, as well as to critics of the Soviet Union within the international Communist movement, another of the principles governing the actual conduct of its foreign policy. To have given the Algerian rebels wholehearted and unqualified support would have greatly strengthened Soviet claims to leadership of the "revolutionary process" because of the passions their struggle had aroused among all radical elements in Africa. But to have done so would have created other complications. It would have jeopardized the important Soviet objective of splitting France from the NATO alliance. It would have created acute problems within the French Communist party, which could not give all-out support to the FLN because of the divided sentiment of its French members. It would have created problems for the Algerian Communist party, which was largely non-Arab and opposed by the FLN. Thus, in the realistic and typically unheroic fashion of a great power attempting to serve contradictory interests, the Soviet Union blurred and muted its efforts in all directions: On the one hand, it avoided direct attacks on the French government. But through the French Communist party and in other ways it attempted to press France toward a negotiated settlement. On the other, it expressed public sympathy with the cause of the Algerian rebels and gave them some help—while privately counseling them to seek agreement and a compromise settlement with France. This convoluted posture, essentially subordinating Algeria to larger policy objectives in Europe, considerably cooled the pro-Soviet sympathies of those Africans who regarded Algeria as a crucial anticolonial struggle.

After 1960 the state of African politics required the Soviet Union to make further public expressions of preference which it would have preferred to avoid. As liberation and independence swept through North and Tropical Africa, it was accompanied by a general upsurge of African political activity, which, as soon as the immediate goal of political independence had been achieved, brought to the surface the many latent divisions of interest and viewpoint among Africans themselves. Events in the Congo and Algeria during 1960 and 1961 sharpened these divisions, which were formalized into the rival Brazzaville (later Monrovia) and Casablanca groupings. Faced with these confusing splits and alliances, Moscow could no longer avoid choices by merely invoking the myth of Afro-Asian or all-African solidarity. A differentiated policy was needed. Grasping the nettle, Moscow decided to reward those states willing to cut their ties to the West, and to draw back from the others. It endorsed the members of the Casablanca group as Africa's only genuine revolutionaries and praised them for leading the fight against neo-colonialism and for true African independence. At the same time it roundly condemned the others, calling them among other things "puppet regimes governed by right-wing elites" and "the Trojan Horse of Western imperialism in Africa." But the profits of this maneuver, if any, were soon erased when, as soon as the heat of the Congo crisis had cooled and the Algerian War had been terminated, the African states found a basis to compose their differences. In a new spirit of compromise and moderation they formed the Organization of African Unity in 1963 at Addis Ababa, again leaving the Soviet Union with one foot in the air.

As early as 1961, questions began to be raised within the Kremlin about the effectiveness of Soviet bloc policy in Africa, and by 1962, in the wake of a series of adverse developments, a reassessment was under way. President Nasser in Egypt had turned from a marked pro-Soviet orientation in the pre-Suez and the immediate post-Suez period to growing conflict with the Soviets. Disagreements arose over the union of Syria with Egypt in 1958, a proposed similar union with Iraq in 1959, the persecution of Communists in the U.A.R., and Nasser's advocacy of an ideology of "Arab socialism" incompatible at many points with Communist doctrine. The promising situation in Guinea had gone sour after December 1961, when the Soviet ambassador was expelled, after his indiscreet meddling in an internal political situation. The following year Sékou Touré veered toward a restoration of relations with the Western countries and appealed to West Germany and the United States for economic assistance.

The Congo, after the first period of turmoil, continued to lurch from catastrophe to catastrophe; but its successive governments, whether military or civilian, offered the Soviet Union no opportunity to retrieve its earlier losses and assuage its humiliation. In Algeria, once the war with France was settled, the Ben Bella regime fell into intense factional quarrels; and although it welcomed both Soviet and Chinese assistance, it also cracked down on all organized Communist activity within the country.[13] In fact, the new African states generally showed very little inclination to regard the Soviet Union as their protector and guarantor of their freedom. They dealt with it only at arm's length and, contrary to Soviet advice, continued to strengthen and develop their economic ties with the West. Nor did intransigent Soviet positions at the United Nations on peace-keeping, financing, and the powers of the Secretary-General win support among the Africans.

Clearly, the outcome of the first few years of direct Soviet involvement in African affairs was discouraging, and earlier Soviet optimism about the prospects gave way to realism, if not pessimism. The Soviet Union thereupon set forth on a new course built upon different and much less hopeful assumptions regarding future African developments. Concluding that socialist regimes were not likely to come to power soon and that revolutionary progress would probably be slow, it determined to expand its contact with the so-called moderate states. By mid-1962 Khrushchev announced, "We are in favor of developing businesslike and useful cooperation and strengthening trust and friendship between all peoples and countries."[14] When the pro-Western Premier of Senegal visited the Soviet Union shortly thereafter, he was able to sign agreements on trade and economic and technical cooperation, a convention on cultural cooperation, and an agreement for the exchange of ambassadors, although the general policy discussions were reserved.

The final engagement in the broad political offensive launched by the Soviet Union in 1957 to exploit its achievements in rocketry was the Cuban missile crisis in October 1962. The Soviet Union's setback in that confrontation with the United States led to a general policy shift from aggressiveness to renewed détente, which Khrushchev acknowledged in January 1963 in a speech in East Berlin before the Socialist Unity Party. A tripartite partial nuclear test-ban treaty was signed with the United States and the United Kingdom; the so-called hot-line was opened between Moscow and Washington; and a series of similar "cooling actions" were taken. Consistent with this turn of policy, the Soviet Union immediately began toning down pronouncements about its readiness to intervene directly in the less developed areas to rescue besieged "democratic revolutions" and ceased repeating Khrushchev's earlier bellicose endorsements of subversion and guerrilla warfare. Instead, the Soviets promised "broad moral, political, and material support" to the national liberation movements,[15] and to areas openly struggling for national independence they offered support only in the form of "constant diplomatic struggle, the unmasking of the colonialists, and the mobilization of public opinion in defense of the oppressed peoples."[16]

The Soviet Union proposed to shelve almost completely its revolutionary objectives in Africa, broaden still further the range of its collaboration, and, if necessary, acquiesce in the dissolution of African Communist parties—which subsequently happened in Algeria and the U.A.R. A letter from the Central Committee of the Soviet party to that of the Chinese party[17] suggested that it might be necessary to collaborate with Third World leaders who might "establish, for a time, reactionary political regimes and subject Communists . . . to persecution." The Chinese retorted that they would even accept certain "kings, princes, and aristocrats" as allies, but the local Communists had to be protected and had to maintain "leadership of the revolution."[18] The Soviet rejoinder coldly placed the burden of proving their right to exist upon the local Communist parties themselves.

The movement away from revolutionary objectives and traditional approaches toward indiscriminate collaboration with non-Communist leaders occasioned extraordinary efforts by party theoreticians, in following the twists and turns in policy, to maintain a degree of rationality and coherence of doctrine. The differences among them, from revisionists at one extreme to dogmatists at the other, were so great that a-condition of ideological chaos developed.[19] Between 1955 and 1960, Soviet practice in collaborating with the new non-Communist regimes of the Third World had raced far ahead of theory. Then, in the 1960 Moscow Declaration of eighty-one Communist parties, the Soviets and the Chinese hammered out a compromise slogan of "the independent state of national democracy," which was further refined and defined in the 1961 Draft Program of the Soviet Communist party. The hope of early Communist leadership of the newly independent countries was not abandoned, but non-Communist regimes were to be embraced whenever they fought Western political and economic influence, maintained military neutralism and friendship with the U.S.S.R., carried out radical economic and social reforms, and permitted local Communist parties to organize and exist. Some conservative theoreticians, such as Boris Ponomarev, the party authority on developing countries, were uneasy even about this compromise. But Khrushchev was prepared to claim that "today practically any country, irrespective of its level of development, can enter on the road leading to socialism."[20]

As the Soviet and Chinese ideologists struggled with the problem of finding new formulations, they had to attempt at the same time to suppress continuous manifestations of heresy by even the most radical of the African nationalists, who continued to insist that African society was classless, contrary to the official Communist view that "recognition of class realities in modern Africa is essential if there is to be any advance towards socialism." In the relatively "progressive" states of Ghana and Mali, the view was repeatedly expressed that socialism could be achieved without class struggle, that socialism and religion need not be incompatible, and that the socialist doctrine necessarily had to be adapted to Africa's special circumstances and requirements.

Moreover, many specifically African doctrines proved unpalatable for the Soviet ideologues, drawing either their criticism or at best their equivocal tolerance. "African socialism," the vague credo endorsed by virtually all African leaders after independence, was regarded by Soviet theoreticians as a concept representing "petty bourgeois illusions about a socialism which excluded class struggle." In African nationalism and particularly in the insistence on the solidarity of colored peoples, the Russians detected racialistic trends, "national egoism and national exclusiveness." Similarly, ideas of African unity and nonalignment were viewed with mixed feelings, some seeing African unity as a "progressive under-taking" but others considering it a force isolating Africa from "progressive influences" from other continents. As a general principle they did not find nonalignment objectionable, but they vigorously rejected the idea that Africa could find some "third path to development" that was neither socialist nor capitalist. And when Africans sometimes equated the Eastern and Western blocs, implying there was little or nothing to choose between them from an African viewpoint, Soviet commentators were indignant.

In December 1963, Khrushchev, impatient with the pettifogging of the theoreticians, turned his back on the restrictions and quali-fications stated in the 1961 Party Program and explicitly endorsed "socialism of the national type." In effect he offered to recognize the revolutionary standing of certain "national socialist" leaders, provided only that they were friendly toward the Soviet Union and stopped persecuting Communists. Following his lead, some revisionist Soviet intellectuals were prepared to concede in 1964 that "the classical path to socialism was by no means obligatory" and contended, leaving a heap of broken ideological crockery around them, that socialism in Africa could leapfrog history and that its achievement need not await the maturation of the prole-tariat and the emergence of Communist parties. There the transi-tion to socialism could be accomplished directly by those "close to" the working class, such as the Convention People's party in Ghana—an ideological somersault the full significance of which is hard to appreciate outside orthodox Communist circles. From then on, until Khrushchev's removal in 1964, revisionism was rampant.

After Khrushchev

As soon as Krushchev had left the scene, his more orthodox and conservative successors moved promptly to further scale down Soviet interest in Africa and to close some of the ideological breaches he had opened. Their revised formulations revealed a more circumspect theoretical view of Africa, as well as a more conservative practical assessment. As one Soviet economist sum-marized the new attitude:

> The failures and setbacks of some African countries which have tried too rapidly to introduce measures of a socialist character showed . . . that it is impossible to introduce socialism by decree, and to jump across the stages of democratic reforms and imme-diately find oneself in a socialist society. The advance to socialism

requires planned systematic work and the gradual creation of the economic and social base of the new social system.[21]

The new policy was reflected in practical programs of collaboration in Africa, notably foreign aid. Enthusiasm for foreign aid was never great in the Soviet Union and became markedly less so after Khrushchev's deposition. His successors made clear their intention to consider all economic projects according to stricter criteria of feasibility and economic payoff. Moreover, under the rearranged priorities of the new regime it became evident that in the future the helping hand of the Soviet Union would reach into Soviet resources only after other domestic concerns had had their turn. According to a *Pravda* editorial of October 27, 1965, the people of the socialist countries believe that they can best fulfill their "supreme international duty to the workers of the whole world" by focusing their energies on strengthening their own national economies. In "concentrating their main efforts on the building of socialism and communism in their own countries" they would be preparing the "decisive condition for increasing aid to other detachments of the liberation struggle." Soviet writers were equally hostile to plans for price subsidization of products from the underdeveloped countries. Any attempt to fix export prices should not, they said, "be effected at the expense of lowering the standard of living of the population of the developed countries."[22]

At the same time that Soviet authorities were making clear their primary interest in their own needs they also undertook to convey to the African nations that it was up to them to assume the burden of their own struggle for political and economic independence. In the words of *Pravda*, "Those who can put an end to all forms of colonialism and neo-colonialism, and raise the economy and culture of the young national states, are above all the peoples of these countries themselves." Consistent with the new note of austerity regarding foreign aid, commitments after 1965 dropped abruptly below previous totals.

The initial euphoria of independence having passed, harsher political and economic issues were breaking the surface throughout Africa at this time. Economic development generally was lagging, and as internal pressures mounted in country after country, military regimes of more conservative cast displaced the more ardent and sometimes more colorful earlier political leadership. Without exception, the more radical African states which the

Soviet Union had favored fell into severe economic distress. On the other hand, some regimes that had been branded as right wing and reactionary began to show both increased internal stability and accelerating economic development.

One result was to impel the Brezhnev regime to extend Khrushchev's earlier efforts to establish cordial relations with the moderate African states. He had reinforced "businesslike" relations with such states as Senegal, Dahomey, Nigeria, and Kenya; the new Soviet leaders went a step further in seeking ties with Africa's least revolutionary regimes. In the past, the Malagasy Republic and Ivory Coast had been favored targets of Soviet propaganda, which charged that they had remained hopelessly tied to their former colonial masters, that their economies under the domination of expatriate capital were no more than an appendage of the metropole's economy; and that their leaders were black capitalists and pawns of imperialism.[23] In turn, these countries had long refused to establish diplomatic relations with the Soviet Union and had publicly expressed the fear that the Soviet Union would exploit its diplomatic presence to interfere in their internal affairs.

But by 1965 Russia's behavior in its dealings with such states as Nigeria, Senegal, and Dahomey had convinced even President Houphouët-Boigny of Ivory Coast that the time had come when diplomatic relations could safely be opened. As he said at the Fourth Congress of the *Parti Démocratique de la Côte d'Ivoire*: "It seems that Russia, preoccupied by the task of raising the welfare of its people and wisened by its failures on our continent, has renounced any intention of dominating Africa through the imposition of its doctrine."[24] Taking advantage of the opening offered, the Soviet Union in January 1967 moved to exchange ambassadors. In the following months a similar arrangement was concluded with Upper Volta. With Sierra Leone, the Soviet Union negotiated long-term trade agreements. New credits were promised Morocco, Nigeria, and Tanzania, all countries which had never previously received Soviet aid. Simultaneously the tone of Soviet comment toward the moderate and rightist regimes of Africa lost all revolutionary edge.* Leaders once described as "collaborators of colonialism" were now praised for introducing progressive reforms. Soviet leaders even congratulated Congolese President Mobutu for severing ties with Portugal and nationalizing

---

* The Soviets in the same period followed the same line in Latin America toward Venezuela, Colombia, and Chile, over Castro's violent objections.

the properties of Union Minière—compliments that must have sounded odd to a man vilified in an earlier period as a "callow little Napoleon" who "had been bought by Belgium" and who had murdered Patrice Lumumba.

The stunning *coup d'état* in February 1966 which deposed Nkrumah in Ghana drove home to the Soviet leadership the fallaciousness of the assumptions governing their initial African policies. For Nkrumah, despite earlier Soviet reservations about him, had consistently been the most eloquent and internationally known spokesman of the radical view in Black Africa. His writings and statements exercised an influence far beyond that of any other African spokesman on younger and "progressive" elements throughout the world. While others among the earliest group of African leaders either turned toward moderation, as Jomo Kenyatta in Kenya, or became deeply mired in their own internal problems, as Sékou Touré of Guinea and Modibo Keita of Mali, Nkrumah became to an even greater extent the African personification and symbol of the anti-Western viewpoint. But his displacement, the popularity of the new military regime with the people of Ghana, and the sordid record of his mismanagement and megalomania, which was revealed after his ouster, forced Soviet analysts, perhaps for the first time, to go beyond the simplistic formulations and rationalizations with which they had treated their earlier African discouragements. After examining the debris of the disaster, they concluded that for all his prowess as a leader of the anti-imperialist struggle, Nkrumah had failed to provide Ghana itself with sound political and economic leadership. He had divorced himself from the people, and his ruling party "remained a ship floating on the surface of society, comprising a group of revolutionary intellectuals and town dwellers."[25] The lessons of the Ghana experience for such states as Algeria, Mali, Guinea, and Congo-Brazzaville, according to Soviet theorists, was that priority had to be given to augmenting each nation's productive forces in order to raise the living standards of the people.[26] Unless this were done, experience had shown that the critical "intermediate social strata" would be alienated. Summoning greater sacrifices from a population in order to extend state control over commerce and industry when the means and cadres were lacking to accomplish the task tends only to generate dissatisfaction and to undermine the essential alliance between "revolutionary democrats" and the middle level of society. The paramount task of the revolution is not, therefore, to aid other people to secure independence; it is not even to launch radical social and economic reforms if these jeopardize the political stability of a "progressive" regime.

Following the new pragmatic line, Soviet spokesmen by late 1966 and 1967 were advocating measures almost indistinguishable from the recommendations of Western experts on technical assistance and economic development. Where they had once urged drastic agricultural reform they now counseled the gradual modernization of agriculture, if necessary by means not entirely along socialist lines. "The essence of the agrarian reform in these countries [of tropical Africa] consists primarily in raising the rural economy to the level of modern production and a gradual advance toward cooperative farming."[27] The trouble with producers' cooperatives, which in the past had represented the Soviet Union's minimum program for agricultural reform, was that they were up against great technical and economic difficulties (shortage of technicians, scientists, administrative and political personnel, shortage of agricultural machinery and implements). Because some African countries had disregarded these difficulties and proceeded hastily to establish producer cooperatives, "many proved ineffective with the result that output dropped."

Concerning the status of the local private sector, always before considered an obstacle to essential economic reform and therefore to be eliminated as quickly as possible, Soviet spokesmen began to express unusual tolerance: "It is often maintained that the emergence and especially the development of a private capitalist sector should be opposed. Only time and the experience of each country can provide the final answer. Everything depends on circumstances but . . . one cannot always categorically deny the need to draw on private initiative."[28]

While economic ties with socialist countries assured these nations of the kind of assistance that would not encumber their development along a progressive path, Soviet spokesmen conceded that it would be "hard to imagine the African countries being able to isolate themselves from the Capitalist world." In consequence, African radicals such as Bouteflika of Algeria were by 1967 expressing a lack of enthusiasm for all the developed nations, saying that the "progressives" (i.e., the Soviet Union) had come to take the same attitude as the "moderates, extreme Right and the capitalists."

Thus, in the brief decade since their direct entry into Africa, the Soviets have undergone a number of trials and made a number of errors. Their twisting policy has successively emphasized peaceful coexistence, cold war, and a return to détente, while the Soviet world-wide political offensive from 1957 to 1963 largely failed in Africa as elsewhere. Ideologically, the Soviet Union came to be extraordinarily flexible in seeking influence in Africa, thereby sowing great and continuing confusion among its theoreticians. To a great extent it has now abandoned immediate revolutionary goals, even to the point of sacrificing the African Communist parties in order to maintain collaboration with new non-Communist regimes.

To implement its zigzag policy to date, the Soviet Union has employed in its own fashion the standard instruments of modern multiple diplomacy, including propaganda, cultural and educational exchanges, economic and technical assistance, trade, and military assistance. A brief recapitulation of the nature and extent of these separate Soviet efforts adds another dimension to an understanding of Soviet objectives and priorities.

SOVIET ECONOMIC AND TECHNICAL ASSISTANCE

Traditionally, the Soviet Union had few economic or commercial relations with Africa, and its limited economic aid programs date from the mid-1950s, after the Stalinist period. By the end of 1967, Soviet offers of credits and grants to the less developed countries totaled some $6 billion. Of this amount, $858 million in aid was offered to the nations of Africa (excluding the U.A.R.). In the 1950s and early 1960s offers were concentrated on a limited number of recipients, usually of radical political orientation, such as Ghana, Guinea, and Mali. The exception was Ethiopia, which was pledged more than $100 million. In more recent years Soviet aid has been distributed much more widely in Africa. By the end of 1967, eighteen states were on the list of recipients, many of them politically moderate or conservative. Likewise, in more recent years few offers have been made and little interest shown in the more radical states favored in the earlier years. Table 14 lists the African states that have been offered Soviet aid and the cumulative amounts from 1954 through 1967.

World-wide aid commitments by the Soviet Union through 1966 were sustained at a relatively high level, but in 1967 there was a sharp drop-off. Most recently, the bulk of new offers has been concentrated on the Asian subcontinent and in the Middle East. In Africa the volume has declined sharply since 1965 when a total

TABLE 14. Soviet Offers of Economic Credits and Grants, 1954–67,
and Years 1966 and 1967

(In millions of U.S. dollars)

	1954–67	1966	1967
Total, all less developed countries	5,989	1,244	69
Total, African less developed countries	858	77	9
Algeria	232	1	
Cameroon	8		
Congo	9		
Ethiopia	102		
Ghana	89		
Guinea	73	3	
Kenya	44		
Mali	55		
Mauritania	3		3
Morocco	44	44	
Senegal	7		
Sierra Leone	28		
Somalia	66	9	
Sudan	22		
Tanzania	20	20	
Tunisia	34		
Uganda	16		
Zambia	6		6

SOURCE: *Research Memoranda*, R-SB-80, July 21, 1967, and RSE-120, August 14, 1968, U.S. Department of State, Washington.

of $230 million was reached. The total dropped to $77 million in 1966, and plummeted to only $9 million in 1967.

Aid commitments are normally long-term, but disbursements are made only after close examination of specific projects. Consequently, actual deliveries of Soviet economic assistance have lagged far behind the amounts extended. World-wide, less than 40 per cent of the aid offered to date has actually been delivered, and the difference cannot be taken to be a currently active pipeline. The record of disbursements in Africa is somewhat worse than elsewhere. Aggregate statistics are not available, but Ethiopia and Ghana can perhaps serve as two representative examples. Neither country had by the end of 1965 come close to spending the Soviet assistance offered: in the case of Ethiopia, $15 million had been delivered out of $102 million offered; and in Ghana, $29 million had been delivered out of $89 million offered.

The principal vehicle of Soviet assistance has been loans, the formal terms of which have been generous, with annual interest rates of 2.5 per cent or less. The technical and educational assistance has been emphasized in recognition that shortages of technical skills and trained administrative and managerial personnel can obstruct the effective implementation of all Soviet aid commitments. Also, it is believed that such efforts help "deprive the imperialists of important levers of spiritual influence . . . on liberated countries and for the dissemination of reactionary, anti-socialist ideas."[29]

In 1965 there were 9,385 Soviet technicians in less developed countries, of whom 2,720 were in Africa. By 1966 the total had grown to 11,730, of which 4,170 were in Africa. In 1967 the total eased off to 11,040, and the number in Africa to 3,800. Most of these technicians were concentrated in Algeria, Mali, and Guinea. Some were at work in vocational schools and at higher-level technical institutes established with Soviet assistance in Guinea, Algeria, and Ethiopia. In addition, a moderate number of technical trainees from Africa—375 in 1967—were receiving instruction in factories and technical institutes in the Soviet Union.

A far larger number of academic trainees were brought to Soviet educational institutions. This aspect of Soviet aid has grown rapidly from its beginning in the academic year 1956–57 when only 46 students from less developed countries were on scholarships. By 1966 the world-wide total reached 11,215, of which 6,305 were from Africa; the following year the total dropped to 10,275, of which 5,750 were from Africa. Training is provided at regular universities of the Soviet Union and at new universities and institutes established especially for students from the developing countries. The average period of training for academic students in the U.S.S.R. is about five years, including one year of Russian-language study. Lumumba University (also known as Friendship University), established to cope with the sudden influx of students brought to the U.S.S.R. in the early 1960s from the underdeveloped world, now has an enrollment of about 4,000, and graduated 535 in 1967 in its third graduating class (470 in 1966 and about 220 in 1965). The yearly number of graduates should soon level off around 700, given the size of the university's enrollment. Most of the new graduates, like their predecessors, are specialists in engineering, chemistry, agronomy, and other technical fields, and there is a high proportion of medical doctors.

These academic programs have been plagued with problems

from the beginning, and difficulties still exist despite many changes and improvements made in response to student protests. A Kenyan student, Nicholas Nyangira, wrote in *The New York Times Magazine* in May 1965 that during his study in Baku, he and his fellow African students were subjected to blatant indoctrination, brainwashing, and constant pressure to join political movements. "We knew that we needed education, but we did not leave Kenya to go to the Soviet Union only to study Marxism-Leninism or revolutionary tactics. We were uncertain whether we had been chosen to learn or to be trained as Communists."

Another cause of discontent has been racial discrimination on the part of Soviet students and other Soviet citizens. Michel Ayih, a Togolese student, wrote, after his educational experience in the Soviet Union, "My disappointment concerning . . . racial equality, about which the susceptibility of a black student is the strongest, was as great as my other illusions. Instead of finding a country of unlimited 'human fraternity, I found myself in the heart of a world dominated by the most elementary and primitive racial reaction. . . . This situation was so revolting that it led to numerous fights and brawls between blacks and whites, not only in Moscow, but also in Warsaw."[30]

Other sources of student disaffection were climatic and living conditions, restrictions on movement and on social intercourse with the local population, and deficiencies in the quality of instruction. However, there are indications that Soviet officials have become sensitive to these problems as well as to the need to devote greater attention to the selection of better qualified students for the available scholarships.

The impact of graduates of Soviet institutions returning to Africa is just beginning to be felt as more students complete their programs. What the long-term value or consequences of Soviet training both in terms of economic development and political attitudes may be cannot yet be estimated, though some African governments are beginning to be apprehensive.

Given the limited amount of Soviet economic assistance, it would be difficult to form any judgment of its over-all impact on African development to date. For those countries which have received relatively large offers, Soviet aid has represented a significant though usually secondary source of help. Moreover, its intent has often seemed to them transparently political, timed and designed to take advantage of a specific political opportunity.

Qualitatively, Soviet economic aid in Africa has represented neither originality of concept nor superiority of execution. The types of projects financed have been of traditional character, and Soviet inexperience in the administration of aid has been reflected in errors of planning and management as well as in the generally low caliber of Soviet technicians. It can be said that Soviet aid in Africa to date has been so limited, so piecemeal, and so poorly conceived and executed that it has made little difference to African economic development and is not looked upon by African leaders themselves as a significant factor for the future, particularly in view of the fact that prospects for growth of Soviet aid are not bright. They are well aware that Soviet aid has always been a matter on which there have been mixed views and characteristically little enthusiasm in Moscow. They know too that in the post-Khrushchev period, the growing preoccupation of Soviet leaders with the internal needs of the Russian economy has diminished further what little previous enthusiasm may have existed, to the point where almost no new offers of aid to Africa were made in 1967.

Soviet Trade

As late as the mid-1950s Soviet trade with all the less developed areas remained at a low level, totaling only about $370 million, or less than 6 per cent of the Soviet world-wide total. By 1965, however, such trade had increased fivefold to $1.8 billion, or 13 per cent of total Soviet foreign trade. In 1967, however, the latest year for which figures are available, no growth occurred. Consistent with the over-all priorities of Soviet policy in the Third World, Soviet efforts in trade expansion have been concentrated in recent years in South Asia and the Middle East, including the U.A.R. This concentration reflects in part the trade momentum generated by deliveries under Soviet aid programs and by repayments in the form of commodities.

With an increasing number of trade agreements signed in recent years, often in conjunction with aid agreements, Soviet trade with Africa has grown considerably in percentage terms at least. But since 1963 it has fluctuated, declining somewhat in 1964, rising markedly in 1965, and falling slightly in 1966. Although the recent level of nearly $200 million per year represents a minor fraction of the total trade of the independent African states, it tends to be concentrated in a few countries, and for them it constitutes a significant element. Table 15 on Soviet imports and exports from the African states indicates that, for Ghana, Sudan, Mo-

TABLE 15. Soviet Trade with Less Developed Countries and
with Africa, 1964–66

(In millions of U.S. dollars)

	Soviet Exports			Soviet Imports		
	1964	1965	1966	1964	1965	1966
Total, all less developed countries:	774.3	910.7	886.3	654.0	845.4	903.2
Total, all African less developed countries[a]:	88.9	115.6	103.8	58.8	84.8	71.5
Algeria	15.7	15.4	18.8	3.8	3.8	5.9
Angola	...	...	...	...	...	...
Cameroon	[b]	0.1	0.1	0.1	0	0.4
Chad	...	...	...	...	...	...
Congo (B)	[b]	2.7	1.3	...	...	0.4
Congo (K)	...	...	...	...	...	...
Dahomey	[b]	0.4	0.4	...	...	...
Ethiopia	3.3	7.8	5.2	2.4	2.6	3.0
Gabon	...	...	...	...	...	...
Ghana	19.5	34.6	14.0	20.7	30.7	24.2
Guinea	9.2	9.7	10.8	2.2	3.6	3.6
Ivory Coast	...	0.3	...	0.9	5.1	...
Kenya	[b]	1.0	1.7	0.1	0.7	1.1
Malagasy Republic	...	...	...	...	...	...
Mali	13.2	9.8	8.6	3.7	2.6	1.6
Morocco	8.1	8.4	10.8	6.5	11.0	9.4
Mozambique	...	...	...	...	...	...
Niger	...	...	...	...	...	...
Nigeria	1.2	3.2	4.6	4.2	5.8	0.8
Rhodesia	...	...	...	...	...	...
Senegal	0.1	0.1	0.2	0.3	0.6	0.8
Sierra Leone	...	0.1	0.7	...	...	...
Somalia	8.3	6.9	8.7	[b]	0	0
Sudan	6.3	7.2	7.4	5.0	12.4	7.3
Tanzania[c]	0.2	0.4	1.0	2.0	1.7	1.8
Togo	0.7	0.8	0.7	0.4	0.6	0
Tunisia	3.1	6.6	8.7	2.2	3.6	3.8
Uganda	[b]	0.1	0.1	...	0	0.3
Zambia	...	...	...	4.3	...	7.1

[a] Excluding United Arab Republic.
[b] Less than $50,000.
[c] Data for Tanganyika only.

NOTE: A leader entry (...) indicates that no figures for trade are known, although some trade may have taken place. Totals are derived from unrounded data and may not agree with the sums of the rounded components.

SOURCE: Data from official Soviet Trade Yearbooks, as reported in *Research Memoranda*, RSB-80, July 21, 1967, and RSE-120, August 14, 1968, U.S. Department of State.

rocco, Ivory Coast, Algeria, Mali, Somalia, Tunisia, and Nigeria, trade with the Soviet Union is not unimportant, although in Ghana, the volume in 1966 dropped off sharply from 1965, especially of imports from the Soviet Union, following the deposition of Nkrumah. From the standpoint of the African countries generally, however, Soviet trade is quantitatively minor and, since it is to some extent related to political objectives, has the disadvantage of being unstable, fluctuating greatly from one year to the next.

The prospects for Soviet trade with Africa are difficult to assess. Soviet writers have repeatedly stressed the importance of trade as an instrument for the development of the poorer countries on a "mutually advantageous" basis; and Soviet economists have estimated the possibility of tripling trade with the developing countries by 1970, an ambitious goal. If the less developed areas are able to draw down the large backlog of unexpended Soviet credits, this should help maintain Soviet exports at relatively high levels in the years to come. Similarly, commodity repayments on past Soviet credits should gradually rise, increasing Soviet import totals.

But apart from the volume of trade stimulated and supported by Soviet aid and credit, there is little basis for expecting a spectacular increase. In Africa the slow growth of the various economies will severely restrict purchases of foreign manufactured and processed goods, including those of Soviet origin. Soviet programs permitting an increase of domestic consumption levels may provide increased requirements for certain African products, including cocoa and cotton. Yet on the whole, it seems most likely that while the growth in trade between the Soviet Union and Africa may continue, it will be many years before it becomes a major factor in the economic accounts of either party.

SOVIET MILITARY ACTIVITIES

The aspect of Soviet policy in Africa which most clearly reveals its meandering quality, as well as its strict control over commitments, is the military. To date, Soviet military ventures in Africa, from the Congo to the U.A.R., have mostly had sobering, even humiliating, consequences. Although the implication of these experiences have not been forgotten, the Soviet Union is clearly not prepared to give up militarily and get out. On the contrary, it appears that increasing reliance is being placed on military actions of a limited, probing, opportunistic type. Military aid programs of various kinds are being carried on where possible with the newly independent states; some help is being given to the liberation movements of the South; and the utility in Africa of certain new capabilities of Soviet air and naval forces is being tested.

Total Soviet military aid to the developing countries over recent years has been estimated at some $4 billion—although all such valuations, particularly of obsolete military equipment, must be treated as the grossest approximations. Of this total, perhaps one-eighth, or less than $500 million, has been delivered to the states of North Africa (other than the U.A.R.) and in sub-Saharan Africa. The annual total has been growing over the past decade but remains a minor factor when compared to the amounts of Western European equipment and training that have been made available. It is comparable, however, to American military aid programs, which are under increasingly severe congressional restrictions as to volume and types of material as well as to the permitted number of recipient countries. Some Soviet assistance is provided in the form of grants, but the bulk is through credit sales at greatly discounted prices. To a degree, assistance has been concentrated in the more radical regimes, including Guinea, Mali, Ghana, and especially Algeria; but some of the moderate and even conservative regimes, including the Sudan and Nigeria, have recently been added to the list of recipients. Increasingly, the Soviet Union appears willing to respond promptly to all African requests for military training and equipment, including aircraft.

The first military aid in Africa was offered to Ghana in 1957 in response to a personal appeal from Nkrumah. In 1959 the Soviet Union concluded its first formal military aid agreement with a sub-Saharan country, namely Guinea, involving some $3 million in arms. Under the agreement, Guinea obtained a few MIG-17's, rifles, pistols, machine guns, radio communications equipment, and some armored cars. Trucks and transport aircraft were offered to Lumumba in the Congo in 1960, and during the same period the first of a series of deliveries of military equipment was made to Morocco where King Hassan, having been unsuccessful in obtaining desired military equipment from the French, turned to the Soviet Union.

In 1961 Mali began to receive Soviet military aid; in 1963 a rebel regime in the northern Congo was provided with arms and training, and a major agreement was reached with Somalia for the delivery of more than $30 million of arms, including a dozen

MIG-17's and some T34 tanks. At about the same time, large arms shipments to Algeria began, which are estimated now to have reached a total value of more than $250 million.[31] Deliveries have included 6 Komar guided-missile patrol boats with C2C missiles, plus two or three Osa guided-missile patrol boats (a slightly larger version of the Komar), 150 MIG's, 15 to 20 Antonov transport planes, and 25 to 30 Ilyushin-28 bombers. About 300 to 350 Soviet tanks are also thought to have been received. Nearly 3,000 Algerian officers have now been trained by the Russians, and the Soviet Union has sent some 600 military instructors to Algeria in addition to 1,500 civilian technical experts.

Military assistance, including aircraft, was extended to Tanzania in 1964, and in 1965 to Uganda. After civil war had broken out in Nigeria in 1967, the Lagos government sought to purchase arms and aircraft from the Western nations, including the United States, but, its requirements not being fully satisfied, turned to Soviet and East European sources, and quickly received at least 6 MIG-15's or MIG-17's and 6 or 7 Czech L-29 jet trainers. In January 1968 an agreement was reached with the Sudan for the delivery of sizable quantities of Soviet equipment.

The motivation behind the spreading Soviet program of arms deliveries in Africa can only be surmised. It would appear that military assistance, because of the speed with which agreements can be implemented and the directness of identification which it provides with the current policy of the recipient country, is considered to be especially effective in opening up general channels of political influence. There is apparently also a conviction in some Soviet official circles that the new military elites in Africa are likely to be the real locus of political power in the future and must therefore be cultivated.*

* Milton Kovner, in his "Soviet Aid and Trade" in *Current History*, October 1967, p. 242, reports that the military of the developing countries has now been promoted in Communist ideology from the most reactionary category of the bourgeoisie, where orthodox Marxism had consigned them, to the status of "backbone of the revolutionary democratic forces" on whom Moscow counts to implement the transition of their countries to socialism. He adds, however, that other Communist analysts continue "to find such military regimes strange and uncomfortable bedfellows." *Izvestia* for January 17, 1967, states that whereas "some authors did not want to assign the Army a progressive role and define political power established through military coups merely as reactionary and fascist, others try to present the Army as just about the only all-national force capable of leading the national liberation movement." *Izvestia* took a centrist position asserting that the armies "may not only play a progressive role . . . but easily become a weapon of the reactionary forces."

There are some observers who consider that one Soviet purpose may be to establish arms depots in Africa—as in the case of Algeria —for the transshipment of military items to revolutionaries and Russia's allies throughout the continent and in the Middle East.[32] Yet it is difficult to find in the varied pattern of the Soviet military aid program any dominant or consistent objective, other than a general anti-Western quality. Wherever a situation of tension or trouble has offered opportunity, the Soviets have entered if it seemed some political profit could be realized, if Western influence could be displaced, or if an American action could be countered.

Because the objectives of the program have not been clear, it is hazardous to attempt to appraise its results. In some instances, Western influence has been displaced: The Soviet Union has become the largest arms supplier to Algeria; the United Kingdom has been replaced in Sudan and Italy in Somalia; Soviet equipment has entered in significant scale in Uganda and Tanzania and has been particularly welcomed by the Lagos regime in Nigeria, which felt itself at the time to be in urgent need. But to what extent Soviet political influence will follow the provision of military aid remains to be seen. The Algerians, who have been major recipients of such assistance, are visibly discontented with some aspects of Soviet policy. The Nigerian government, despite its gratitude for Soviet help, seems highly unlikely to respond to Soviet political guidance. And earlier Soviet efforts in Ghana and Guinea, of course, produced only bitter fruit. Whether the extensive training being provided to African military personnel will in time offer a new base of Soviet influence likewise remains to be seen. If one purpose of Soviet military assistance has been to encourage arms races and consequent instability in Africa, the results of its efforts in such terms are also equivocal. On the Horn, for example, where great tension existed between Somalia and Ethiopia, and where Soviet arms were provided in quantity to Somalia, the nations directly involved have recently been able to reach agreements that have considerably reduced the likelihood of open conflict.

Apart from open military assistance to the independent African states, Moscow also provides arms and financing to some of the

Which of the two tendencies, the democratic or the reactionary, will prevail at any given historical stage, it said, will depend on how effective is the revolutionary influence exerted on them.

liberation movements working to displace the white minority governments in the south.* However, after the fiasco of its support to the subversive activities of Nkrumah in Ghana and with the shift in its general policy toward collaboration with moderate regimes, the Soviet Union appears to have now cut off its financial and military assistance to subversive and opposition groups in the independent states of North and Tropical Africa. Its aid to the southern liberation movements, though continuing, has been kept within rather low limits. Enough has been provided to maintain lines of communication and to save face in the Soviet Union's competition for revolutionary honors in Africa with the Chinese. But not enough has been given either in the form of effective guerrilla training or weapons to enable the liberation movements to mount major campaigns, except possibly in the case of the Mozambican Liberation Front (FRELIMO). Such reserve on the part of the Soviet Union is attributable to the weakness, disunity, and ineffectiveness of most of the liberation groups. The Soviet Union may also be inhibited by growing awareness that effective action in Southern Africa will necessarily have to be on a major scale, thereby creating the risk of U.S. intervention and pre-emption—an eventuality which the Soviets seem desirous almost above all else to avoid.

The presence of a Soviet fleet in the Mediterranean following the six-day Arab-Israeli war in mid-1967, has recently drawn attention to another aspect of Soviet military policy and aroused speculation as to the implications for Africa of the growing air- and sea-lift capability of Soviet forces. Following their setbacks in both the Cuban missile crisis and the Congo confrontation, the Soviets have given high priority to the development of long-range logistical capacity. In taking this decision, the Soviets did not necessarily have in mind any specific eventual use in areas of the Third World or elsewhere. It may well have been a more generalized response to repeated demonstrations (including Viet Nam) of their inferiority in this respect in comparison with the United States. Their determination may be simply to overcome a weak-

---

* The liberation movements (of which each country has at least two) that are believed to receive Soviet assistance are: in Mozambique, FRELIMO (the Mozambican Liberation Front); in Angola, MPLA (the Popular Movement for the Liberation of Angola); in Rhodesia, ZAPU (The Zimbabwe African People's Union); in Southwest Africa, SWAPO (the Southwest Africa People's Organization); and in South Africa, ANC (the African National Congress).

ness which, if accomplished, could enlarge their role on the world scene and open up a range of new possibilities.

Now that a Soviet fleet is in the Mediterranean and further development of Russian long-range naval power (including submarines) seems under way, experiments in deployment are being carried out both in the Mediterranean and, according to some reports, in the Persian Gulf, from which British air and naval units have begun to withdraw. Soviet naval forces may before long also begin to cruise the western and eastern flanks of Africa, and the question therefore arises as to what political consequences might flow from this new factor in the African context.

Emergency military assistance available to troubled African countries in the past has been almost entirely Western, and such external military intervention, though limited, has been able to tip the balance in various instances in favor of pro-Western regimes. But, now that Britain and even France have greatly reduced their military presence in Africa, will an increased Soviet naval and air capability, available to appear quickly at given points, be able to produce disproportionate political consequences?

Because of the precarious balance of power within many of the new African states, governments have been, and in even more cases could be, toppled by a mere handful of armed men in a matter of hours. For the Soviet Union, the temptation to act might be very attractive. The Soviet military and political leadership may now see Africa as an area in which the U.S.S.R. can use its new capability without too great a likelihood of confrontation with the United States. Certainly, for local revolutionary groups in Africa, the availability of Soviet military assistance— a totally new factor—could greatly change their calculations of the prospects for success and, as a result, add greatly to the instability and fragility of an already unstable situation. Whether the availability of Soviet naval and other forces off the African coast might cause the number of sudden coups to increase in the future is an open question. How many dissident groups might call for Soviet help and in how many cases and in what ways the Soviet Union might be willing to respond likewise remain to be seen.

For the Soviets, any decision to intervene would of course involve fine calculations. They have already been humiliated in Africa by their inability to maintain a position in direct confrontation with the United States, and they would not lightly run the risk of a repetition of such experience. On the other hand, it would be no inconsiderable advantage for them to be able to help install a certain number of pro-Soviet and dependent regimes in various parts of Africa if that could be accomplished without incurring undue financial burdens or military risks.

Should radical political changes be precipitated by Soviet military action, especially if they were to occur in a sequence of instances, rather urgent new questions would be presented both to the United States and to the countries of Western Europe concerning the response they would feel obliged to make. Still larger questions would arise about the impact of such incidents on the over-all political situation in Africa, the turbulence of the general international atmosphere, and the world-wide interests of both the Soviet Union and the United States.

Such a destabilizing impact in Africa of new Soviet logistical capability seems hypothetically possible. At present, however, Soviet military policy on the continent generally remains one of restraint, opportunism, minimum risk, and the avoidance of any major commitments or confrontations.

An Evaluation

The Soviet Union moved into Africa late—only little more than a decade ago—and did so under heavy disadvantages. It began with little direct experience on the continent and almost no knowledge of its special characteristics and problems. Without qualified personnel of its own and with no indigenous Communist apparatus or cadres of any consequence to work through, it had to compete with a massive Western presence, pervasive and long-established. The new nations of Africa remained heavily—and willingly— dependent on Western European advisers, technicians, and administrators. Their leaders, although familiar with the vocabulary of Marxism, had been deeply infused with Western concepts in the process of their educational development; and their economies were heavily dependent on Western sources of supply and outlets for their products. The Soviets, moreover, began with a set of rigid doctrinal concepts that only impeded their understanding of Africans and African problems, nor did they have cordial personal relations with the new African leaders for whom, individually and as a group, Communist leaders had long felt distrust and distaste.

After the advent of Khrushchev, Soviet activities in Africa and elsewhere in the Third World were intensified as part of a dynamic new effort to spread Soviet influence and compete with the West. In many important respects, at least during the Khrushchev period, Russian policy was flexible and innovative. But however much boldness was displayed in breaking old doctrinal molds, in the substance of its policies the Soviet Union has behaved conservatively as the kind of nation-state it is—a great power with its own vested interests, heavily bureaucratized, and constrained constantly by the necessity to reconcile conflicting objectives, establish priorities, and calculate costs.

Particularly in their initial ventures in Africa, the Soviets manifested their inexperience by misjudging certain situations and by overreacting and mishandling others. But more important than their early mistakes is the fact that, when attempts have proved misguided, they have corrected course. In the short space of a decade they have not only shifted policy, they have overhauled it repeatedly; indeed, the frequency and amplitude of change have become its distinguishing characteristic.

Although the Soviets have now learned to avoid some of the amateurish errors of which they were guilty earlier, the results of their policies have not yet noticeably improved. Throughout Africa the countries and leaders on whom they have gambled have frequently faltered and defected, while those they opposed have in many cases survived and prospered. No African regime has become Communist yet, nor have attempts been made to apply rigorous Leninist concepts to the development of an African state; and everywhere, regardless of the general political orientation of regimes, Communist activity and organizations have been restricted or suppressed.

Forced to face the intractibility of African realities to their theories of history and development, the Soviets have had to profoundly reexamine their own policies and priorities in the context of the general difficulties of their foreign policy over the past decade in Eastern Europe, in relations with China, in the competition with the West, and in the drive to build influence in the Third World. As a result, Africa has now been downgraded. The Soviets have shifted to a policy of dealing indiscriminately with all elements, radical or reactionary, and of placing small bets on every available horse. They are investing some resources in the training of civilian and military youth; they are spraying propaganda in all directions; they are conducting a few cultural programs and some organizational activity; they are giving a small amount of economic assistance and are encouraging the development of trade; they are delivering some military aid to existing governments and limited assistance to revolutionary groups of the south. But being ideologically in a state of some confusion and preoccupied with major internal problems of economic reorganization, they are doing nothing with conviction or serious commitment. Above all, they seem determined to avoid major costs or the risk of serious confrontation with the United States.

In independent Africa, therefore, the Soviet Union has suspended any immediate revolutionary objectives and shifted essentially to a policy of "wait and see." In the words of a Chinese proverb, it now appears to have accepted the view that the best cure for muddy water is time. But the Communist Chinese, who entered Africa at about the same time as the Soviets and have likewise suffered many reverses, have come to quite different policy conclusions. To them, their own proverb is unpersuasive.

7

The Chinese Involvement

Communist China's involvement in Africa began even later than that of the Soviet Union and with an even more modest base of previous interest in or experience with the continent's special characteristics. Although in the initial years after the Bandung Conference in 1955, from which the beginning of China's direct interest in Africa might be dated, Peking essentially followed Moscow's lead and cooperated in a common policy, the Chinese approach has consistently shown distinctive features. With the passage of time, it has departed more and more widely from Soviet policy in both methods and objectives. On the whole, the Chinese have been both more bold and more ambitious, less concerned than the Soviets with the adaptation and reformulation of doctrine to specific African conditions, less concerned to obscure the contradictions between the separate branches of its African policies, and less restrained in taking political risks. In Africa as elsewhere the Chinese have tended to go at their work with fervor and conviction in their revolutionary mission, and even the evidence of failures and defeats has not, thus far at least, deterred them from their dogmatic approach.

At the level of "normal" diplomatic relations, Peking has sought to win formal recognition by the new nations of Africa in order to strengthen its claim of being the sole legitimate government of China, to blunt the comparable effort being made by the Chinese Nationalist government, and eventually to wrest China's seat at the United Nations from the Taiwan regime. In pursuit of these objectives, China has presented itself in polite and cordial terms, has offered economic favors and cultural displays, and—for a time at least—has achieved some success.

In pursuit of its parallel revolutionary and ideological objectives, however, China has disseminated great quantities of revolutionary propaganda in Africa, has attempted to encourage the Africans whenever possible to put their faith in violence and intransigence, has encouraged and supported various liberation movements, and has become involved in the internal political struggles of a number of independent African states.

The objectives of Chinese policy in Africa have increasingly become entangled with and obscured by the growing political rift with the Soviet Union, especially after 1963. The manifestations of this world-wide struggle have become more and more obvious and disquieting to the Africans—to the point where many are wondering whether the African objectives of China, whatever they may be, have not been subordinated to the requirements of the conflict with Moscow and in relation to which Africa may have become simply an available theater of maneuver and display.

To follow the winding trail of Chinese involvement in Africa after 1955 is instructive because of how it contrasts with that of the Soviet Union. China's entrance was prepared diplomatically at Bandung in April 1955 and was consummated with the opening of its first embassy on the African continent in Egypt just over a year later. At the Eighth Congress of the Chinese Communist party in September 1956, Mao Tse-tung declared, "We must give active support to the national independence and liberation movements in Asia, Africa, and Latin America, as well as to the peace movement and righteous struggle in all countries throughout the world." In pursuit of this policy China undertook to develop relationships throughout the Horn and North Africa. Once the Permanent International Secretariat of the Afro-Asian Peoples' Solidarity Conference was established in Cairo in December 1957, China was able to open up direct lines of contact with radical and revolutionary groups elsewhere in the continent. Somalia was a situation of special attraction because of the festering conflict between it, French Somaliland, and Ethiopia. North Africa was even more immediately attractive because of the Algerian War, then a scene of massive violence stirring anticolonialist passions throughout Africa.

Because of its proximity and relationship with the Algerian struggle, Morocco was a natural focus of interest, and throughout 1958 and 1959 China intensified contacts with Moroccan leaders and offered credits and arms to leaders of the Algerian FLN operating from Moroccan bases. During this period, an early but clear signal was given of a developing difference of view between the Russians and the Chinese on the question of violence in Africa. Moscow, because of concern over Soviet relationships with France, argued that "the only realistic way to solve the Algerian problem is by the opening up of direct negotiations,"[1] while Peking continued to warn the Algerians of the dangers of negotiation and urged them to continue their war to a victorious end.[2]

Chinese Meddling and the Sino-Soviet Split

Once its involvement in North Africa had been established, China turned its attention to West Africa and to the three radical new states, Guinea, Ghana, and Mali, which had already attracted Soviet interest. After Guinea gained its independence, in October 1958, China moved rapidly to establish close relations. Ambassadors were exchanged; high-level visits and cultural exchanges were arranged. In September of 1959 President Sékou Touré visited Peking and signed a treaty of friendship, an agreement for cultural cooperation, an economic and technical cooperation agreement, and a trade agreement. Mali became a separate independent state in September of 1960, and by early 1961, Peking had signed a trade and payments agreement, made a substantial interest-free loan, and established an embassy. Although Ghana became independent in 1957, it did not become a republic until July 1960. Shortly thereafter diplomatic relations were established with China, and Nkrumah went to Peking on a state visit. He concluded a ten-year friendship treaty, received an interest-free loan of nearly $20 million, signed a trade and payments agreement, and received other promises and assurances.

On the whole, Chinese policy at the time generally paralleled that of the Soviet Union. However, the treaty signed between Peking and Guinea and the circumstances surrounding its conclusion suggested a Chinese desire to establish a special relationship, clearly independent of Guinea's relationship with the Soviet Union. The terms of economic assistance offered were extraordinarily generous, and the publicity with which the occasion was celebrated was most unusual in the cordiality of its tone.

When the Congo crisis erupted in mid-1960, new signs of Soviet-Chinese disagreement developed. Although it refrained from saying so publicly, Peking clearly disapproved of U.N. intervention and was critical of Moscow's blunder in having helped bring it about. In Peking's view, U.N. intervention could only open the door wide to U.S. imperialism. At the time, it confined its attacks to the United States although later, after the long-smoldering Soviet-Chinese rift had become public, its spokesmen were almost equally critical of the line Moscow had taken. Three years later, China, like the Soviet Union, recognized the dissident Stanleyville government of Antoine Gizenga as the "legitimate central government of the Congo Republic." When Gizenga subsequently agreed to take part in a reunited government under moderate Cyrille Adoula, with Moscow's unreserved support, Peking flatly refused to go along. The differences between Peking and Moscow were becoming more and more open, but the point of direct, sustained hostility had not yet arrived.

Peking established a diplomatic mission in Dar es Salaam in January 1962, thereafter extending its contacts throughout East and Central Africa. With bases of political operation functioning in North, West, East, and Central Africa, in addition to regular diplomatic missions throughout the continent, the Chinese proceeded more aggressively to carry forward their general programs of diplomatic and cultural relations, trade, aid, and technical assistance with the newly independent states, and at the same time to become directly implicated in specific situations of political conflict and disorder.

Both aspects of Peking's split-level policy were intensified by the visit of Chou En-lai with a large entourage to ten African countries in late 1963 and early 1964. In its timing, it coincided with the decisive rupture of Chinese-Soviet relations, following Moscow's return to a basically conservative policy line of détente after the Cuban missile crisis.

By the time of Chou's visit, China had already been accorded recognition by nine African states, not including the U.A.R. To advance the diplomatic objective of putting China forward as the friend of African independence and development, Chou adopted a benign tone embodied in the Eight Principles to which he referred repeatedly during his trip and which he declared were the basis of Peking's foreign assistance policy:

1. The Chinese Government consistently abides by the principle of equality and mutual benefit in providing aid to other countries. It never regards such aid as a kind of unilateral alms but regards aid as always mutual.
2. In providing aid to other countries, the Chinese Government strictly respects the sovereignty of the recipient countries, and never attaches any conditions or asks for any privileges.

3. The Chinese Government provides economic assistance by giving interest-free or low-interest loans and where necessary extends the time limit for the repayment so as to alleviate as far as possible the burden of the recipient countries.
4. The purpose of the Chinese Government's foreign aid is not to make the recipient countries dependent on China but to help them to embark on the road of self-reliance and independent economic development step by step.
5. The projects which the Chinese Government helps the recipient countries build are those which will, as far as possible, require less investment while yielding quicker results, so that the recipient governments may increase their income and accumulate capital.
6. The Chinese Government provides the best quality equipment and material of its own manufacture at international market prices. If the equipment and material provided by the Chinese Government are not up to the agreed specifications and quality, the Chinese Government undertakes to replace them.
7. In giving any particular technical assistance, the Chinese Government will see to it that the personnel of the recipient country fully master such techniques.
8. The experts dispatched by the Chinese Government to help in construction in the recipient countries will have the same standard of living as the experts of the recipient countries. The Chinese experts are not allowed to make any special demands or enjoy any special amenities.[3]

But the other face of Chinese policy, namely meddling in political affairs within and between African states was re-emphasized when Chou, on the eve of his departure from Somalia, declared as one of his major conclusions that "Africa was ripe for revolution." This aspect of Peking's policy had been detectable in Africa from the beginning, even during the period of close cooperation with the Soviet Union and of priority in the drive for diplomatic recognition. Examples of Chinese subversive activity had repeatedly come to light and attracted great attention, partly because of the aura of oriental intrigue that surrounded them. For example, Félix Roland Moumié, leader of the revolutionary Union des Populations du Cameroun in the French Cameroon, after making two trips to Peking in 1959 and 1960, died mysteriously in Switzerland of "an overdose of rat poison administered by persons unknown."[4] Another Chinese beneficiary, Mohamed Harbi Farah, a leader of the National Pan-Somali Movement, was killed in an airplane crash between Geneva and Rome in late 1960. A

dispute thereafter between two of his followers over a bank account resulted in an investigation which revealed he had received
more than $4 million from Communist China in support of his
clandestine activities. In Zanzibar in 1962, the Chinese gave their
backing to the radical elements of the Arab minority of the island.
In January of 1963, however, the black African majority took
power in a bloody coup, drastically reducing the influence of the
group Peking had gone to such lengths to cultivate, and incidentally uncovering evidence of extensive Chinese bribery and
subversion.

One of the more bloody of the Chinese efforts to meddle in
African trouble spots occurred in 1963 in the two tiny nations of
Rwanda and Burundi. Sensing an opportunity in the bitter tribal
conflict between the minority Watusi, who had traditionally ruled
the area, and the Bahutu majority, Peking established diplomatic
relations with Mwami Mwambutsa IV, the Bahutu King of Burundi, and concurrently made contact with the leaders of the
thousands of Watusi refugees in the area. As a result of Peking's
assistance and encouragement, a series of guerrilla raids were
launched by the Watusi from Burundi and the eastern Congo
against Rwanda in 1963 and early 1964. These were followed by
appalling reprisals by the Bahutu in Rwanda against the remaining
Watusi of that country. During the same period, the Chinese
Embassy in Burundi attempted to compound the confusion in the
region by also supporting a recrudescence of rebel activity in the
eastern Congo, supplying propaganda materials, small arms, and
money.

In 1964, Zambian officials disclosed a Chinese plot to overthrow
that government the day after independence was declared,[5] and
in the same year Dr. H. Kamuzu Banda of Malawi carried out a
purge and cabinet shakeup following a scandal in which Chinese
agents had allegedly offered $50 million in exchange for Malawi's
recognition of Peking.[6] In the fall of that year, in Niger, where
they had been involved in training activities, the Chinese were
implicated in an attempted coup.

These revolutionary activities of Peking, injudicious, ill-planned
and ill-timed, have produced sharp reactions because they have
touched two tender points. Nearly all the leaders of the newly
independent states are faced with dangerous problems of internal
dissent, tribal conflict, or territorial secession, and thus regard any
exacerbation of these tensions by external elements to be a direct

threat to themselves and their own power. Furthermore, all the new African states are sensitive and insecure about respect for their independence and take foreign political interference to be a grave affront.

Nor has it been only the subversive activities of China which have caused anxiety and produced resentment. The general bellicosity of the Chinese posture in world affairs is worrisome to the African nations, nearly all of which feel that a minimum condition of their survival is to keep great-power confrontations out of Africa and to avoid the outbreak of another general war.

In this context of African apprehension, the increasing brutality of the Sino-Soviet split as reflected in Africa has produced strong negative reactions. In the late 1950s the Chinese-Soviet differences, although indicative of basically different points of view on important questions of strategy, were still only occasional, indirect, and relatively dignified. But what began as hardly more than a clear lack of coordination later developed into an all-out ideological struggle in which the Chinese have been the aggressors. The turning point came about 1959, when the Soviets and the Chinese broke on the crucial question of priority as between coexistence diplomacy and revolutionary action, although the split did not become public until late 1963. The Chinese have charged repeatedly and with increasingly violent language that Mocow's general willingness to subordinate the "struggle against imperialism" to coexistence is a betrayal of the colonial liberation movements and the people of the underdeveloped countries. Russia is not merely accused of collaborating with capitalism but is described as a rich, powerful, industrialized country whose conduct is less and less distinguishable from that of the former colonial and imperialist powers. Russian "revisionism" is insistently identified with American "imperialism." The shrillness eventually reached in the tone of the attack is reflected in the following dispatch of the New China News Agency of May 24, 1967:

> At present the imperialists, aided by the modern revisionists, are making frantic attempts to carve up Africa into their own spheres of influence in order jointly to continue exploiting the African toiling masses. While the U.S. imperialists are pouring in so-called aid, the revisionists are peddling the Tashkent spirit and emphasizing the need for economic development of the so-called underdeveloped African countries through *imperialist* aid. [Emphasis added].

China's violent criticism of Soviet economic assistance is intended in part to discredit the idea that socialism can be reached through gradual evolutionary change. Soviet aid has been condemned as a "nostrum for all the ills of the oppressed nations."[7] The content and the purpose of Soviet foreign aid, the Chinese insist, should be questioned by the recipient countries. In giving aid, Soviet leaders "often take an attitude of great power chauvinism and national egoism"; they attach conditions which "harm the economic and political interest of the receiving countries"; and they give aid for "ulterior motives."[8] Finally, threaded through the attack is the steady theme of race—of the identification of the Soviet Union with the "white nations" and of China with the nonwhites of the world.

This unremitting barrage has been disseminated in Africa via radio broadcasts, the New China News Agency, a flood of subsidized pamphlets and books, and various "friendship societies" which operate in at least ten independent African states as cultural organizations rather than political parties. But perhaps the main arenas in the ideological battle have been the two international Communist-front organizations, the World Peace Movement and the Afro-Asian Peoples' Solidarity Organization and their many affiliates and appendages, with the Soviets championing the former and the Chinese the latter. At the Stockholm meeting of the World Peace Council in late 1961, Chinese spokesmen declared that disarmament slogans were inapplicable to nations struggling for liberation and that national liberation movements should not sacrifice their objectives for the sake of "peaceful coexistence." Although the Soviet view prevailed on that occasion in the final wording of the resolutions, the Chinese pursued their charges at the Conference of Afro-Asian Writers held in Cairo in February 1962, where neutral participants described the Chinese performance as "Russian-baiting." It was in the lobbies of this Conference that Chinese representatives were first reported to have talked of the need for the "colored nations" to band together against "the whites."[9]

The third Afro-Asian Peoples Solidarity Conference met at Moshi, Tanganyika, in early February 1963 in a highly charged atmosphere of factional struggle. Throughout the conference, the Chinese attacked every Soviet position, every Soviet-sponsored organization, and all Soviet representatives. At the fourth meeting held in Algiers in March 1964, the same tactics were pursued, leading one member of the Kenyan delegation to complain:

We are not Marxist–Leninists and most of us have never read a single line of *Das Kapital*. So what interest do you have in our participating in your doctrinal quarrels? I have had enough, when I am eating a sandwich, of being accosted by someone who asks me what I think of the Soviet positions and, when I am drinking coffee, by someone who questions me about the Chinese arguments. I would like to be able to eat in peace.[10]

By any ordinary measure it would appear that after a good beginning in winning diplomatic recognition in Africa, China has now sacrificed most of those gains and has generated widespread resentment and fear as a result of its political and propaganda tactics. In this sense, Chinese policy, at least in the short run and as regards present African leadership, has been a failure. The evidence of the failure is so obvious that the Chinese cannot be unaware of it; and the fact therefore that the present policy line is not only being maintained but intensified raises important questions regarding the time scale and objectives of Chinese strategy. Before exploring these, certain details of Chinese military and economic programs in Africa merit review.

CULTURAL, EDUCATIONAL, MILITARY, AND ECONOMIC PROGRAMS

Chinese programs in general have been severely limited by a lack of resources and logistical capability. Unlike the other major powers, for instance, China does not even have its own air services with Africa. One task of its planners and administrators has therefore been to make maximum impact with minimum outlay in behalf of Chinese objectives. For this reason, perhaps, considerable emphasis has been given to the more showy forms of cultural relations and diplomatic contact. In 1966, for example, Peking received no fewer than 143 African "cultural" delegations and sent 162 groups and delegations to Africa, including acrobats, music and dance ensembles, and a basketball team. Another preferred activity has been state visits by Chinese leaders to Africa and of African leaders to China. The large-scale receptions and celebrations that have greeted Africans on their arrival in Peking have apparently made a considerable impression on some of them. Likewise, China has regularly organized mass rallies of its own citizens in support of African causes to impress Africans with their interest and concern. Thus hundreds of thousands of Chinese gathered in late November 1964 at the Gate of the Heavenly Peace in Peking to protest the U.S.-Belgian airdrop into Stanley-

TABLE 16. Communist China's Trade with Less Developed
Countries and with Africa, 1964–66

(In millions of U.S. dollars)

	Chinese Exports			Chinese Imports		
	1964	1965	1966	1964	1965	1966
Total, all less developed countries:	389.4	438.1	555.4	299.2	385.6	335.9
Total, all African less developed countries[a]:	48.9	85.7	104.7	41.3	68.9	44.8
Algeria	4.2	5.6	7.0	. . .	2.6	3.2
Angola	b	. . .	. . .	0.2	b	. . .
Cameroon	b	. . .	0.3	0	. . .	. . .
Chad	0.5	. . .	0.6	. . .	. . .	. . .
Congo (B)	. . .	. . .	. . .	0.3	. . .	. . .
Congo (K)	. . .	. . .	. . .	n.a.	n.a.	n.a.
Dahomey	. . .	0.5	0.6	. . .	. . .	. . .
Ethiopia	1.8	2.7	2.6	0	0.1	0.5
Gabon	. . .	. . .	. . .	. . .	. . .	. . .
Ghana	2.7	14.7	7.5	2.8	5.7	5.2
Guinea[b]	n.a.	n.a.	n.a.	n.a.	n.a.	n.a.
Ivory Coast	0.5	. . .	0.2	. . .	. . .	b
Kenya	1.9	2.7	5.4	1.1	1.8	2.6
Malagasy Republic	0.3	1.6	2.9	. . .	b	n.a.
Mali	2.8	9.8	10.0	2.0	b	b
Morocco	11.8	11.9	16.4	12.3	9.2	7.8
Mozambique	b	b	b	0.2	. . .	. . .
Niger	0.5	1.8	2.5	. . .	. . .	. . .
Nigeria	8.8	13.6	14.1	1.6	2.0	. . .
Rhodesia	. . .	0.1	0.1	. . .	b	. . .
Senegal	3.3	3.0	4.1	. . .	. . .	. . .
Sierre Leone	0.8	1.3	1.5	. . .	n.a.	n.a.
Somalia	. . .	. . .	. . .	n.a.	n.a.	n.a.
Sudan	6.6	6.6	10.5	4.9	15.4	11.2
Tanzania[c]	0.9	4.9	10.4	6.5	12.1	9.5
Togo	0.6	0.6	1.3	. . .	. . .	. . .
Tunisia	0.2	1.6	1.7	0.3	2.5	0.8
Uganda	0.7	2.7	4.8	9.1	17.5	3.4
Zambia	. . .	. . .	0.2	. . .	. . .	0.6

[a] Excluding United Arab Republic.
[b] Less than $50,000.
[c] Data for Tanganyika only.

ville, an action which had aroused much agitation in Africa at the time.

China has made a considerable effort in Africa to reach the youth through the establishment of book shops, publications programs, and friendship societies. However, the more costly forms of educational and technical assistance have been severely restricted. As of 1966, only a handful of technical trainees from Africa were in China, and less than three hundred African academic students were estimated to be in Chinese institutions of higher education. At the end of 1967, some fifty African trainees were estimated to be in China, while the number of academic students dwindled to almost nothing as the turmoil of the Cultural Revolution continued to disrupt all academic life.

In its military assistance, China has been willing to make limited offers to certain selected states: Guinea, Mali, Somalia, Zanzibar, and later Tanzania. But on the whole, it does not seem inclined to provide military help to the armies of the present governing elites. Moreover, Chinese industrial limitations are such that it is unable to offer large quantities or sophisticated types of equipment. China has been ready, even eager, however, to offer military aid (essentially small arms and communications equipment) to the guerrilla forces of various southern liberation movements and to a few rebel groups in independent Africa, including the Congo, Cameroon, and reportedly Kenya. To date, however, such assistance, though it has helped emphasize China's revolutionary image, has had little more than a nuisance value from a military standpoint.

Chinese economic activities in Africa until very recently have also been on a minor scale. The total volume of Chinese trade with less developed countries is relatively small, though it has been growing in percentage terms at a lively rate. The volume of $688 million in 1964 jumped 19 per cent to $824 million in 1965, and to $891 million in 1966. Of this, about one-fifth, or $155 million,

---

NOTE: Data are based on official trade statistics of the Free World involved —that is, Communist exports and imports indicated are the Free World countries trading partners' reported exports and imports. In some cases where such data were not available, independent estimates were made. A leader entry (...) indicates that no figures for trade are known, although some trade may have taken place. Totals are derived from unrounded data and may not agree with the sums of the rounded components.

SOURCE: *Research Memorandum*, RSB-80, July 21, 1967, U.S. Department of State.

was with Africa in 1965, concentrated on Algeria, the Sudan, Tanzania, Uganda, Morocco, Ghana, and Nigeria. Table 16 indicates the scattered and limited character of the movement of trade taking place between 1964 and 1966.

China has sought to conclude trade agreements with all the less developed countries, and by 1965, according to a report by China's Foreign Trade Department, such arrangements had been completed with sixty African and Asian countries.[11] In general, the totals set as goals in the various trade agreements with the African countries have not been reached; indeed, trade has typically fallen far short of anticipated levels. Internal Chinese problems have limited its imports from Africa, and in a number of instances African buyers have found Chinese goods to be inferior in quality and not advantageous in price.

Table 17 indicates that Chinese economic aid in Africa for the continent as a whole until the year 1968 was as inconsequential as Chinese trade. Through 1967 China had made aid offers totalling only $296 million, the bulk of it concentrated in the more radical

TABLE 17. Communist China's Offers of Economic Credits and Grants, 1954–67, and Years 1966 and 1967

(In millions of U.S. dollars)

	1954–67	1966	1967
Total, all less developed countries:	893	31	49
Total, African less developed countries:	296	11	21
Algeria	50		
Central African Rep.	4		
Congo (B)	25		
Ghana	40		
Guinea	25		
Kenya	18		
Mali	23	3	
Mauritania	4		4
Somalia	22		
Tanzania	53	8	
Uganda	15		
Zambia	17		17

SOURCE: *Research Memorandum*, RSB-80, July 21, 1967, and RSE-120, August 14, 1968, U.S. Department of State, Washington.

states—Algeria, Congo-Brazzaville, Ghana, Guinea, Mali, and Tanzania. Kenya, Uganda, Somalia, and Zambia had also received offers because of special political circumstances in those countries which the Chinese were seeking to exploit. In 1967 the only significant Chinese offer, one of $17 million, was to Zambia. But if Chinese aid through 1967 had distinguishing characteristics other than the insignificance of its scale, they were essentially its relatively heavy emphasis on the support of technicians working in Africa (of whom there were 2,600 in 1965 and slightly over 3,000 in 1966 and 1967), and the effectiveness with which a number of small individual aid projects selected for their possibilities of producing quick and visible results had been executed. Chinese technicians have been competent and hard working, but on the whole the aid given has been of such a nature and scale as not to have made any fundamental difference to African economic development—a fact of which the Africans generally are well aware.

In a spectacular move in the early months of 1968, however, the Chinese offered a huge credit of $300 million (value estimated by Western experts on the basis of construction costs) to Tanzania and Zambia to build a railroad from Dar es Salaam on the Indian Ocean to the copper-producing areas of northern Zambia. Although preliminary indication of the action had been given in September 1967, Western observers and many Africans had been doubtful that it would ever be made, and even after its formal announcement they were skeptical of its seriousness. It was doubted that any considerable proportion of the offer would ever be drawn down, partly because of a suspected inability of the Chinese to deliver and partly because of expectations that Tanzania and Zambia would be unwilling to accept the political conditions which would probably be demanded by the Chinese as the *quid pro quo*. Within weeks, however, Chinese technicians by the hundreds began to arrive in Dar es Salaam, and preliminary surveys for the construction for the new rail link were begun. Since then, further evidence has accumulated that the project is seriously moving forward.

Apart from whether or not the Tan-Zam railroad is ever completed by the Chinese, the offer itself is suggestive of the assumptions and objectives of the world's leading revolutionary power regarding the future of Africa. At least since 1960 China seems to have operated on the theory that the present regimes are on the whole transitory, incapable either of retaining power or of solving the development problems confronting them. It has appeared to be a matter of indifference to China therefore whether its actions were popular or unpopular with the existing regimes so long as they confirmed the Chinese revolutionary position in the eyes of dissident groups and the general populace.

This suggests that not only is China gambling on revolution rather than evolution in Africa, but also that in its judgment the most imminent point of eruption is in the south over the issue of race. The offer to finance the Tan-Zam railroad can, therefore, be read as a summary statement in specific assistance terms of the Chinese assessment of the prospects for Rhodesia, race relations, and political stability in Africa in the years ahead. It represents a gamble of grand proportions—which could produce spectacular failure or the kind of success whose repercussions would extend the length and breadth of Africa and beyond.*

CHINA'S ROLE

Judged by their most obvious appearances and effects, with the exception of the Tan-Zam railroad, Chinese efforts to date in Africa might be written off as minor, contradictory, and largely unsuccessful. They have scattered about bits of economic assistance and propaganda; they have meddled and probed; they have made a few spectacular diplomatic gestures. But they have also been caught in a number of scandals. Although they have made many loud and harsh noises about other foreign aid to Africa, they themselves have on the whole failed to deliver meaningful economic, military, or even political support to matters the Africans cared about. They have gained some diplomatic recognition, but they have few real supporters among present African leaders and have now an increasing number of opponents. They have not been able to establish either mass parties or effective front organizations in independent Africa. With the various Southern African liberation movements the Chinese have been able, by giving financial support and arms, to create a Sino-Soviet split in some of them, but their penetration is still far short of control.

It would be plausible, therefore, to dismiss the short-term and

* In late May 1968, a second major Chinese railroad project was reported, namely, a $50 million offer to construct a rail link between Guinea and Mali. This raised interesting new questions regarding long-term Chinese objectives in West Africa. But, before the project could get under way, a military coup in Mali changed the political complexion of that government and resulted in the ousting of Chinese representatives and technicians from the country.

immediate significance of the first decade of Chinese programs in Africa in this fashion, and it may prove to be correct that the Cultural Revolution has immobilized Chinese policy in Africa as elsewhere. But, in a somewhat longer time perspective, the Chinese revolutionary potential in Africa should not too readily be dismissed. Whatever the successes or failures of the total Chinese performance in Africa to date, the present Chinese regime has repeatedly indicated that it attaches great importance to its relationships with the underdeveloped countries and believes it can operate to advantage in them. As long ago as 1949, the Chinese announced their claim to ideological leadership of revolutionary movements in "colonial and semi-colonial countries." Since then, China has worked to shift the center of the world revolution to the zone of the Third World and the so-called national liberation movements.

In ideological terms, China asserts that Africa, Asia, and Latin America are today *the main focus of world contradictions* and that the struggle of the nationalist movements in these ex-colonial, colonial, and underdeveloped countries against imperialism will be decisive for their own victory and for the victory of the Communist proletarians in the advanced countries as well. Lenin of course has assigned the role of savior of the world to the "internal proletariat" of the developed countries, under whose leadership the colonial peoples would gain their liberation. In this respect the Chinese have turned Lenin inside out.

In strategic terms as well, Maoist China sees the importance of the Third World as crucial. In the words of Marshal Lin Piao, the Chinese Minister of Defense:

Taking the entire globe, if North America and Western Europe can be called the "cities of the world," then Asia, Africa, and Latin America constitute the rural areas of the world. Since World War II, the proletarian revolutionary movement has for various reasons been temporarily held back in the North and West European capitalist countries, while the People's Revolutionary Movement in Asia, Africa, and Latin America has been growing vigorously. In a sense, the contemporary world revolution also presents a picture of the encirclement of cities by the rural areas. . . . Comrade Mao Tse-tung's theory of the establishment of rural revolutionary base areas and the encirclement of the cities from the countryside is of outstanding and universal practical importance for the present revolutionary struggles of the oppressed nations and peoples and particularly for the revolutionary struggles of the oppressed nations and peoples in Asia, Africa, and Latin America against imperialism and its lackeys.[12]

Africa and Latin America constitute for Peking areas of priority interest in both the short and the long term second only to that of the Asian mainland itself and markedly more important for Chinese objectives than for the short-term objectives, at least, of the Soviet Union. Moreover, China believes that it can operate advantageously in these areas in competition with both the Soviet Union and the Western powers. It sees itself as a nation—impoverished, underdeveloped, non-Western, and nonwhite—in basic harmony with the problems, outlook, and emotions of the underdeveloped world.[13] It believes that they share the view that all international objectives, including the diplomatic struggle for peaceful coexistence, must be subordinated to the general struggle against imperialism, and China is not worried about the risks if conflicts in distant countries are pushed to the brink and even beyond. Herbert Dinnerstein effectively summarizes this viewpoint:

> For the Chinese in areas far from the mainland of China, the encouragement of revolutionary activity in underdeveloped countries is the only way they have of coping with the totality of American power, whereas the Soviet Union has a varied range of instruments at its disposal—e.g., technological advances, especially in missiles and space; military preponderance in Europe; weapons test moratoria; the partial test ban treaty . . . this [Chinese strategy] is, in essence, an international variant of the strategy of the Chinese Revolution: the weaker force wears down the stronger by guerrilla tactics until the latter's strength is reduced and it can be directly engaged.[14]

Another fundamental element in the Chinese approach to Africa has been an unquestioned confidence in the validity and applicability of the Chinese revolutionary experience to other underdeveloped areas and in eventual victory through the pursuit of these methods. The Peking regime sees its "stupendous, sublime, glorious and victorious revolutionary movement"[15] as the "prototype of the revolutions in colonial and semi-colonial countries."[16] In turn, it holds the view that revolutionary movements must be violent in order to generate and release—under the party's control —what Mao sees as the miraculous energy of the masses, the "spiritual atom bomb." This concept of mobilizing the "revolutionary will" of the oppressed masses—i.e., their rage and hatred for an enemy—is the basis of Mao's military thinking. The masses are galvanized by a "reign of terror," which is to say, by abnormal conditions of insecurity and stress which makes possible the conversion, liberation, or salvation of individuals and nations.

This conviction, arising from their own direct revolutionary experience, causes the Chinese leaders to affirm that in Africa, as elsewhere, the basic struggle requires a tough, unyielding, disciplined approach without compromise, moderation, or concession to achieve short-term advantage. Their view, for example, that there should be no cooperation with bourgeois or democratic elements unless the Communists are firmly in control, is rooted in their own history. In 1927 their collaboration in a subordinate role with Chiang Kai-shek led to bloody repression of the Communist party. From their own experience, likewise, they are convinced that the peasantry is the mainspring of revolution in countries at the stage of economic development of most of the Third World. Their contempt for moderation and short-term solutions has to be interpreted in light of the fact that they unleashed civil war in China after 1946 in disregard of the U.S.S.R.'s advice to find compromise and a collaborative solution—and they won.

In pursuing a hard line the Chinese appear satisfied that nearly all the present governments in Africa are inherently incapable of solving the problems of development and that in time they will inevitably disintegrate in confusion and be forced to rely increasingly on repression. Therefore Peking should make no concession to them and should not assist them or even be disturbed by their disapproval or hostility. The faith of the party in a final revolutionary outcome remains undisturbed. Thus, *The People's Daily*, commenting in 1967 on the situation in the Third World, said: "Although the patriotic guerrilla forces in Asia, Africa, and Latin America may be weak and small and may face a multitude of difficulties today, they will assuredly be able to grow in strength and size, win major victories after winning minor ones, and establish with guns a land of the people provided they rely on the people and persist in struggle."[17]

Finally, in interpreting the Chinese reaction to the results of their activities in Africa to date, the growing and decisive importance of the ideological and organizational struggle between the Russians and the Chinese for control of the international Communist movement must be kept in mind. The fact that Burundi may withdraw diplomatic recognition from China may be of small moment to Peking if the actions provoking the rupture helped score a point in its favor in the world-wide ideological arena.

China's dedication to its own conceptions of violence and revolution, confidence in the long-term victory to be achieved in the underdeveloped areas of the world, and determination to wrest the torch of Communist and revolutionary leadership from Russia, are at present the distinctive features of its foreign policy. So long as that policy continues, Africa remains an obvious focus of interest. Given its chaotic internal situation, such energies as China is currently able to apply beyond its borders are being directed very largely, but not entirely, to the adjacent areas of Southeast Asia. But, over the longer term, China must be considered a factor of continuing and disturbing potential influence in Africa unless and until political changes within China should bring a new leadership prepared to heal the rift with the Soviet Union and to turn fully and definitely inward to concentrate on the stabilization and development of China itself.

Communism's Performance and Prospects in Africa

The brief decade in which the Soviet Union and China have been directly involved in Africa has been one of many problems and many changes for both countries and for the world Communist movement generally. The period began with the advent of Khrushchev in Russia and of coexistence in Communist policy. In the years since, centrifugal forces have fractured the unity of the Soviet bloc and opened a gulf between the Soviet Union and China. Both Communist powers in these years have faced severe internal political strains and major economic difficulties. Both have also made great advances in their military technology. The Soviet Union has added hydrogen bombs to its atomic arsenal and intercontinental ballistic missiles to deliver them, and has seen China, its erstwhile partner, undergird an increasingly antithetical policy position with atomic and then hydrogen weapons and most recently with the beginnings of a long-range missile-delivery system.

In the mid-1950s world communism turned to the nations of the so-called Third World as a great field of opportunity, an arena of contest with the West in which it believed it enjoyed fundamental advantages and where it could score decisive victories. The direct entry of the Communist powers into Africa was part of this offensive. But the results, insofar as they can be judged at this early date, cannot be particularly gratifying either to the Soviets or the Chinese. There has been some progress; diplomatic relations have been developed, operating experience has been gained, some conceptions have been refined, and a quality of realism has displaced an earlier optimism. Yet on the whole, the failures have outnumbered the successes, and the instances of plain nonaccomplishment far outnumber both. Communism has attracted few adherents in Africa; neither Communist parties nor Communist-front organizations have developed any strength or substance; no African government has become Communist or attempted seriously to apply Marxist-Leninist principles in its planning and development, nor has any even unequivocally associated itself with "the Socialist camp." Communism has remained an intriguing topic of discussion and occasionally a fleeting object of enthusiasm. But it has made little detectable impact thus far on the actual shape of political evolution in Africa, on the nature or outcome of development efforts, or on the relationship of African states with one another or with the outside world.

The reasons for this are perhaps not so difficult to identify. First, the Communist powers, despite their protestations of support for African independence, development, and liberation, have in the event played it safe and given little. Their contribution to the education or practical training of young Africans has been inconsequential. With few exceptions, their economic assistance has been minor. In trade, they are neither a major nor a particularly attractive market for African products. In the liberation struggles of the countries of the south, the Communist powers have not used such economic capacity as they have to exert pressure on the existing white minority regimes; nor has their material support of the revolutionary movements been of a scale or character to make a decisive difference.

The Africans have not been slow to recognize that the policies of the major Communist powers are directed primarily to the service of their own interests and ends. Leaders in the new states have proved unusually impervious to Communist penetration and ideology. They have insisted on defining their problems in their own terms and finding their own solutions. Even where major Communist arms shipments have encouraged dangerous tensions, as between Morocco and Algeria and between Somali and Ethiopia, the Africans have been able to defuse the situations through their own cooperative efforts. And in the case of the Nigerian civil war, when the federal government in Lagos was obliged to turn to Communist sources to buy arms, the terms of the transaction provided neither Czechoslovakia nor the Soviet Union with a political *quid pro quo*.

The consequences of the Sino-Soviet split and the subsequent bitter struggle for control of the world Communist movement has further weakened the Communist position in Africa. As the contest has moved from the level of ideological debate to organizational rivalry and as the contestants, particularly China, have resorted to increasingly crude and vicious attacks on the motivation, objectives, and character of each other, African sympathizers with communism have reacted not by taking sides but by generally recoiling in disgust. In consequence, the tendency is to believe the worst of the allegations about both: that the Russians in Africa have been stingy, are racial-minded, and have behaved as an arrogant great power; and that the Chinese are a sinister influence with a predilection for subversion and violence which had best be kept out of Africa. The losses for communism in Africa over the past decade are probably even greater than the aggregate negative results of Soviet and Chinese policies and the detrimental effects of the Sino-Soviet rift. In the most fundamental sense, the image and the ideal of communism have been injured.

As a model for development, communism has been undercut not only by the general inapplicability of Communist economic formulas to African circumstances but still more basically by the failure of the Communist countries to sustain their own dynamism of development at a time of extraordinary economic growth in the capitalistic economies of Western Europe, Japan, and the United States.

Communism as a revolutionary model has similarly been undermined, partly because of the inapplicability of both the Soviet and the Chinese revolutionary experience to African circumstances and partly because of the unheroic response, particularly of the Soviet Union, to revolutionary struggles such as Algeria's over which African passions were aroused. The invasion of Czechoslovakia in 1968 further dimmed the Soviet image in Africa—though the spectrum of public reactions, ranging from silence (the Arab states in the North, plus Guinea and Mali) to muted criticism (Nigeria) to more outspoken dismay (most countries), seemingly were dictated by the extent to which countries had become involved in aid and general political relations with the Soviet Union.

In a more special and yet important sense, the attractiveness of communism has faded because it has lost its mystery and its abstraction. For the ardent and radical young African, communism can no longer be thought of simply as an ideology or an ideal.

It is Soviet technicians leaving for home, their suitcases laden with Western-produced soap and stockings. It is Chinese representatives endlessly squabbling with the Russians at an international conference. It is the Russian delegate denouncing the United Nations and blocking its budget at a meeting in New York. It is an African student returned from Bulgaria or Moscow complaining of racial discrimination even more bitterly than his compatriots back from study in the United States. Communism has, in sum, become a plain reality embodied in powerful foreign governments and their attendant bureaucracies, which behave in the ordinary fashion of governments and bureaucracies according to their own interests and requirements. Because of its growing familiarity, communism is now seen not in an aura, but in the light of common day, to be judged not only by its ideals but also by its practical performance.

If this negative estimate of the results of a decade of Soviet and Chinese effort in Africa is accurate, it does not follow, however, that communism in Africa has no future. Three circumstances might readily lead to its resurgence. The first and perhaps least likely would be some degree of reunification in the world Communist movement. Should the Sino-Soviet breach be healed and the Communist countries achieve a surging and sustained economic growth, such a demonstration of the power of the Communist approach would speak more persuasively in Africa than any propaganda. Second is the possibility that present regimes of Africa may clearly fail in their efforts to provide stability, educational opportunity, and economic improvement. In that event, internal pressures of discontent could bring about great disorder and open the way to extremist leaders and doctrines of all kinds. Depending on the world situation when and if such calamities befall the new nations of Africa, a new wave of Communist interest in the continent could develop and under those conditions Communist initiatives might find an unprecedented reception. The third circumstance would be the outbreak of violent revolution along racial lines in the presently white-dominated countries of Southern Africa. Such an eventuality, which cannot be expected soon but which seems almost inevitable over a longer span of time, would present major opportunities for both the Soviets and the Chinese. The struggle of those black populations for freedom, democracy, and self-government would win the sympathy of a great many individuals throughout the world. The spectacle of massive repression and the killing of blacks fighting in behalf of ideals which have become a hallmark of the twentieth-century world would inflame passions throughout the underdeveloped world and elsewhere. For both the Soviets and the Chinese, the situation would present great attractions and promising opportunities, and neither power, if it retained any hope of claiming leadership of revolutionary and progressive forces in the world, could permit the other to outdo it in the speed or vigor of its intervention.

The game of international politics is never over. The two Communist powers may have little to show for their efforts in Africa to date, but neither has given up. A Soviet fleet is cruising the Mediterranean, and Soviet arms are piling up in Algeria. Chinese surveyors and railroad technicians are at work in southern Tanzania and Zambia. The Soviet Union, as a major and established industrial power, is watching and waiting and, in the fashion of a conservative banker in an uncertain situation, is making a large number of small, carefully hedged investments. But China, as one of the dispossessed, has to gamble. Its few chips have been boldly placed on the prospects for race war and revolution. Either or both of the great Communist powers may well prove to be wrong; but the influence of both is a part of the complex of forces in Africa which the nations of Europe, the United States, and Africans themselves will have to take into account in shaping their own plans and policies for the future.

Part Three

The Evolution of Postwar U.S. Policy

8

The Truman-Eisenhower Period

Through most of American history—indeed until rather recently —Africa essentially did not exist as an independent concern of foreign policy. The first contacts between the two continents were made by elements hardly reflecting the finer qualities of either— American slave traders raiding African coasts and African pirates attacking American merchantmen in the Mediterranean. But apart from such occasional encounters, American-African relationships through the eighteenth and most of the nineteenth centuries were indirect and extremely limited. Militarily, economically, and politically, Africa in American governmental policy was only an adjunct to relationships with Europe.

Limited though the interest was, however, American policy early and steadily reflected that duality of approach, that intertwining of idealistic declamations with hard-headed pursuit of national interest, which has been the trademark of American foreign policy. American leaders repeatedly expressed sympathy for the subject peoples of Africa and opposition to colonialism. In parallel, they sought to assure access to the markets and raw materials of the colonial territories for American industry. The price they were prepared to pay in pursuit of each of these separate objectives in terms of risk or obligation was markedly different. In behalf of anticolonial principles they were ready—sometimes eager—to issue pronouncements but unwilling, at least through the nineteenth and the first part of the twentieth centuries, to accept formal commitments or international responsibility. Thus the United States accepted an invitation to attend the first international meeting on Africa, the Congress of Berlin in 1885, but

on the stipulation that it would not be bound by any of the conclusions that might be reached. Likewise, after the First World
War, President Woodrow Wilson's declarations concerning national self-determination and the League of Nations were not
followed by formal American acceptance of the international
agreements subsequently reached. In behalf of commercial and
economic objectives, however, the United States was not only
prepared to sign formal agreements but repeatedly made it clear
that it was prepared to send military forces, if necessary, to enforce
what it considered to be its rights.

THE SECOND WORLD WAR

With the outbreak of the Second World War, American isolationism in its traditional form gave way to a new approach to international affairs. But the duality of the attitude toward Africa
with its contrasting and often contradictory aspects of cloudy
idealism and concrete self-interest survived to a considerable extent. During the past twenty-five years or so, a continuing evolution of American policy has taken place which is fascinating to
retrace not only for what it reveals of the changing relationship
between the major continents, but also for what it suggests about
the kind of nation the United States has become in the latter part
of the twentieth century and the values and priorities which now
appear to control its conduct in the international community.

President Franklin D. Roosevelt gave strong emphasis to the
anticolonial aspect of the dual tradition during the Second World
War. He repeatedly and insistently—even during the most intense
phase of the combat—made clear to the European allies his
conviction that the Age of Imperialism was over and that it would
become essential after the war for them to loosen their control
over their colonies and to improve the condition of the indigenous
peoples. His purpose in pressing these ideas seems to have been
more than purely altruistic, believing as he did that if the harsh
imperialism of the older colonial powers were replaced by a more
liberal and humane American penetration, there would be advantages to American comerce as well as to the natives.[1] While the
fighting was going on, however, these long-term political objectives
had to be reconciled with immediate military necessities, which
at times intersected them at right angles. When in 1942 the Allies
were preparing the North Africa landings as prelude to an eventual
invasion of the southern flank of Europe, the thorny problem arose

of formulating a line of policy that would accommodate the pledges of the Atlantic Charter, the interests of the rising forces of nationalism in the North African territories, and the practical need to lessen the likelihood of active Vichy French resistance to the Allied landing. The problem was resolved, consciously or unconsciously, by the method of plain inconsistency.

Secretary of State Cordell Hull, a vigorous supporter of President Roosevelt's anticolonialism, said on July 23, 1942:

> In this vast struggle, we Americans stand united with those who, like ourselves, are fighting for the preservation of their freedom; with those who are fighting to regain the freedom of which they have been brutally deprived; with those who are fighting for the opportunity to achieve freedom.
>
> We have always believed—and we believe today—that all peoples, without distinction of race, color, or religion, who are prepared and willing to accept the responsibilities of liberty, are entitled to its enjoyment. . . . It has been our purpose in the past—and will remain our purpose in the future—to use the full measure of our influence to support the attainment of freedom by all peoples who, by their acts, show themselves worthy of it and ready for it.[2]

Later, on December 19, 1942, speaking of American relations with France in North Africa, he said, "With the victory won and freedom restored to those who have lost it or are seeking it, there would then arise under Point Three of the Atlantic Charter the fullest opportunity for each people to select their leaders and their forms of government."[3]

Meanwhile, back at the front a rather different line of policy was being developed during that same year. In late summer General Eisenhower, the Allied Commander for the North African invasion, had received specific instructions to avoid embittering the French authorities then in control of the area. The arrangements worked out with General Henri Giraud, the French representative, put the Allies clearly on record in favor of the full restoration of French sovereignty with no mention of concessions to the local Moslems or their leaders. Ambassador Robert Murphy, then a special diplomatic representative of the President, conducted the negotiations which led to the so-called Giraud-Murphy Accords. On a visit to General Eisenhower's headquarters in London in September of 1942, he explained the reasons for Giraud's insistence that the command in North Africa be French: "This was not personal ambition, which Giraud never had, but a matter of guaranteeing French sovereignty and of demonstrating to the Arabs and Berbers American acceptance of it."[4] Then on November 2, 1942, Ambassador Murphy in a letter to General Giraud gave an iron-bound guarantee to the French which was in direct contradiction to the policy statements of Secretary Hull of the same period:

> I am in a position to assure you that the restoration of France, in all her independence, in all her grandeur and in all the area which she possessed before the War, in Europe as overseas, is one of the aims of the United States.
>
> It is well understood that French sovereignty should be reestablished as soon as possible over all territories, Metropolitan as well as colonial, over which the French flag waved in 1939.
>
> The Government of the United States considers the French nation as an ally and will treat it as such.
>
> I add that in case of military operations on French territory (either Metropolitan or colonial), in all instances where the French collaborate, the American authorities will in no way intervene in affairs which are solely the province of the national administration or which derive from the exercise of French sovereignty.[5]

Anticipating the need, even while the fighting was still in progress, for a more coherent basis of American policy toward Africa in the postwar period, the State Department issued a significant statement on the subject on August 19, 1943, in the form of a speech by Henry Villard, Assistant Chief of the Division of Near Eastern Affairs. Villard unequivocally reaffirmed the determination of the United States to ensure for itself and other nations equal access on equal terms to the trade and raw materials of Africa. Second, he ventured to suggest that opportunities for American aid to Africa after the war would be very great in fields of education, medicine, and social welfare in general, and he seemed to imply the possibility of U.S. government assistance in addition to that of missionary and philanthropic societies.

Third, he raised forthrightly the delicate problem of American interest in the political aspects of the colonial question. Although it was "improbable that the United States would alone accept jurisdiction or control over any part" of former enemy territories in Africa, he nonetheless asserted plainly, almost aggressively, the American right to interest itself in the future treatment of Africa and its inhabitants.

> We reserve to ourselves full liberty of discussion on such important questions affecting the advance of mankind. But in fairness to the

colonial powers who are our allies, and for the sake of greater unity in war and peace, we would do well to reflect that we have minorities and territories under the United States' flag who call for self-government. . . . If we consider how thorny are the problems in our own territories, we will be less hasty in reaching conclusions about Africa.

The Villard speech constituted a declaration of intention by the United States to protect its economic rights in Africa in the postwar period, to involve itself in the political issues of the continent, and to accept at least a degree of responsibility in assisting economic development. In the context of the time it was a bold statement that must have given encouragement to nascent African nationalist movements and produced no little disquiet in the European colonial capitals.

In the closing days of the war, delivery date on a number of American wartime pledges concerning self-determination was approaching and more specific policy determinations had to be made, again requiring the reconciliation of competing or conflicting interests and objectives. One of the most acute of these was the question of the future status of ex-enemy territories. On March 25, 1944, Secretary Hull had stated:

There rests upon the independent nations a responsibility in relation to dependent peoples who aspire to liberty. It should be the duty of nations having political ties with such peoples, of mandatories, of trustees, or of other agencies . . . to help the aspiring peoples to develop materially and educationally, to prepare themselves for the duties and responsibilities of self-government, and to attain liberty.[6]

During this same period, American military authorities, determined to fortify the former Japanese islands in the Pacific that had been captured by American forces, wanted a free hand. The upshot was that at San Francisco in 1945 in the negotiations which led to the creation of the United Nations and its trusteeship system, the United States initially stated a strong position in favor of international responsibility but later began to pull back. Thus, Edward Stettinius, Mr. Hull's successor as Secretary of State, declared on May 15, 1945:

It is and has been the unanimous position of the U.S. delegation . . . that one of the basic objectives of the trusteeship system should be to promote the political, economic, and social advancement of the trust territories and their inhabitants, and their progressive development toward self-government in forms appropriate to the varying circumstances of each territory.[7]

But on June 3, 1945, he added the following:

In all the discussions on trusteeship, the United States has continued to stand fast for provisions which will fully safeguard the control by the U.S.—within the trustee system, but on conditions satisfactory to us—of those strategic points in the Pacific which are necessary for the defense of the U.S. and for world security.[8]

A few months later on January 27, 1946, President Truman, speaking on the same subject at a press conference, placed his emphasis entirely upon the Stettinius qualification, saying, "Those islands we do not need will be placed under U.N.O. trusteeship, and those we need we will keep, as long as we need them."

THE TRUMAN YEARS

That crisp comment was an accurate indication of the balance which was to be struck by the Truman administration between the objectives of anticolonialism on the one hand and of U.S. security requirements on the other. For a short period after the war, the spirit of wartime collaboration with the Soviet Union had persisted in the policy councils of the American government, although even in the closing months of the war the new Truman administration had become conscious of increasing Russian aggressiveness. In a succession of moves in Eastern Europe and around the whole periphery of the area under its control—from Berlin, Trieste, Greece, and Turkey to Iran, Southeast Asia, and Korea—the signals of a new policy course were unmistakable. With the aid of native Communists, Russian troops converted Hungary, Poland, Yugoslavia, Bulgaria, and Rumania into satellites, and in East Germany, the Russians quickly tightened their political and military grip. Countering the Soviet threat became overwhelmingly the most urgent concern of American foreign policy, and President Truman undertook a series of decisive moves to rebuild American military forces (which had fallen by January 1947 to roughly one million men from their wartime peak in 1944-45 of more than eleven million), to restore the economic and military strength of Europe, and to deal with the most ominous specific outbreaks of violence—beginning with the Communist-supported civil war raging in Greece by early 1947. A major credit to Britain in 1947, economic and military assistance to Greece and Turkey under the Truman Doctrine in the same year, the launching of the Marshall Plan in 1948, and the formation of the North Atlantic Treaty Organization in early 1949 were among the major milestones along the road to what came to be called "containment."

Although President Truman had on occasion reaffirmed the Rooseveltian objectives of economic and political advancement for the colonial areas of the world, these were thrust into the background—indeed the distant background—by the intense focus upon measures to cope with Soviet expansionism. Africa was of little direct concern throughout most of his administration. And yet, the programs of economic and military assistance to Europe had highly significant side-effects upon Africa. An American policy toward Africa therefore existed, but it was derivative if not inadvertent.

In terms of economic development, the war itself as well as the American Lend-Lease program had resulted in an infusion of resources, the scale of which had never previously been known. Military supplies flowed in a steady stream to the African terri- tories; modern roads and railways were constructed, airbases were developed in many places, and ports were enlarged and improved. Wartime demand for African products of all kinds swelled, re- sulting in a rapid growth of trade limited only by the desperately overburdened shipping facilities of the Allies. In turn, the stimulus provided by high prices and a growing market caused far-reaching changes in methods of production and the utilization of African labor.

Subsequently, the Marshall Plan indirectly made possible a resumption of the flow of supplies and development resources to Africa after wartime programs had ended. Launched in mid-1948, it was an American commitment to underwrite European recovery over a four-year period to the extent of $17 billion. In its funda- mental approach, the Plan emphasized the mutual and self-help of the European participants and was designed and administered with careful respect for their sovereignty and sensibilities. It left largely to the European partners the formulation of economic plans, the allocation of American assistance, and the specific control of expenditures. The colonial powers insisted, and Ameri- can authorities accepted, the proposition that aid for the develop- ment of their dependent overseas territories—largely African—was an indispensable adjunct of and requirement for their own eco- nomic recovery.

The Marshall Plan contribution to the development of these areas was provided, in part, from regular program funds, which could be freely employed for this purpose. Three additional special sources could be drawn upon: (1) a fund designed to help accelerate basic economic development through grants and loans for road and railway construction, river and port improvement, reclamation and irrigation, and the construction of power plants and other projects; (2) a fund for the development and procurement of strategic materials through loans—repayable in materials —and through long-term procurement contracts; and (3) a limited technical assistance fund to finance resource surveys, soil analysis, the improvement of transport, and agricultural and health programs.

Although the European governments welcomed American financial assistance for these purposes, they gave no encouragement whatever to American participation in development activities in the territories themselves. Nor did they cooperate with one another in joint planning of transport, power, and other territorial projects of a regional character. On the contrary, they attempted in a variety of ways to preserve their exclusive presence and control in their own domains.

The amounts expended under the Marshall Plan in the colonial territories totaled hundreds of millions of dollars. Andrew M. Kamarck, a respected economist of the World Bank, has in the absence of precise data estimated the volume in these terms:

> The United States came on the African aid scene for a brief period during the Marshall Plan and after, mostly because of the use of local-currency counterpart funds generated in the European aid programs. The amounts of the American aid contribution are lost or obscured in the intricate accounting of these counterpart funds— particularly in France, where a strict division was not maintained between the use of funds in France and overseas. Since during this period France and the U.K. were receiving aid from America and simultaneously extending aid and exporting capital to their currency areas, it is admittedly arbitrary to identify one final user as the "recipient" of aid. But in any case, about half a billion dollars of real resources made available to France and the United Kingdom under the Marshall Plan were passed on to Africa. Most of this went to North Africa, but as much as 100 million dollars of the French and British aid to Sub-Saharan Africa might at least be ascribed to the Marshall Plan. That is, the 100 million dollars is essentially an accounting estimate of the amount of counterpart funds generated by Marshall Plan aid that were made available to

Sub-Saharan French and English colonies. In general economic terms, one could just as well argue that the aid given to African countries by Britain and France during this period was a marginal use of resources, and that if the Marshall Plan aid had not been received in the first place, there would have been no aid to Africa. On this basis, one could label all the French, British and Portuguese aid to Africa during this period as indirect American aid.[9]

Similarly, the side-effects of American military assistance to Western Europe after the formation of the North Atlantic Treaty Organization in 1949 were enormous upon the colonial areas. This was particularly true in the case of France, which during that period was conducting major military undertakings first in Indochina and later in Algeria. The aid received took several forms. Nearly half the bilateral military aid given to NATO countries went to France as part of the effort to build barriers to Soviet expansion in Europe. In addition, while the Indochinese War lasted, the United States paid an increasing share of its annual cost. In 1952 and 1953, special U.S. financial support was granted to the French military budget because of the strains of this effort, and by 1954 the United States was assuming close to three-quarters of the total burden. Promptly after its defeat in that contest, France's principal military interest shifted to Algeria where fighting had by then intensified. Under the terms of the NATO Alliance (by which Algeria was considered a part of France itself for defense purposes) France was able to divert to Algeria more and more of the troops it had committed to NATO, and more and more of the military equipment that had been supplied to it for the defense of Europe. The wide gap which progressively opened between the military priorities of NATO and those of France provoked no audible protest from the United States.

NATO arrangements also provided France with important additional economic benefits. Within the framework of the Mutual Assistance Program, the instrumentality developed under American policy for strengthening the NATO structure, large quantities of French armaments were purchased through the "offshore procurement" program, which, while strengthening the French military establishment, also helped France indirectly in its foreign exchange balance.[10] It can fairly be said, therefore, that the American government during the Truman administration was to a large degree the financier and the arms supplier for two major French colonial wars, in Indochina and Algeria, and the financier of France's effort in the first postwar decade to restructure its empire and consolidate its colonial control through programs of economic development.

The American drive to regenerate the Western alliance and develop united resistance to Soviet policy had not been greeted with universal enthusiasm within Western Europe. As a necessary price to be paid for their cooperation in the primary task, the European recipient countries were permitted to employ a significant proportion of U.S. economic and military aid in their own dependent territories. The magnitude and the consequences of such diversion of resources has often been overlooked both by American defenders and European critics of alleged American anti-colonialism.

Two other consequences of the programs of economic and military cooperation between the United States and Western Europe were important for colonial developments and should also be noted. The first was psychological: by the financing and the arms provided to France and Britain, the United States permitted and indeed encouraged them (particularly France) to prolong their illusions of world power and empire, thereby impeding readjustments of attitude that their gigantic war losses would surely have forced upon them much earlier. The second effect was to reduce the independence of U.S. policy in general. By the urgency of its concern to rebuild the Western Alliance and erect defenses against the Soviet danger, it made itself particularly vulnerable and responsive to the wishes and requirements of the Western European powers on secondary issues, such as those relating to the colonial areas.

Nonetheless, even under the stress and strict priorities of the cold war the Truman administration did not completely abandon concern for the political and economic advancement of colonial peoples. Supporters of that goal within the Executive Branch were, although subordinated, still active and determined, and their arguments became more persuasive as evidence accumulated of a probing interest on the part of the Soviet Union in extending its influence in the colonial areas. Thus, President Truman was led to assert in the Fourth Point of his Inaugural Address of January 1949: " We must embark on a bold new program for making the benefits of our scientific advances and industrial progress available for the improvement and growth of underdeveloped areas. . . ." Although Congress was slow and restrained in providing appropriations for the Point Four program (not until September 1950 was an appropriation of $34.5 million approved), the legislation further defined the U.S. attitude toward its international role and provided a basis for new programs in later years. In President Truman's view, the program had strategic and economic purposes as well as idealistic. "The Point Four Program," he wrote in his memoirs, "was a practical expression of our attitude toward the countries threatened by Communist domination. It was consistent with our policies of preventing the expansion of Communism in the Free World, by helping to insure the proper development of those countries with adequate food, clothing, and living facilities."

President Truman stated the economic objective in the following terms: "Common sense told me that the development of these countries would keep our own industrial plant in business for untold generations. The resources of such areas as Mesopotamia, Iran, India, North Africa, and huge sections of South America have hardly been touched, and their development would be as beneficial to American trade as to the areas themselves."[11]

American interest in the more difficult issue of political advancement for the colonial areas was also flickeringly manifest during the Truman years, particularly in connection with a series of problems concerning the disposition of the former Italian territories in Africa of Libya, Somaliland, and Eritrea. In these discussions the United States attempted simultaneously to placate its European allies, especially Britain and Italy; to counter Soviet moves to exploit the issue for the benefit of the Italian Communist party; to safeguard American strategic interests and facilities; to keep the friendship of Ethiopia; and to satisfy the reasonable aspirations of the colonial populations. The result, not surprisingly, was a posture somewhat contorted and unsteady. Finally, in late 1949 after a long period of fruitless debate and confusion, it joined in turning the matter over to the United Nations. The General Assembly then decided on early independence for Libya, a ten-year trusteeship under Italian administration for Italian Somaliland, and the federation of Eritrea with Ethiopia. But this result was not reached before the United States and the Soviet Union had changed and even reversed positions several times.

Another arena in which the United States had to take a position on issues of self-determination was the Trusteeship Council of the United Nations. In the late 1940s, as the cold war progressed and the anticolonial attacks of the U.S.S.R. in the Council grew in intensity, the alignment of administering versus nonadministering states tended to sharpen and solidify. Although the United

States, for the most part, felt compelled to support the views of its Western allies on specific issues, it played a somewhat more positive role in the discussions on self-determination than did the other administering authorities. As for its own territorial acquisitions during the war, the United States, despite sharp disagreements between political and military elements within the government, took the initiative in submitting a draft Trusteeship Agreement for the Pacific Islands in 1947. It favored requiring the colonial powers to submit political information on their dependent territories despite the strong opposition of Britain and France. It took the lead in asking the International Court of Justice for an advisory opinion on South Africa's international legal responsibilities for South West Africa in 1949. And in the case of Indonesia, the United States pressed hard on the Netherlands government to accord independence to that populous Southeast Asian colony.

By 1950 the effort of the United States to maintain a generally united front with its Western European allies and at the same time to identify itself with the aspirations of the colonial populations of the world was becoming almost unmanageable. Cold war concerns had intensified after the Soviets detonated their first atomic bomb in 1949 and provoked an outbreak of war in Korea. Awareness of the spreading wave of revolt in the underdeveloped areas also grew. The Nationalist government had collapsed and the Communists had taken over in China; fighting was raging in French Indochina; independence was impending in Indonesia; and many indications of brewing disorders were apparent elsewhere. An address on African policy given in mid-1950 by Mr. George McGhee, then Assistant Secretary of State for Near Eastern and African Affairs,[12] provides graphic evidence of the contradictory and complex concerns of the administration at the time. He began by saying in effect that the United States could not allow Africa through neglect to meet the same fate as China— and that there was still time to act. Looking ahead, however:

> . . . if this is one area in the world where—in the broadest sense— no major crisis exists, then it is imperative that advantage be taken of the absence of pressure to plan against the time when such pressure may be applied.
>
> Advantage must be taken of this period of grace to further the development within Africa of healthy political, economic, and social institutions, to create an understanding on the part of the Africans of the forces of communism which are disturbing the

peace and security of hundreds of millions of peoples elsewhere in the world, and to inspire a determination to resist these forces. . . .

In an unusual and revealing digression, Mr. McGhee commented on the equivocal attitude of Africans toward the United States:

Racial discrimination in the United States has produced unfortunate reactions on the part of many educated Africans. In addition, our ECA [Marshall Plan] program is an important object of suspicion, since there is some tendency to regard this program, as it applies to the overseas territories of the European powers, as a device to strengthen or perpetuate the hold of the European powers over the African territories.

With equal awareness of European sensibilities, he went on to say:

. . . these powers are fearful of what they regard as an apparent American tendency to give indiscriminate and uncritical support to movements toward self-government or independence without adequate consideration of the experience and resources of the peoples concerned. . . . The European powers are convinced that the rate of political advancement for their dependent peoples must be carefully geared to the tempo of progress in economic, social, and educational institutions. They feel that they understand the situation better than we, and they are, in many cases, proud of the progress which has been made.

To indicate that Washington did not intend to behave recklessly in encouraging African nationalism, he said that the United States had to

. . . keep in mind the fact that we are not in position to exercise direct responsibility with respect to Africa. We have no desire to assume the responsibilities borne by other powers and, indeed, our principles, our existing commitments, and our lack of experience all militate against our assumption of such obligations.

With this nuanced reassurance to the metropolitan powers he went on to identify the objectives of American policy:

First, to see that the peoples of Africa advance toward full independence and in accordance with the principles of the United Nations Charter. In the attainment of this objective, however, the United States could play "only a cooperative role with the administering powers."

Second, to assure the development of mutually advantageous economic relations between Europe and Africa in the interest of contributing to the restoration of a sound European economy and of furthering the aspirations of the African peoples.

Third, to preserve the right of the United States to equal treatment and access in the development of the continent.

Fourth, to help provide "an environment in which the African peoples will feel that their aspirations can best be served by continued association and cooperation with the nations of the free world."

The instrumentalities to be employed in pursuit of these goals were primarily economic assistance through the Marshall Plan and technical assistance through the proposed Point Four program, plus information- and educational-exchange programs.

McGhee's statement was an interesting synthesis of earlier American objectives in Africa, such as access to markets and raw materials, the preoccupations of 1950 with communism and the cold war, and the anticipation of coming problems of independence and economic development. It was realistic and candid in its appraisal both of European and African attitudes, and although it was considerate of European sensibilities, it did not back away from the fact of continuing American concern both for political change and for economic and social advancement of the African territories.

President Truman's State of the Union Message to Congress on January 7, 1953, summed up the record of his eight years. He reminded Congress that he had taken office the month before the Nazis surrendered in May of 1945, and that in August the first atomic bomb was detonated over Japan. Building a durable structure of security and avoiding the holocaust of atomic war had been, above all else, "the task of our Republic since the end of World War II." After describing the military efforts he had taken to confront the Soviet offensive, the President asked:

> Did this mean we had to drop everything else and concentrate on armies and weapons? Of course it did not: Side by side with this urgent military requirement, we had to continue to help create conditions of economic and social progress in the world.
>
> There will be no quick solution for any of the difficulties of the new nations of Asia and Africa—but there may be no solution at all if we do not press forward with full energy to help these countries

grow and flourish in freedom and in cooperation with the rest of the Free World.

In these words there was reflected an appreciation of the problems of the emergent areas, but as President he had been preoccupied with rebuilding the defenses of the Western world against Russian aggression. His monument in history would be the bold new policies framed for the United States summed up in the term "containment." Though he was not unaware of, or unsympathetic to, the problems of the colonial territories, these had to be of relatively minor concern in his time and in his policy.

THE EISENHOWER ADMINISTRATION

President Eisenhower took office early in 1953 in an international atmosphere still dominated by the confrontation with the Soviet Union. By the beginning of his second term, however, profound changes had begun to take place within the Soviet Union and the Communist world and throughout the less developed areas, which led to the emergence of a new and more intricate world balance and, in the case of Africa, called for far-reaching revisions of American policy. The adequacy and the timeliness of the Eisenhower administration's response to the new requirements led to great disputes and eventually made Africa for the first time a major issue in American politics.

Stalin's death one month after the new President made his first foreign policy address to the Congress was an omen that the Eisenhower years were destined to be a time of transition in world affairs. By fall of the same year, Malenkov, who had succeeded Stalin, announced that the American monopoly of hydrogen bomb production had been broken, a scientific triumph with important strategic and political consequences. This news added to the fears, suspicions, and divisions in American life which had developed as a malignant by-product of the cold war. The State Department and the Foreign Service were under attack; McCarthyism, loyalty investigations, and the China Lobby were symbolic of the sickness of the times; and a substantial minority in both houses of Congress, distrustful of the Executive Branch, favored passage of the so-called Bricker Amendment intended to redefine and restrict the powers of the President in making treaties and executive agreements.

Faced with challenges abroad and division at home, the new administration essentially continued the Truman policy of containment, changing only some details of substance. But the style and emphasis with which its approach was presented by the incoming Secretary of State, John Foster Dulles, produced great misunderstanding. His references to "liberation" and "rolling back communism" in Eastern Europe stirred disquiet abroad as did his declaration of the doctrine of "massive retaliation" and his avowal of the practice of "brinksmanship." To the less developed countries, it appeared that the United States had become even more obsessed with the Communist threat and less responsive to their particular needs and outlook than it had been during the terms of President Truman. Dulles repeatedly indicated his intolerance for neutralism and "nonalignment," tendencies then increasingly favored by nationalist leaders and the heads of the various Afro-Asian states as they attempted to insulate themselves from—and take advantage of—the competition of the cold war. Likewise, the dogmatic emphasis given to private enterprise in the credo of the new administration ran counter to the prevailing socialistic sentiments of Afro-Asian leaders. From the beginning, therefore, they felt little warmth or sympathy toward the new group in Washington despite the fact that in earlier times both Eisenhower and Dulles had expressed themselves clearly in favor of eventual independence for the colonial areas.

The first major policy statement on Africa made under Secretary Dulles was delivered on October 30, 1953, by Henry A. Byroade, at that time Assistant Secretary of State in charge of the Bureau of Near Eastern, South Asian and African Affairs. Byroade had to wrestle with the same cold war and Western-unity versus anticolonialism dilemma that had been the crux of the problem of American policy toward Africa for nearly a decade. But his formulations suggested that the match was now likely to end in a stalemate. His speech was an ambiguous, self-contradictory, "balanced" statement which satisfied neither the Africans nor the Europeans, but which in the judgment of responsible officials of the American government, or at least the most influential of them, best served the needs and interests of the United States at the time.

Professor Vernon McKay, then a State Department official, subsequently wrote a classic analysis of the Byroade address:

If we strip away the excess verbiage in which the essence of the statement is obscured, however, we will find the following ten passages, five of which tend to nullify the other five:

1. This movement toward self-determination is one of the most powerful forces in twentieth century affairs.
2. We ourselves believe that peace, prosperity, and human freedom can be assured only within a concert of free peoples. . . .
3. We hope that the peoples now seeking self-determination will achieve it. . . .
4. We recognize that the disintegration of the old colonialism is inevitable. We believe that much blood and treasure may be saved if the Western world determines firmly to hasten rather than hamper the process of orderly evolution towards self-determination.
5. The clock of history cannot be turned back. Alien rule over dependent peoples must be replaced as rapidly as possible by self-determination. Of this there can be no question.

And now the reverse:

1. It will be one of the great tragedies of our time if the peoples of Asia and Africa, just as they are emerging from generations of dependence, should be deluded by the fatal lure of the new [Soviet] imperialism and return thereby to an age of slavery infinitely more miserable than they have ever known before.
2. It is a hard, inescapable fact that premature independence can be dangerous, retrogressive and destructive.
3. Unless we are willing to recognize that there is such a thing as premature independence, we cannot think intelligently or constructively about the status of dependent peoples.
4. Premature independence for these peoples would not serve the interests of the United States nor the interests of the dependent peoples themselves.
5. . . . let us be frank in recognizing our stake in the strength and stability of certain European nations which are our allies. They share many common interests with us. They will probably represent, for many years to come, the major source of the free world defensive power outside our own. We cannot blindly disregard their side of the colonial question without regard to our own security.[13]

McKay also concluded:

The careful reader will note that the first five passages quoted above pay appropriate tribute to the principle of self-determination in rational but colorless prose. In the second five passages, however, the "dangers of premature independence" are heavily stressed in emotion-laden words which give the speech its tone—"fatal lure," "blindly disregard," "infinitely more miserable," "hard, inescapable fact," and "dangerous, retrogressive and destructive."

In its evident anxiety about the dangers of "premature independence" in Africa, the Byroade speech seemed to reflect not only the precedence of European over African interests that had been characteristic of American policy in the postwar period, but also a sense of dismay at the growing danger of disorder in the underdeveloped world from Indochina, Iran, and Egypt to many parts of Africa at the very moment when an ominous advance in Russian strategic capability had been announced. The address ended in bafflement and a recommended policy of no-policy: "It is no secret that these problems confront America with a dilemma. The present situation therefore calls frankly for a middle-of-the-road policy which will permit us to determine our position on practical issues on their merits, as they arise."

In the following two years, as the end of the first postwar decade approached, powerful new forces began to shake both the Communist countries and the less developed areas. Within the Soviet Union, Nikita Khrushchev assumed leadership and launched new domestic programs emphasizing agricultural development, consumer goods production, and de-Stalinization. In foreign policy he made "peaceful coexistence" the new party line. In Eastern Europe, strains in relations between Moscow and the satellites increased and threatened to erupt in violence. The war in Korea had been brought to a conclusion; the French had been humiliatingly defeated in Indochina; and the Red Chinese in company with the Soviet Union moved forward with a broad new political, cultural, and economic offensive directed to the colonial and newly independent areas. The Bandung Conference of Afro-Asian states in 1955 gave heightened prominence to the collective political and economic objectives of the underdeveloped countries and to the revolutionary policies of Communist China. In Africa, decisive events were occurring which were shortly to bring the wave of independence and the breaking of colonial control to its crest.

George V. Allen, who had, in the meanwhile, succeeded Henry Byroade as Assistant Secretary of State, delivered on April 21, 1956, the second major policy speech on Africa by an official of the Eisenhower administration.[14] It is a laboratory specimen of the agony of a bureaucratized foreign policy establishment attempting to respond to new circumstances and also of the capacity of the old-line professional diplomat, if afflicted by timidity in the face of change, to make a bad situation worse. In substance it contained little that was new, but it added three embellishments to familiar themes, all offensive to African sensibilities at the time. Fortunately, the speech attracted little attention; otherwise, its effects would have been worse. But because of the revealing nature of some of its phraseology, it is instructive to review.

First, at the moment when a lessening of tensions had just begun to be detected in the international atmosphere, the Allen speech gave crude stress to the cold war and implied that American interest in Africa was essentially strategic.

> The United States' attitude toward colonialism is known. . . . But the application of this principle to present-day foreign policy problems all over the world requires patient understanding and a high sense of responsibility regarding the ultimate and basic security interests of the United States. . . . All of the so-called colonial powers represented on the continent of Africa are our friends and allies in the world-wide contest between the Free and Communist worlds. . . . A strong, free, and friendly Africa is extremely important to United States security.

Second, at a time when the leaders of both the newly independent African nations and the various nationalist movements anticipating independence were especially eager to break free of all remnants of colonial domination, Allen urged the preservation of European links and influence in Africa even after independence. He emphasized the great harm which would result for the European allies if ties with the African territories should be violently disrupted, as well as the dangers of a sudden break of the European "lifelines" for Africans themselves. "Our security interests and our moral interests are both effectively served by the same general line of action—we need friendly and cooperative relations with Europe and Africa, just as their own interests require the maintenance of intimate ties with each other."

Third, and most unfortunate, was Allen's implicit disparagement of the struggle against racism in Southern Africa as the work of "extremists" if not of Communist agents: "Again it behooves us not to become identified with any of the conflicting factions, but rather, while preserving our adherence to our own basic principles of racial equality, to attempt to exert a moderating influence upon the extremists, and to oppose those who are exploiting these tensions for ulterior purposes."

The Allen speech made the administration's policy, which he presumably was seeking to defend, seem worse than it was—at least in African eyes—for in the course of President Eisenhower's first term some shift toward a cautious support for nationalism, as in the cases of Morocco and Tunisia, had emerged. And ironically, this policy statement, which was so backward-looking and immobile in its general approach, was made just when the accumulating pressures for change in many parts of the world were beginning to break through the surface of older arrangements. Early in 1956 three African states became independent, Morocco, Tunisia, and the Sudan; and France, by its enactment of the *loi cadre* in response to mounting nationalist discontents, made far-reaching political concessions to its African territories. Then, later in the year, two occurrences challenged the whole concept of a bipolar world: Disunity within the Soviet bloc was exposed by riots in Poland and revolt in Hungary. Almost concurrently, the unity of the Western bloc was rocked by the decision of Britain and France to join Israel in an attack on Egypt in late October and early November. The United States took an immediate and firm position against the Anglo-French operation and ranged itself with the Soviet Union in forcing them to withdraw without having achieved any of their objectives.

In terms of African policy, the events produced two results: First, the importance of the underdeveloped areas in the general confrontation with communism became greater. The Eisenhower Doctrine was formulated to enable the United States to fill the "power vacuum" resulting from the destruction of British influence in the Middle East with military and economic assistance. Second, the rupture which had occurred between the United States and its most important allies in Europe seemed to have major implications for the future balance to be struck in American policy between conflicting European and African interests. In the reactions of the principal political figures of the Eisenhower administration could be sensed strong feeling, even anger, that Britain and France had proceeded independently on a matter vitally affecting American interests.

Some strain in relationships had long been apparent, as in the statement of Secretary Dulles in the early 1950s threatening the European nations with an "agonizing reappraisal" of American policy and commitments if their performance in the alliance were not improved. Perhaps because of the furious reaction that resulted, a more carefully modulated tone had been adopted thereafter despite continuing serious disagreement on many points of military and economic policy. After the Suez attack, these long repressed feelings again exploded. Both President Eisenhower and

Secretary of State Dulles let it be known that they personally felt let down, even betrayed. Going still further, Vice President Nixon told an audience in Hershey, Pennsylvania, that "for the first time in history, we have shown independence of Anglo-French policies toward Asia and Africa which seem to us to reflect the colonial tradition." Far from being the impetuous outburst of an over-wrought political campaigner, one White House official subsequently revealed that the text had been authorized and written for Nixon by Secretary Dulles himself.[15]

That a breaking away from Europe on colonial questions might be forthcoming in American policy seemed to be confirmed by the fact that in December of 1956, after Suez and after President Eisenhower's re-election, the United States and Russia for the first time voted side by side in the U.N. Trusteeship Council on a procedural question regarding a new status for French Togoland which the French opposed.[16]

Other indications in early 1957 also made it appear that the American government, both in Congress and the Executive Branch, was beginning to be more Africa-conscious. In February Senator Green, Democrat of Rhode Island, issued a report calling for a revision of American policy. Noting that the drive for political independence in Africa was gaining momentum, the Senator called it a "continent in ferment" and said that American policies had failed to keep pace with developments. He called for a new assessment of American interest in the continent and urged that new aid programs, broad in scope and of long-term commitment, be adopted.[17] In February and March of the same year Vice President Nixon paid a month-long visit to eight African countries— Morocco, Ghana, Liberia, Uganda, Ethiopia, Sudan, Libya, and Tunisia—on the occasion of Ghana's independence.

High administration officials as well as prominent members of the Republican party apparently had become convinced that the force of nationalism in Africa was about to explode in a fashion similar to the political changes in Asia in the immediate postwar period. Conscious of their success in making political capital out of the Communist take-over of China during an earlier Democratic administration, they became uneasily aware of a possible boomerang effect if the Asian pattern were repeated in Africa under a Republican regime. They concluded that some new effort —which hopefully would cost little—was required to stop communism from taking root in the new African nations. Even before the Vice President's departure in February, the decision had been taken to create a new Bureau of African Affairs under its own Assistant Secretary of State, and legislative proposals to this end were prepared for presentation to Congress.

The report of the Vice President on his return accelerated the new trend of thinking and precipitated some action within the Executive Branch in the direction of upgrading Africa.[18] In it, he stated that Africa was the most rapidly changing area in the world and that its emergence from colonial status to independence and self-government "could well prove to be the decisive factor in the conflict between the forces of freedom and international communism." He praised the caliber of the new leaders of Africa and recommended that the United States come to know them better, understand their aspirations, and support their plans. He urged that the United States have the strongest possible diplomatic and consular representation to the new countries and consult them on a basis of equality on all matters affecting mutual interests.

Vice President Nixon stressed the importance of eliminating racial discrimination in the United States in order to maintain the good will of Africa; but he did not go so far as to urge U.S. action of any kind with respect to racial issues in Africa itself.

Recognizing the great needs of the new African nations for development, he recommended that the United States provide assistance first by drawing the "attention of private American capital to opportunities for investment," then by supporting "applications before the appropriate international agencies for financing sound economical development projects," and finally by direct U.S. economic and technical assistance, but only "to the extent that our resources and the demands of other areas permit."

His report contained two rather striking departures from previous policy statements: About the maintenance of European-African links after independence, he said they should be continued only "where they are considered mutually advantageous by the states concerned." Second, in contrast to the deference habitually expressed by American spokesmen to the primacy of European relationships to Africa, he said, "We should take them into account in formulating our own policies to the extent compatible with the fundamental requirement of conducting our own relations with these states on a fully equal and independent basis." He also took special note of the importance of trade union developments in Africa, urging that diplomatic and consular representatives get to know African trade union leaders, and he paid tribute to the effectiveness of American trade unions in working with their African counterparts to prevent Communist penetration.

The Nixon report was a mixture of things: a new acceptance of the sovereign place of the African states in world affairs and in American policy; a side-stepping of the touchy issues of Algeria and racism in South Africa; and a concern for African development—but without costly commitments. Nevertheless, it was a milestone in the development of American policy toward Africa in the postwar period. Although it did not fundamentally change the pro-European orientation of the State Department as a whole, it brought African affairs out of bureaucratic limbo and invested them with new dignity; and it accelerated a number of organizational changes which were to be of long-term importance. If his visit and report had a negative aspect in terms of African reactions, it was in its fixation upon the dangers of communism, the implication that Africans alone were incapable of recognizing and resisting the danger, and that American interest was not in Africa itself but as a means for the achievement of U.S. anti-Communist objectives.

Indicative of the tangled threads of American policy at the time, during the very period of Nixon's trip, the U.S. delegation to the United Nations clearly retreated from the post-Suez posture of "anticolonialism" on a number of African resolutions before the U.N. General Assembly. Forsaking the easier alternative of abstention, the United States stood with the colonial powers as they were heavily and repeatedly outvoted by the Soviet and Afro-Asian blocs. Ambassador Lodge told the General Assembly on February 6, 1957 that no "international initiative" should be taken in respect to Algeria, where a colonial war was then raging. On February 26 the United States opposed resolutions which in effect (1) urged France and Britain to give passports to petitioners to the United Nations from the Cameroons; (2) asked administering countries (a) to estimate the time required for trust territories to be given self-government and (b) to insure that self-government would come at an "early date"; (3) asked France to restore political "normalcy" in the Cameroons and; (4) asked Britain to state plans for developing democratic self-government in Tanganyika.

That there was something less than perfect harmony within the foreign policy establishment on African policy issues was also exposed in some curious events that involved Mason Sears, a member of the U.S. delegation to the United Nations. In April 1957, while he was serving on the Trusteeship Council, the United

States co-sponsored a resolution with India calling for free elections in French Togoland. A month later, however, the United States turned an awkward somersault by voting against its own proposal. According to press reports, Washington had learned of the motion and put its foot down after the delegation had already committed itself. Some in New York were amused; officially, Washington was not; and the incident provided evidence of a policy struggle in process.[19]

Developments in Africa were proceeding swiftly. After Britain accorded independence to Ghana, it became obvious to observers everywhere that some kind of watershed had been reached and that a dramatic succession of political events could be expected. From Washington, a series of congressional committees began to visit Africa and came back with reports confirming the general conclusions which had been expressed earlier by Vice President Nixon.

Then on July 2, 1957, the young Senator from Massachusetts, John F. Kennedy, made a speech on the Senate floor about U.S. policy toward Algeria, which was to have a profound impact. No American leader had ever before challenged with such powerful logic and in plain public view the fundamental assumptions and underlying values which had long dominated American policy toward colonialism. Moreover, the speech signaled unmistakably that African issues were on their way to becoming a focus of dispute in partisan politics.

After a detailed review of the failures of French policy in Algeria, Senator Kennedy declared:

> This dismal recital is of particular importance to us in the Senate . . . because of the attitude toward the Algerian question which has been adopted throughout this period by our spokesmen in Washington, Paris, and U.N. headquarters. Instead of contributing our efforts to a cease-fire and settlement, American military equipment—particularly helicopters, purchased in this country, which the natives especially fear and hate—has been used against the rebels. Instead of recognizing that Algeria is the greatest unsolved problem of Western diplomacy in North Africa today, our special emissary to that area this year, the distinguished Vice President, failed even to mention this sensitive issue in his report.

At a later point in his speech Kennedy made an even more sweeping attack on the ideas and tendencies which had come to characterize the foreign policy of the Eisenhower administration:

If we are to secure the friendship of the Arab, the African, and the Asian—and we must, despite what Mr. Dulles says about our not being in a popularity contest—we cannot hope to accomplish it solely by means of billion dollar foreign aid programs. We cannot win their hearts by making them dependent upon our handouts. Nor can we keep them free by selling them free enterprise, by describing the perils of communism or the prosperity of the United States, or limiting our dealings to military pacts. No, the strength of our appeal to these key populations—and it is rightfully our appeal and not that of the communists—lies in our traditional and deeply felt philosophy of freedom and independence for all peoples everywhere.

Kennedy then went on to attack not only the Republican administration, but also the basic concepts of earlier Democratic administrations. First he questioned the feasibility of attempting to ride two horses—of courting the friendship of the colonial powers and the colonial peoples at the same time. Second, he sharply questioned the practical effectiveness of efforts to carry water on both shoulders in the form of what was then called a "balanced" position. He denied that there was any value

> in the kind of discussion which has characterized earlier United States consideration of this and similar problems—tepid encouragement and moralizations to both sides, cautious neutrality on all real issues, and a restatement of our obvious dependence upon our European friends, our obvious dedication nevertheless to the principles of self-determination, and our obvious desire not to become involved. We have deceived ourselves into believing that we have thus pleased both sides and displeased no one with this head in the sand policy—when, in truth, we have earned the suspicion of all.*

Finally, he denied that the policy had been balanced at all and charged that it had in fact been biased in favor of the colonialists: "No matter how complex the problems posed by the Algerian issue may be, the record of the United States in this case is as elsewhere a retreat from the principles of independence and anti-

---

* President Eisenhower's evaluation of the same line of policy was rather different: "America has preserved its position as the friend of all. . . . We have not been drawn into the position of being so completely on one side of a quarrel—any quarrel—due to emotion or sentiment or anything else that we are incapable of carrying out our proper role of mediator, conciliator and friend of both sides when there is any possibility of settling a quarrel." Quoted in Lincoln P. Bloomfield, *The United Nations and U.S. Foreign Policy* (Boston: Little, Brown, 1967), p. 193.

colonialism regardless of what diplomatic niceties, legal technicalities, or even strategic considerations are offered in its defense."[20]

Because of the excellence and courtesy of its style as well as the cogency of its reasoning, the speech amounted to far more than a partisan blast. It was a fundamental criticism of the ideas and judgments which through the whole postwar period had governed American policy in those situations where concrete economic and strategic interests and alliance commitments had to be weighed against American political interests in the emerging areas of the world where independence and human freedom were the issues.

Despite the recommendations for a modified policy toward Africa made by Vice President Nixon early in 1957, the powerful attack by Senator Kennedy in midyear, and repeated minor zigzags of the American position on various U.N. votes affecting Africa, the State Department branch primarily responsible for African affairs remained essentially unmoved. On December 12, 1957, Joseph Palmer 2nd, then the Deputy Assistant Secretary for African Affairs, in a public address once again cautioned Africans of the dangers of "premature independence," and with respect to racialism in Southern Africa he repeated the Allen thesis that the United States should remain uninvolved.[21]

By early 1958 political events in Africa were rushing toward a climax. Several key states had already become independent. The British colonies, following Ghana, were moving at an accelerated rate toward independence, and changes in French policy had opened the way for rapid movement of its territories in West and Equatorial Africa in the same direction. Moreover, a series of precedent-setting international conferences beginning with the first Afro-Asian Peoples' Solidarity Conference held in Cairo on January 1, 1958, drew dramatic attention to African developments. But in Washington, adjustments of policy to the changing circumstances came slowly and hesitantly and were camouflaged by much oratorical obfuscation.

Early in the year, Julius C. Holmes, who was another career officer of long experience, was named to succeed Palmer as interim head of the State Department's Africa unit. His statements during his six-month tenure contained much that was familiar, although some hints and traces of a change of course could be found. He continued to warn of the "dangers of premature independence" and had kind words to say for colonialism, asserting that "both

Africa and the world owe the Metropolitan powers a great debt for the administrative techniques, methods of economic development, the great capital investment and construction, and the educational and public health measures they have brought to the area." On the crucial Algerian question he would go only so far as to say that the United States sincerely hoped that "no avenue will be left unexplored" to bring about a peaceful, democratic, and just solution. On the question of racism in Africa he persisted in the Allen thesis that we should be humble in our approach and that we should exert a "moderating influence upon extremists and oppose those who seek to exploit racial tensions for ulterior purposes." He then added a further caveat, namely that we should avoid "unwarranted interference in the internal affairs of other countries."[22]

But in his speech of May 1, 1958, there was a different note: "However, let there be no mistake about the African atmosphere of 1958, for, although the manner of expression will vary with the area, the general theme is "better the ragged shirt of self-government than the warm blanket of colonial protection."[23]

Finally, in July 1958, Congress authorized the new post of Assistant Secretary of State for African Affairs, to which a prudent and experienced foreign service officer, Joseph C. Satterthwaite, was appointed.*

His first public address was delivered on September 10, 1958. The occasion might have been appropriate for enunciating a visible break with the older line of policy, but such was not Satterthwaite's impulse. Instead, he recited standard themes, and, essentially, he repeated what George McGhee had said eight years before: "We of the West have no time to lose. We must anticipate events, sympathetically understand African aspirations, and help to meet them. . . . The opportunity to develop a sound base for enduring friendly relations and mutual cooperation with an emerging Africa is ours today. We must makes the most of this opportunity without delay." If he struck any new note it was in

---

* Apropos the "mirror image" phenomenon which many observers have remarked in the interaction of U.S. and Soviet foreign policy, it is interesting that in the same week as Satterthwaite's appointment, the Soviet Union announced the creation of a new Department of the Soviet Foreign Ministry to deal solely with African affairs. The Director named was A. A. Chvedov, an experienced professional diplomat previously Deputy Chief of the Middle East Department.

suggesting that the American attitude toward African "nonalignment" should be one of "sympathy and support."

Even though the oratory seemed stuck in the same groove, some actual policy changes were beginning to occur. Economic assistance to Africa, which had totaled $100 million in fiscal 1958, nearly doubled to $185 million in fiscal 1959. At the U.N. General Assembly in 1958, the United States voted consistently for a series of resolutions designed to pave the way for independence of the several U.N. trust territories in Africa.

By early 1959 the new approach began to be reflected in the tone of the new Assistant Secretary's public statements. On the problems of race relations in Africa he dropped most of the unfortunate elements of the earlier official formulations and struck a more positive note in asserting that "the United States cannot ignore the serious dangers inherent in any failure to meet the problem of harmonious and just race relations in Africa's dependent and independent territories. . . . We must regard them with understanding while at the same time continuing as in the past to stand steadfast in all international forums for the principle of non-discrimination and racial equality throughout the world." There was a note of urgency, almost of passion, in his statement:

> As the old Africa refashions its visage and the new, vibrant and politically articulate Africa evolves the United States recognizes the challenge of the hour—a challenge to contribute to the stability and orderly evolution of this giant continent; to be responsive to its needs and sympathetic to its legitimate aspirations. . . . The West must show dedication and imagination and build a new relationship with the dynamic twentieth century Africa based on principles of equality, justice, and mutual understanding.

As 1960 approached, the United States had passed through fifteen years of major foreign policy undertakings in reconstructing Europe and organizing a powerful Western Alliance and other security commitments in Latin America, the Middle East, South Asia and the Pacific. Along with these primary preoccupations it had tried to reconcile its conflicting obligations and interests in relating itself to the emergent colonial areas of the world. Until 1950, hardly the fragments of a policy existed, although in the following decade segments were developed but on a piecemeal basis. Little by little a new approach to Africa was fashioned, but the process was singularly sluggish and uninspired. To read the successive policy formulations over those years is to discover how hopelessly bogged down in word games a bureaucracy and its committee system can become if it lacks the benefit of clear conviction and a sense of direction from the top.*

The Hinge Year—1960

But 1960 was to change everything. That year, seventeen new African nations were admitted to the United Nations—including the Congo, which became independent at the end of June and within a matter of weeks had become the chaotic center of an international confrontation. Impelled by the drama of what was taking place in Africa as well as by the mounting pressures of a domestic political campaign, the Eisenhower administration in its final year scrambled to break free of its earlier paralyzed and contradictory policy. As the months went on, a number of important new steps were taken, significant and constructive decisions were made, and a new and more positive tone toward African affairs and African leadership was introduced. More in fact was done than the administration has generally been given credit for. But what had been lost before action came could not be recaptured.

First, important initiatives were taken in the field of foreign aid. For fiscal 1961, the administration requested from Congress $150 million in special assistance for Africa, $24.3 million in technical assistance, and a new fund of $20 million for grant aid to Tropical Africa. Assistant Secretary Satterthwaite, in telling the House Foreign Affairs Committee on March 9, 1960, that the initial appropriation of $20 million was an attempt to meet a new situation in a fresh manner, candidly specified the criteria which had led to the proposal:

> First, we wanted something which would provide a close identification of the United States with the African people. Second, we wanted to find some way of encouraging closer cooperation and interchange between the many African countries. Third, knowing that Africa's need for economic help is almost unlimited, we wanted to concentrate on the key problem area, one which stands as a

---

* That the State Department in those years "spoke with a European accent" and had a deep, built-in bias in favor of European as against African viewpoints is generally accepted by American Africanists. Whether certain racial attitudes common among the older members of the Foreign Service were also an impediment to the more timely development of new African policies is a matter of some disagreement. But because this view is strongly held by many knowledgeable persons, including a number of American Negroes familiar with the government at the time, it deserves to be noted.

major block to development. Fourth, we wanted to avoid competition with large-scale assistance from Europe but serve rather as a catalyst for stimulating an even higher level of this assistance. Fifth, we wanted as much as possible to avoid getting into a position of annual aid-level negotiations with many new countries pressing for external assistance. Finally, we wanted a program which would provide sufficient flexibility to permit effective adaptation to a very fluid situation.

He went on to say that he himself considered these amounts conservative and minimal. With them, however, "I believe we can demonstrate our sympathy with the newly emerging African countries and respond to the varied and complex demands the African Continent makes in this first year of a new and epochal decade for Africa."

Second, in midyear after the independence celebrations in the Congo and the disorders which followed, the Eisenhower administration laid down the basic lines of policy which have guided American involvement in that troubled country ever since. Although Premier Patrice Lumumba appealed to the United States for military aid after internal order broke down and Katanga province under Moïse Tshombé announced its secession, President Eisenhower decided that direct intervention by the great powers should be avoided and that the United Nations should deal with the situation. In this, the American viewpoint corresponded with that of most of the independent African states, whose self-appointed spokesman at the time was Kwame Nkrumah of Ghana. Subsequently the United States gave steady support to Dag Hammarskjöld, the U.N. Secretary-General, in his skillful and tireless efforts to persuade the Belgians to withdraw their forces and to keep other states, including the Soviet Union, from intervening directly. Moreover, although Britain and France were reluctant to support strong U.N. measures in the first months of the crisis, the United States not only gave its diplomatic backing but provided substantial material assistance as well. As the Congo crisis re-erupted in later years, additional and difficult choices then had to be taken by the United States; but the original decisions of the Eisenhower administration remain a sound axis of policy.

Third, on September 22, 1960, President Eisenhower made an address to the U.N. General Assembly in which he proposed a plan for military protection and for economic and educational development in Africa under the United Nations. No more comprehensive or constructive statement of broad American policy toward Africa has ever been made. Even *The Washington Post,* a consistent critic of the administration's foreign policy, called the address "serious, positive, and constructive without arrogance or synthetic showmanship . . . one of Mr. Eisenhower's very best efforts."

In his speech the President publicly abandoned the earlier hostility of his administration to "neutralism" and "nonalignment" in asking for a pledge by all member nations "to respect the African peoples' right to choose their own way of life and to determine for themselves the course they choose to follow." All nations should also pledge noninterference "in these nations' internal affairs—by subversion, force, propaganda, or any other means." He urged concerted action to "choke off competition in armaments" among the new nations and promised U.S. support for a proposed $100 million U.N. fund for the emergency needs of the Congo. He proposed increasing to a similar level the Special U.N. Development Fund and suggested an expanded U.N. Technical Assistance Program to which the United States would be prepared to contribute increased amounts for training permanent administrators for the new African states. He called for "an all out U.N. effort" to help African countries launch such educational activities as they wished, and he pledged additional U.S. aid to support various U.N. organs designed to give the African people "the fundamental tools to preserve and develop their freedom."

Finally, on the question of African security he endorsed the Secretary-General's recommendation for the creation of a qualified staff within the Secretariat to assist in meeting future needs for U.N. forces, and he repeated the proposal he had first made in 1958 for the establishment of stand-by arrangements for a U.N. emergency force. He added that the United States was ready to earmark substantial air and sea transport facilities to help move contingents when requested by the United Nations in any future emergency.

These were important new proposals. The Eisenhower administration, which had had such difficulty in addressing itself realistically to the changes taking place in Africa, had finally made a decisive shift. But the shift came when the hour was already late, and the impact of the President's proposals was greatly diminished by the fact that he was about to leave office. Moreover, there was a quality of near panic in the last minute efforts of an administration which had come to fear that its temporizing on African policy had perhaps opened the floodgates to widespread Communist penetration of the suddenly independent nations and incidentally had exposed a long flank of the administration's foreign policy to a telling Democratic political assault at home.

Fully aware of their opportunity, the Democrats did not delay in capitalizing upon it. After the nomination of John F. Kennedy for the Presidency at his party's convention in July of 1960, a full-scale attack on the African policy of the Eisenhower administration was mounted, largely following the themes of criticism which Kennedy had outlined in his speech on Algeria in the Senate three years earlier.

To dramatize the failure of the Republican administration to provide a greater number of scholarships to African students, the private foundation of the Kennedy family financed an airlift in the summer of 1960 for 250 young Africans coming to American universities. In late summer Kennedy sent W. Averell Harriman on a fact-finding mission to West and Central Africa. Upon his return, Harriman urged increasing efforts to aid the new states and hammered on the theme of the Eisenhower administration's failure to keep pace with events. The result, he charged, was that Africans had come to believe that "we will not be interested in a country unless a communist threat exists."

In his campaign speeches Kennedy made literally hundreds of references to Africa and used it as a point of attack in his television debate with Vice President Nixon on October 21, 1960: "I have seen us ignore Africa," he said, "There are six countries in Africa that are members of the United Nations. There is not a single diplomatic representative in any of those six. When Guinea became independent, the Soviet ambassador showed up that very day. We did not recognize them for nearly two months. The American ambassador did not show up for nearly eight months."

Republican presidential candidate Nixon had been put on the defensive, and three days later, Assistant Secretary Satterthwaite put forward the general case in defense of the administration's record. The official U.S. presence in Africa, he reported, had been built up swiftly, with the United States then maintaining twenty American embassies, ten consulates general, eight consulates, three branch offices, and one consular agency on the continent. He said that the State Department had announced the establishment of embassies "very soon" in six additional capitals and that Deputy Under Secretary of State Loy Henderson was at that moment visiting them in order to expedite the opening of the new posts.

Other elements of our official programs he said, were expanding equally rapidly. The American foreign aid agency was conducting technical assistance programs in fourteen African countries and "had sent or was about to send" teams to survey the needs of ten additional ones. The U.S. Information Service had a total of thirty-one offices in Africa and was engaged in expanding its African programs generally. He reported the expansion of various kinds of capital assistance, including loans by the Development Loan Fund and the Export-Import Bank. Exchange programs to bring Africans to the United States for study and training, as well as to send American leaders and specialists to Africa, were being enlarged.

In addition to these points directed presumably to the American electorate, he repeated the tolerant new tone toward neutralism, saying, "If neutralism as adopted reflects a wish to remain aloof from East-West tensions it does not necessarily mean indifference. The African nations prize their independence; they have a vested interest in freedom and they are unlikely at the decisive moments to mistake the enemies for the friends of freedom." As for the United Nations, which had been largely ignored in many policy speeches in the earlier years of the Eisenhower administration, Satterthwaite gave a detailed citation of U.N. activities in Africa and made repeated references to President Eisenhower's proposals before the United Nations in September.[24]

Clearly, the administration in its closing weeks was making haste to regain lost ground. But the final touch put by the Eisenhower administration on its African record was a smudge. In December of 1960, forty-three Afro-Asian states presented an unusually significant resolution to the U.N. General Assembly calling for immediate steps to end colonialism throughout the world. The vote on the proposal was interpreted as a crucial test of great power attitudes on this issue of consuming interest to the new nations, and in their view, the United States dismally failed it. The final vote was eighty-nine to zero with nine abstentions, the United States ranging itself with the colonial powers in abstaining. According to press reports, the President himself made the decision following a personal appeal from Prime Minister Macmillan of Great Britain. But whatever the cause, this final action threw into question in the minds of many the genuineness of the policy shifts which had been observed during the preceding year.

To Africans, looking backward from the events of the climactic year of independence, 1960, the hesitant and cautious evolution of postwar U.S. policy meant that during the critical years of the process of their decolonization, the United States was an indifferent, almost irrelevant, factor. But from the perspective of policy councils in Washington, those same years were a time when the United States had moved from nonexistence of an African policy, to fragmentary policy, to a first approximation of a general position and a more comprehensive view of the continent.

During the earlier part of the period, a Democratic administration was in power, and during the latter, a Republican. The similarities and contrasts of the responses of the Truman and the Eisenhower governments to African requirements are instructive to consider. The Truman administration inherited power from Franklin Roosevelt, whose anticolonial sentiments were vigorous and outspoken (though not shared by all his principal associates). The Truman foreign policy was bold, innovative, and effective—but not on African questions. Traces of the Rooseveltian anticolonialism remained, but were visible only occasionally.

The Eisenhower administration took office in an atmosphere of continuing international tension and bipolarity and also of domestic difficulty and distrust of government. To a considerable extent, particularly in the early years, the general lines of policy followed were a continuation of those established in the previous administration. Insofar as Africa commanded attention, it was essentially because of a fear that the dislocation of European control in Africa and in other colonial areas might lead to disorder and Communist penetration.

To the general containment policy which it inherited, the Eisenhower administration, however, did add certain new subsidiary themes which, as far as Africa was concerned, were not helpful. These included an attitude of stern moralistic disapproval of neutralism; strong, ideological emphasis on free enterprise and a corresponding disapproval of socialistic tendencies; and a quality of pious detachment from such matters as racial discrimination in Southern Africa. But in the course of President Eisenhower's second term, after sweeping political changes had already begun to occur in Africa, basic alterations in African policy were introduced. Machinery was established for the first time in the Executive Branch to deal specifically and consistently with African questions. American official representatives were deployed throughout the continent, and new programs were hastily constructed and set into motion. The growth in the volume of economic assistance to Africa during these years was one indication of the change:

Over the four-year period 1953–57, loans and grants to Africa totaled only $120.3 million. But in a fiscal 1958 the total jumped to $100 million; in 1959 to $185 million; and in 1960 to $211 million.

In the final months of President Eisenhower's second term, interest in Africa shot upward under the impact of political events both in Africa and at home. The administration at that point scuttled its reserve. Policy toward Africa for the first time commanded the attention of the highest level of American leadership and was stated in an unequivocal voice, most notably in President Eisenhower's statement to the United Nations in September 1960 on the Congo problem, the dangers of great power confrontation in Africa, and the peace-keeping and developmental role of the world organization.

But the deathbed conversion of the Eisenhower administration did not greatly alter its over-all record on Africa, which was one of passivity, caution, and hesitant reaction to events which had already occurred. African matters remained to the end systematically subordinated to the interests of the European partners in the Western alliance. The policy was not adventuresome; and though it honored in studiously modulated language the principles of self-determination and racial justice, it excluded the taking of any significant risks or the incurring of any substantial costs in their behalf. The Eisenhower administration thereby managed to make the least of what it on the whole considered a limited opportunity.

The methods by which it chose to deal with Africa are open to criticism on at least four counts:

First, until 1958, although African issues were cropping up with increasing frequency, no machinery for dealing expeditiously with them was created. Part of the delay was due to inaction by Congress on administration proposals; but some was due to the chosen method of working through a cumbersome hierarchy of committees in the Executive Branch.

Second, responsibility for dealing with African questions typically was placed in the hands of professional diplomats whose experience and orientation was European not African, and whose age, personality, and outlook had little in common with that of African leaders at the time. If the choice of such officials was to insure a conservative cast to American policy toward Africa, that was accomplished. But it was achieved at great expense in terms of rapport with the Africans.

Third, these officials for some reason became addicted to the habit of lecturing Africans on various matters such as the hazards of "premature independence." The object of such attempts at moral suasion may have been to reassure European allies rather than to persuade the Africans to moderate their political demands. If such was the purpose, there is no evidence that it lessened European anxiety about American anticolonialism; while, on the other hand, it effectively infuriated the Africans.

Fourth, the style of presenting the American viewpoint on many issues during the Eisenhower years made the policy seem worse than it was. High-level declarations had a quality of dogmatism, arrogance, and righteousness, while those emerging from lower echelons bore all the marks of having been produced by leaderless functionaries endlessly exchanging memoranda, squabbling over petty points of punctilio, and working out in committee laborious verbal compromises, which in the end were meaningless or after the fact.

Even if the Eisenhower administration was guilty of various faults of timing and style—of procrastination, lack of concern, and stuffiness—and though it lacked those qualities of foresight, boldness, and clarity so venerated by many critics of U.S. foreign policy, it does not necessarily follow that in substantive terms the policy was a failure or that any feasible alternative approach would have done better.

The evidence is not conclusive, nor can it be, but, on balance, three conclusions inconvenient to critics of the Eisenhower administration probably can be supported:

First, through most of the years it held power, any attempt to press vigorously for clear-cut support for African self-determination would in all likelihood only have produced a clear-cut defeat for the proposition since neither the public nor Congress were ready to back such a departure.

Second, even if the United States had attempted to play a more active role in behalf of independence in North and tropical Africa in the crucial transitional years up to 1960, it is doubtful that the result would have been significant in terms of influencing either the pace or the outcome of events.

Third, the hesitant and pro-European cast of U.S. policy during those years produced no enduring damage or impediment to workable relationships with the new African states once they had become independent.

As long as support for self-determination within the Executive

Branch and the foreign-policy establishment spoke softly, and as long as specific issues could be dealt with on a day-to-day basis at the staff level, compromise settlements of various arguments with the European bureau of the State Department could sometimes be achieved by the African bureau, and occasional victories in the form of pro-African votes at the United Nations could be scored. But had the issues been pressed to the point of direct confrontation at the highest levels of government, the over-riding priority of Europe and of security policy would have come into operation in the decision. Quite probably, it was only because support for African self-determination within the Executive Branch was low key and its objectives limited that it was able to obtain the modest success which it did.

The United States did little during the Eisenhower years to press the European metropoles to accelerate decolonization. Secretary Dulles had declared on several occasions that the United States was "pushing for self-government more than appears on the surface," and, in at least one specific instance, involving the return of the Sultan to Morocco, it seems that an American official representative was able to exercise effective private influence upon French policy. But a great deal more could have been done through quiet diplomacy and in other ways than in fact was.

To consider, however, that such efforts would have made any real difference in the general course of events is grossly to overestimate the actual significance of U.S. influence in African matters at the time, and equally to underestimate the powerful historical forces, both in Europe and in Africa, which were in control of the process of decolonization then under way. It would be romantic to consider that the United States could have persuaded the European powers to alter their basic approach. It is highly unlikely even that they could have been persuaded to modify or intensify their efforts to prepare the colonies for self-government. In the event, since almost all of the colonial structure in most of North and Tropical Africa collapsed within the space of less than five years, such small alterations in European programs and policies for the colonies as might have resulted from greater American efforts of persuasion would only have been lost in the onrush.

Finally, the question of "costs"—if any—of the Eisenhower policy cannot, of course, be judged in purely African terms: Gains may well have been made in terms of U.S. national security or relationships with Western Europe for example, which many would consider sufficient to justify any demonstrable "losses" in Africa. Even within the African context, those losses do not seem to have been great or enduring. Without question, the United States soiled its image in the eyes of many nations by its complicity with France in the Algerian War, and some African nationalist leaders expressed strong criticism of American policy during the Eisenhower years. But, without exception, once the new African nations became independent, the United States was able to establish workable and in most cases cordial relationships with them—including Algeria, Guinea, Mali, and others among the then so-called radicals. This may have been due to a characteristic pragmatism and flexibility of the Africans and their recognition of the indispensability of maintaining relations with the richest and most powerful state in the world; or it may have been, as some would argue, the result of the new style of the following Kennedy administration in dealing with them. In either case, whatever damage might have been caused by the Eisenhower approach was readily and quickly reparable once independence came. Thus, not so much because of the skill or wisdom of its authors but principally because of the course which history took, the Eisenhower policy toward Africa, in the realistic terms by which practicing diplomats are inclined to judge, worked out reasonably well. Or, putting it somewhat more harshly, the United States was of such little consequence in African events at the time, a good policy could not have made much difference, and a poor policy produced little harm.

9

African Policy Under Kennedy and Johnson

When John F. Kennedy took office as President in January 1961, Africa as a foreign policy issue was commanding a level of attention and interest never known before in Washington. The collapse of the colonial structure which reached its climax in 1960 had brought Africa regularly into the headlines; and the laggard performance of the Eisenhower administration in dealing with opportunities in a changing continent had enabled the Democratic candidate to score telling points during the Presidential campaign. After President Kennedy's victory in November, some officials in Washington who were sympathetic to the new African states had high hopes that the continent was finally to become the object of much greater interest in U.S. foreign policy. Others were frankly fearful that the African enthusiasm of the new administration might endanger what they regarded as basic elements of American interest in European security arrangements. Likewise in Europe and in Africa, because of the long interest and strong views of Mr. Kennedy himself on colonial questions, both anxieties and expectations had been aroused.

It was a time of change, and many changes did in fact occur. But as with all other aspects of the brief and dramatic Kennedy administration, its record on Africa—composed as it is of intangible as well as of more readily measurable factors—is not easy to appraise. Events have not yet sufficiently receded in history to give adequate perspective, and the analyses and evaluations which have been written to date by persons directly involved in some of the decisions provide valuable insights but are not distinguished for their objectivity.

283

THE KENNEDY ADMINISTRATION AND AFRICA

Beginning with President Kennedy's Inaugural Address, the new administration got off to a fast start in a deliberate effort to display warmth and cordiality toward Africa and the Third World, as marked by a clear shift in vocabulary and the abandonment of some characteristic themes of the Eisenhower administration. Many Africans had come to identify American policy with a kind of pathological anticommunism and an interest in Africa not for itself but only as a counter in the cold war. In his Inaugural Address, the President took pains to dissociate himself from this approach. "To those people in the huts and villages of half the globe struggling to break the bonds of mass misery, we pledge our best efforts to help them help themselves, for whatever period is required—not because the Communists may be doing it, not because we seek their votes, but because it is right."

Eschewing the attitude of moralistic disapproval of neutralism, Kennedy was careful to say to the new states, "We shall not always expect to find them supporting our view. But we shall always hope to find them strongly supporting their own freedom." Similarly, doctrinaire disparagement of socialism and praise for free enterprise were themes conspicuous by their absence from the initial policy statements of the new administration.

Whereas President Eisenhower had seemed detached if not indifferent toward Africa, his successor showed an intense personal interest. After taking office, President Kennedy welcomed a stream of African leaders to the White House. In lengthy conversations with them he displayed knowledge of their countries and sympathy with their problems. For the leaders of the newly born African nations to be so received by the head of the most powerful state in the world made a deep and favorable impression.

Kennedy's appointments to key foreign policy posts also reinforced the appearance of a shift in approach. The new Secretary of State, Dean Rusk, was an articulate intellectual who had had long experience in the problems of overseas education and agricultural development as head of the Rockefeller Foundation. Chester Bowles, appointed Under Secretary of State, was outspoken in his friendly attitude toward the underdeveloped areas, Africa included. Adlai Stevenson, named to head the U.S. delegation to the United Nations, was regarded as more liberal in attitude than his predecessor, Henry Cabot Lodge. As Assistant Secretary of State for African Affairs, Kennedy turned not to another career foreign service officer but to an energetic and personable politician, the former Governor of Michigan, G. Mennen Williams, widely known for his ties with the labor movement and for his militant support of civil rights in the United States. The fact that Governor Williams was the first major foreign policy appointment announced by the new President strengthened the public impression that African affairs were to be given new emphasis. As deputy to Williams, the President took the equally unusual step of naming an outsider to the foreign policy establishment, Mr. Wayne Fredericks, whose experience had been in private business and philanthropy, and who personally was strongly pro-African.

In the closing days of the Eisenhower administration, the President-elect's brother Robert, together with Chester Bowles, reportedly blocked an effort by the State Department to place senior foreign service officers as ambassadors in the growing number of embassies in Africa. In subsequent weeks, once President Kennedy took office, he filled those posts largely with able noncareer men. With the help of Ralph Dungan, of the White House staff, a creative series of appointments was made over the next two years: Philip Kaiser, a former Rhodes scholar and labor expert to Senegal and Mauritania; liberal activists John Ferguson and James Loeb to Morocco and Guinea; journalists William Attwood and Edward Korry to Guinea and Ethiopia; and Edmund Gullion, an independent-minded career officer who had been out of favor during the Eisenhower administration, to the Congo. Such appointments implied a desire to upgrade Africa; and in fact as a result of the personal relationships between many of the men named and the President, the State Department was exposed to a far greater degree of initiative and pressure for action from the field than would normally have been the case. In this sense the appointments had substantive as well as stylistic importance.

Amid these many encouraging indications, Africans waited with unusual interest to see what actions the Kennedy administration would take on the two issues of greatest concern to them, namely, independence and development.

As for independence, echoes of President Kennedy's 1957 speech on Algeria were still audible both to African nationalists and to Europeans when he took office, and in statements immediately thereafter he indicated that his basic attitudes had not changed. He told the President of Finland, for example, "The strongest force in the world is the desire for national independence. . . . That is why I am eager that the United States back nationalist movements, even though it embroils us with our friends in Europe."[1] In February 1961, during his first trip to Africa, Assistant Secretary Williams was quoted as having said in Nairobi, Kenya, that "Africa should be for the Africans," a statement which though applauded by African nationalists stirred up a hornet's nest of criticism by white British settlers in East Africa and by Foreign Office officials in London and Lisbon. President Kennedy at a news conference on March 1 clarified the reference to "Africans" as encompassing "all those who felt themselves Africans whatever their color might be," but he essentially backed Williams' statement.

Later in March at the United Nations the first opportunity arose for the new administration to support its statements about African independence with specific action. In the preceding weeks, disorders had broken out in Angola, followed by bloody repression imposed by the Portuguese government. In the wake of these events, Ceylon, Liberia, and the United Arab Republic submitted to the Security Council a resolution calling upon Portugal to introduce urgent reform measures in the colony and to prepare it for independence. After thorough consultation between the U.S. delegation to the United Nations and the Department of State, and after specific approval by the Secretary of State and the President, the United States vote was cast in favor of the Afro-Asian resolution. Even though it failed of adoption (five votes in favor, none opposed, six abstentions), the American action rang like a pistol shot and was interpreted as a repudiation of the position taken in December 1960 by the outgoing Eisenhower administration on the question of anticolonialism. Essentially the same resolution was subsequently submitted to the General Assembly, where it was adopted overwhelmingly, the United States again voting in favor.

In the following weeks in public statements throughout the country, Secretary Williams repeatedly called for Portugal to make step-by-step preparations for self-determination in its African territories. The American position was welcomed enthusiastically by Afro-Asian diplomats and was considered the more significant and appreciated the more fully because it involved a risk of rupture in the impending negotiations with Portugal for continued rights of U.S. access to the strategic facilities of the Azores, which were due to expire in 1962.

In less public fashion, the new administration moved simultaneously to open lines of communication with the nationalist political movements of the Portuguese territories. Although rebel leaders were not formally received in the State Department, they were regularly consulted on an informal basis by high government figures, including the President's brother, then Attorney General. In addition, early in 1961 a special interdepartmental committee was formed in Washington to study feasible and appropriate means by which the United States could develop closer links, through scholarships and other measures, with young political refugees from Portuguese territories who were then going principally to the Soviet Union and Eastern Europe for special training and indoctrination.

The willingness of the administration to break new ground and take gambles with previously untouchable political elements was confirmed by the nature of its response to events in the Congo. Patrice Lumumba, the Congolese leader, was assassinated in early 1961 under circumstances which gave grounds for belief that the act had been done by or with the complicity of the African and Belgian supporters of Moïse Tshombé in Katanga. Reactions were furious throughout Africa, and the U.S.S.R. made every effort to exploit the situation in behalf of its attack on the United Nations, Secretary-General Dag Hammarskjöld, and "the colonialists." President Kennedy remained firm in his backing of the U.N. effort to maintain the unity of the country and warned the U.S.S.R. against unilateral intervention. But in the subsequent struggle for political leadership in the Congo, American policy shifted to acceptance of a coalition of the Center and the Left against the forces of the Right led by Moïse Tshombé, as a result of which a few months later Cyrille Adoula became Prime Minister with leftist Antoine Gizenga as Deputy Prime Minister.

This "opening to the left" in U.S. policy in the Congo was consistent with the approach being taken toward some of the "radical" states of West Africa. The cordiality of the conversations between President Nkrumah of Ghana and President Kennedy in Washington in March 1961 was taken as evidence of the genuineness of the new administration's attitude. And when the President a few months later wrote Nkrumah that the United States would go ahead with its share in financing the costly Volta Dam project, many Africans normally cool to the Western countries were greatly impressed because they were well aware not only of conservative opposition in the United States on grounds of Nkrumah's political orientation, but also of sharp disagreement even within the circle of the President's close advisers.

In May, Ambassador Attwood, then posted to Guinea, returned

to Washington after his first assessment of the situation in that country, which had become a base of Soviet and Chinese activities in West Africa. He recommended that the United States offer increased assistance; and as a first step in that direction a month later, Mr. Sargent Shriver, who had been named to head the newly created Peace Corps, visited Guinea to work out the details of an agreement for dispatching volunteers.

The first six months, then, of the new Kennedy administration were a time of bright beginnings: Africa commanded the President's personal interest; he had placed men sympathetic to Africa in key positions in Washington and in the field; and with remarkable perceptiveness the new administration had managed to avoid the obtuse formulations of its predecessor in discussing African questions. By its actions it had convinced even the skeptics in Africa that something different in American policy was beginning to happen. Bourguiba of Tunisia, Hassan of Morocco, Nkrumah of Ghana, and Nyerere of Tanganyika, among others, expressed their praise for the "definite change." In a number of quarters at home and in Africa, expectations even developed—fed in part by the dashing pronouncements of Assistant Secretary Williams —that a fundamental shift in American foreign policy priorities had occurred.

But such an evaluation proved premature. Events in other parts of the world—from the Bay of Pigs fiasco in Cuba in mid-April to ominous new tensions in Berlin after midyear—tended to drive Africa once again into the background and to bring to the fore those political and strategic considerations which had been consistently predominant in American foreign policy since the end of the Second World War. As a result of those developments, plus the fact of a closely balanced and balky Congress, the more ambitious objectives of the administration regarding Africa quickly had to be compromised or scaled down. Moreover, the kinds of issues relating to African self-determination that arose after midyear at the United Nations faced the administration with particularly hard choices, some involving relations with European allies and others requiring decision whether to go beyond general declarations of attitude to the support of concrete actions to hasten independence. At this point unrestrained pro-African generalities gave way to qualifications and even contradictions.

Thus, in May of 1961, Secretary Williams told a conference: "We intend to stand up and be counted when issues of political self-determination and racial equality are debated in the United

Nations." But in August, following a bloody encounter between French and Tunisian troops at the naval base of Bizerte, a resolution was presented in the United Nations calling for the withdrawal of all French forces from Tunisian soil. It was adopted by the General Assembly on August 26 by a vote of 66 to 0 with 30 abstentions, including the United States. President Kennedy himself, who in 1957 had so slashingly attacked the American tendency to give lip service to self-determination but to side with the colonialists when the chips were down, made the decision in this instance that the United States should abstain out of deference to the delicate position of General de Gaulle in France, who was then trying to arrange a settlement of the Algerian issue.

On October 31, in reference to the Algerian question, Secretary Williams told the Overseas Press Club in New York: "We feel that the key to a solution lies in negotiations between France and the FLN [National Liberation Front]. We hope these negotiations can soon be resumed and that a settlement based on the principle of Algerian self-determination will be achieved."[2] But when the General Assembly on December 20 adopted a resolution calling for such a resumption of negotiations, France boycotted the debate and vote and the United States once again abstained.*

If renewed consideration for the sensibilities of U.S. allies in Europe was one tendency becoming manifest, the other was a sharp distinction between general condemnations of colonialism and racism in Southern Africa as against any kind of direct economic or other action. Thus on November 28, on a General Assembly resolution condemning the South African government for *apartheid* and asking that all states take "separate and collective action" to try to bring about abandonment of the policy, the United States voted in favor, but only after the resolution had been shorn of provisions calling for U.N. sanctions.

The second general area in which policy affecting Africa encountered difficulty after the first few months was foreign aid. In his State of the Union Message in January, President Kennedy

---

* Yet the record of U.S. compliance with European wishes on colonial questions that year was not without exception: On November 27, 1961, the United States broke ranks with Britain and France in voting for a General Assembly resolution to create a 17-nation special committee to examine the actions taken by member states to implement the United Nations' 1960 declaration for the immediate abolition of colonial rule. The resolution was considered to have been directed primarily against Portugal, however, and British and French objection to it was apparently not vigorous.

had urged a "towering and unprecedented" effort to build sound and expanding independent economies in the emergent countries. Based on the recommendations of task forces of economists and development experts which had been set to work to devise a revamped aid program, he recommended to Congress the consolidation of various governmental agencies into a new Agency for International Development (AID), and the adoption of a long-term approach to the planning and administration of assistance.

Because of his extremely close election victory, President Kennedy had to work with a paper-thin Democratic majority in both the House and Senate, and conservative elements on both sides of the aisle were ascendant. He was able to win congressional support for the creation of the Peace Corps and for an expansion of shipments of agricultural commodities to many countries overseas. But his proposals regarding the foreign aid program as such immediately encountered heavy opposition, especially his request for authority to make long-term loan commitments based on Treasury borrowings, which ran head-on into a jealous congressional defense of its control over annual appropriations.

In their attempt to get the proposal through, administration spokesmen eventually had to put aside the fresh themes of the Inaugural Address and argue for the aid bill in terms which an economy-minded and cold-war-minded Congress would understand. In contrast to the idea that the United States stood ready to cooperate generously with the new African nations in their development efforts, administration witnesses returned to the older line of argument that other nations of the Free World—that is to say, the former colonial powers—would be expected to play the primary role, not the United States, and that private enterprise should be expected to carry much of the burden. In contrast to President Kennedy's declaration that help would be given not because of Communist competition but "because it is right," administration witnesses before House and Senate committees in May and June essentially relied on the thesis that "all of the African countries are going to require some consideration to keep out the Communist influence."

President Kennedy had asked a "rock bottom figure" of $4.8 billion, of which $2.9 billion was for economic and $1.9 billion for military aid. In the end, Congress ignored his urgent appeals and cut more than $1 billion from the request. The appropriation battle was hard-fought, and administration forces in the end had to call on every resource, including the support of former President Eisenhower, to prevail against congressional opposition.

In brief, within the short span of twelve months, most of the high hopes and expectations entertained by Africans and pro-African elements in the United States had run aground on the hard realities of the cold war, conservatism, and cost. Although a new and warmer atmosphere of African-American relationships had been created, in the substance of African policy under President Kennedy there was less change than met the eye. The appearance was greater than the reality.

During the following year, 1962, the "return to normalcy" in regard to the place of Africa in American foreign policy was confirmed and consolidated. Events in Laos, Berlin, and Cyprus and the Cuban missile crisis later in the year kept the spotlight off Africa and fixed it on more familiar concerns in Latin America, Europe, and Asia.

Within Africa the Congo remained in danger of imminent disintegration and was the object of increasing concern and controversy in the United States. In other regions, however, encouraging developments occurred. Orderly progress toward independence was being made in East and Central Africa; and the Evian Accords were signed between France and the Algerian Nationalists on March 19, 1962, bringing the seven-year war to an end. When Algeria became independent in midyear, President Kennedy moved quickly to extend recognition, post an ambassador, and offer food and other assistance. The policy of cooperation with the more radical states paid a clear profit during the Cuban crisis in the fall, when Guinea and Algeria refused to permit Soviet aircraft to land for refueling on their way to Havana—even on airfields which the Soviets had financed.

At the United Nations the increasingly numerous Afro-Asian members were beginning more insistently to demand actions to force the pace of independence in Southern Africa. The pre-Kennedy pattern of American behavior, which had begun to reassert itself the year before, became more definite. In the case of Rhodesia where the prospects for evolutionary political change were visibly deteriorating, the United States expressed its fear that conflicting attitudes would harden into complete intransigence, making a disaster inevitable. But out of deference to the wishes of London, it repeatedly abstained from resolutions calling upon Great Britain to take actions of various kinds.[3] At the fall session of the General Assembly, it refused to go along with resolutions calling for a boycott and break in diplomatic relations with South Africa and for a ban on the sale of arms to Portugal. It likewise voted against a resolution setting a time limit on decolonization. On October 19, 1962, Ambassador Plimpton of the U.S. delegation argued against the imposition of sanctions on South Africa before the Special Political Committee of the General Assembly in these words:

> . . . the adoption of a sanctions resolution which would not be fully implemented and which would not achieve the desired result would seriously weaken the authority of the United Nations, debase the effectiveness of its resolutions, and generally impair its reputation. . . . Members of this Committee will recall that last year the General Assembly adopted, with near unanimity, a resolution which called on all members to take such individual or collective actions to end *apartheid* as were open to them in conformity with the Charter. The United States has supported that resolution and has complied with it. . . . To be concrete, the United States has already adopted and is enforcing the policy of forbidding the sale to the South African Government of any arms, whether from governmental or commercial sources, which could be used by that government to enforce *apartheid* either in South Africa or in the administration of South-West Africa.

He omitted to mention, however, that, the previous June, Washington had agreed to sell certain kinds of weapons to South Africa, in return for which South Africa permitted the establishment of an American space-tracking station on its soil. That the arms were supposed to be used exclusively against "Communist aggressors" did little to diminish the jarring impact on other African representatives, however, after the news of this gesture of collaboration with the South African regime leaked out.

In its 1962 proposals on foreign economic and military aid, the Kennedy administration fared no better in Congress than it had the year before. A total of $4.8 billion was requested; and after a grim congressional struggle, an appropriation of $3.9 billion was enacted. Congressional discontent had clearly reached dangerous proportions, and in an attempt to keep it from becoming still worse, the President transferred his able and respected budget director, David E. Bell, to be head of the AID, to reorganize it and to rebuild confidence in its program. On December 10, 1962, in a less happy move, he named a private committee, with General Lucius D. Clay as chairman, to review the entire assistance effort. The gambit of having the aid program studied and subsequently endorsed by a group of leading private citizens was an old and familiar one in the game of cooling congressional criticism, as was the tactic of selecting a prominent conservative figure to head such a group. Just as Kennedy had named a Republican, Clarence Randall of Chicago, to review and recommend financing of the Volta Dam project in 1961 to blunt anticipated congressional opposition, so he named a military officer who had become prominent in private business after distinguished service in postwar Germany to execute his protective maneuver in 1962 for the AID program. But the exercise was to backfire the following year.

As 1962 drew to a close, it was becoming evident that African matters in the councils of the U.S. government were the object of active controversy. Some of the points at issue were of long standing and had become almost institutionalized. In regard to the Portuguese colonies, for example, support for self-determination had to be weighed against the strategic importance of the Azores base and U.S. commitments to NATO. The Joint Chiefs of Staff considered the base essential to American security; the U.S. delegation to the United Nations argued that the political costs of concessions to Portugal because of the base were excessive and might cost equally important military rights in other parts of Africa. The Africa Bureau within the State Department was locked in a prolonged wrangle with the European Bureau on the same issue. Similarly, opinions were divided on American bases in Morocco, which President Eisenhower in the closing months of his administration had agreed to evacute within a three-year period. The Department of Defense not only wished to maintain them for the full three years but to extend the base rights if possible. Others in the White House and the State Department, as well as a number of influential Democratic senators, argued that the bases were a political liability and should be evacuated even before the end of the period agreed upon.

In these and many other on-going discussions within the Executive Branch, the pro-African viewpoint was often inadequately defended. Assistant Secretary Williams, who swung an effective broadsword in the arena of general salesmanship and political speech-making, had neither the taste nor the talent for the fine épée work required in day-to-day internal staff debate. Within the government, he came to be opposed by virtually the whole old-line Foreign Service establishment and his influence as a policy voice steadily declined. Outside it, he became the target of a sustained barrage of criticism by Republicans in Congress, much of the press, and certain influential Democrats outside the administration.

But Williams' flamboyant personality was only an incidental cause of the growing opposition in Washington to responsiveness to African viewpoints. African members of the United Nations who had moved from general resolutions to calls for voluntary action were beginning to approach the forbidden zone of Security Council action under Chapter VII of the U.N. Charter. Demands to declare the political problems of Southern Africa formally as "threats to peace," thereby justifying mandatory sanctions and possibly the use of force, caused not only those officials concerned with NATO relationships but many others as well to dig in their heels.

The long-festering Congo situation, which by mid-1962 was plunging toward a violent climax, was an additional source of concern. The United States was for the first time heavily engaged in an action in the heart of Africa which, as it grew in scale and danger, raised grave doubts among many persons whether the United States had become overcommitted, and indeed whether the basic objectives of its policy were realizable. As the final struggle with the Katanga secessionists approached, George McGhee, Under Secretary of State for Political Affairs, was sent on a special mission to the Congo to make a complete reappraisal of the situation to allay misgivings which had arisen even among some high members of the administration. Following the report of his findings, the official position was reaffirmed. The year 1963 opened with certain positive developments but ended with the Kennedy administration effectively immobilized on most major issues relating to Africa. In January the Katanga secession was broken by U.N. forces, with the full financial and logistical support of the United States. With the most immediate threat to dismemberment of the Congo at last overcome, the difficult but less dangerous phase of national reconstruction and rehabilitation could begin— and public anxiety as well as interest in the question quickly subsided. A second encouraging development was the decision of the independent African states (of which there were 33 by early 1963) to heal their factional differences and agree to create an Organization for African Unity (OAU), a step which the United States applauded.

But at the United Nations, the issues of Southern Africa were becoming even more acrimonious. The United States was under steady and growing pressure to join in forcing Britain, Portugal, and South Africa to act in bringing about political change. As

J. Wayne Fredericks, Deputy Assistant Secretary for African Affairs, said in a speech on July 18 in St. Paul, Minnesota, "In our relations with the rest of Africa, we may find ourselves having to acquiesce in more extreme action or face sharply reduced influence, to the detriment of other important objectives. At the United Nations, we shall more and more be branded as hypocrites by the Afro-Asians and branded as traitors to the West by their opponents."[4]

The actual pattern of voting by the United States at the United Nations that summer and fall reflected a sharpened discrimination and careful balancing of diverse considerations in handling the issues presented, but no capitulation to Afro-Asian demands. The United States abstained on a resolution passed in July by the Security Council that asked member states to refrain from the sale or the supply of arms and military equipment to Portugal for use in the Portuguese overseas territories in Africa. In the initial form of the resolution the United States objected to language declaring that the situation in the Portguese territories constituted a "threat to the peace." But after that language was modified, the United States was still unwilling to vote for the proposal. In abstaining, the U.S. representative went to some lengths to explain that although much of the substance of the resolution was acceptable, its wording was objectionable because it would not encourage "needed dialogue between the Portuguese and the Africans." Regarding the proposed arms ban, a sticky matter because of U.S. military commitments to Portugal under the NATO Treaty, the U.S. statement said:

> The United States has felt that arms supplied to Portugal for other purposes and used in its overseas territories might well contribute to an increase in friction and danger. With these considerations in mind, the United States has for a number of years followed a policy of providing no arms or military equipment to Portugal for use in these territories. And with these same objectives in mind, we have also prohibited direct export of arms and military equipment to the Portuguese territories. The United States will continue to adhere to this policy.[5]

The United States thus put itself in the curious position of refusing to vote for a resolution asking all the members of the United Nations to do what the United States, according to its own statement, had already put into effect. The reason, according to subsequent reports, was that the nuclear test-ban treaty with the

U.S.S.R. was at that moment on the verge of signature, and President Kennedy wished to avoid any risk of endangering U.S. rights to the Azores base—which could have strengthened congressional opposition to the treaty.

In early August the Security Council debated a resolution calling for a ban on the sale of all arms to South Africa, in the course of which the United States attempted a somewhat overly clever finesse. In essence, before voting for the proposed ban, which it did, the United States hurried to announce that it had already and unilaterally put such a ban into effect—either to avoid the appearance of complying with a U.N. action, or to gain credit for initiative, or to create a smoke screen behind which to fulfill military commitments made to South Africa in June of 1962. U.S. Representative Adlai Stevenson on August 2, 1963, announced the action as a major new policy step. He reminded the Security Council that several months before, the United States had adopted a policy of forbidding the sale of arms and military equipment, whether from government or commercial sources, which the South African government could use to enforce *apartheid* or in its administration of South West Africa.

We have carefully screened both government and commercial shipments of military equipment to make sure that this policy is rigorously enforced.

We expect to bring to an end the sale of all military equipment to the government of South Africa by the end of this calendar year in order further to contribute to a peaceful solution and to avoid any steps which might at this point directly contribute to international friction in the area.

Yet he went on to say, "There are existing contracts which provide for limited quantities of strategic equipment for defense against external threats, such as air-to-air missiles and torpedoes for submarines. We must honor these contracts." Five days later, Ambassador Charles Yost, Stevenson's deputy, in explaining the U.S. vote, did not atempt to reconcile the contradictory positions taken by the United States on the successive Portuguese and South African resolutions. But he emphasized that in the U.S. view the situation in South Africa was not such as to justify mandatory sanctions and, moreover, that the sanctions called for under the resolution were voluntary in character.[6]

The United States, in dealing with these resolutions, clearly felt itself coming dangerously close to mandatory action and measures of force, and it therefore took care to draw distinct lines of demarcation around its position, while at the same time giving way in some degree to growing Afro-Asian pressures. The resulting posture resembled one of straddling the fence, with an ear to the ground, an eye to the future, and a finger in the dyke.

In the case of Southern Rhodesia, however, the United States firmly and consistently backed Britain against all efforts by the United Nations to press for more decisive action. Unquestioningly—and so far as can presently be determined, passively—the United States followed Britain's lead even as the Rhodesian situation began to head unmistakably toward a political disaster. Although U.S. representatives reportedly urged the United Kingdom in private to use its special position to try to broaden the franchise and eliminate racial discrimination in the colony, strong doubts have persisted as to the vigor and persistence of such attempts to influence British policy. In late June the United States refused to support a decision in the 24-member Committee on Colonialism to call the attention of the Security Council to what it termed the deterioration of an explosive situation then prevailing in Southern Rhodesia. After the African states protested decisions made in connection with the dissolution of the Federation of the Rhodesias and Nyasaland to turn its military forces over to Rhodesia, Ambassador Stevenson, on September 11, told the Security Council: "We are confident that the United Kingdom will exercise its full authority to assure that these forces whether nominally pertaining to the Federation as they are now or pertaining to the government of Southern Rhodesia will not pose a threat to the security of Southern Rhodesia's neighbors in Africa or the peace and security of that Continent." Evidently the U.S. delegation accepted at face value official assurances that Britain had the Rhodesian situation under control and that it was embarked on a course to "stimulate a political climate favorable to liberal and orderly constitutional development." Subsequent events suggest that there was little basis for such unqualified confidence in Britain's capacity to fulfill its declared responsibilities.

While struggling with policy dilemmas in Southern Africa, the Kennedy administration was in even worse trouble on its proposals for economic assistance. In 1961 and 1962 a combination of congressional opposition to the aid bill and ineffective White House support for it had resulted in substantial and damaging cuts. On March 20, 1963, the Report of the Clay Committee, created presumably to defend the aid program, was issued. It proved, however, to be a booby trap for the program, especially the African aspects, because in its fundamental viewpoint and in many of its specific recommendations it undercut the basis of assistance to those new nations. This outcome was almost foreordained by the terms of reference which President Kennedy had set for the Committee. He placed its tasks specifically within a cold-war framework and asked the group to examine the scope and distribution of U.S. foreign and military and economic assistance in terms of "its optimum contribution to strengthening the security of the U.S. and the Free World," omitting any reference to other possible assistance objectives or justifications. Judging the aid program, therefore, by what the Committee Report called "the sharp, hard criterion of immediate strategic interests," it relegated African aid to insignificance. Since the African countries were not contiguous to the territory of the Communist bloc, they were not part of the "frontier of freedom." On this basis the Report recommended that the new African nations should look essentially to their former colonial masters for help in development. It was recommended that the limited U.S. grant programs already in operation in Africa be reduced and new grant projects be discouraged. Loans were to be permissible only after severe screening.

By its assertion that the United States had been "trying to do too much for too many too soon," the Clay Report seemed to aim its fire directly at assistance programs for the large number of new African nations whose development programs were just beginning to get under way. In nearly every respect it reached back to the most negative, narrow, and unperceptive attributes of an earlier time in American policy. By implication it endorsed the view that much of American economic and foreign aid had failed to produce results; it revived the idea that development in the impoverished countries was a short-term problem from which the United States could and should soon withdraw; it manifested no understanding of the neutralist viewpoint in the underdeveloped countries; and it not only returned to the emphasis of the Eisenhower period upon free enterprise, but actually recommended that American aid be withheld from public "socialistic" projects.

After the Report appeared, it was indicated that the Committee as a whole had seldom met and that some of the most prominent members who signed the final document had taken virtually no part in its proceedings. In any event, that the Report represented to a very large extent the personal views of General Clay, whose antipathy to the spirit of President Kennedy's Inaugural Address was apparent in every line.

Congressional critics of foreign aid immediately seized upon the document as showing the program to be so rotten that even the President's hand-picked Committee could not defend it. Officials of AID and the Department of State were in the embarrassing predicament of having to contest many of the Report's conclusions without being able to disavow the Report itself or its principal author. As a result of the fiasco, congressional action on the aid bill in 1963 was delayed for six months after the end of the fiscal year. It was not until President Johnson took office following the assassination of President Kennedy in November that passage of a lacerated and amputated bill could be completed.

AN EVALUATION

During the three brief years of the Kennedy administration, Africa was still in the morning of its emergence. The changes which continued to occur with great rapidity, though somewhat less dramatic than those culminating in 1960, were in some cases hopeful, in others not. The ugly war in Algeria ended, secession in the Congo was crushed, important areas in East and Central Africa progressed toward independence, and the Organization of African Unity was formed. But in many of the newly independent states, economic development failed to make sufficient progress to check the spread of unrest. Old tribal and other antagonisms began to reassert themselves, and the first signs began to appear of what subsequently developed into an epidemic of coups, military take-overs, and constitutional crises.

In Southern Africa, racial discrimination became worse, and prospects for peaceful political evolution dimmed. The enforcement of *apartheid* in South Africa became more harsh as that government remained utterly unmoved by the appeals of the world community to ease its policies. In the Portuguese territories, some reforms were introduced after the Angolan disorders in 1961, but thereafter the resistance of the Portuguese government to any political concessions stiffened. In Rhodesia, what had at one time seemed to be a hopeful possibility for political evolution and racial reconciliation polarized and hardened. By 1963 Africa had become a confused and complicated political scene. American policy, while of little consequence in altering the powerful dynamics of African evolution itself, nevertheless resulted in a number of specific and tangible achievements.

It continued the buildup of personnel and diplomatic missions in Africa already under way in the closing months of the Eisenhower administration. By the quality of his appointments, President Kennedy infused into the bureaucracy a new freshness of spirit.

It launched and obtained substantial financing for that happy innovation, the Peace Corps. The new African nations were in acute need of teachers and technicians, which the Peace Corps helped provide. Even more important, the enthusiasm, energy, idealism, and friendliness of the young volunteers showed the new leaders of Africa an attractive aspect of American life which in their habitual dealings with American business, diplomatic, and military representatives they had not encountered before.

President Kennedy's decision to try cooperation with the more radical and pro-Communist African states also bore fruit. From 1961 through 1963, relations with Guinea, Ghana, and Mali generally improved, and workable relations with the new Algerian government were established.

Administration policy in the Congo likewise achieved its immediate objectives and must be judged a success. The dismemberment of the country was prevented, and a direct great-power confrontation was avoided. Beyond that, however, the results were mixed. Africans agreed with the United States and the United Nations in opposing Moïse Tshombé and the Katanga secession, but on most other questions their views were divided. The more militant states—primarily Ghana, Guinea, and Algeria—vociferously supported those U.N. activities which tended to strengthen the Lumumba faction and opposed those that did not. The moderate states of Nigeria, Ethiopia, and Tunisia, on the other hand, were important mainstays of the U.N. effort, both politically and with contribution of troops. But even they came to feel that the strong U.S. support of the U.N. action derived basically from concerns about the cold war and communism, not Congolese independence as such. By the time the crisis had run its course over a period of 30 months, even some members of the Kennedy administration had begun to doubt whether direct Soviet involvement had been overestimated as a threat and whether the problem should not have been viewed in more limited African terms with American involvement and support scaled accordingly.

President Kennedy's own evaluation of the complex situation is described by his biographer and colleague Theodore C. Sorensen in these words:

> The unification of the Congo was consistent with over-all American policy in Africa. U.N. pacification of Katanga was preferable to a bloody civil war that could drag in other African states on both sides—the black nationalists against the white supremacists—and ultimately drag in the great powers as well. He was concerned, however, that the U.N. did not have the means to achieve this goal, and he wanted no undertakings launched which would shift the burden of achieving it to direct American action. He recognized the unpopularity in this country of supporting with funds and planes a U.N. peace-keeping operation that was neither peaceful nor aimed at Communists. He disliked disagreeing with the British, French and other Allies who were more inclined to protect Katanga —although Belgium's Paul Spaak, he felt, had shown great courage and restraint in reversing that nation's encouragement of Tshombe's secession. But backed by his able Ambassador, Edmund Gullion, he believed that world peace, the effort to keep communism out of Africa and our relations with the other African nations were all best served by opposing all tribal secessions in the Congo, and by supporting instead the U.N.'s precedent-setting role as a nation-builder.[7]

Another significant achievement of the Kennedy administration in a more general area should also be noted. Through the indefatigable efforts of Mennen Williams and Wayne Fredericks, an American "constituency" for a constructive and informed African policy was being built for the first time. Leading Africanists were enlisted as consultants by the State Department, and various American Negro organizations were encouraged to take more active interest in African issues, a step which, though sound in concept, produced few short-term results and seemed premature. Fredericks, quietly but steadily, through many private conversations, educated and involved a small but growing number of senators and congressmen of both parties in African questions while Secretary Williams stumped the country speaking to all kinds of business, labor, professional, and civic groups about Africa—explaining "African socialism," defending one-party regimes and neutralism, and attempting valiantly to leaven the massive ignorance of the American public about Africa.

But in other fields of policy and action affecting Africa, the Kennedy administration achieved little tangible success. On the problems of political progress toward self-determination, which arose principally in the forum of the United Nations, the administration, after early indications of more forthright and consistent support of Afro-Asian proposals, was quickly confronted by the old necessity of balancing U.S. interests and objectives in Africa against those in other parts of the world. A period of serious crisis in East-West relations which manifested itself in Cuba, Berlin, and elsewhere, made Africa once again subordinate in foreign policy priorities to broader security considerations. Moreover, a qualitative change began to take place in the nature and implications of the African proposals at the United Nations on which voting positions had to be decided. Whereas in earlier years the Afro-Asian states were pressing the Western powers to take general condemnatory positions toward racial discrimination and colonialism, by the early 1960s—the previous efforts having succeeded—they were calling for more concrete action: boycotts, arms bans, and economic sanctions. Thus, the United States returned essentially to the line of policy followed in the latter months of the Eisenhower administration—namely, to court the favor of the newly independent states, but not to the point of endangering existing security commitments and European relationships. It attempted to do so essentially by the same method—namely, declaratory support on broad questions of principle such as majority rule, self-determination, and racial justice—but it showed the traditional Washington disinclination to take risks or incur commitments in behalf of those objectives in concrete cases. Whenever its French or British allies were on one side of an issue (e.g., Algeria or Southern Rhodesia), the United States consistently voted with them or abstained. It had confidence that France and Britain would ultimately act in behalf of self-determination—a confidence which proved justified in the case of Algeria but not in the case of Rhodesia.

On issues involving the Portuguese territories or South Africa, however, it had to follow a more complex course. Having no confidence that Portugal or South Africa would move in the direction of majority rule, the United States could not simply side with them. At the same time, various U.S. military and strategic interests were at stake. As a result, the United States largely voted against Portugal and South Africa on "verbalisms"; but it generally voted against boycotts and against all mandatory measures. On arms bans it voted for one against South Africa but refused to vote for one against Portugal. And it stood flatly and firmly against declaring the issues of Southern Africa to be "threats to peace" within the meaning of the U.N. Charter.

In the vital area of economic assistance the Kennedy administration made only limited progress toward the ambitious goals it set for itself. Organizationally, it brought about definite improvement of the AID program. But the attempt to put assistance on a long-term basis did not win congressional support. No basic change occurred in the policy habit of considering American assistance as secondary and supplementary to that of the ex-colonial countries of Western Europe. On the other hand, the amount of assistance to Africa was somewhat increased, and the proportion of total U.S. aid given to Africa nearly doubled during the Kennedy years. Whereas in the period 1956 through 1960, 4.9 per cent had been allocated to Africa, the percentage for the period 1961–64 rose to nearly 10 per cent.

If any specific failures of policy could be attributed to the Kennedy administration—that is, failure to take feasible action on problems which it might have significantly influenced—these would probably relate to the Portuguese territories and to Rhodesia. In the former case, the demands of the Pentagon for preservation of access to the Azores facilities were on balance heeded, with a consequent halfheartedness in efforts to persuade Lisbon to initiate movement toward self-government in the colonies. Particularly in 1961, more determined action by the United States could have been taken to try to get Portugal to budge. It might not have succeeded, but an opportunity to try harder was lost.

Similarly in the case of Rhodesia, even many of those who believed that the proper course for the United States was generally to back Britain came to feel that the United States under President Kennedy was excessively passive in following the British lead. With the benefit of hindsight, it now appears that the United States might have been a better friend to Britain and would have far better served its own interests if it had recognized the deterioration of the Rhodesian situation earlier, had understood the implications, had indicated more vigorously the necessity of British action to head off the possibility of rebellion and breakaway by the white settlers, and had been prepared to strengthen the British hand by firmer commitments of its own.

At present, such specific judgments, made without benefit of access to secret diplomatic papers, are necessarily somewhat impressionistic and therefore open to argument. But the available evidence supports the over-all assessment that the Kennedy administration altered basic U.S. policy toward Africa far less than is commonly supposed. The same fundamental concerns of national security, the same web of international commitments, the same preoccupation with communism and the cold war reasserted themselves a few months after President Kennedy's inauguration. The enthusiasm and interest of the Kennedy administration in Africa was, from an African viewpoint, a lovely but short-lived phenomenon; its record of actual contribution to African independence and development becomes less impressive the more closely it is examined.

To say, however, that the Kennedy record was more shadow than substance is simply to raise the question of the role of illusion in international affairs versus more concrete factors. Moreover, illusion can become—and in Africa in more than one instance has become—a kind of reality.

For there can be little question in the mind of anyone who has maintained close contact with African leaders of all political viewpoints over the years that the Kennedy myth—if that is all it was—has, nevertheless, been a thing of power and durability. Though many of them were confused and troubled by various attitudes and actions of the American government under President Kennedy, and in fact on numerous occasions were sharply critical, he personally continued to enjoy their confidence and nearly all felt that he had manifested a warmth, a respect for their dignity, and a genuine sympathy for their problems which no American President had ever shown before. Perhaps because of their own need for acceptance, their own insecurity at the time, these qualities made an unusually deep impression. After President Kennedy's assassination, the expressions of grief throughout Africa were remarkable to witness. West Africa, a leading publication which had frequently criticized Kennedy's policies, carried an editorial eulogy which was typical:

> In the face of Congressional criticism, Mr. Kennedy was unable either to increase the amount of U.S. aid to Africa to the extent he wished, or to secure authority to offer it on more advantageous terms. In particular, he failed in his early endeavor to make U.S. aid "long-term" so as to assist its recipients in their planning. But African leaders while alive to the great importance of the American contribution to their countries' development, probably considered that Mr. Kennedy's political attitudes were even more important than his efforts to aid their economies. . . . No American can again

win in Africa the status of the President who understood so well and who shared the African attitude to the world.

The Kennedy personality and the aura of his spirit continue to be major and favorable elements in the attitudes of Africans and the new African nations toward the United States.

THE JOHNSON ADMINISTRATION AND AFRICA

Lyndon B. Johnson assumed the American presidency after the Dallas tragedy in November 1963, and held power during one of the most troubled periods in U.S. history. His five years in the White House were a time of increasing racial strain and violence in American cities, mounting economic problems of domestic inflation and a continuing international exchange deficit, and, above all, deepening division and dissent caused by the war in Viet Nam. During the last two years of his tenure, a national mood of disillusionment and anxiety over events abroad and discontent over neglected problems at home led to intensified constraints upon U.S. foreign policy and to a deep-running re-examination of all commitments abroad.

Only in relation to these overpowering trends can the evolution of U.S. policy toward Africa during the period from late 1963 onward be understood. Although Johnson's immediate predecessors had not found it easy to give attention to African needs in the face of competing foreign policy demands, his administration found itself mired in a set of crises of such intractability that they threatened to absorb virtually all available resources, paralyzing the capacity for maneuver, initiative, and response in secondary areas. That the Johnson administration was not an utter failure in Africa and that the generally negative trend of relationships was punctuated by a few brilliant strokes and positive achievements entitles it at least to the distinction of having conducted a skillful holding action, or more accurately, retreat.

Not all of President Johnson's problems were inherited from the past, but as regards Africa specifically, he assumed responsibility at a most unpropitious moment. His predecessor had been a man of grace and glowing style, which had produced much good will and great expectations in Africa—and had also obscured the extent to which his major pledges had gone unfulfilled. He had died tragically at a moment when African disenchantment with American policy had just begun to crystallize and when a wave of grave political and economic difficulties had just begun to sweep across the newly independent African states. In the circumstances it was virtually inevitable that the policies of President Johnson would suffer by comparison and seem disappointing.

Initially, his course was to leave intact the Kennedy team, the Kennedy programs (including the increasingly extensive operations of the Peace Corps), and the elements of what was probably the essential Kennedy strategy, namely, to keep commitments on the issues of Southern Africa to a minimum, to try to maintain rapport with the independent African states essentially by utilizing the instrument of economic assistance, and otherwise to deal with problems as they arose pragmatically rather than on the basis of broad concepts or rigid principle.

Thus, on November 30, 1963, as one of his first acts as President, Johnson, in a message to President Nkrumah of Ghana, stated that his administration would continue active efforts in behalf of African independence. On April 20, 1964, in a speech to the Associated Press in New York, he reiterated American support for African independence and also for sustained assistance to development in these emphatic terms:

We began a revolt from colonial rule which is now reshaping continents. . . . Having helped create hopes, we must now help satisfy them or we will witness a rising discontent which may ultimately menace our own welfare.

Let there be no mistake about our intention to win the war against poverty at home, and let there be no mistake about our intention to fight that war around the world. . . . The world must not be divided into rich nations and poor nations, or white nations and colored nations. In such division, I know you must realize, are the seeds of terrible discord and danger in decades to come. For the wall between rich and poor is a wall of glass through which all can see.

In North Africa, the decisions taken under President Kennedy to accept the ultimate loss of military bases in Morocco and Libya and to concentrate U.S. development assistance on Tunisia were not altered. Cooperation with the neutralist regimes of Ghana, Mali, Algeria, and Guinea was maintained. On Southern African issues, the Johnson administration not only held the policy boundary at which the Kennedy administration had stopped, or at least paused, but in an early test went a step beyond. In the Security Council on June 18, 1964, the United States voted for a resolution to create a special committee of experts to "undertake a technical and practical study" of measures which might be employed by the Security Council against South Africa because of its racial policies. In itself the resolution contained no hazardous commitments, but by voting for it the United States conceded the possible applicability of mandatory sanctions in the future and in this sense edged closer to their eventual acceptance. Its action was therefore more than a minimal and purely negative response to a challenge, and marked a turn in the evolution of U.S. policy which has been underrated.

In the spring of 1964, as President Johnson began to burn his own brand on his administration, he made procedural changes of some importance in the handling of African issues. As part of a general shift away from the personalized manner of President Kennedy, he re-established the practice that African questions, as all others, should be channeled upward through the State Department before reaching the White House. In early April he designated Ambassador-at-Large W. Averell Harriman to take special responsibility for Africa, which to some observers seemed an implicit demotion of Assistant Secretary Williams. But whatever the bureaucratic significance of the move, the immediate practical effects were not injurious. Harriman had a sensitive understanding of African problems, and in addition, because of his immense prestige within the government, he was able to influence decisions and get action where Williams could not.

The longer-run effects of Johnson's decision to "regularize" the handling of African questions, however, was to subject them completely to the priorities, procedures, and perhaps the prejudices of the old-line professionals and to deprive Africa of that slight advantage it temporarily enjoyed under Kennedy of being able to escape the foreign policy hierarchy whenever the President took interest in a specific matter, as in Guinea or the Congo, or had a personal relationship with the U.S. ambassador involved. Whether the irregular handling of certain foreign policy questions by the White House is good or bad is of course an issue on which views differ sharply. But President Johnson's preference for more standard practice became evident rather early, first by his re-establishment of State Department control and coordination and later by his increased reliance upon career foreign service officers. And just as the kind of men drawn in by President Kennedy helped give a distinctive coloration to his policy in Africa, so the men utilized by President Johnson served to give his policy its increasingly gray cast.

In early November 1964, while he was serving out the final year of Kennedy's term, Johnson was elected President in his own right by a massive majority. Personally, such evidence of his popularity could only have been gratifying; politically, it meant ample Democratic majorities in both House and Senate, which greatly strengthened prospects for legislative support and funding of his domestic and foreign programs. Kennedy's hand had to be played from a position of political weakness; Johnson could play from strength, strength which from long experience on the Hill he knew as well as anyone how to mobilize and use. In terms of practical results, therefore, more could reasonably be expected of him and his administration.

But in the same month occurred the event in Africa which decisively marked the end of the Kennedy atmosphere in U.S.-African relations and the beginning of the Johnson period. The place was Stanleyville in the northern Congo. There, on November 24 and 26, 1964, in joint operations with Belgium, U.S. aircraft and personnel conducted an airborne rescue of several hundred white hostages being held by rebel forces. Even in the context of the tangled and emotionally charged history of the recurrent Congo crisis, the operation aroused an astonishing volume of angry debate in Africa and throughout the world. It provided a classic example of how a given set of facts can be interpreted in diametrically opposite ways, depending upon national viewpoints, and illustrated how a specific event can bring to the surface all manner of fears, anxieties, prejudices, and assumptions which not only underlie but in certain situations can control the behavior of nations.

From the American point of view, the national conscience was clear: The United States had steadily opposed breakup of the Congo by secessionist movements of any kind; it had consistently opposed direct foreign intervention; it had steadfastly supported the United Nations and its operations, both military and civil; and largely as a result of U.S. financial and other support, law and order had been maintained, secession crushed, and some advance toward political stability and economic rehabilitation made. The United States had backed Lumumba as well as his moderate successor Adoula, and his successor, the controversial Moïse Tshombé, who was Premier at the time of the Stanleyville airdrop. The rescue operation had in advance the explicit approval of the Congolese government and was undertaken only after negotiations for the release of the hostages had broken down. In the American view, it was, therefore, a necessary and appropriate humanitarian action, and U.S. representatives regarded African charges which were subsequently made at the United Nations and elsewhere that the airdrop was "wanton aggression" and a "mere pretext for military intervention" as incomprehensible and outrageous.

By Africans, however, the event was seen in a different light. They were distrustful of any action of Belgium in the Congo and therefore of any collaborator of Belgium. Many considered Tshombé not a true African leader but a hireling of the "Western imperialists" and dismissed as dubious the defense that the intervention was "authorized"; instead they noted with resentment that the airdrop had occurred while the Congo Conciliation Commission established by the OAU was still at work to try to bring about a negotiated release of the hostages. Confirming their worst suspicions about the motives both of the Belgians and of Tshombé was the fact that white mercenary forces (largely Belgian) of the Léopoldville government, in what appeared to be close coordination with the airdrop, immediately advanced upon the Stanleyville stronghold of the rebel movement and killed thousands of Africans. Probably most upsetting of all, the so-called humanitarian rescue operation exposed the frightening weakness of the new African states in attempting to control their own destiny and seemed to demonstrate the readiness of powerful outside nations, including the United States, to violate African sovereignty and exploit that weakness. Individual dignity and national independence—two raw and sensitive African nerves— were thus stung by Stanleyville as by an electric shock. The result was that, for many Africans, the incident ranged the United States for the first time openly with the colonialists and to a degree with the racists, while, for Americans, the wild charges that were made seriously and durably damaged both public and official good will toward the new African states.

The harm done to African attitudes toward the United States might have healed with the passage of a few months, but other events interfered. Foremost among these in its direct and indirect consequences was the escalation of the war in Viet Nam. In early August of 1964, two American destroyers were reportedly attacked by North Vietnamese forces in the Gulf of Tonkin, as a result of which Congress accorded the President a free hand to take such military measures as he might judge necessary. In the following months American forces were for the first time directly committed to the fighting, their number began sharply to increase, bombing of the North began, and the costs of the war began to skyrocket. Then in May of 1965, to deal with a situation in the Dominican Republic that was appraised by the White House and the State Department as an imminent threat of Communist take-over, intervention by American military forces was ordered. As a result of this combination of developments, many in Africa as elsewhere began openly to question whether military considerations had not come to dominate the nonmilitary in the shaping of American foreign policy, and whether the United States had not taken a sharp new turn toward aggressive unilateralism.

Such feelings and fears, following on the emotions aroused by Stanleyville, brought a sudden and almost palpable change in the African perception of American policy. The Era of Good Feeling which began with the Kennedy Inaugural ended, and American actions as well as their underlying motivation began consistently to be questioned. Most of all, Africans sensed that a chill of independence had begun to settle over American policy. Wherever they looked they began to find evidence to support their suspicions that, at the moment when their problems were growing more disquieting, the United States was pulling back and, in many cases, out.

The annual difficulties of the foreign aid program in Congress, which year by year were intensifying, were taken as evidence of declining U.S. responsibility and interest in African development. Africans read, perhaps inaccurately, into congressional opposition to "scatteration" in the foreign aid program specific opposition to meeting the special needs of the many new African states. Even in the Congo and Ethiopia, which had long been favored with substantial U.S. economic and military assistance, they saw what they took to be signs of American cutbacks. In the Congo, once the Tshombé government and its mercenary forces had brought the immediate threat of the Stanleyville secession to an end, American policy seemed to reflect a desire to reduce both military commitments and economic and technical assistance. In Ethiopia the provocative action of the Soviet government in providing large quantities of arms to neighboring Somalia was not sufficient to reverse the tendency in American policy to hold military aid to Emperor Haile Selassie to a minimum and to provide only such economic assistance as might be necessary to protect American access to its large military communications facility at Kagnew.

Similarly, signs seemed to point discouragingly toward an immobilization of American policy on the key political issues of Southern Africa. Portuguese repression of black rebellions in Angola and Mozambique was becoming more effective, but American pressures on Lisbon for political advancement in the colonies had apparently diminished, not increased. In South Africa, the racial situation continued to worsen, but American response to the deterioration seemed to African leaders almost one of passive acceptance. In Rhodesia, they were convinced the white settler government was determined to declare its independence from Great Britain, illegally if necessary, to block political advancement for the Africans; and they saw American policy as contributing to the impending disaster by its docility in support of the British position.

Under the circumstances, some were disappointed, others resentful, and most shared the gloomy anticipation that the situation would probably get worse, that the Johnson administration would be increasingly caught in the toils of its Viet Nam enterprise and in its problems at home. Many expressed the view that so long as those problems commanded attention, nothing more could be expected of the United States than a holding action, that no-cost and no-risk would become the twin touchstones of U.S. policy in Africa thenceforward. Assistant Secretary Williams and other official spokesmen labored throughout the year in numerous private conversations and public speeches to persuade the Africans of the contrary, but their efforts were largely unavailing. Nor did events and U.S. actions in the following months diminish African skepticism.

In November 1965, after many months of tension and dispute, the Ian Smith regime in Rhodesia not unexpectedly declared its independence, unilaterally and illegally. The British government which had done little more than wring its hands to head off the event thereupon reacted with great indignation. Prime Minister Wilson declared the Rhodesian action to be treasonable and asserted full British legal responsibility for all that took place in the colony. Britain immediately imposed sanctions on Rhodesia, blocking its sterling accounts, and took other retaliatory measures. At the same time it asked for an emergency meeting of the United Nations Security Council, which took place on November 12. Resolutions were adopted calling on all member states not to recognize the rebel regime and to impose economic sanctions, and urging the United Kingdom to enforce punitive measures with "vigor." The United States joined Britain in voting for the resolutions and took independent action in terminating diplomatic relations with the rebel regime, imposing an arms embargo, and suspending the U.S. sugar quota for Rhodesia.

Even those who defended the American action, however, could hardly call it daring. To support Britain, a major ally, in dealing with a fractious colony was an obvious necessity if British support in Viet Nam and in the great issues of Europe and East-West relations were to be safeguarded. Since Britain requested only voluntary sanctions before the United Nations, no policy line had to be breached. Moreover, because U.S. trade with Rhodesia was of microscopic volume, the imposition of sanctions would cost very little, and to get rid of the Rhodesian sugar quota was a positive convenience in view of the eagerness of other friendly states such as the Philippines to increase their lucrative allotments. Still, actions were taken, but in the view of most Africans they earned little credit either for Britain or the United States. Rather, they were judged as probably futile and after the fact, and in effect not much more than a confession of failure.

Early in March 1966, Assistant Secretary Williams made a major presentation on American policy to the Africa Subcommittee of the House Foreign Affairs Committee; whatever its impact on the Congress, it struck Africans as further proof of a standstill in American policy toward Southern Africa. Williams used strong terms to denounce South African racial policy and reaffirmed earlier policy decisions to maintain a ban on the sale of arms, ammunition, and military equipment. Conceding that the United States had significant economic and military interests in the country, he asserted that these did not override the American political objective of seeing an end to *apartheid*. But white South Africans and black Africans alike carefully noted that he did not propose any new steps whatever either in restricting U.S. trade and investment or in reducing scientific collaboration—including nuclear research—with that country. In the evolution of U.S. policy his statement was not a step backward, but neither did it represent a step forward. It conveyed the impression that the administration —faced both with the manifest deterioration of relationships in Africa and with the growing impossibility of winning congressional support for a meaningful response to African political demands and needs for economic assistance—was attempting to camouflage with low-cost rhetoric the immobility of its posture.

President Johnson made his personal contribution to this effort in the form of the first major presidential address in American history devoted exclusively to African questions. His audience was a group of African ambassadors who had been invited to the White House on May 26, 1966, to mark the third anniversary of the founding of the Organization of African Unity. The President stated strongly his repugnance for "the narrow-minded and out-moded policy which in some parts of Africa permits the few to rule at the expense of the many. . . . The government of the United States cannot, therefore, condone the perpetuation of political or racial injustice anywhere in the world. We shall continue to provide our full share of assistance to refugees from social and political oppression." On the question of human rights, he said, "We will not live by a double standard—professing abroad what we do not practice at home, or venerating at home what we ignore abroad."

Concerning the troubles in Southern Africa:

> We are giving every encouragement and support to the efforts of the United Kingdom and the United Nations to restore legitimate government in Rhodesia. The disruptive effects of current sanctions fall heavily upon Zambia, adding a difficult burden to that young republic's efforts to strengthen its national life. I have informed President Kenneth Kaunda that we will work with him in trying to meet the economic pressures to which his country is being subjected.

Finally, he offered continuing American economic assistance for African development. But he scrupulously avoided any promises, specific or implied, of an increased volume of such assistance.

American newsmen at the time reported that in their White House briefing before the speech was given, official spokesmen were obviously caught between their desire to emphasize its importance and their need to stress that no policy departures were being made. The President himself, caught in the same quandary, tried his earnest best to make something that was familiar and faded seem fresh. The result was that the African ambassadors present, though enormously flattered by the special White House ceremony, were fully aware of the noncommital nature of the President's words.

By coincidence, Secretary of Defense Robert McNamara that same month made a major policy address in Montreal, Canada, in which African representatives detected the same note of studied caution, particularly in his comment that "the United States has no mandate on high to police the world and no inclination to do so. There have been classic cases in which our deliberate nonaction was the wisest action of all." To Africans, by then ardently pressing Great Britain to use force in deposing the illegal Rhodesian regime, McNamara's statement not only seemed a transparently veiled promise of the administration to congressional critics not to embark on intervention again, as in Viet Nam, but it was also read as a clue that in the unlikely event Britain might employ military measures in Rhodesia, the United States would not join. To them, viewing developments through African spectacles, their pessimistic expectations about American policy were becoming a disheartening reality. The appointment of a career foreign service officer in the same period to replace Assistant Secretary Williams, who was considered by Africans as a dedicated friend and as a bearer of the Kennedy tradition, re-enforced the impression that caretakers if not undertakers had been put in charge. However, in the latter months of 1966 the United States was required to deal with three concrete and difficult African problems, which it did in skillful and constructive fashion, thereby turning the declining curve of relationships with Africa briefly and unexpectedly upward.

The first problem arose from the deposition of President Kwame Nkrumah of Ghana by a military coup on February 24, 1966. The event, which was of great practical and symbolic significance, removed from the political scene a man who had been the most flamboyant spokesman for radical Pan-Africanism, a dangerous meddler in the politics of other African states, and during his final years a willing instrument of Communist efforts on the Continent. President Kennedy had gambled heavily in agreeing to finance the Volta Dam project in Ghana as a means of restraining Nkrumah's extremism and maintaining workable relationships with his country—a gamble which failed. But Nkrumah's megalomania and dictatorial methods in time undermined his political base in Ghana and to a lesser degree his international prestige; while his mismanagement of the Ghanian economy, a critical factor in his downfall, resulted in the dissipation of the country's once considerable financial reserves and the accumulation of heavy indebtedness. After Nkrumah's removal, the Johnson administration promptly increased food aid to meet an imminent danger of famine; and to help the new regime find its way back to solvency, it also cooperated fully with multinational efforts to work out a rescheduling of debts. In May 1967, a $20 million loan was authorized to ease Ghana's problems with the balance of payments and debt repayment. As a result, relationships with the new military regime became, and have since remained, close and cordial.

The second concrete issue which arose in 1966 to which the United States made a response gratifying to many Africans concerned the territory of South West Africa, a former League of Nations mandate administered by South Africa. Ethiopia and Liberia, two original members of the League, filed suit before the International Court of Justice in 1960, asking the Court to find that South Africa had, by applying its discriminatory racial laws, failed to fulfill its obligation under the mandate "to advance to the utmost the moral and material well-being" of the people of the territory. The case was quite possibly the most significant ever presented to the Court, and its judgment was awaited with great anticipation. For the African petitioners and the Afro-Asian states generally, it represented a test of the possibility of resort to international law and judicial procedures to end colonialism and racial discrimination. For the United States, the judgment of the Court —which was generally expected to be favorable to the plaintiffs— was awaited not only with anticipation but with some unease because of its dangerous implications if South Africa should refuse to comply with the ruling.

On July 18, 1966, the Court after six years of litigation handed down its decision, or nondecision. By a close vote it dismissed the suit on the grounds that the two sponsoring countries lacked sufficient legal right or interest in the matter to require a ruling on the merits of the issue.

The consequences of this action were considerable. Many Western observers were dismayed that the Court, in the handling of a crucial political case, was sharply divided and that its decision was questionable on a variety of legal and technical grounds. The outcome was even more shocking to the Afro-Asian states. It undermined their confidence in the Court itself and in the further utility of the legal approach in dealing with the international issues which most vitally concerned them. Moreover, they had a strong suspicion that prejudice and quite possibly racial prejudice had played a part in the Court's decision. The final vote was a close eight-to-seven. The President of the Court, who happened to be an Australian, cast two votes because of a technicality of procedure; and one of the Asian members of the Court did not participate in the decision because, according to his public statement, he had virtually been obliged by the President to disqualify himself.

Frustrated and angry over the outcome of the costly six-year litigation, the African states promptly turned to the political organs of the United Nations to find remedy. Their hope was to terminate South African control over South West Africa by formal resolution, to transfer political authority to the United Nations temporarily until the area could be prepared for self-government, and to obtain Security Council enforcement measures if necessary to replace South Africa's control with international authority.

The major parties involved—South Africa on the one hand, and the black African states on the other—were adamant in their opposed positions. The African states were determined to press the matter to its ultimate point, and South Africa clearly indicated it was prepared to use force if necessary to resist African and U.N. intervention. It then further inflamed the situation after the Court's decision by promptly taking additional measures to extend the application of *apartheid* to the territory.

For American policy makers, the matter could hardly have arisen at a more inconvenient moment. Congressional and public opposition to any new foreign confrontation had risen steadily as Viet Nam became a more and more divisive issue. Beyond that, many Americans, both privately and officially, had become rather bored with Africa and its pestiferous, unrelenting problems and thoroughly irritated by the sniping and skepticism of African critics of American policy. In addition, coups and bloody disorders occurred in a number of the newly independent African states during the period preceding the U.N. debate on the South West Africa issue, developments which were discouraging even to the few supporters in Congress and the Executive Branch of a positive policy in support of African self-determination. Firm American backing, therefore, for African demands regarding the remote wasteland of South West Africa thus appeared most unlikely.

But, in this unpromising setting, the head of the U.S. delegation to the United Nations, Arthur Goldberg, by a feat of almost single-handed leadership succeeded in winning endorsement of just such a policy. He first persuaded his delegation to accept a draft proposal declaring that South Africa had forfeited its rights to continue to administer South West Africa; that a commission should be formed to recommend means for creating a U.N. administration for the mandated territory to prepare its inhabitants for self-determination; that the United States would be prepared to serve on such a commission; and that the Security Council should be asked to take appropriate action to carry out the commission's report. Goldberg then obtained the support of Secretary of State Rusk and of the President for his bold recommendations. In an unusual instance of American initiative, they were submitted to the U.N. General Assembly during the week of October 10, 1966; the resolution lifting the South African mandate, adopted on October 27 with the United States voting in favor, corresponded closely to the original American draft. The incident was a pointed example—one of the few in recent times—of the potential role of the U.S. delegation in policy formulation if its chief is sufficiently energetic, persuasive, and determined. To Africans it was the finest performance by an American head of delegation in years.

The third in the 1966 series of concrete cases in which the United States had to face a complex decision heavy with future implications concerned Rhodesia, where the situation from both the British and African points of view was obviously worsening. The program of voluntary sanctions instituted in late 1965 was failing a year later. Despite a sequence of overly optimistic statements by officials from London about the effectiveness of the leaky and partial sanctions effort, the Ian Smith regime had both survived economically and had strengthened its position politically. African demands upon Britain for more decisive action steadily increased, and in response Britain turned once again to the United Nations, this time requesting the imposition of selective mandatory economic sanctions by the Security Council. The African states were critical of the British proposal not only because it continued to exclude the possible application of force to re-establish British authority over the rebellious colony, but also because the sanctions proposed did not extend to petroleum, which Africans as well as others considered to be the lifeline of the Rhodesian economy. In the British view, however, to attempt to block oil supplies would involve the possibility of a direct showdown with South Africa, an eventuality which Britain was unwilling to contemplate in its frail economic condition. In the vote at the Security Council on December 16, 1966, the United States followed Britain and voted with the majority in imposing the sanctions requested. In so doing, the United States grasped the nettle and agreed that the situation in Rhodesia was a "threat to the peace" within the meaning of the United Nations Charter—thereby opening the way for the first time to mandatory economic measures and conceivably to eventual measures of force. Africans were gratified to see Britain take the United States across that portentous threshold, even though they were fully aware that the practical effects of the actual sanctions voted in deposing the Ian Smith regime were likely to be inconsequential. Within the United States, however, the aftermath of the action was stormy. As in the curious Stanleyville incident of two years before, the United States' vote on Rhodesia detonated a surprisingly large display of fear, resentment, and prejudice—this time by right-wing groups in various parts of the United States and by some normally dispassionate and even estimable individuals.

Perhaps the most eminent and articulate of these was Dean Acheson, who stated his position in the form of a letter to *The Washington Post* on December 11, 1966. His letter and the subsequent rejoinder by Arthur Goldberg on January 8, 1967, constitute an instructive pair of statements reflecting contrasting viewpoints on the fundamental issues presented.

Acheson formulated his attack in essentially legal terms: The United Nations had no jurisdiction to deal with the Rhodesian situation, which, in his view, was a purely internal matter. He contended that Rhodesia under Ian Smith was a *de facto* "state" and not a dependency subject to British authority; that the action of its tiny white minority in seizing control of the government to the detriment of the political rights of the black majority was done wholly within Rhodesian borders and therefore "affected no one else." Speaking of what had been called in the press "the white minority's transgressions," he asked: "Transgressions against what? What international obligations have they violated?" In his view, therefore, the U.N. action was illegal intervention, nothing less. Insofar as the situation constituted a "threat to the peace," he held that such danger arose purely from the demands of the African states that force be used against Rhodesia and not from any aggressive action by Rhodesia itself.

Goldberg in his rejoinder dealt point by point with Acheson's legal arguments, and then he took up the larger moral and political problems that he believed were involved. He asserted that Rhodesia was not a "state" within the meaning of the Charter and pointed out that it had not been recognized as such by any government in the world. The situation was not "domestic" since it involved the international responsibilities of the United Kingdom to safeguard the well-being and interests of all the inhabitants of one of its colonies. The action of the Security Council therefore did not constitute "intervention" in the internal affairs of a state since the Council acted at the request of and with the concurrence of the legitimate sovereign, the United Kingdom. Nor, he argued, did the United Nations action against the Ian Smith regime represent a denial of the principle of self-determination, since the rebel group which had seized power represented at most only 6 per cent of the Rhodesian people.

Like most constitutional documents, and all workable ones, the Charter is sufficiently general in its key provisions to provide ample basis for both sides of most arguments. But the significance of the Acheson-Goldberg correspondence extended beyond mere legalistic dispute. To Acheson the heart of the matter was the sanctity of the sovereignty of the individual nation-state. What went on within its boundaries was no one else's business, and whatever its political practices, the world community had no grounds to interfere through the United Nations.[8] Moreover, only by an army crossing a border could aggression occur and a "threat to peace" be said to exist which would justify international action. Thus, within this framework of reasoning, Acheson attached little importance to the effects of the illegal seizure of power in Rhodesia upon the political and human rights of the black majority; to the pledges of the United Nations Charter relevant to these matters; to the repercussions of the political events in Rhodesia on race relations and the climate of international relations throughout the world; to the demand of the Afro-Asian nations that Britain fulfill its responsibilities to all the inhabitants of the colony; and—most unexpected perhaps in view of Acheson's experience as Secretary of State and his often-expressed position regarding the importance to the United States of the Atlantic Alliance—to the acute need of Britain, faced with the possible collapse of the Commonwealth, for American support in its predicament.

Goldberg's position in its essence was quite the opposite. He considered that the world community through the United Nations had the right and the responsibility to concern itself with violations of human rights within nation-states, and he considered that flagrant violation of such rights could constitute a "threat to peace" and to the climate of tranquil international relations as real and as dangerous as the more traditional forms of military aggression across frontiers. Goldberg envisaged the United Nations not only as a policeman upholding law and order, but also as an instrument for political change and development in the direction of the human goals stated in the Charter.

Beyond such constitutional and conceptual questions relating

to the United Nations, Goldberg saw the Rhodesian case as presenting questions of moral and political principle for American
policy toward which the United States could not honorably adopt
an evasive position. He believed, as he pointed out in answer to
Acheson's disingenuous question "Transgression against what?"
that the provisions of the United Nations Charter concerning
self-determination and human rights are not mere exhortations
but solemn treaty obligations of the member states, including the
United States.

Acheson, who began the debate in the polished and dignified
language of a jurist, later descended to *ad hominem* argument,
ungenerously comparing Ambassador Goldberg to the one-time
Soviet spokesman Andrei Vishinsky and Britain's conduct in dealing with its rebellious colony to that of the Soviet Union in as-
saulting South Korea.[9] But, in his position of flatly opposing any
extension of American risks or responsibilities in an area such as
Southern Africa, he accurately reflected the inward-turning mood
then beginning to infect large segments of the nation. The essential
cause was Viet Nam, and as that conflagration raged on, the Johnson administration by 1967 could already see most of its original
foreign and domestic objectives being consumed in the flames.

One of these had been the maintenance of an effective and
adequate foreign assistance program. Because of the heavy congressional attack on the program in the last Kennedy year, President Johnson was obliged to submit a considerably reduced
appropriations request in fiscal 1964, which was further slashed by
the House and Senate. In fiscal 1965, the same story was repeated.
What made the situation particularly disturbing to administration
officials and supporters of the aid program generally was that
habitual opponents in the House and Senate were being re-
enforced by former supporters who, because of Viet Nam, had
become hostile to all aspects of the Johnson foreign policy. In
the Senate this took the form of opposition to the "proliferation
of aid." A number of "doves," led by certain members of the
Senate Foreign Relations Committee, argued that bilateral commitments for economic assistance tended under Johnson policies
to lead to dangerous and unregulated involvements abroad—a
sequence which they contended had occurred in Viet Nam.

Since the drive to cut the number of recipient countries would
necessarily have its principal impact in Africa, the President, in
a familiar move, set up a committee to study that aspect of the aid
program and to make recommendations that might blunt the

congressional attack. The committee was headed by Edward M. Korry, then the Ambassador to Ethiopia. It made a skillful attempt to reconcile the irreconcilable—congressional opposition to proliferation and the need to keep aid flowing to the many needy new African states—by an emphasis on regionalism and regional projects. President Johnson accepted the committee's recommendations and incorporated them in his aid message in early 1967— which went beyond the usual request for appropriations and undertook to state a new aid philosophy, the first such attempt since President Kennedy's ill-fated effort in 1961. And because of the urgent need for economic assistance in Africa, his proposals in a certain sense constituted the most far-reaching statement of policy toward that continent during his administration. The unintended result was to undermine much of the remaining position of U.S. influence there.

Congress was neither persuaded by the President's call for increased aid nor appeased by his refurbished proposals for regionalism, burden-sharing, and self-help. It wrangled for many months over the administration's appropriations request, and in the end once again cut it drastically. At the same time, apart from Latin America, it imposed a world-wide limit of twenty on the number of countries to receive development loans and of forty on the number to receive technical assistance. For Africa, the congressional actions meant that only a handful of countries thereafter would be able to receive significant capital assistance for their development programs and that bilateral activities of the Agency for International Development would be closed down in about twenty-five African countries.

With this blow of the broad-axe, the foundations of cooperative African-American relations were gravely weakened. The new African states were faced with increasing difficulties in their economic development and with growing internal pressures and problems, as a result of which a number had collapsed and been taken over in military coups. Adequate assistance to their bogged-down economic efforts might enable them to follow more moderate and responsible courses and to preserve their stability. But a sympathetic and generous response from the United States, at least, was not to be forthcoming.

Later in 1967, in this atmosphere of disillusionment in Africa and distraction in the United States, two policy problems had to be faced which once again demonstrated the capacity of the Johnson administration to deal with concrete cases with discriminating judgment and a steadiness of nerve, despite the general deterioration of its African policy.

The first related to the Congo, that huge, unhappy nation in which the United States had since 1960 made such heavy political and economic investment. By the summer of 1967 revolt had once again broken out, and a group of white mercenaries formerly in the hire of the central government claimed control over the eastern portion of the country. President Mobutu called on the United States for help, this time in the form of military transport. Three aircraft and 150 operating personnel were provided, with the result that Congolese troops were able to bring the revolt quickly under control, and the aircraft were recalled within a few months. American assistance, although small in scale, had helped dissipate another threat to the territorial integrity of the country; it checked a problem which could have caused the collapse of the Mobutu government with all the unpredictable consequences which might have followed; and the support given a black African government in suppressing the illegal action of a group of whites helped spare the Congo's 70,000 law-abiding white residents—including some 1,700 Americans—from a serious danger of racial retaliation. The incident was a superb example of limited, controlled, purposeful, and invited intervention on a timely basis, which helped prevent a localized problem from growing into a major international crisis.

But distrust and dislike of the foreign policy of the Johnson administration in general was such that in the United States the immediate result of the decision to dispatch the C-130 aircraft was an outcry from all sides in Congress and the press—hawks and doves, liberals and conservatives, Republicans and Democrats. Some accused the administration of repeating the kind of foreign meddling which could lead to "a new Viet Nam in the heart of Africa"; others objected that resources and energies were being drained from the crucial struggle in Asia; and still others merely capitalized on general public discontent to score political points against an increasingly unpopular president.

In parallel with the Congo decision, officials in Washington had to cope with an even thornier choice of response or nonresponse to a mounting crisis in the most populous and powerful of the new African states, Nigeria. That country, which after its independence in 1960 was considered by many to have the brightest prospects of any on the continent for development and Westminster-style democracy, had, beginning in early 1966, erupted in a series of coups, political murders, and massacres. As it began to drift toward disintegration, the United States quietly kept in contact with all parties, urging negotiation and peaceful settlement. Then in October 1966 in the northern part of the country an outburst of long-festering tribal hostilities precipitated a critical rupture. Thousands of members of the Ibo tribe were killed, and hundreds of thousands of others in fear for their safety fled as refugees back to the traditional Ibo homeland in the eastern region. As the price of their remaining within the Nigerian federation the Ibo thereafter demanded a degree of decentralization amounting to fragmentation. Finally, on May 30, 1967, having failed to win their objective by negotiation, they seceded and set up the so-called state of Biafra, with a colorful and ambitious military officer, Colonel Odumegwu Ojukwu as its head. Last minute efforts to head off the secession broke down, and on July 7, 1967, the first shots were fired in what was to become an increasingly ugly and tragic civil war.

In formulating its policy, the United States faced a triple decision: which party to the dispute to back, by what means, and within what limits. As to the first, there were many in Washington who strongly opposed any breakup of the Nigerian Federation, despite its great inherent frictions, essentially because of the possibility that a successful secession could trigger a disastrous wave of civil wars throughout much of Africa. They believed that the United States should therefore unequivocally back Lagos and the central government. There were others who believed that the more prudent tactic for the United States was to hedge and back neither party, to take a neutral or "even-handed" position, on the grounds that the Biafrans were likely to win their struggle. The basis for this judgment was the belief that Yoruba-Hausa tensions within the Federal government would tear it apart before the secession could be brought under control. The supporters of Nigerian unity prevailed, and Washington publicly gave its backing to the Lagos regime and refused recognition to the breakaway group.

That basic issue having been decided, however, others had to be faced immediately. As soon as military operations began, the Lagos government sought to purchase certain types of arms and aircraft from the United States. Its needs were urgent, as the Biafran regime had taken steps well in advance of the outbreak of hostilities to obtain arms through private international arms dealers, a number of whom were American.

The response of the United States was to refuse to sell arms or military equipment to the recognized government in Lagos and at the same time to attempt to shut off the unauthorized flow of arms to Biafra through private sources, an effort vigorously pursued but largely unsuccessful. The reasons underlying the decision were several: a desire not to create conditions for a Soviet-American competition in supplying arms to the two antagonists; a belief that the United Kingdom, the traditional military supplier to Nigeria, could and should sell the equipment needed; and an apprehension that there would be strong public and congressional criticism if the United States should become militarily involved, even to the extent of selling arms to a friendly government.

The policy adopted obviously pleased neither the Biafrans nor the Federal government; and the latter promptly turned to other suppliers, including the Soviet Union and some of the Communist states of Eastern Europe, especially for aircraft, which Britain refused to make available. When Czechoslovakian and Soviet aircraft and technicians began to arrive in Nigeria, the United States made an ill-considered public statement that implied criticism of the Lagos government for turning to Communist sources for the matériel which it had refused to supply, but it was not stampeded, as it might well have been a few years before, to reverse its policy on cold-war grounds.

In following months, its preponderant resources and military forces enabled the Lagos government to drive more and more deeply into rebel-held territory. But Colonel Ojukwu, because of the fear and fighting spirit of his people, combined with an extraordinarily skillful international propaganda effort, was able to maintain a protracted resistance and to arouse great sympathy in many parts of the world, including some states in Africa, for the plight of the Ibos. Humanitarian agencies, including certain religious groups, contributed to the confusion by becoming involved not only in providing relief supplies, but also in gun-running and politics and applied great pressure upon the United States to intercede diplomatically on behalf of Biafra. Although the United States made offers of food and medical supplies to the war victims, it maintained a clearheaded distinction between the humanitarian and political aspects of the problem and held fast in its commitment to the territorial integrity of the country. Nor did it succumb to the temptation to offer unwanted mediation in the conflict.

The risks in following such a fine line of policy were considerable: the risk of offense to both sides and rupture of relations with Lagos; the risk of permitting the intrusion of Communist arms, personnel, and influence in a vital region of Africa; and the risk of a frozen posture of over-restraint in the event sudden opportunity should arise whereby American influence might be applied to bring about a settlement. Nice judgments and steady nerves in an atmosphere of passion, danger, and confusion were required; and fortunately they were forthcoming.[10] Imperfect as the U.S. policy course may have been in certain respects, its basic virtue was that it reflected restraint and responsibility in the behavior of a superpower. It combined a principled concern for the unity and stability of an existing African state with a determination to leave largely to that state itself the major burden of regulating its internal difficulties.

Both the Congo and the Nigerian cases, though they evoked little public praise, were examples of creditable professional performance in foreign policy. They were of unusual significance, moreover, not only because of the importance of the nations involved but also because the United States in the years to come would be faced again and again with precisely such choices and decisions in Africa.

Nevertheless, they produced only jiggles in the downward curve of African-American relations as the final months of the Johnson administration approached. In May 1967, in an effort to symbolize continuing American interest in Africa, the Under Secretary of State, Nicholas deB. Katzenbach, made a short and hurried visit to twelve African countries. Then in late December 1967 and January 1968, Vice President Humphrey visited eight African states in an equally brief and highly publicized tour. Personally both men made favorable impressions, Katzenbach because of his identification with the domestic civil rights programs, of both the Kennedy and the Johnson administration and Humphrey because of his long liberal record, as well as his great vitality and enthusiasm. But, given the state of African needs and the disappointment of their hopes for serious political support and economic assistance from the United States, what whirlwind goodwill tours could accomplish in repairing relationships was inconsequential.

By 1968 the Johnson administration was hopelessly caught on the anvil of Viet Nam under the hammer blow of domestic crisis.

More than 400,000 American troops were in Viet Nam; the cost of the war had soared to more than $2 billion a month. American cities were being swept by racial disorders, and the rising discontent of the Negroes, the poor, and much of the youth of the country was approaching the point of a social revolution.

The national economy was endangered by a combination of inflationary pressures and a persistent international exchange deficit which, it was feared, might undermine the position of the dollar. To cope with these economic problems the President proposed the unpopular step in an election year of a 10 per cent increase in income taxes. As the price of its assent, the Congress forced him to accept a mandatory cut of $6 billion in federal expenditures. Urgently needed domestic programs were seriously pinched—and the foreign economic aid program, always unpopular, faced mutilation if not worse. In deference to the mood of the Congress, the President requested an appropriation of only $2.5 billion, the lowest figure in the postwar period. But even this was slashed and slashed again in the House and Senate, the eventual appropriation for economic aid totaling only $1.38 billion. Among President Johnson's other failures, he had seen the level of the AID program during his term in office fall by nearly 50 per cent.

The President's political problems growing directly out of the Viet Nam war were even more pressing and painful. Opposition to his war policies began to mount; and in February in the New Hampshire primary the extent and depth of national division on the issue—and of dislike and distrust of the President himself—were shockingly revealed. In an extraordinary gesture to help restore unity in the country and bring about peace talks to end the war, the President on the night of March 31 dramatically announced new measures of de-escalation of the bombing of North Viet Nam and simultaneously his own withdrawal as a candidate for renomination for the Presidency.

During its last months, his administration, and American foreign policy with it, lay dead in the water. To Africans watching from the other side of the globe, the spectacle of the most powerful nation in the world in such a cataleptic condition was profoundly discouraging. Their need for both political support and material assistance from the United States was great, and the drying up of both threatened to make their arduous labors of nation-building very much more difficult.

EVALUATION OF THE JOHNSON PERIOD IN AFRICAN POLICY

Together the Kennedy and Johnson administrations largely spanned the post-independence era in Africa; and of the two, the latter was responsible for policy for nearly twice Kennedy's "thousand days." The contrasts of manner and political fortune of the two Presidents are of course many and obvious: Kennedy reached office by a razor-thin majority, having been the object of much suspicion and prejudice as a candidate. But by the end of his abbreviated term he had become a tragic and beloved figure to his own people and to much of the world. His successor was swept into office by a massive majority in 1964 in a political atmosphere of national consensus. Four years later the country had been torn into more dangerous division than at any time in a century, and he had become the least revered President in generations.

Even when regarded from the special angle of Africa and African policy, their contrasting fortunes are apparent: With his Inaugural Address, Kennedy launched a courtship of the Third World, and the affection thereby aroused in Africa survived all subsequent disappointments with his performance. President Johnson's first major decision on Africa after his election in 1964, the Stanleyville airdrop, backfired excessively, and the doubts and resentments it produced in Africa persisted for years.

Such gross public reactions at great distance may well contain an overestimation of the nature and content of the Kennedy policy in Africa just as they may proceed from an underestimation of that of Johnson. For, on close examination, the Johnson record is not very different and in most aspects not inferior.

During the year in which Johnson finished out Kennedy's first term, he essentially and consistently held to the course set by his predecessor. In its handling of a considerable series of difficult African problems over the following four years, his administration demonstrated a high level of professional competence in following a prudent, skillful, and yet not inert or minimal policy: assistance to Ghana in recovering from the disastrous effects of the Nkrumah dictatorship; leadership in the revocation of the South African mandate over South West Africa; steady support of Britain in its painful efforts to retrieve its Rhodesian mistakes; selective military assistance to the Congo in putting down rebellion in 1967; and adherence to a deliberate and unswerving line of noninterference in the Nigerian civil war.

But however commendable, even the best of these specific actions were but small upward steps on an escalator that was going down. For the African policy of the Johnson administration, as virtually everything else, was overtaken and overwhelmed by two accidents of truly historic proportions—one at home and the other abroad—for which even the President's many critics would agree he was not wholly responsible. The tragedy which struck President Kennedy was senseless and instantaneous and it made him a hero. The tragedy which struck President Johnson was of a grinding, inexorable, more Grecian kind; and he became its Creon.

Viet Nam and the new American social revolution, with all their political, economic, and international effects and repercussions, form not merely the backdrop of the Johnson policy toward Africa; they were to a decisive degree the direct causes of its ultimate paralysis and failure. Together they deformed the image of the United States into something militaristic, racialist, and brutal. Beyond intangibles, they also combined during the Johnson administration to undercut congressional support for its various specific diplomatic actions and aid efforts and eventually threatened the very basis of public and political support for an internationalist and responsible foreign policy. The mood of anxiety and disenchantment produced by 1968 a general and almost indiscriminate opposition in Congress and many sectors of the public to all new foreign commitments, expenditures, and risks.

In African policy, these trends translated directly into constraints of a nearly compulsory character. For the Johnson administration, the decision in 1964 to vote in the United Nations to set up a committee to study the feasibility of sanctions against South Africa was an act of executive choice; for the same administration three years later to lend three transport aircraft to the Congo had become almost an act of political recklessness. In regard to the brewing racial and political problems of Southern Africa, the United States under President Johnson attempted at the beginning to play a principled and positive role, but by his last year in office, lack of initiative, indecision, and noninvolvement had come to be the most striking qualities of his policy. Even in the case of Zambia, where the President had personally promised help in relieving the economic pressures to which that young country was being subjected as a result of the crisis in neighboring Rhodesia, hardly more than a cupful was actually provided.

Similarly, on the crucial question of African development, the initially expressed goals of the Johnson administration to provide significant capital assistance had simply and shamefully to be abandoned to satisfy the claims of war and domestic crisis. The foreign aid program, always in disfavor with congressional conservatives, was caught in the crossfire of attack from many additional sources: those opposed in general to the administration's foreign policy, those demanding greater governmental economy to lessen inflationary pressure and to defend the dollar, and those demanding greater emphasis on expenditures for domestic urban and racial problems. Assistance to Africa was withered by the successive shrinkages in the annual aid appropriations and was even more seriously affected by the congressional limitations upon the number of nations receiving direct U.S. assistance, a restriction which necessarily fell most heavily on activities in Africa with its numerous and needy claimants. The result was a double loss: To the new African states, the cuts and restrictions meant the removal of one of their major hopes for financing their lagging development programs. For the United States, it meant that in nearly two-thirds of the new African states the useful, indeed the almost indispensable, instrument of bilateral economic aid to its diplomacy had been badly blunted.

There were those who felt it remarkable that an administration as deeply in trouble as that of President Johnson could give even the limited attention it did to African issues and needs after 1965. But, to Africans faced with the mounting urgency of their own problems, the principal fact about American policy on the issues that concerned them most was that by 1968 it had been gutted of its substance.

Twenty-five years after the end of the Second World War and ten years after the outburst of independence in Africa, American policy and African-American relations had reached bottom. For Africans, the nadir was marked not by vehement feelings of hostility but by a sad and growing conviction that despite their earlier hopes, the United States was not likely to be a very important or very helpful factor in their difficult future. However, with preliminary peace talks between the North Vietnamese and the United States under way, and with the advent of a new year and a new American President in 1969, the hope of some improvement remained alive.

SUMMARY AND CONCLUSIONS

In the twenty-five years since the United States discovered Africa diplomatically, the actual course of American policy under four Presidents—three Democrats and one Republican—has been traced out by a long succession of specific actions and reactions. Each is of interest because it represents in a concrete way the resolution arrived at by the makers of foreign policy of the complex of factors—pressures and counterpressures, arguments and counter-arguments—relevant to the particular issue at a given moment of time. The succession of these cases makes a curving but not discontinuous profile of American policy, which also reveals a good deal about the successive administrations that have held power in Washington in recent years and of contemporary American society and values.

For the first fifteen years of the period, as the forces of African nationalism gathered, the United States was essentially a sympathetic though somewhat fretful onlooker, not an active participant in the deep historical process under way. As the moment of probable European-African rupture approached, the inconvenience and hazards of a period of rapid and somewhat chaotic transition had to be faced. The reaction of the United States was an awkward, uncomfortable ambivalence—of counseling both sides to patience and moderation, of opening new relationships in Africa while paying careful heed to sensibilities in Europe, and of tortuously attempting to reconcile its habitual policy formulations to the new realities. The shift, as for any large and responsible government with manifold and contradictory interests, also encountered much bureaucratic friction and inertia.

But, as the wave of independence began definitely to crest in the late 1950s, the tone of American policy evolved from one of uneasy circumspection, to acceptance, to positive cordiality. And once the new states were in being, the United States could turn from the task of general policy reformulation, in which it was demonstrably inept, to the task of building staff and programs for Africa, which it accomplished with both great energy and skill.

In the years since, Africa has come for the first time within the radius of direct U.S. foreign policy concerns and has also become an integrated element in the American foreign policy apparatus, with specialized staff, bureaus and programs. Whereas it was once possible to appraise that policy essentially by an exegesis of occasional official statements, it has increasingly become necessary to review also the growing number of operating programs in Africa, from the Peace Corps to economic and military assistance.

The contrasting styles of successive administrations in coping with the challenges thrown up by developments are intriguing to observe—from the plain-speaking of Truman to the preachiness of the Eisenhower administration to the felicity of Kennedy to the earnest heavyhandedness of Johnson.

Despite stylistic differences, significant though they can sometimes be, the most important fact about American policy toward Africa over the past quarter-century is not its change but its continuity. This in turn derives from the stability of the two basic premises on which that policy has rested and continues to rest. The first premise is the belief that the United States has no vital economic or strategic interests there. It has, of course, interests in trade, investment, and access to African raw materials, but none are considered to be of compelling importance. Likewise there is some strategic interest in Africa, at least in particular locations and facilities, but these again are considered to be less than essential. Indeed, Africa tends to be placed rather low in the list of those various areas even of secondary interest in American policy; and this general evaluation has rarely been modified over the years and then only briefly—as in the short lifetime of the era of the Intermediate Range Ballistic Missile, when the northern portion of Africa was believed by some military leaders to be crucial in the strategic defense of Western Europe.

The second premise has been that whenever European and African interests intersect or conflict, as they frequently have, Africa must be subordinated. Prior to independence, Africa was only a subsidiary aspect of relations with Europe, and since the late 1950s more in this regard has remained the same than has changed. The United States continues to define its role as secondary to that of the former metropoles, frequently defers to their wishes, and to a considerable extent conceives its diplomatic relations and various African programs as complementary to theirs. Understandably, as time goes on, as European powers withdraw gradually from Africa and as U.S. relations take deeper root, the American role becomes more independent. But the older pattern largely persists, along with the underlying reasons for it.

Given this continuity, the general characteristics of American policy in recent years can be stated in the form of the following five propositions:

First, official concern for Africa at the highest levels of Amer-

ican government is extremely vulnerable to distraction when crises appear elsewhere in the world. In the intense competition among various foreign policy interests and objectives for the limited time, energy, and resources of an administration, Africa tends to be almost the weakest claimant. It readily becomes the Peter that is robbed to pay almost any Paul.

Second, U.S. policy in the main has been shaped and controlled by events outside of Africa, including developments within the United States, rather than within Africa itself. In the late 1940s and early 1950s such little interest as Washington displayed in Africa arose largely out of cold-war anxieties, and American policy was strictly guided by the requirement not to undermine the Atlantic Alliance. From 1958 to 1961 the dramatic surge of independence in Africa made the continent the object of serious policy interest partly because of continuing preoccupation with the Communist confrontation, partly because of partisan political pressures at home. But within a relatively short time a new challenge by the Soviet Union, increasing disarray in the Atlantic Alliance, and troubles in Latin America quickly pulled the focus of official attention back to more familiar objects. In more recent years and particularly since 1965, urban and social troubles at home, a continuing trade deficit, and above all, Viet Nam, with all its repercussions, have not only pushed Africa once again into the shadows but have brought about a new atmosphere of hesitancy and reluctance in facing African problems.

Third, American policy has to an unusual degree tended to be pragmatic rather than doctrinaire, and reactive rather than active. Because of the secondary nature of American interests, the United States has never made Africa the object of clear, dominant, long-range purposes. It has instead tended to cope with problems as they arose. This pragmatism and relative passivity have been responsible on the one hand for neglecting some matters until they drifted out of control, as may well have been the case in Rhodesia. On the other hand, a number of the finest accomplishments of American diplomacy in Africa have been the outgrowth of effective handling of specific problems that arose, rather than the execution of a planned or prefabricated line of policy.

Fourth, the basic posture through the tumultuous changes of recent years has been to maintain contact and communication with all parties, to avoid long-term commitments wherever possible and to keep costs, risks, and responsibilities to a minimum. This has meant, in turn, lavish verbal support to African aspirations but great restraint in political, military, and economic undertakings. On occasion the United States has been forced into a temporary leadership role, as in its support of U.N. activities in the Congo; in Southern Africa it is becoming increasingly difficult for the United States to remain as passive and obscure as it might wish; and in a few specific countries, as Tunisia, U.S. economic assistance has become a primary factor. But the general disposition of the United States to attempt to avoid a primary role and responsibility in Africa remains intact.

Fifth, in the totality of American policy, elements of idealism and a broad conception of international responsibility coexist with traditional and narrower considerations of economic and strategic self-interest. Practical considerations and limited definitions of self-interest and of national role have clearly predominated, and in this sense U.S. policy has been almost the antithesis of a crusading or revolutionary program in behalf of African national independence and human rights. However, though true, this is true only up to a point. The United States does not deserve the lurid reputation for anticolonialism and sympathy for the underprivileged which European colonialists and conservatives believe. But at the minimum the United States has constantly affirmed its support for democratic and humane principles; it has never condoned racism or repression; and both Africans and Europeans have been well aware of the American tendency at crucial moments to put the weight of its influence on the anticolonial side of the balance. This double quality of pragmatism and principle has indeed been the distinguishing mark of American policy at its finest moments in recent times.

In its evolution over a span of years, American policy has become more familiar with Africa and somewhat better shaped to its special requirements. But the needs in Africa, where over the past five years a huge double crisis has been emerging, have nonetheless outraced the American response. In the south the problems of racial injustice and minority political control have hardened and become more explosive; while the newly independent states, already faltering in their efforts at economic and social development, are weakening in their capacity to maintain political stability and constitutional government. Economically and politically, Africa hangs precariously on the edge of an abyss. But in Southern Africa, U.S. policy has come to a dead end, and its aid programs to independent Africa are tapering sharply off as the development crisis deepens. To make matters worse, this tendency of withdrawal and cutback in U.S. policy is also apparent in the policies of the other great powers.

Now, after a momentous quarter-century, American policy and prestige in Africa are drifting steadily downward. The situation could readily get worse; but if it is to get better, the moment calls for basic rethinking about a new American policy toward Africa, grounded on rational objectives and conceptions of national interest, governed by some over-all framework of priorities, and inspired by some sense of national principle and responsibility.

Part Four

A Future U.S. Policy
Toward Africa

10

The Unassembled Triangle: Europe, Africa, and the United States

Foreign policy in the modern era has for the first time become global, and relations between Africa and the rest of the world are now part of this great living web of action, reaction, and interaction. Perhaps the only conception that approaches adequacy for comprehending the dynamism and complexity of the processes traditionally known as "international affairs" is that of an elaborate system of simultaneous equations, the terms of which are variable and interdependent, each perpetually affecting and being affected by all the others.

The functioning of all those equations has been altered by the emergence of Africa as a sovereign international factor in the past quarter-century. And every element, within Africa and outside, is in ferment and flux. The new African states are actively at work to build workable relations with one another and to find new patterns of cooperation among themselves. Between them and the former metropoles a process of disengagement is under way, but much old debris remains to be cleared off before more relevant and durable new relationships can be formed.

For the European powers, not having found a satisfactory role for themselves in the postwar world, the altered status of Africa is an important added complexity. For the superpowers, it is a relatively new and unfamiliar feature on the horizon of their diplomacy. In terms of their protracted and multiple competition with each other for world pre-eminence—a competition that has formed the context of all international developments since the war—Africa has been, by turns, intriguing, exasperating, exciting, worrisome, and fatiguing. But both have now, after their initial probings and experiments in Africa, begun somewhat to draw back—the Soviet Union possibly because of its failures and the United States despite its successes—while a new evaluation and reformulation of policies takes place.

These parallel and interconnected movements and tendencies constitute a historical change that, because it is so near in time and so vast in scope, becomes extraordinarily difficult to see as a whole. If the present analysis has succeeded in bringing together in some coherent and comprehensible fashion the several major elements and the emerging trends in the major outside powers' policies toward, and relationships with, Africa, it has accomplished its primary objective. The corollary objective is to attempt to draw some useful guidance from all that has taken place in this telescoped quarter-century to strengthen and improve American policy toward Africa in the future.

The Crucial Issues

In looking over the impending issues four can be identified that are of special concern to American policy.

First, there is the question of the desirable and feasible relationship to be encouraged between Europe and Africa; it leads directly to the broader question of the kind of structured relationships to be fostered between the developed regions in the Northern Hemisphere and the underdeveloped regions to the south.

Second, there is the question of American interest in, and responsibility for, initiative in unfreezing the situations of arrested political development in Southern Africa. These impasses present arduous conceptual and practical problems for American diplomacy in attempting to influence internal political and constitutional change within other sovereign entities. They present especially difficult problems of coordination with our European allies. They inevitably touch the even larger and more profound problems of the American position regarding racial injustice throughout the world, and the eternal dilemma of the balance to be struck between immediate considerations of self-interest and general idealistic principles in the shaping of American foreign policy.

The third crucial issue concerns American strategic and military policy in relation to African stability and security. This raises highly complex questions of the preferable methods and the limits of U.S. intervention in an unstable underdeveloped area now essentially unprotected by any external security umbrella and, beyond that, of the role and feasibility of multinational peace-keeping arrangements in the future.

Fourth, there is the question of what the United States should do in its own interest and in conformity with its own principles about the environmental problems of poverty and underdevelopment in Africa, and by what means—whether unilateral or multilateral, or both. The answer to this must obviously be related to the question of the American posture toward the progress of the underdeveloped areas generally. Some tentative ideas and suggestions bearing on each of these four important issues are set forth in this and the three following chapters.

A REVOLUTONIZED INTERRELATIONSHIP

The most obvious necessity, if a viable American policy toward Africa is to be developed for the years ahead, is that it be conceived as an integral part of the whole of U.S. foreign policy and that it be fitted within that framework. To a large degree this means in practical terms that the roles and interrelationship of Europe and the United States in Africa be better defined and deliberately proportioned.

During the colonial period, Europe was the dominant presence in Africa; and today, a decade after independence, it remains the principal foreign factor, economically, politically, militarily, and culturally. Yet, important as the continuity of the European influence in Africa may be, the severance of former ties has, nonetheless, profoundly affected the premises of American policy. Independence obviously brought about a shift from indirect to direct U.S. relations, but its significance reaches far deeper than diplomatic procedures; it touches and in fact transforms the very nature of the policy choices presented. With the upsurge of African nationalism in the colonial period, European and African aspirations and objectives were antithetical. The Europeans wished to maintain or at least protract their privileges and control; the Africans wanted to end them; and essentially, the United States had to choose between the parties. Accordingly, because European relationships were central to the major and urgent goals of U.S. security at the time, the outcome was foreordained: American policy steadily—with only a few exceptions and aberrations—opted for Europe.

But with the fact of independence, the issues which now arise in most of Africa do not present themselves in the bald form of a choice of Europe versus Africa. The old mold has been shattered; and so likewise, in making decisions, has been the possibility of resort to a simple rule of regional priorities—Europe first, Africa second. In some parts of the continent, as in the Portuguese colonies, the problem remains one of conflicting European and African objectives and the necessity therefore to choose between them. But in most of North Africa and Tropical Africa, and in those portions of Central and Southern Africa where independent African states exist, African and European interests and objectives are no longer inherently irreconcilable. Frictions and differences on all manner of specific issues remain, but a broad area of common interest and concern has opened up—in the expansion of trade and investment, in economic and social development, and in political stability. This transformation in the form in which most African issues now present themselves is of surpassing importance. In it lies the essence of a new opportunity for U.S. policy—of reconciling and interrelating its African and European interests in all of new independent Africa.

Mr. Ball's Bold Thesis—A Critique

The fluidity and diversity of the problems being cast up in the several regions of Africa, independent and not yet independent, has predictably produced a variety of reactions within the United States. Many whose concern centers on those areas where European and African objectives remain in conflict, where self-determination is the issue, tend to plead for a line of American policy more independent of Europe. To them, to deal with the problems of contemporary Africa in a spirit of subservience to Europe, or even of parallel concern for European sensibilities, is a hangover of the past, a failure to understand and to come to grips with the present. Rather than the maintenance of European-African ties, they tend to feel the United States should seek to offer the new African nations an alternative to former dependence on the metropoles, another Western option in external ties and assistance.

To other Americans, fearful of an over-extension of American commitment or simply uneasy about the destabilizing effects of European removal from Africa, it appears that the United States is drifting toward too heavy and direct an involvement in Africa, thereby encouraging a European withdrawal from responsibility.

The more moderate of these seek, therefore, a cutback in American efforts and a stronger emphasis on the primacy of the European role. The more extreme, restless under the many present international burdens of the United States, seem inclined to want to toss the whole bothersome matter back to Europe, to unload on someone else the costs and cares of assisting and protecting a continent as large as Africa and as troubled as it is likely to be in the years ahead.

But many of those who, sorrowfully or gladly, accept the inevitability and necessity of an international leadership role for the United States have begun to search for some better pattern of U.S. policy in Africa which will serve U.S. interests and African needs, and at the same time contribute to closer U.S.-European ties—still the pivotal security alliance of the United States.

The most provocative of the ideas in this regard that have recently appeared are those of George Ball, Under Secretary of State under Presidents Kennedy and Johnson and later head of the U.S. delegation to the United Nations. Long an advocate of European unity and of greater U.S.-European cooperation, Ball holds views on American policy toward Africa that are a by-product of that interest. His proposals regarding a future pattern of European-American relations in Africa provide a concrete basis for analysis which brings out sharply both the potentialities and the limitations of trying to construct a new triangle of cooperation between Europe, Africa, and the United States.

The first public expression of Ball's ideas came in connection with a discussion of U.S. foreign economic policy before the Joint Economic Committee of the Congress on July 20, 1967. In commenting on the spreading net of preferential trade arrangements with Africa at that time, he suggested that perhaps the United States should depart from its traditional universalist approach and become reconciled to the advent of some kind of a "closed system" between Europe and Africa in economic affairs. Perhaps, he said, we should go even farther and seek some fuller "geographical division of responsibilities" between the United States and Europe in Africa.

His statement promptly made waves, particularly among economists concerned with international trade expansion and economic development. But Ball, unrepentant, proceeded during a brief interval in 1967 and early 1968 between official assignments to elaborate the implications of his congressional statement into a full-blown proposal for the restructuring of global relationships.

In his widely publicized book, *The Discipline of Power,* he presented the proposition that world order in the future requires the development of a strong and united Western Europe as a third power center, the present bipolarity as represented by the Soviet-U.S. confrontation being inherently and excessively unstable; and that the United States, as a matter of the highest importance, should therefore seek to encourage an integrated and federated Europe closely linked to the United States. Applying his general approach to the specific problem of the American attitude toward the broadening of European membership in the Common Market, he argued that the United States should accept the enlargement of this preferential trading area only on terms that would contribute to European political unification, his central objective. Thus the United States should oppose the admission of additional Western European countries to membership unless they were prepared to accept the full obligations of the Rome Treaty. Otherwise, from the American point of view, such an arrangement would create discrimination against our own production without a compensating contribution to European cohesion.

Turning then to Africa, he argued for the same notion of preferences-with-responsibilities: As a matter of justice and logic, any acceptable preferential trade arrangements between Europe and Africa had to be coupled with the assumption of substantial obligations going beyond commercial convenience or advantage on the part of the industrialized countries. This line of reasoning led him into a brief and fanciful speculation about the possibility of some kind of a general take-over of the problems of Africa by Europe:

> If the European Economic Community continues to expand its system of preferences for Africa we should, I think, make it emphatically clear that we will look to the nations of the Community to carry the burden of economic assistance and, where necessary, political tutelage for those African countries. In practice, this would mean an American recognition of the primacy of the European interest in Africa—and consequently the primacy of European responsibility for the economic assistance, education, health and defense of the African people.

But he indicated at the same time his awareness of the disadvantages of and impediments to such a sweeping "delegation" of responsibility to Europe, and he stopped far short of giving it his unqualified endorsement. At most, he was prepared to concede it could have some advantages and that it might, *faute de mieux*, have to be accepted:

> It would, of course, be to our interest to have relations between North and South so organized that all the industrialized nations of the North assumed a generalized responsibility for the whole less-developed world of the South. . . .
>
> There are, of course, serious disadvantages to sectioning the world as one might an apple, cutting it into slices that define the special relationships between particular Northern and Southern areas. Clearly this is not the best way to allocate responsibilities for the poorer nations of the South. It is structurally reminiscent of colonialism, and when it is based on Closed Systems of commercial relations it interferes with the most efficient use of resources.
>
> Nonetheless, we may in the long run be forced into it, since it may prove to be the only means of defining for Europeans a manageable area in which they can concentrate their foreign aid while looking after the education, health and defense of the African people.
>
> Any Closed System such as I have suggested is bound to create hardship and resentment even among the members and it is particularly offensive to nations that are left completely out of the regime of Closed Systems. I recognize all this and do not like it. Nonetheless, if Closed Systems continue to develop, as in the case between Africa and the European Community, we may well find it sensible to stop fighting the trend and undertake to draw up a rational scheme that takes account of it. Certainly the present situation in which the key nations of Europe belong to a Closed System while we do not, is far from perfect.

In the end, Ball's specific recommendation was more limited, more tentative. But its meaning was nevertheless loud and clear. The United States should take a fresh look at the European-African nexus of its foreign policy, and should explore new possibilities of U.S.-European collaboration in Africa and the Third World:

> It is time to review again with the European nations how we should design the structure of our relations between North and South. This might, I think, be the occasion for some serious discussions regarding the allocation of political and strategic responsibilities— particularly in Africa, where the Europeans do have considerable experience, large investments, and a great geopolitical interest. Such talks would be addressed primarily to responsibilities for Africa north of the Limpopo River, thus excluding the so-called White Redoubt countries (Portuguese Africa, South Africa and Rhodesia)

and south of the Atlas Mountains (thus excluding the Maghrebian countries, Morocco, Algeria, and Tunisia).[1]

The general workability of this concept of a restructured, multipolar world as a basis for international peace and order in the future need not be evaluated for the purposes of the present analysis. But Ball's suggestion of a reopening of basic questions about the framework of U.S.-European-African relations and of formal, high-level discussion of American and European roles in Africa deserves serious consideration on a number of grounds, including the extraordinary credentials of their author as international lawyer, businessman, and diplomat.

His proposed approach has at least three major virtues. First, he addresses the problem of reformulating American policy toward Africa in the context of global U.S. interests and responsibilities, the only adequate point of departure.

Second, he views the problem not only in breadth but in a long-term perspective and with a definite point of orientation. Specifically, what the United States does in Africa should, if possible, contribute both to European unity and to a sense of continuing European responsibility for Africa. This approach is both useful and relevant. To the extent that such European-African ties can be strengthened on the basis of mutual agreement, the advantages for Africa, Europe, and the world could be considerable. Nor is it impossible, once the wounds of colonialism have fully healed, that a new coming together of Europe and Africa may occur, that some limited, balanced, and mutually acceptable kind of European-African structure might emerge. To help keep open that possibility, and to encourage it as a long-term goal of American policy, is desirable.

Third, his acceptance of special links between Europe and Africa takes into account certain present trends and existing assets. Europe is a major factor in Africa; the EEC, with its Associated African States, is an existing structure; the network of preferential trade ties between Europe and Africa is spreading; the predominance of European assistance continues. The Ball approach means that such realities neither be ignored, nor uprooted, nor sacrificed on the altar of theoretical alternatives. The newly independent African states urgently need help, need shelter from the impending storms. For American policy to recognize and attempt to strengthen such useful relationships as now obtain with Europe makes plain good sense for all concerned.

However valid the general approach, it would nevertheless be well from the beginning to recognize both the rather limited objectives which it may be feasible to pursue in the short-term and the major obstacles standing in the way.

These relate, first and foremost, to the present states of mind in Europe and in independent Africa—European reluctance on the one hand to undertake, and African reluctance on the other to accept, wider European responsibilities. For Africans, their new states having finally achieved independence, the desire is to reach out for new international ties, not to throw themselves back into the embrace of Europe. Similarly, the European nations at present are strongly disinclined to assume new burdens in Africa. Faced with urgent problems of internal development, preoccupied with local and regional issues, Europe is in a mood of self-obsession, materialism, and a kind of isolationism approaching international irresponsibility. Nor can it be assumed the European nations are eager to join forces with one another in Africa. Indeed, to a large extent Europe remains competitive and separatist in its approach. The mechanisms and commitments of the Common Market are a counterforce, but Britain and France, the two major elements, are still far apart in their programs and policies in Africa and will not readily or quickly be brought together.

Such an atmosphere of reluctance, resistance, and division means that any American efforts to encourage greater European-African collaboration and a continuing sense of European responsibility in Africa are likely to be far more productive in certain functional areas than in others. There are, for example, some prospects for success in the area of trade: Europe is disposed to offer trade preferences which much of Africa is prepared to accept. Likewise in development aid, the nations of Europe have to a remarkable degree continued to accept the principal responsibility of providing financial, educational, and technical assistance. The present prospect is for gradual decline, but conceivably, this might at least be checked by some new forms of American inducement or commitment.

On the other hand there is little likelihood of success from any American effort to bring about an extension of European responsibilities to embrace, in Ball's words, "the defense of the African people." Any such attempt would very likely founder on grounds of double unacceptability. It is difficult to defend Africans or anyone else if they themselves do not desire such protection. And on the whole, despite the existence of a certain number of limited military arrangements with Europe, Africans are passionately convinced that their continent belongs to them and that their new nations must remain free of foreign military infringements upon their sovereignty. With only a few exceptions, they are opposed to foreign military bases on their soil. Should the need arise for military assistance, they have indicated a strong preference to receive it either from "neutral" states or from the United Nations rather than from the former European metropoles. The Nigerian crisis, and the eagerness of the Lagos government for more ample supplies of British arms, indicates that in extremis, help from the former metropole is welcomed, but African reservations about such military dependence remain. It is equally difficult to foresee circumstances under which the nations of Western Europe, individually or collectively, would be prepared to broaden their military and strategic commitments in Africa. They are all, in fact, moving at present in just the opposite direction.

If broader military and strategic links between Europe and Africa have rather little immediate prospect of acceptance, the idea of European "political tutelage" of Africa has even less. To press for immediate progress in this direction would be an exercise in futility, or worse.

The second general limitation in any American attempt to define and encourage a wider European role and responsibility in Africa is that however fruitful it may prove in certain fields and with some of the independent African countries, it will not lessen or dispose of many of the most dangerous problems facing American policy, especially in the south. Ball himself seems to have grave doubts about turning over to the Europeans responsibility for those African matters which could have real importance to the United States. This is implicit in his recommendation that in talks with the European nations in designing a new structure, the United States should concentrate on the area south of the Sahara and north of the White Redoubt. He is not ignorant of the fact that in a world ridden with racial strife, the United States can hardly refuse to be concerned with the issues posed in Southern Africa. With a Soviet fleet now cruising the Mediterranean, and with Libya having become the second largest oil-producing country in the non-Communist world, he is likewise aware that the United States cannot neglect some direct involvement there. His proposal thus comes down to the possibility of greater American deference to the nations of Europe in those parts of Africa where we presumably have lesser concern, namely the Tropical Center. But even there, question arises as to the extent to which a global power such as the United States can entrust its interests entirely to others. If dangerous eruptions or foreign intrusions should occur in Nigeria, Zambia, or the Congo in the future, could the United States at that point refuse to act to protect its interests if the European nations should fail or decline to? Certainly, at present the degree of actual clash of policy, particularly as between France and the United States, makes any notion of general U.S. deference to Europe in Africa seem premature and any assumption of an identity of interests quixotic. But even with Britain, where severe policy conflicts do not exist, it is doubtful whether that nation is ready or able to serve as the protector of U.S. and Western interests and positions in Africa.

Thus, however desirable, the achievement of greater European-African cooperation will not come soon, and the practical possibilities should not be overestimated. The labor will be long and difficult, and many of the most acute problems of African policy will not thereby disappear for the United States. These considerations in turn lead to the third basic implication of Ball's suggestion. Nothing will be accomplished by a mere "allocation" of new responsibilities to Europe or by a simple act of American backing-off. On the contrary, progress will be achieved, if at all, only by vigorous, continuous American effort, by the exercise of effective American persuasion upon Europeans and Africans, and by the acceptance of continuing and perhaps additional costs and commitments. The need is for *working with* and not *withdrawal from* the other parts of the fateful triangle. There, then, is the rub: American action and initiative is essential. But the Atlantic Alliance is in disarray, partly as a result of a failure of American leadership. And U.S. influence in Africa has been undercut by many factors, from its policies in Viet Nam to its weakening contribution to Third World development.

Inducing a greater degree of European cooperation and responsibility in Africa will not be any easier than any other aspect of the whole task of revitalizing the Atlantic Community. It is in fact an integral part of, and cannot be accomplished without some progress on, the total problem. Moreover, it has to be done, if it can be done at all, by the same method: not by scolding or sermonizing or threatening to walk out, and not by static formulas "allocating" European and American responsibilities, but by wholehearted and continuing American cooperation with Western Europe in helping Africa in its efforts in economic and educational development, in dealing with its problems with trade and attraction of investment, and in other common tasks. With cooperation, slow but significant progress can be made. Without it, Europe, Africa, and the United States can only drift apart, to the detriment of each and all and of the prospects for a stable and progressive world.

11

Southern Africa: Smoldering Catastrophe

One of the special complexities of Africa for American policy is its relationship to Europe and the consequent necessity of achieving wherever possible a coordinated, proportioned, European-American approach. One of the special dangers of Africa is the problem centered in the so-called White Redoubt, where, paradoxically, the possibility of a coordinated European-American policy is already severely limited and with the passage of time may well become impossible.

The Redoubt, a U-shaped cauldron consisting of five geographically contiguous areas at the southern tip of the continent, under the control of white minority regimes, is an area simmering with discontents which could boil over in massive bloodshed at some point in the future, arouse violent emotions throughout the world, and almost inevitably attract great-power involvement, thereby presenting major hazards to peace. It is the most blatant and brutal example in the contemporary world of denial of the human and political rights on the basis of race.

For the Communist powers, it is a most attractive opportunity for unmasking the democratic pretensions of the West and for identifying their own policies with the aspirations of the vast number of ex-colonial and nonwhite peoples of the world. For most of the nations of Western Europe, the situation is an international nuisance and embarrassment but not much more. But, for the United States, the problem has far greater significance. It is a challenge pointed directly at the political ideas and ideals which it symbolizes and on which its international prestige in major parts rests. Moreover, the challenge which it presents

349

reaches deeply into American society itself, already dangerously troubled by racial questions. The United States cannot, therefore, merely follow a passive European lead on the issues or concern itself primarily with maintaining close coordination with its European allies without risk of major damage to its world position and perhaps even greater damage to its own internal strength and unity in the future. If the United States were to shift to bolder, more independent action, the damaging impact on some of its European allies could be considerable; and yet the United States may well be obliged in its own vital interests to strike off more and more on just such a course.

Even apart from the dilemma of widening European-American divergence on the problem, the African South presents American policy with one of the most inherently baffling and frustrating problems in the world today. What the United States should try to achieve is not easy to define. And how to go about achieving it—given the risks flanking all sides of every possible course of action and the world-wide repercussions which could follow an ill-considered move—is both obscure and intimidating.

FACING THE FACT OF PRESENT FAILURE

Among nearly all those who feel something should be done about Southern Africa—African nationalists, independent African states, much of the world community, including the United States— there is agreement that the goal of all efforts should be the open- ing, or reopening, of a political dialogue, not the provocation of war. Yet if future efforts toward this objective are to bear fruit, the starting point for a re-evaluation of policy must be candid recognition of the utter failure of all that has been attempted to date. For twenty years, no other issue has so commanded the gen- eral disapproval of the world, no other issue has been dealt with so relentlessly and repeatedly at the United Nations and elsewhere over so many years. And yet, despite all the efforts of quiet bilateral diplomacy, of noisy multilateral diplomacy, of moral suasion and condemnation, and of ostracism and sanctions, the political predicament of the blacks in the Redoubt is today worse than in 1945, not better, and the prospects for violence and a worsening of the situation in the future are greater, not less. Before better approaches can be formulated, some hard questions have to be put about what has gone wrong and why.

Fundamentally, it would seem that the very nature of the

problem has been misjudged and misunderstood; and, as a result, the measures taken have typically been inadequate and sometimes almost irrelevant. From the beginning, the operative premise, explicit or implicit, of those hoping to alter the situation in Southern Africa has been that the problem was one of modifying political relationships between whites and nonwhites in a setting if not of mutual rapport, at least of communication and potential negotiation. Because there were supposedly some available constructive outlets for the forces of change and a degree of malleability, it was further assumed that some combination of gestures from the outside plus pressures from inside organized by nonracist whites and by the blacks would suffice to bring about the desired results. One basis for this expectation was an assumed parallel between the situation in Southern Africa and that in Northern and tropical Africa, where, except in Algeria, such methods had resulted in decolonization. Another was the assumption that "natural forces"—e.g., economic development and industrialization in South Africa—would necessarily work on behalf of the gradual improvement of the political as well as the material position of the blacks.

Whether such assumptions were ever an accurate or adequate conception of the problem, they are now neither accurate nor adequate. Anything resembling political dialogue between the contesting parties within the area has been interrupted. Polarization of attitudes has increased. What little flexibility in positions may have existed has given way to rigidity. Any existing avenues of evolutionary political development for the blacks—whether through the Bantustan concept in South Africa, or what is called assimilation in the Portuguese colonies, or the procedures of some new multiracial constitution in Rhodesia—are very limited, if not indeed fictitious. As to the effect of "natural forces," twenty years of economic boom in South Africa have brought modest material benefit to the blacks, but a steady worsening of their political position.

Likewise, the imagined parallel between the former situations in other parts of Africa and that now obtaining in the Redoubt does not stand scrutiny. In the British and French territories, and even in the former Belgian colonies, the controlling powers were modern, industrialized states. By their exposure to the Reformation, the Enlightenment, and the Industrial Revolution they had been deeply affected by conceptions of individualism, socialism, and democracy. They were therefore more or less "soft" to the moral and political demands for freedom and self-determination by peoples of the colonies. France tried for a time to behave otherwise in Algeria but, as a result, tore its society and institutions to ribbons and in the end had to make its conduct conform to the values of a twentieth century Western nation. But in Southern Africa, such responsiveness and responsibility on the part of the controlling white groups does not prevail. Portugal, an antiquated, authoritarian country, which has long been cut off from the mainstream of European political and intellectual development, remains ideologically fixed like a fly in amber in the sixteenth century. Although Portugal may in time give way to force, it is unlikely to be moved by moral pressures or democratic ideas as long as its present political system prevails. South Africa, for a complex of ethnic, religious, and historical reasons, is likewise politically impervious to such influences and is capable of imposing repression and exploitation virtually without restraint on its nonwhites over a sustained period. Rhodesia has now passed under the control of a group of whites of such racist convictions that its responsiveness to counterarguments is now likely to be imperceptible. Therefore, while some superficial, cosmetic changes in policy may be accomplished by external appeals or condemnation, though even that is far from certain, all these areas are basically disposed to the limit of their economic and if need be their military strength to try to hold on.

Realistically, then, the problem as it has developed is not one of mere political adjustment but of a radical transfer of political power to be accomplished between antagonistic and extremely unequal groups. It is in this sense nothing less than a revolutionary problem. That is why the application of appeals and indirect pressures has not worked. That is why it is so dangerous. That is why the choices it poses for American policy are so painful. But recognizing frankly and intelligently the kind of change being called for and the means by which it probably has to occur may at least make it possible to reintroduce some relevancy in the approach of the African nationalists, their Afro-Asian sympathizers, and some of the Western nations, including the United States.

If the problem is of this stark and obdurate character, the question arises whether the United States, by its own efforts or in company with other nations, can find measures which will be sufficient to cause the present regimes to make basic political concessions to their black majorities without the use or the threat of force and therefore of the risk of war. The chances are not too bright that it can, but not to make a further search for them is to make a possibly avoidable disaster probably inevitable.

CREATIVE TENSION—A NEW AMERICAN APPROACH

The issue of Southern Africa for American policy is so unorthodox and complex, and so overlaid with prejudice and emotion, that it is essential to begin by etching with the greatest possible clarity the controlling postulates of a suggested new American policy, which even under the passions engendered by crises must not be compromised. First, the goal must continue to be to help bring about a political settlement of some kind by negotiation or at least by means other than naked force. Second, negotiation or settlement can only be accomplished, practically and in principle, by the parties directly involved. What has ultimately to be done cannot be done by third parties or elements alien to the areas in question. Third, in exercising its influence, the United States must for reasons of self-interest and self-respect continue to support without qualification the principles of self-determination and equal human rights. Fourth, the United States must withhold absolutely the use of its own military force or military assistance to either side.

A number of the reasons for these postulates are self-evident and have been frequently emphasized: Any resort to force would be contrary to commitments under the U.N. Charter; and in a world already cursed with too much war and with nuclear as well as other military dangers, it would be unacceptably dangerous and irresponsible for the United States to contribute to still another breach of the peace. But there is an additional practical reason of great human meaning which deserves to receive greater emphasis than some who are impatient for more direct action tend to give. The present fact within the Redoubt is one of a total disparity of armed strength between the whites and the blacks. This disparity, plus the moral climate prevailing among the whites who monopolize the modern weapons, has made it possible on at least one occasion in recent years for tens of thousands of blacks to be killed within a period of a few weeks in a reprisal action.* If by

* The situation was in Northern Angola in early 1961. Because of tight censorship, adequate data on the massacres carried out by the Portuguese after an armed uprising by blacks and half-castes are not available. But foreigners who were in the area at the time, including a number of American businessmen (some of whom politically were sympathetic to Portuguese

A FUTURE U.S. POLICY TOWARD AFRICA

the sudden introduction of a major new external military factor the extremity of life-and-death struggle between whites and blacks in the region were precipitated, the immediate result could be an appalling loss of life—black life—because of the present inability of the blacks to defend themselves and the practical impossibility of outside forces to rescue or protect them. Over a longer term, even if African guerrilla action with powerful foreign support might gain "victory," the problems of subsequent occupation, pacification, and the re-establishment of functioning political systems in a passion-laden and blood-soaked atmosphere are fearful to contemplate.[1]

Thus, in effect, the United States must continue to pursue a peaceful and reasonable goal which, for the present at least, seems beyond reach; it must stand firm and uncompromisingly on its political principles; it must begin to show a more vigorous and purposeful kind of concern; and yet it must put aside the one element of its power which might make a decisive difference, its armed strength. Quite obviously, such stipulations are nearly self-contradictory. But not totally. In the narrow space between lies the zone of possible and appropriate action. That zone, though limited, is sufficient for much more to be done. What is called for is a line of policy operating on several levels simultaneously, requiring fine distinctions as well as great patience, and seeking not a spurious tranquility but the deliberate stimulation of creative tensions out of which some genuine political settlement might come.

First and more concretely, the U.S. government should continue its full and active participation in multilateral efforts through the United Nations and otherwise to condemn discriminatory practices and infringements of human rights, and to employ limited measures other than force to attempt to persuade the present regimes to alter their course. Such multilateral action is not in itself likely to have a decisive, or even significant, effect. But the principles embodied are those which the United States symbolizes and which the international community, if it stands for anything, must assert. So long as efforts are directed to activating a political process, rather than the imposition of a formula or the use of

---

policy), have estimated the number of deaths by burning, machine-gunning, and bombing to have ranged from 75,000 to 150,000 over a six-week period. Given the number of deaths resulting from French repression of uprisings in Madagascar in 1947, such figures are not improbable.

force, they deserve backing, Moreover, it is not inconceivable that over the longer term, despite the general intractability of the situation as it now exists, they can result in some gains as circumstances change. Combined with other efforts, the possibility of their effectiveness greatly increases.

Second, with respect to its own national action, the United States must do two kinds of things: (a) begin to evaluate more critically the limited utility to itself of the maintenance of normal "friendly" diplomatic relations with the regimes of the Redoubt, and in the interest of its own world-wide prestige and credibility be far more careful than before to avoid even the appearance of collaboration with them; and (b) begin to give greater attention to the vulnerability of the adjacent African states to the developing political counteroffensive of the Redoubt.

In regard to the former, direct relations with Rhodesia have now been cut off. But the full benefits of normal relations with the United States are still accorded to South Africa and Portugal— not necessarily to the net advantage of the United States. A fresh and hardheaded review of all remaining forms of cooperation and assistance with these regimes is called for to determine which are essential to maintain lines of communication and the avoidance of outright rupture, which are expendable carry-overs from the past, and which are on balance compromising or dangerous to the broader interests of the United States. The review should embrace all economic and military aid to Portugal (which necessarily would require re-examining the desirability or undesirability of continued Portuguese membership in NATO) and the full range of present cooperation with South Africa—from official uranium purchase contracts, to space-tracking facilities agreements, to the flow of U.S. private investments. To insure that sufficiently broad criteria of judgment are employed, such review might best be made by a group commissioned by the President and representing not only government and business, but also church, Negro, and other interested U.S. elements. The point of cutting back certain present kinds of cooperation is not "to bring the present regimes to their knees," which is a futile hope. In fact, the economic or other impact upon them would probably be negligible. But the action would give some substance and credibility to the American posture of moral disapproval of their policies.

Beyond taking better care of its own interests and world-wide reputation in the handling of direct relations with the Redoubt, the United States must begin to give greater attention to helping protect the adjacent areas from demoralization and disorganization as a result of pressures from the Redoubt. Should such disorganization occur, it could greatly increase the instability and explosiveness of the situation in Southern Africa and perhaps well beyond. The purpose basically would be to keep the area of danger from spreading. Measures, essentially economic and financial, are called for to re-enforce the frail new governments of Botswana, Lesotho, and Swaziland, which now are vulnerable to South African demands. If they are to survive, they have no alternative to a policy of accommodation with their overpowering neighbor; but they should not be abandoned to it. Likewise, the states of Zambia, Tanzania, the Congo, and Malawi must be assisted in greater degree to reduce their vulnerability to Rhodesian, Portuguese, and South African pressures and controls and to buffer them against the impact of any international economic sanctions.*

These actions will be of value—but they leave the core of the problem almost untouched. They will do almost nothing to accelerate political change within the Redoubt itself. Essentially, such change can only come from an increase of *internal* pressures on the present white regimes to negotiate political concessions with their nonwhite citizens. Although external multinational efforts of a nonmilitary kind can perhaps help to create an atmosphere of tension conducive to political change, at best they can only be supplementary and ancillary. Pressures strong enough to bring the present regimes to the point of negotiating or conceding real political power to the blacks can only be generated by the blacks themselves—by internal political activity, combined perhaps with external nationalist, political, and, in all probability, military or guerrilla action.

* For the responsible policy-maker, the gnawing question then has to be asked: "Yes, but at what cost?" To this, only a general and logically unsatisfactory a priori response can be given: "Limited and reasonable, but enough to make a significant difference in giving these countries the *feeling* of having an alternative to submission, of not having been abandoned." In the case of Lesotho, for example, with a majority of its working force employed in South Africa, some meaningful contribution to its development program should be made, but to insure it against all the effects of possible South African economic pressure would be out of the question. In the case of Zambia, a few million dollars to help ease its transport problems in circumventing Rhodesian control would be significant and reasonable, but tens of millions of dollars to enable it to develop military and air forces superior to those of Rhodesia would be unreasonable. The fact that the costs in theory might be enormous if not controlled is—in the uncertain calculus of foreign policy—not a conclusive reason for doing nothing.

As of now, the internal political base for black nationalist efforts to bring about change in Southern Africa remains extremely weak. Because of the backwardness and tribal divisions among the populations, and because of the ruthless measures directed against them by the white regimes, indigenous political movements have never been strong and under the frustrations and harassments of recent years have become even weaker. Nor have most of the liberation groups operating from outside the Redoubt been much more effective. Small, inexperienced, and impoverished, they have faced almost hopeless tasks of simultaneously pleading their case before various international bodies, training and disciplining their fragmentary political organizations and liberation "armies," and attempting through all the obstacles of frontier controls, censorship, police spies, and other problems to organize support at home. Their efforts have not been helped by persistent tendencies for internal factions to quarrel and to form splinter groups, or by the strong preference of some leaders for the pleasures of speechmaking and the diplomatic high life rather than the unglamorous work of staff development and administration or the dangers of fighting in the bush. There are some brilliant exceptions, but on the whole the nationalist forces remain frail and ineffective—and still trapped to an inversion of proper priorities, giving their primary effort to arousing international sympathy and gestures of support rather than to building their own organizational, political, and military strength.

But first things are now beginning to be put first. The illusion that some *deus ex machina* in the form of international or great power intervention is going to bestow liberation as a kind of gift upon their peoples is fast melting away, replaced by a growing recognition that if change is to come, it will have to be largely as a result of their own efforts and sacrifices. They will have to develop the skills, create and lead the organizations, impose the discipline—and insofar as that may be necessary, shed the blood. Hopes that there could be revolution by proxy, that the sacrifices and risks would be borne by others, and that indirect political and propaganda action would be enough have all proven false. What they can count on in the form of material help rather than symbolic expressions of support from their friends in the international community—except possibly from the Soviet Union and China— all of whom have more than enough troubles of their own, is likely to be precious little. Even that cannot be effective except in relation to driving, courageous, unified, sustained, intelligent effort by the nationalist movements themselves. If a way to political dialogue is to be found, the single most essential need therefore is to strengthen these nationalist political forces.

Assuming that the proper and responsible course for the United States is to refuse to do this by supplying them with arms or military equipment, the sharp-edged question which then arises is: Can and should the United States government undertake to do it by financial and other nonmilitary means? The question is heavy with implications.

There is no doubt about the need of these movements for help. At present they are confronted with every conceivable handicap: lack of training facilities for their cadres; lack of facilities for communicating among themselves and with their adherents within the Redoubt; lack of resources to provide even minimum health, education, and welfare services to the areas (e.g., Northern Mozambique) already under their physical control; lack of funds even to meet the costs of their tiny staffs and of sending their representatives to the United Nations and other international bodies.

What limited assistance the United States government has so far given in the form of relief supplies and scholarships for refugees, however welcome to the individual recipients, has represented humanitarian concern, not coherent political purpose. It has been insignificant in checking the drift of the nationalist movements into bitterness, extremism, and growing dependence on Communist support.

For the United States to begin officially to provide more ample assistance to them—even of a strictly nonmilitary kind—will, of course, promptly raise cries of interference in the internal affairs of the white-controlled countries. These charges will, moreover, be massively amplified by the extensive propaganda and lobbying system these regimes currently maintain in the United States.[2] Quite apart from such self-interested charges, however, the question of intervention and its proper limits must be carefully weighed in all its subtlety. Even the term "intervention" is elusive to define: Has the American economic and military assistance given to Portugal under NATO arrangements and otherwise, despite restrictions on its use, not constituted "intervention" on the side of white control in Africa? Similarly, have the highly sophisticated weapons (including aircraft and submarines) provided to South Africa in the past not amounted to intervention? Does *nonintervention* by the United States on behalf of the blacks under present circumstances not in effect amount to intervention on the side of the existing regimes?

Obviously, nonintervention is not an absolute principle governing the actual policies of actual governments. Numerous precedents of intervention in U.S. policy can readily be cited from Cuba to China to Eastern Europe, where every form of U.S. assistance has at one time or another been given to groups opposed to the present regimes. The policy issue presented, therefore, cannot be dealt with in purely scholastic or legalistic terms. Realistically, the questions to be asked and answered are: Is it wise and proper to intervene abroad against a security menace (or, as in the Dominican Republic, what is designated a security menace) but not in behalf of other national commitments or interests? Are some new forms of, or a different bias in, U.S. intervention in Southern Africa now required? What forms of intervention, if any, would be useful and appropriate to U.S. interests and responsibilities?

The case for increasing such help rests on these grounds: Without it, there is no reasonable prospect of achieving the stated objective of American policy—namely, a political process rather than race war in Southern Africa. Despite their present weaknesses, the existing nationalist movements are embodiments of the universal human impulse to freedom and self-determination, which the United States in principle has committed itself to defend. Not to give them help is to condemn them to extremism, to prolong oppression in the Redoubt, and basically to position the United States on the side of the present white regimes in the coming struggle for power. The reasons for helping the black political movements are therefore related to American self-interest, political principles, and moral responsibility.

If the case for intervention in this sense is conclusive, then specific corollary questions arise of what help and through what means. There are kinds of nonmilitary assistance which would be important to improve the political effectiveness of the movements, and such help can prudently be given by the United States if one rule is followed: the help should not be given directly—which would present both disadvantages for the movements by subjecting them, or appearing to subject them, to U.S. pressures if not control; and disadvantages to the United States by involving it in endless factional dissensions among competing nationalist elements, as well as other avoidable problems. The better method would be to provide any assistance through responsible existing African governments—individually or through the OAU.

More concretely, the following kinds of assistance deserve consideration: First, grants of funds to the government of Tanzania, Zambia, and the Congo to enable them to give greater financial assistance to the movements operating on their soil and incidentally to relieve these governments and the movements themselves of the heavy burdens of refugee support which have been imposed on them as a result of political oppression in the south. Second, grants of funds to the OAU for its allocation in support of the educational, medical, and administrative needs of the several movements. Third, and of very great importance, special funds to enable the nationalist movements to develop their contact and communication with the black populations within the Redoubt by means of programs of informational and educational publishing and broadcasting. It would be both unwise and unnecessary for the U.S. government to become as directly involved in the support of such activities as it has long done, for example, in the case of "unofficial" broadcasting to the Soviet Union, Eastern Europe, and Communist China. But grants to the OAU or to an existing responsible black African government to help support such activity are called for. Without such action by the United States, the black populations of the south are abandoned to the present smothering totalitarian controls which are imposed on all media of communication; and the nationalist movements are cut off from contact with the mass of their people.

SOME FURTHER QUESTIONS

The altered U.S. policy as proposed includes continuation of many of the basic elements of present policy, a more rigorous examination of all relationships with the regimes of the Redoubt, greater help to the endangered black states on the borderline, and increased assistance to the black political movements to help them generate greater internal pressure on the present white minority governments. If it is assumed that these actions will help accelerate progress toward evolutionary political change in the Redoubt, when could change come? What changes would be accomplished? And, in the world-wide context which this analysis has emphasized, what would be the costs of such a policy to the United States outside Africa, especially in relations with Western Europe?

As to the first, no one can say. The timetable is inherently indeterminate. There are reasons to think it may extend over many years, perhaps decades: The labor of political organization and

politicization of the black populations will be long, and fundamental alteration in the human values and organized will for
resistance of the whites will not come quickly. But it conceivably
could be rather short. How long Portugal can stand the strain
of its present program of military repression cannot be foreseen.
A single triggering event could produce political unheaval in
Portugal itself at any time. There could be a sudden shift in the
level and type of assistance given by the major Communist powers
to some of the nationalist liberation forces. These and other
possible developments could sharply change expectations. Given
the inherent unpredictability of the situation, the approach proposed is one of multiple and parallel efforts, of staying in close and
waiting for whatever breaks may come.

Equally unpredictable is the eventual nature and form of any
change. Hitherto, the implicit single goal of the advocates of
change has been the transfer of decisive political authority in the
existing political units to the black majorities—over some relatively
brief period of time. As a goal, such a formulation is reasonable;
but as a description of what is likely to happen, it is illusory. Even
if the present regimes can be persuaded or brought to accept some
modification of the *status quo*, there are available a large number
of alternative or intermediate forms of concession: the transfer by
Portugal of self-governing status to its colonies on some basis of
local, restricted multiracial control; or in Rhodesia, further constitutional modification altering the pace and limits of increase in
African political participation; or in South Africa, the establishment of additional Bantustans on its own territory, and the "spin-
ning off" of portions of South West Africa into supposedly
self-governing units. If and when change comes, it is most likely
to be in the form of such murky, controversial compromises. In
the end, the Africans themselves will have to decide whether and
which of such imperfect solutions they will accept.

A revised U.S. policy will hopefully produce gains for the black
populations of the Redoubt, for the long-term climate of world
peace, and for the American position throughout Africa and in many
other parts of the world. But it will also impose costs and possible
losses, especially in relations with Western Europe. More particularly, Portugal and the United Kingdom would be significantly
and directly affected, the former because of its position in Angola
and Mozambique and the latter because of its position in Rhodesia
and its many commercial and investment interests in South Africa.

There are those, including some prominent Portuguese, who feel that increased American pressure to force that government to make progressive political concessions to the African colonies would be a boon to Lisbon by sparing it from repeating the error of rigidity, which previously caused Portugal to lose completely its once great South American possessions. The present Portuguese government, however, is not likely to take such a detached and philosophical view. American encouragement to the nationalists would officially be regarded as antithetical to Lisbon's interests. For practical diplomatic purposes, the proposed change in the U.S. course must be expected to encounter sharp official opposition by Portugal, and conceivably could lead to the loss of U.S. base rights in the Azores and to Portuguese withdrawal from NATO.

The consequences of the suggested U.S. policy shift for Britain and British-U.S. relations would probably be more subtle and more mixed. Greater U.S. pressure on the Ian Smith regime could be helpful to present British policy and might be welcomed—tacitly if not publicly—by the British government, most members of the Commonwealth, and some elements of the British public. Similarly, greater American pressure on South Africa would be consistent with the present principles of British policy, or at least would not be objectionable. If, however, Britain were to be directly implicated in some U.S. action of a highly offensive or frightening character to the South African government, retaliatory action against British trade or investments might result. In turn, the economic impact on Britain could be serious. This implies the need for close private consultation with Britain in the implementation of any new policy toward South Africa, careful timing, and a readiness to buffer Britain from damaging economic penalties, if necessary.

The general impact of a shift in American policy on the NATO alliance can only be assessed in still wider terms. Greater pressure on Portugal for a change in its colonial policy would meet with more support among various NATO members than the statements of some advocates of "NATO solidarity" might lead one to suppose. The Scandinavian countries, for example, have repeatedly indicated their discontent with Portuguese policy in Africa; and major political groups in most of the principal Western European countries (including some Christian Democrats, Labor, the Socialists, and other elements of the Left) would not object even to Portugal's exclusion from NATO. Militarily, they argue, Portugal's contribution is inconsequential; and if the NATO alliance is ever to be reconstituted politically and revitalized along modern lines, it must purge itself of affiliation with dictatorships and reaction as exemplified by the Salazar tradition in Portugal. At the least, it can be said that the impact of an American policy change in Southern Africa upon NATO would be mixed and that the negative effects could be greatly reduced and the positive effects increased by the means in which the change was introduced, the terms in which it was explained, and the methods employed in prior consultation with allies.

In effect, therefore, the policy modifications proposed involve some concrete risks and costs in the hope of achieving certain basic but rather uncertain, intangible, and possibly slow gains. Is the danger of the situation really so ominous as to necessitate, on the part of the United States, more than passive concern and symbolic action at a time when so many other dangers beset the world? Can the United States take the risk of further unsettling still another region by aiding and abetting black political activity in Southern Africa, which can in the end only be disturbing to the *status quo?*

These are the bedrock questions, and they can be answered only by other and still more troublesome ones: Can the United States, in the face of a situation which is offensive, explosive, and deteriorating, consciously hold to a line of policy which is clearly inadequate to alter the situation? Can the United States, even apart from questions of principle, wisely throw the causes and the majority political movements of Southern Africa to the extremists and the Communists by a policy of aloofness? Can it, in a revolutionary world, commit its future and its interests not only to the *status quo,* but in Southern Africa to a *status quo* which by every avowed principle of the United States is indefensible? Can the fabric of American society itself stand the consequences of another protracted situation in which major elements of U.S. society deeply feel that the nation is committed to a fundamentally immoral line of policy? For, let it be plainly recognized: The issues of Southern Africa, once the Viet Nam agony is finished, are going to be the next foreign policy focus of the moral indignation of youth, the Negroes, and the American left. A policy of passivity and compromise now—though it may seem to some a prudent course for the moment—can only reap another terrible harvest of bitter division in the United States in the future. Only the issues and the dangers are clear-cut. But, amid all the uncertainties and obscurities, it is difficult to believe that there is either dignity or wisdom in a policy limited to words and pious posturing.

12

Peace-Keeping and Security Policy

That the United States cannot be policeman for the world is a proposition which an increasing number of Americans are coming to believe. Yet, because of its vital interest in an orderly and peaceful international system, the United States cannot view with indifference the outbreak of violence and spreading disorder in any major region. The prospect and attendant problems of such disorder is the third great challenge which Africa presents to U.S. policy.

The dangers are not merely hypothetical. Despite the generally peaceful character of the process of decolonization, Africa has in recent years contributed its full share of disturbances to the disordered state of the world. These have included one major colonial war, a large-scale civil struggle, a bloody racial uprising, several ongoing anticolonial revolutions, instances of aggression by one state against another, several violent secessionist attempts, and literally dozens of coups, counter-coups, political murders, and army mutinies and revolts.*

In Africa, these outbreaks of internal violence have repeatedly drawn in foreign military forces—French, British, and Belgian troops. They have required the intervention of a multinational force under the United Nations on one occasion. And the United States, the Soviet Union, and China, though avoiding direct confrontation

---

* The growing number of such conflicts is probably a world-wide phenomenon. As Robert McNamara, then Secretary of Defense, pointed out in a speech in Montreal, Canada, on May 18, 1966, "At the beginning of 1958, there were 23 prolonged insurgencies going on about the world. As of February 1, 1966 there were 40."

thus far, have repeatedly played an indirect or background role, sometimes active and substantial. Two facts are quite clear: Africa is an area of instability, and the instability which has thus far occurred has often produced wider international repercussions. Looking to the future, there is every likelihood that the number of outbreaks will grow, and the crucial cases will cause far-reaching international disturbances.

Within the newly independent states, the frequency of internal violence since about 1963 has been increasing, and this trend can be expected to continue for identifiable reasons: The expectations of material improvement following independence have on the whole not been satisfied. The unifying political factors that were operative during the period of anticolonial struggle have now progressively lost their adhesiveness. Tribal antagonisms from an earlier era have continued, and the crazy-quilt of inherited political boundaries is another very likely source of future frictions. A climate of lawlessness and resort to force has been created as leaders, faced with growing threats to their power in the form of public discontent, factionalism, and resurgent separatism, have typically taken measures of dubious constitutionality in repressing opposition. Until effective governmental institutions take firmer root and some new political equilibrium can be achieved, the prospect is for a rising number of coups, secessions, civil wars, and, though less likely, violence by one new state against another. Many of the outbreaks will be purely internal and localized. But others could arouse much greater international concern, such as an attempt by Egypt to seize or subvert Libya or the region of Eritrea in Ethiopia, or fighting between Guinea and Ivory Coast, or a new break-up in the Congo. In this respect, the worst dangers by far lie, of course, in the south. There the racial revolutions, however slow and erratic their present pace, are already under way and the possibilities of military escalation are very considerable. For international peace, therefore, Africa represents both a gigantic new Balkan problem and an open boundary of East-West confrontation.

Given these prospects, the need for the United States is to define the extent of its interests and responsibilities and to determine what peace-keeping role it should play. Formidable in themselves, the security problems of Africa are an integral part of the still broader range of such problems presented by all the restless, impoverished nations of the Third World. Some of them can, in principle, best be left to the individual African states themselves to deal with. But their capacity to do so may be a matter of legitimate U.S. concern, for it will take some time and considerable investment before internal security forces in independent Africa are adequate to fulfill the tasks formerly carried out by colonial forces. Some of the impending problems will call for multilateral action; but the OAU has yet to develop a peace-keeping capability, and the United Nations has now been financially and politically handcuffed in its peace-keeping function. Some problems may call for U.S.-European cooperation; some, for East-West cooperation; and possibly some, for direct U.S. intervention.

The problem of peace and order in Africa is formidably varied and complex, and it provides an example, *par excellence*, of the necessity in American policy of viewing and dealing with African issues in a global context.

U.S. SECURITY POLICY IN EVOLUTION

From a strategic and military viewpoint, U.S. interest and activities in Africa to date form a generally coherent and consistent pattern. The continent has been considered to be of relatively little importance in terms of U.S. military plans and requirements, and with the advances in military technology in recent years, the strategic significance of Africa—probably to its great good fortune —is decreasing. The United States's security is considered not to be directly involved, and Africa itself poses no threat; nor does the pursuit of other world-wide U.S. objectives, now or in the foreseeable future, require a direct or substantial American military presence in Africa. Likewise, to the converse question of whether Africa would be of significant value militarily to the Soviet Union, the answer is generally considered to be negative, and for the same essential reasons: Certain African bases and facilities could be of value, but highly vulnerable. Africa has no military forces which would make important contributions to Soviet requirements; communications lines across Africa would be unreliable in time of war; and the U.S.S.R., like the United States, is not economically dependent on African supplies in peace or war.

The military activities of the United States in Africa are a logical reflection of these strategic judgments. After World War II the United States largely gave up the bases it had used in North Africa for the landings in Southern Europe. The defense perimeter of NATO was originally drawn to include Algeria, but since the independence of the North African countries it no longer includes any part of Africa. In 1950, with the Russian entry into the nuclear field, the United States built three new Strategic Air Command bases in Morocco, became a joint user of North African naval facilities, and obtained the use of Wheelus Field as a year-round training facility in Libya. In Ethiopia, it also developed a major military communications facility at Kagnew. But with the passing of the era of the B-47, the Moroccan bases have now been closed down, and Wheelus is being phased out. Only Kagnew remains and, though important, is no longer considered indispensable.

U.S. policy has been consistent in avoiding formal mutual security pacts with the new African states, except for a limited agreement for military cooperation with Liberia, which included the use of a military airfield near Monrovia. Military assistance figures in independent Africa have also been severely restricted. The volume from 1950 through 1967 totaled only $227 million, and for 1968 and 1969 is likely to average less than $25 million per year. Seventeen countries at one time or another have received such aid. Some former French territories were briefly included, but strenuous French objections brought a prompt cessation. At present there are only six countries which receive equipment and training; of these, Ethiopia receives nearly half the military assistance funds allocated to Africa. Tunisia and Morocco are also relatively large recipients, partly in consequence of sizable Soviet military assistance to their neighbor, Algeria. The Congo, Libya, and Liberia complete the list. The program has been a form of base rental in Ethiopia, in Liberia and, until 1963, in Morocco. To a lesser extent it has been a riposte to Soviet actions. In the Congo it has been supplementary to Belgian assistance, designed in part to maintain the involvement of the former metropole in the strengthening of Congolese internal security forces.

Because of strong congressional sentiment against stimulating arms races in the underdeveloped regions, military assistance to Africa has been subjected not only to financial limitations but also to restrictions on the type of arms provided and the purposes for which they can be used. Section 508 of the Foreign Assistance Act requires that "no military assistance or sales shall be furnished . . . to any country in Africa, except for internal security requirements or for civic action requirements," except as specifically authorized by the President. The so-called Symington Amendment to the same act is intended to discourage "excessive" military expenditures by underdeveloped countries, including the use of foreign exchange for such purposes; and it directs the President to terminate U.S. economic assistance to any such countries which divert their resources to "unnecessary" military expenditures. The Conte-Long Amendment further prohibits assistance to all underdeveloped countries for the purchase of "sophisticated weapons systems" such as missiles or jet aircraft and, in the event of such purchases, directs the President to withhold U.S. economic assistance by an equivalent amount.

One of the purposes of the United States in not drawing the new African states into direct participation in its military alliances and in keeping its military assistance small has been to emphasize insofar as possible the primacy of European responsibility for African security. When outbreaks have occurred, it has tended to stay in the background in deference to European, African, and U.N. responsibilities. On the whole, therefore, it can convincingly be claimed that the United States has no important military or strategic designs on Africa; it has behaved with severe restraint in not contributing to arms races and military expansion in independent Africa; and it has tried to keep the direct military aspect of the cold war out of Africa. The record is a creditable one; the policies followed provide some of the elements of a sound and promising course for the future.

ELEMENTS OF A FUTURE U.S. ROLE

For a combination of mutually re-enforcing reasons, the basic approach of the United States to the prospective security problems that will arise in Africa must be one of minimal military and unilateral involvement. Simple prudence in the allocation of U.S. resources requires it. Moreover, in the vast majority of the situations to be dealt with, a direct U.S. presence would be likely to aggravate the political atmosphere of the conflict and quite possibly would draw in opposing great power resources and thereby set in train a dangerous escalation. The intrusion of external forces would also tend to inhibit and undercut the growth of African skills and responsibility for dealing in the first instance and insofar as possible with their own security problems.

Adherence to a policy of minimal military and unilateral involvement will oblige the United States to put aside some of the criteria for Third World intervention which it has sometimes asserted in the past. One criterion has been opposition to illegal seizures of power by dictators, military or nonmilitary. This is not to say that the appearance of such regimes should be fostered or their practices condoned, but direct attempts to suppress or replace them would be both indefensible and futile. The past twenty-five years have demonstrated the fruitlessness of attempting to implant an alien idea of Western-style parliamentary government in the present environment of the underdeveloped areas, including Africa. It will likewise be necessary to re-examine the whole pattern of U.S. thinking about counterinsurgency and "liberation wars." In contrast to past over-reaction to such incidents, it will in the future be wiser in many cases to accept the existence and activity of revolutionary and sometimes Communist-oriented or affiliated groups without automatic hostility or opposition. It will even be necessary to watch aggressions committed by one African state against another and, in the typical case, to limit the American response to verbal censure.

The United States will probably be repeatedly faced with appeals from African regimes subjected to internal subversion or external aggression, whose own defenses are being overwhelmed and who are in desperate need of external assistance if they are to survive. Though it cannot wisely turn a deaf ear to all such appeals, it will have to do so to most of them. For, in reacting to disorders in Africa, the United States must draw a crucial distinction between security and stability. To attempt to suppress most of the many disorders would be preposterous; in the interest of fundamental growth and long-term security in Africa, it would also be wrong. A certain amount—indeed, a considerable amount—of disorder must be permitted to occur for the sake of African progress itself.

Many of the independent African states as they exist at present, institutionally and in some cases even geographically, are not viable or even potentially stable entities. They are provisional, largely artificial products of the accidents and aftermath of colonialism. Their governmental systems and their power structures have yet to be fully reshaped by indigenous African forces, traditions, and values, which alone can give them validity and durability. Their borrowed and ill-adapted institutions are just beginning to become workably African, and the process of transition to new forms is both indispensable and unlikely to be smooth. Likewise, it is entirely possible that the boundaries of some of the present African states will have to be adjusted to accommodate geographical, historical, economic, or ethnic realities. Thus it is conceivable, however undesirable, that some of the very large states which are tribal conglomerates may break up; and that, regardless of the growth of functional groupings now occurring, economic necessity alone may drive some of the mini-states to join together or be absorbed into the larger neighboring entities. In this sense, any kind of imposed stability in Africa, even if briefly successful, would not constitute security. The kind of African security relevant to the broad interests of the United States is more likely to arise out of the largely unrestricted interplay of deep and powerful indigenous forces of change.

For the United States to attempt to impose on these situations a kind of order based on force would undercut African sovereignty, interrupt a necessary process of historical evolution, drain off vast quantities of American resources, and generally expose the United States to risk and criticism without any compensating gains for U.S. or international interests.

CREATING A STRATEGICALLY STERILE ENVIRONMENT

In pursuing this fundamental approach of permitting the forces of change to operate short of the point where African disorders could produce major international dangers, the first task of U.S. policy should be to help create a strategically sterile environment in Africa. Essentially, this objective will require taking the initiatives to remove Africa as an area of direct or indirect cold war military competition and to buffer it against disruptive intervention by external powers. This, in turn, means attention to the possibility of an understanding or agreement between the United States and the Soviet Union, tacit or explicit, regarding security matters in Africa. Such an understanding cannot readily be reached; in fact, the possibility of it after Soviet intervention in Czechoslovakia in 1968 has probably receded, but it is not inconceivable.

There is one line of plausible reasoning which rejects the search for such an accomodation as hopeless. At a time of nuclear stalemate, when a direct confrontation has become suicidal, the superpowers, it is argued, will inevitably compete for influence in the Third World. Communist endorsement of "wars of national liberation" proves that seeking strength in the underdeveloped areas is an indispensable ingredient of Communist ideology and policy, and therefore any effort to place Africa off-limits in the global strategic struggle is bound to be fruitless, or even dangerous if the outcome were a spurious agreement that would be unequally respected and in effect handcuff the United States. Further, it is argued that even if the Soviet Union might be willing in terms of its own national interests to make an accord, it could not afford to do so simply because of the challenge to Soviet world revolutionary leadership posed by the Chinese, one major focus of which is in Africa.

But there are other grounds, equally or more persuasive, for believing that the Soviet Union might possibly be receptive to American initiative in this direction. Africa is not a region of primary importance to Soviet strategic objectives. Like the United States, the Soviet Union is not bound by any general strategic commitments in Africa and has a relative freedom of maneuver. Soviet economic, political, and military programs on the continent to date have produced no great profit; and in the Congo, where a near-confrontation with U.S. forces occurred, Russia was humiliated. In actual fact, a degree of withdrawal by both the United States and the Soviet Union from head-on competition in Africa has been noticeable in recent years. Soviet behavior in relation to some current security issues, such as nuclear proliferation, suggests the possibility that, to advance its own vital objectives, the U.S.S.R. may be prepared to help ease tensions in certain secondary areas and reduce the scope of its present exposure and burdens. Africa would seem a likely place to begin.

If an approach along these lines were decided to be desirable and perhaps feasible, the broadest possible area of agreement should be explored. An understanding to reduce any further supply of arms and military equipment might be the first objective. Agreement on the total and permanent removal of military, naval, and air installations on the African continent might be another. A third would be agreement to desist from military intervention—directly or by surrogate—when disorders erupt in independent Africa and from attempts to change boundaries or political regimes by force.

The limitations of such possible understandings—even under the most optimistic assumptions—are obvious. Even if some general agreement regarding military operations could be reached, competition in covert, propaganda, and political activities could not be controlled. And Chinese programs, military or otherwise, are at present beyond reach of any agreement, formal or informal. But the possibilities are nonetheless sufficient to justify the effort.

Such a pattern of Soviet-American cooperation or, short of that, of parallel action, if it could be achieved, would be a step of fundamental importance both in protecting Africa from external damage and in shielding the climate of world peace from the effects of future African disorders. Moreover, there is some urgency in attempting to bring it about. The opportunities for external meddling in the unstable African political atmosphere are not decreasing, and with the rapid development of long-range Soviet air- and sea-lift capacity, a new and upsetting series of interventions in the coming few years can be anticipated, with the possibility of equally upsetting countermeasures by the United States. The opportunity for a timely, new initiative in Soviet-American co-operation in Africa would seem to be considerable.

A separate but related problem in the strategic sterilization of the African environment is the danger of military intervention by Western European powers and, in consequence, the policy to be followed by the United States in regard to this very real possibility. The military ties between Europe and Africa, though weakening, remain considerable. To date, repeated European interventions have taken place. Is it in the broad interest of the United States to seek to encourage the maintenance of such military links between Europe and Africa, or to discourage them? If not, and if it is desirable in principle to weaken or replace present European-African military ties, is there a practical possibility of doing so by American initiative?

It might be argued by some that removal of the European military presence from Africa automatically creates a "power vacuum"; that such vacuums historically have tended to be dangerous and destabilizing to international peace (e.g., the "weak states" of the Balkans, Turkey, and China before the outbreak of the First World War); and that the present decline of the European military presence is therefore to be discouraged, not encouraged. That standard syllogism as applied to present-day Africa is unconvincing. First, if a strategic "power vacuum" now or potentially exists, it is not filled by the kind of European military presence which is available in Africa. Undoubtedly, the European presence can make a crucial difference in the outcome of struggles for power within African states, or disputes between one independent African state and another. But if and when superpower interest should be attracted to an African crisis, the European presence would be more likely to trigger trouble, as in the case of Belgian forces in the Congo, than to prevent it or cope with it. Second, it cannot be assumed that the European military presence in Africa in the post-independence era has necessarily been stabilizing. In some instances it was, but in others—the Congo, Biafra, and the Portuguese territories—it has been tension-creating and destabilizing.

Henceforth, the propensity of the European states to take military action in Africa will probably decline, as will African resort to European help—at least if other, more acceptable sources are available. As the years pass and the new African states move beyond their immediate post-independence instabilities, the positive values of European intervention are reduced while the negative effects increase. But not always. Various situations may arise—as in the case of reprisal attacks on Tanzania, Zambia and the Congo by Portugal, Rhodesia, or South Africa—in which the African call for European or other external military assistance may be urgent, and a positive response may be warranted.

In practical terms, therefore, the indications for American policy would seem to be three: to view the present tendency for a decline in bilateral European military links with Africa with equanimity and seek neither to accelerate nor retard such decline; to attempt to discourage—though with no great expectation of success—European efforts to meddle in African quarrels and to sell military equipment of all kinds and quantities to the new states; and generally, as part of comprehensive U.S.-European cooperation, to consult closely with the Western European states on all African security problems.*

But the problem of buffering Africa against the dangers of external military intervention cannot be solved by a purely negative or preventive approach. Parallel efforts are needed to encourage and assist the new African states to mediate their differences and, in the event of breakdown, to make available external military assistance when required and justified, but on a safer and better basis than either direct superpower or Western European intervention. This calls for exploration of the possibilities of wider multilateral action.

Strengthening Multilateral Peace-Keeping Capabilities

The specific tasks are two: first, to help strengthen African capacity for the self-regulation of outbreaks of disorder and, second, to

---

* Such cooperation does not, of course, exist at present, nor does an effective vehicle for it. It is doubtful that NATO would be an appropriate or effective mechanism for this. The complex nature of the organization's policy- and decision-making procedures, as well as its other preoccupations, constitute one kind of difficulty; the presence of Portugal as a member, another.

reconstruct and rehabilitate the peace-keeping machinery of the United Nations.

The practical possibilities for the former are moderately encouraging. In recent years, the antagonistic divisions among the new African nations have somewhat decreased, along with the tendency of certain militant and radical states to sit in righteous judgment of, and sometimes to attempt to subvert, those with whom they disagreed.

With the formation of the OAU in 1963, the principle of non-interference in one another's affairs was made a part of the charter of the new organization.* Since then, despite its financial and other weaknesses, the OAU has been able to play an important conciliatory role in easing tensions and averting clashes in a number of potentially dangerous situations. To help maintain and develop the capability of the OAU to do this effectively, the United States might appropriately offer to provide facilities and general financial aid to the organization, if requested. Furthermore, it might indicate its readiness, if and when the OAU should decide to create some kind of inter-African peace-keeping force, to provide transport, communication, and other equipment. Obviously, the creation of such a force would be a matter requiring the most extensive preparatory discussion and the development of careful controls and procedures by the African member states. But, if it is established on an acceptable basis, the United States should give the most sympathetic and generous consideration to making it effective.

In addition to Pan African approaches, it seems likely that situations will arise in the future, as in the past, where mediation or other necessary action can best be accomplished by the formation of *ad hoc* groups of neighboring states, or by the involvement of those nations which are members of some common functional or regional economic or political grouping. In such instances, action or assistance by the United States could sometimes be essential to their success.

The proposal has recurrently been made that the United States could usefully press the independent African governments to join in a disarmament pact. This is questionable. By the restraint

---

* By the terms of the OAU Charter, the member states agree to coordinate and harmonize their general policies "in the fields of defense and security" (Article II, Paragraph 2). They also pledge to settle all disputes among themselves by peaceful means and "establish a Commission of Mediation, Conciliation and Arbitration" (Article XIX).

of its own military programs in Africa, the United States can avoid leading the new states into excessive military expenditures. But, beyond that, any American effort to press for African disarmament is likely to be pointless and most probably counterproductive for an obvious and basic reason: Its intentions would be suspect. The United States acquiesced in the transfer of the military forces, including aircraft, of the former Federation of the Rhodesias and Nyasaland to Rhodesia; prior to the imposition of its present ban on arms to South Africa, it made available highly sophisticated military equipment, including submarines, jet aircraft, and missiles; and it continues to provide, directly and through NATO, advanced technology and some equipment to the armed forces of Portugal, which, though not for use in its antinationalist campaigns in Africa, nevertheless, contribute to the general military competence of the country. It would be futile for the United States under present circumstances to attempt to persuade the regimes of the Redoubt to disarm, and it is most unlikely that it would be inclined to try. And without such an effort, capped with some success, the United States could not with clean hands or persuasiveness attempt to promote disarmament in independent Africa.

The United Nations as Peace-Keeper. For the full variety of crises which will possibly arise, the United Nations is not only the most appropriate but in principle the only adequate peacekeeping instrument for Africa. Pan African efforts, understandings between the superpowers, or European or Atlantic arrangements all have inherent limitations. Only the United Nations can deal with the problems of the control and reduction of national armaments, the enforcement of such agreements, and the arbitration and if necessary the enforcement of peaceful settlements of disputes on an almost universal basis. Until the necessity of a far stronger U.N. peace-keeping capacity is generally recognized and understood, the national insecurity that now eats at the core of international order will remain. All other, less comprehensive measures can only provide partial solutions, which does not mean, however, that they are valueless.

But, if the peace-keeping potential of the United Nations is great, its actual capability at present is extremely limited. Its organs for decision in security matters are paralyzed or in low repute: the Security Council because of the veto, and the General Assembly because of the irrelevancy if not irresponsibility of some of its actions on past security issues. The authority of the Secretary-General to negotiate peaceful settlements, even to carry out Security Council decisions, has become increasingly restricted. It has no standing armed force of its own and must rely on national contingents of doubtful availability in situations of need. In addition to procedural impediments, those members opposed to effective peace-keeping have succeded in imposing severe financial limitations on the organization.

The catalogue of what must be done to re-establish the capacity of the United Nations in this field is the reverse face of its list of present weaknesses. But to a large degree, the problem of enabling the United Nations to take decisions on security matters which can lead to prompt and adequate action is unsolvable until there can be a new recognition of common interest by the Soviet Union and the United States in some basic stabilization of world affairs. One of the special attributes of Africa may lie in the possibility it offers of a beginning in that direction. It should be among the highest objectives of U.S. policy to strengthen the U.N.'s effectiveness in peace-keeping. Yet at best the effort may require many years, and perhaps some horrifying international disasters, before it can succeed.

The Residual Problem of Direct U.S. Responsibility for Action and Intervention

After all has been done that can be done to encourage multilateral measures and agreements to deal with future African disorders, there will remain the problem for U.S. policy of its own national action or nonaction in the crises that will occur. Even if a firm line of policy is followed to let historical processes of change, even violent change, take place insofar as possible without American involvement, and to make minimum response to various internal and even international disputes that arise, there will be those few cases—the hardest and most dangerous, unfortunately— where the wisest course does not appear to be nonaction, and where resort to multilateral measures is in practical fact inadequate or unavailable.

In general terms, the kinds of situation that might provoke U.S. action would be those which clearly threatened to produce epidemic disorders in a whole region; those in which an external power, especially the Soviet Union or China, is directly involved in some form of aggression against African states; those in which American interest or prestige is significantly threatened; those where massive humanitarian considerations, such as starvation or genocide, are present; and above all, those in which a racial and colonial issue is sharply drawn, as in the south.

The declared general principles of present American policy might seem to be relevant to some of these issues, i.e., "to support free peoples who are resisting attempted subjugation by armed minorities, or by outside pressures," and "to give help to victims of aggression who request our help and are willing and able to help themselves." But, in the event, broad principles for dealing with foreign policy crises are about as useful as general rules for playing shortstop. In the dynamics of the actual situation, circumstances and contingency are likely to be controlling. In almost every instance of coming conflict in Africa, nonintervention by the United States will be the wiser course. But not absolutely and without exception.

In the aftermath of Viet Nam, it will be all too easy for many to conclude that because the United States cannot be policeman everywhere in the world, it should not be policeman anywhere; and that the best contribution the United States can make to peace is to withdraw its influence from every danger-spot. Beguiling though such a stance might seem in a moment of disenchantment, it offers little safety. For the world—including the continent of Africa—will in all likelihood go on for some time being a disorderly and dangerous place. If it is to continue to be habitable, its many separate nation-states with their deadly weapons, their fears and ambitions, and their illusions of unfettered sovereignty must somehow be subject to stabilizing influence. That influence must derive basically from the achievement of some wider ground of agreement between Russia and the United States—and eventually China—to neutralize or isolate from their competition at least certain areas of the world, of which Africa should be one. Initiative toward that objective is the first contribution the United States can make. The second is to work closely and cooperatively with the new African states to develop their capacity to cope to the maximum feasible extent with their own conflicts and breaches of the peace. And the third must be the overwhelmingly important and difficult task of rebuilding a universal peace-keeping instrumentality through the United Nations.

But between the dangerous now and the stabilized future lies a span of many ominous years; only the smallest beginnings of Soviet-American agreement on security matters are now detectable; only the rudiments of an African regional peace-keeping capacity now exist; and this capability of the United Nations which a few years ago seemed to hold such promise is for the present almost in ruins. During the period ahead, therefore, the United States will have to maintain that most difficult stance of alertness and restraint in Africa, neither plunging itself into situations unnecessarily nor standing frozen and immobilized while small dangers grow into large and uncontrollable ones. The extent to which the United States will be capable of this new kind of international behavior in the quest for security—far more subtle in its requirements than the relatively straightforward requirements of "containment" in its time of relevancy—will to a great degree determine the prospects for security in Africa.

13

The Linchpin: The U.S. Role in African Development

Physical security is one face of a coin; the other and more positive face is development. Each is a necessary but not sufficient condition if Africa is to be a healthy, contributing part of a peaceful and progressive world. Both are essential, and each is a precondition to, and consequence of, the other not only in general theory but in practical diplomatic fact as well. Just as African development efforts would be ruined by the continent's becoming an active cold war battleground, so any agreement of the superpowers to limit their military and political intrusions is unlikely to work unless there is reasonable economic advance in Africa. Assuming that their ideological competition does not fade away completely, a stagnant Africa will simply be too tempting, or too disquieting, to resist. No understanding between them, explicit or implicit, is likely to survive unrelieved hopelessness in Africa and the politics it would produce. Total withdrawal—military, political, and economic—could only be temporary and would lead rather quickly to military and political re-involvement. Thus, paradoxically, military and political withdrawal by the superpowers from Africa can be maintained only at the price of their constructive involvement in African development.

But development itself is not a simple task or concept. If it can be achieved, it will be the complex result of African efforts of planning, organization, and capital formation and acquisition; of the functioning of the international systems of trade and finance and of their impact on Africa; and of foreign aid programs directed to Africa—of which some are bilateral, and some are multilateral.

The contribution of the United States to African development, therefore, functions as one element within a multiple system of other national and international efforts and is itself made up of several elements ranging from the flow of private investment to U.S. trade policy to the various sub-programs which go to make up what is called "foreign aid." To define the wise and proper U.S. role in African development, one must take into account these several interrelated elements. And to evaluate the U.S. contribution to date, one must consider not only simple statistical trends of the volume of aid, for example, but also the impact of American economic policy on African efforts of self-development and on the policies and contributions of the other donor countries and multilateral agencies in that complex phenomenon called "assistance to African development." As with all the major issues presented by Africa, an adequate American policy must be conceived in a global context and executed with full use of and regard for the various other national and multilateral programs and policies simultaneously at work.

For most African leaders, development is their central preoccupation because it is considered indispensable to their objectives both of retaining their own positions and power and of extricating their countries from powerlessness and constant disruption. There are instances in which traditional elites may be indifferent or even opposed to it, but these seem less common in Africa than elsewhere in the Third World. To a great degree, therefore, the shape and nature of African internal economic and political institutions and their orientation in international affairs will be determined by what is regarded as the more advantageous course in terms of the urgent need for material improvement and modernization. For American policy, concern with African development is a *sine qua non* if workable, friendly, and influential relations with the new states are to be maintained.

The seriousness of the African economic predicament is not fully grasped by most Americans. The general difference in income level and material standards of life between the developed and underdeveloped nations is so great as to be virtually one of kind rather than degree. As a group, the former enjoy a per capita income more than seven times as large as that of the poor nations, and in the case of the United States, nearly fifteen times as large. This gap is widening, not decreasing, despite the considerable development efforts—and the still more considerable talk about development efforts—in recent years. For example, in the next decade the average citizen of Western Europe or the United States, already in affluence, is likely to increase his annual income by ten to fifty times as much as his African counterpart. Economic data on gross national product and individual income in the less developed countries can normally be taken with a large pinch of salt; but differences such as these, whatever discount for error is applied, are still awesome, even ominous.

More precisely, the world is not divided into rich and poor— or even rich, middling, and poor—but into a spectrum of differences in wealth. Along this spectrum the relatively more developed nations are advancing the fastest, and the relatively least developed nations tend to be the most stagnant, as the figures in Table 18 show. The importance of this fact for Africa, and for American

TABLE 18. Estimated Annual Growth Rates of Less Developed and Developed Areas, 1960–67

	Per Cent Change in GNP			Per Cent Change in GNP Per Capita		
	1960–65 Annual Rate	1966	1967	1960–65 Annual Rate	1966	1967
Less Developed Countries:						
Latin America	4.6	4.3	4.5	1.5	1.3	1.5
Europe and Near East	6.5	7.1	5.0	3.8	4.7	2.4
South Asia	4.0	2.6	8.3	1.2	0.1	5.6
East Asia	4.6	6.8	5.5	1.9	4.1	2.7
Africa	3.4	3.4	4.3	1.1	1.1	2.0
Average	4.9	4.9	5.4	2.3	2.4	2.9
Developed Countries:	5.1	5.4	3.4	3.9	4.3	2.4

SOURCE: U.S. Agency for International Development, *Gross National Product*, RC-W-138, July 25, 1968, Washington.

policy toward Africa, is fundamental. The new African states, already among the poorest in the world, are lagging badly in their development; and even among them, the relatively richer and most developed states are fast moving ahead of the more backward.

Africa then is an extreme case of a world-wide problem—a problem which in many respects is the crucial challenge of the twentieth century to the international community, and to the United States as the richest country of the world—a challenge beyond and even more elusive than the historic quest for peace.*

As their understanding of the nature of the development process has become more refined and realistic, economists have come to shun earlier sweeping theories and to give greater attention to those practical measures that have now demonstrated their effectiveness—such as technical assistance, educational development, and specially designed economic incentives to alter production habits. Whatever their differences as to the efficacy of such specific measures in triggering change, all economists agree that if development programs are to succeed, it is essential that the new states find or produce greater resources of capital. In this regard the poor countries at their present stage are caught in a trap, within a cage, within a prison. Even if they had the social attitudes and institutions necessary for the accumulation of savings, their poverty is such that, however much they may tighten their belts, they are incapable of generating such capital in suficient quantity. Nor are their possibilities of obtaining it by increased export earnings, or by influx of foreign private investment, or by economic aid encouraging.

Again, the African countries are illustrative. Since independence, they have had extreme difficulty in attracting new foreign private investment. Similarly, their efforts to increase earnings have encountered great obstacles. Although their exports have

---

* There are some who seriously question whether the problem is solvable. They are inclined to the belief that the poverty which exists reflects national deficiencies of character and intelligence and that neither foreign aid nor anything else—except perhaps the passage of centuries—can do much about it. See, for example, Hans J. Morgenthau in his A New Foreign Policy for the United States (New York: Praeger, for the Council on Foreign Relations, 1969), p. 96: "To put it bluntly, as there are bums and beggars, so there are bum and beggar nations." Despite the general unpopularity of foreign aid programs, this is a minority, even an eccentric, view. Since the period of the Great Depression and the advent of Keynesian and other modern economic doctrines, there is widespread confidence that just as economic fluctuations within the developed nations can be dealt with by monetary and other measures, so the problem of stagnation in the less developed areas is subject to remedy by purposeful economic action—at least to some degree. This confidence is increasingly substantiated by the evidence being produced in those pre-industrial and impoverished nations that as a result of planned development programs and foreign aid, have in fact reached dynamic and self-sustaining growth: Formosa, South Korea, Pakistan, Turkey—and in Africa, Ivory Coast, Kenya, and Uganda—are cases in point.

increased somewhat in quantity over the years, the prices obtained have been unstable and in general decline. To make the pinch more severe, a high proportion of the manufactured goods they need must be imported, the prices of which have been rising steadily. Thus, an African farmer today must produce a substantially greater quantity of cocòa, sisal, or palm oil than five or ten years ago to buy the same imported tractor or electric motor.

Economic assistance likewise has become more, not less, difficult to obtain. The total of foreign aid, which bulged in the early 1960s, has leveled off and is now beginning to fall. Moreover, the proportion of their export receipts and foreign assistance funds which can be used for development is shrinking as their debt burdens and consequent debt-servicing requirements rapidly grow.* Thus the three major sources from which Africa might hope to obtain additional resources for development—trade, private investment, and foreign aid—are either stagnant or in decline. They show little prospect of meeting the requirements of even the most minimal development goals.

The Threefold Flow and the U.S. Record

As one of the several external sources of assistance, the U.S. contribution to African development is in financial terms the total of these three flows of resources, and its performance in each must be reviewed if its over-all record of performance is to be appraised.

Historically, Africa has not been an area of extensive interest on the part of American investors (see Table 19). As of 1967, only 3.8 per cent of total U.S. foreign investment had been placed in Africa. Of a total American investment on the continent of some $2.1 billion, nearly 30 per cent has gone to one country, South Africa; of the remainder, a large proportion has been concentrated in a small number of other countries, such as Libya and Liberia, with rich petroleum and mineral resources.

The possible contribution of private investment to foreign development has been extolled over the years in many official

---

* The World Bank has estimated that in the decade of 1956–66 public debt of all underdeveloped countries increased from $10 billion to more than $41 billion, and the annual service charge on this debt during the same period rose from $800 million to nearly $4 billion. In the Bank's annual report for 1967–68, it was reported that for all of Africa except Egypt and South Africa, outstanding public debt increased from $3.1 billion in 1963 to $5.1 billion in 1966, and service payments from $192 million in 1963 to $413 million in 1967.

TABLE 19. Total Direct U.S. Investment in Africa,ᵃ 1950–66

(In millions of dollars, at year end)

	Libya	Republic of South Africa	Other	Total, Africa
1950	—	140	147	287
1957	24	301	339	664
1961	177	311	576	1,064
1962	265	357	649	1,271
1963	304	411	710	1,426
1964	402	467	817	1,685
1965	428	529	962	1,918
1966	389	601	1,087	2,078

ᵃ Excluding the U.A.R.

SOURCE: The U.S. Department of Commerce, *Survey of Current Business*, various issues.

statements, and U.S. foreign aid legislation has long provided certain inducements to such investment. But relatively little has been accomplished, despite some interesting and imaginative efforts by the government and private organizations in recent years. On the whole, American investors in other than extractive industries have been hesitant to move into Africa, partly because of unfamiliarity with the area, partly because of more attractive alternatives in Western Europe or at home. The inducements offered by U.S. legislation in the form of investment guarantees and other measures have not been sufficient to overcome these inhibitions, nor have the measures taken by African governments. It remains possible that bolder and more determined private and governmental efforts on both continents can rechannel some of the present movement of private capital and make it a major force for African development.* But that must be judged unlikely in the short term, not only because of the record of the past but also because new factors, such as the U.S. balance-of-payments problem, strongly encourage American capital to stay home.

The long-term trend, now that colonial control has ended and

* The next major invention in U.S. foreign aid may well relate to this problem. Private and official planners are now seriously considering the possibility of creating a new governmental or mixed public-private corporation to promote and underwrite American private enterprise in the developing countries.

Africa has been opened to U.S. investment, will probably be in the direction of a slow increase in private capital flow. Until now, U.S. private capital has made relatively little over-all contribution to African development, and in the near future it is unlikely that the volume of such investment can have a major impact, except perhaps in a handful of countries. Moreover, private investment tends to flow after a country has shown a good record of growth and stability; it is not normally available when the development problem is most severe, namely, at the start.

For American traders, Africa historically has been as inconsequential as for American investors; as of 1967, only 3.5 per cent of U.S. foreign trade was with Africa, 1.1 per cent being with a single country, South Africa. As a market and as a source of imports, the United States remains far less important to Africa than the former European metropoles. But in a larger sense the United States is of vital importance to African trade prospects.

Caught in the grinding gears of the present international trading system, the less developed nations as a group have struggled through UNCTAD and other mechanisms to persuade the developed countries to concede new advantages to them to help redress their competitive weakness and to shield them against the destructive fluctuations in world commodity prices to which they are all now exposed. In their drive, the attitude of Washington is crucial because of the preponderant influence of the United States in world trade. But in common with virtually all the other developed nations, the United States has shown great reluctance to intervene in altering the functioning of the system.

To date, the main concern of American policy has been to bring about a maximum universal reduction in trade barriers. In pursuing this objective in recent years, U.S. trade officials have been primarily concerned with the threat to American interests posed by restrictionist developments in some of the industrialized countries, especially the European Economic Community. President Kennedy in January 1962 proposed, and Congress passed, new legislation permitting the administration to make a major effort to persuade the EEC to lower its outer tariff wall. The negotiations which followed, known as the Kennedy Round, culminated in 1967 in a series of agreements which represented highly compromised settlements on all major points but which at least may have avoided a wave of protectionist measures that could have swept around the world if negotiations had broken down. However, from the viewpoint of the developing countries, including those in Africa, one major stated objective of the negotiations, namely, stimulation of their lagging exports, was shunted aside. In their opinion, the outcome was little more than a bargain among the wealthy countries in their own interest.*

In certain respects, the trade policy of the United States has been somewhat more liberal than others, such as France and the EEC countries, in giving access to its markets to the less developed countries. It has eliminated all duties on tropical products, such as cocoa, coffee, tea, and bananas, and has urged others to do the same. But the possibility of widening this access has been carefully hedged. The Trade Expansion Act of 1962 makes reference to encouraging imports from the least developed areas, but gives the President little authority to carry out this objective: it does not permit departure from unconditional most-favored-nation treatment for the benefit of less developed countries; it does not authorize the elimination of such nontariff barriers as quotas, where they exist. Nor in the authority granted the President is the need recognized for correcting cases of high concealed protection afforded to domestic processors of industrial materials by the spread between the tariff rates on materials in raw and processed forms.[1]

In regard to certain other trade problems, however, such as stabilizing the prices of primary products, the United States has been less prepared than some other developed countries to join in international remedial efforts. It has supported arrangements in the International Monetary Fund to provide prompt balance-of-payments assistance to those countries experiencing severe shortfalls in export earnings because of factors beyond their control, and it has participated in the International Coffee Agreement, which for Africa has been of importance, helping make possible an increase in export earnings from coffee from $360 million in 1962, before the agreement, to almost $700 million in 1966. But traditional reluctance has only slowly and gradually given way to a more favorable disposition toward efforts to regulate production and prices for other commodities, including, most recently, cocoa. Moreover, the United States has not favored preferential trade arrangements such as those presently existing between Africa and

* In the view of some economists from the developed countries, the less developed countries received concessions as important as those the developed countries gave to each other. Even if true, however, this does not satisfy the demand of the former for special consideration of their particular needs and weaknesses.

Europe which presently provide for stabilized demand, support prices, and other economically interventionist measures.

On the whole, therefore, the United States has represented a somewhat mixed but basically conservative viewpoint on maintaining the present world trading system. And because of strong doctrinal commitments to the principle of universality, the general weakness in the position of the dollar, and the powerful influence of American commercial interests and their congressional spokesmen in shaping trade policy, the United States is unlikely to become a bold and innovative leader in modifying it to the advantage of the less developed countries. Indeed, given the present ground swell of protectionist sentiment in the United States, similar to that appearing in most of the developed countries, it will be fortunate if even the small and precious gains made by liberalized trade advocates over past years can be held.

Thus, there is no prospect for any marked increase in the near future in the flow of U.S. private investment to the new African states, or for new American initiatives to permit a major improvement in the volume or stability of their export earnings. This being so, the matter of U.S. foreign assistance policy becomes crucial if African capital requirements for development are to be met.

U.S. foreign aid programs were born and have lived for more than twenty years in controversy, and the fierceness of the debate has produced a great deal of misunderstanding about them. To appraise their results it is first necessary to cut through this thick accumulation of mythology, self-delusion, rationalization, and exaggerated praise and criticism which now envelops the subject and to state in reasonably factual terms what the United States has so far given to Africa and for what purpose. On this basis five general propositions can be defended:

First, the U.S. aid program in Africa has specifically been designed as secondary and supplemental to those of the former European metropoles; their responsibility, in the American view, remains primary. The U.S. aid program therefore does not constitute a fully independent assistance effort. In effect, the policy adopted has led to a tailoring of American assistance in most African countries to accommodate existing European activities. At best, the policy has been a means of avoiding possible duplication of effort and the displacement of European resources; at worst, it has amounted to filling gaps left in the pattern of European activity and rushing in to salvage situations in the wake of disasters of European policy. At the same time, the systematic and continuous operational coordination of U.S. aid policy in Africa with that of other major donors, particularly European, has been of very limited effectiveness because each contributing country, the United States included, has had specific national purposes and priorities which it has not been prepared to compromise for the sake of a more unified effort.

Second, quantitatively the United States has provided a relatively small fraction of the total foreign assistance received by the new African states since their independence; and this fraction is declining. Direct U.S. assistance has accounted for roughly a quarter of the total aid received by Africa in the past; and currently the American contribution has fallen to about one-fifth. The major national donors to Africa have been Britain and France. Most of the principal external sources of assistance to Africa, which together provided the continent with a larger per capita volume of aid than any other region of the world, have begun to cut back their programs. In recent years Britain, despite economic difficulties, has managed to sustain the level of its aid with only gradual reduction, while France, though faced with growing internal stresses, has so far succeeded in keeping the downward trend of its aid program from becoming a sudden plunge. The Common Market Development Fund continues to be a significant source of assistance and is likely to be renewed in 1969, though perhaps at a somewhat reduced level. The world-wide total of U.S. aid has recently declined sharply, but proportionately less reduction has been made in the African aspects of its program than in some others. Africa has not suffered the most damaging blows of the economy drive, possibly because the total of aid to Africa was rather limited to begin with.

On the other hand, assistance from some of the smaller donors, including West Germany, the Scandinavian countries, and Canada, has been increasing in recent years, which helps fill a portion of the gap being created by the decline in the major donors' aid programs. Of great importance, the World Bank under new leadership has taken an aggressive and daring approach in increasing its lending to underdeveloped countries, which, so long as the credit standing and the ability of the Bank to raise capital in international markets is not weakened, can be of vital importance in maintaining a flow of development resources. In its increased lending, the Bank plans to concentrate heavily on Africa, where it expects to raise its rate of investment threefold in the coming five years.

Third, in dollar size, U.S. economic assistance to Africa has been a small proportion of its total foreign aid, has fluctuated greatly, and since 1962, has been in general decline. Table 20 gives the official U.S. figures of the transfer of governmental assistance —both in the form of funds and commodities, by gift and loan— over the past decade.

Though generally fair and accurate, these figures may somewhat overstate the economic value of the assistance to the recipient countries because of the substantial proportion now given in the form of agricultural commodities. Such assistance, though useful, is less flexible in meeting the requirement of the African states than aid in financial form. Also, nearly half the total has been provided in the form of loans rather than grants; and the interest charged on such loans has tended upward, now being fixed at an average of about 3 per cent per year as of 1967.

Fourth, U.S. assistance to Africa has been focused on a minority of countries of special interest and has not been addressed to the continent as a whole. Thus, beginning in 1958, of the total of $87 million of U.S. assistance, $74 million was allocated to three countries, Libya, Morocco, and Tunisia. In 1959, $112 million of a total of $161 million was allocated to those same three, plus Sudan. In 1960, $150 million of a total of $178 million was concentrated on the same group. In 1961, $175 million of $212 million went to the three North African states, plus the Congo. This pattern of concentration, only slightly diluted, has continued through the most recent years. Through 1967, nine African countries have received two-thirds of all U.S. assistance—Morocco, Tunisia, Congo, Nigeria, Ethiopia, Liberia, Ghana, Sudan, and Guinea. The other thirty received one-third, and for many of them, U.S. assistance has been almost microscopic.

Fifth, U.S. aid to Africa has been used largely to support various military and political objectives. Apart from its technical assistance aspects, it has not on the whole been motivated by development objectives. Among the major receivers, the decision to accord aid to Morocco, Libya, and Ethiopia was heavily influenced by the desire to assure U.S. access to military facilities; in Guinea and Ghana, cold war political objectives weighed heavily, as they did in the Congo; in Tunisia and Liberia special considerations have been operative—the abrupt removal of French assistance in one case and historical ties and special U.S. economic and military interest in the other. The concentration of U.S. assistance on these "priority" countries has sometimes been defended in official state-

TABLE 20. U.S. Economic Assistance to Africa and Other Less Developed Areas, 1958–68[a]
(U.S. fiscal years, in millions of U.S. dollars and percentages)

	1958	1959	1960	1961	1962	1963	1964	1965	1966	1967	1968
Total, commitments to all LDCs:	$2,900	$3,400	$3,200	$4,100	$4,700	$4,600	$4,400	$4,500	$5,200	$5,300	$5,701
Total, commitments to Africa[b]:	100	185	211	460	489	473	359	329	384	389	408
Of which aid to Africa in form of Agricultural commodities:	13	24	33	148	99	210	133	118	138	165	182
Percentage of aid to Africa in form of Agricultural commodities:	13%	13%	16%	32%	20%	44%	37%	36%	36%	42%	45%
Percentage of total U.S. aid to LDCs committed to Africa:	3.4%	5.4%	6.6%	11.2%	10.4%	10.3%	8.2%	7.3%	7.4%	7.3%	7.2%

[a] Includes AID and predecessor agencies, Food for Freedom, and Export-Import Bank Loans.
[b] Excluding U.A.R.

SOURCE: Statistics and Reports Division, AID, Washington; various publications. Senate Foreign Affairs Committee Hearings.

ments in terms of their alleged role as economic "bellwethers," or as areas of exceptional promise in development or of effective self-help. Only in the case of Nigeria, perhaps, until the outbreak of its civil war, could such a rationale hold much water. Once the decision to accord aid was taken, however, administrators have done their best to direct it to projects of greater rather than less relevance to development. Also, over time, developmental objectives have been given greater emphasis, partly because of the increasing urgency of African needs, and partly because of the relative decline in urgency of U.S. military requirements, particularly in North Africa.

The U.S. economic assistance program to date in Africa has therefore had a clear and consistent character: In the tradition of rich and powerful countries throughout the centuries, the United States has used economic gifts and loans as a flexible, multipurpose instrument in the service of political, military, and economic interests and objectives.[2] Though economic in form and called "aid," it has been neither lavish nor designed or distributed with primary regard to African needs or opportunities for economic development.

Given the actual, multiple purposes of U.S. aid in Africa to date, the evidence of its value to U.S. national interests is rather impressive. The assistance to the countries in which it has been concentrated has made it possible to utilize military and communications facilities considered of great importance to the United States. In Guinea, Ghana, and the Congo, American assistance was initially intended largely to support cold-war objectives; and in two of the three at least, it can be said that substantial success was achieved. The limited financing given Zambia to develop new transport routes for its exports and imports emphasized U.S. opposition to the rebel racist regime in Rhodesia and thereby served an important political objective. Measured in these specific terms, the aid program has fully achieved its actual primary purposes. But it is perhaps in the maintenance of a general rapport and an atmosphere of cooperation in American political and diplomatic relationships with independent Africa that the modest U.S. assistance program has paid off the most richly. It is after all remarkable that a very rich nation which took little active part in the winning of independence by the new African states, and which since independence has not come forward with any great support for African development, should have been able to maintain workable and, in many respects, cordial relationships with them. A very different situation might well have emerged. The fact that they have on the whole chosen a rather moderate and pragmatic course in their international relations is due primarily, of course, to their own good sense. But American economic assistance, limited though it has been, has been an indispensable factor without which all relationships would have been far stickier and less amicable.

Thus, the conclusion of the Clay Committee that in regard to Africa the United States has been "undercompensated" in results is not in accord with the evidence. On the contrary, the United States has probably gained dollar-for-dollar as much benefit to its several foreign policy objectives as a result of its aid expenditures in Africa as it has in any part of the world and with any of its activities in recent years. This being so, it should be of as much concern to those primarily concerned with the strengthening of the American position in the world as to the African recipients themselves that the program has now been severly crippled. Ironically, by its inept use of the budget knife the United States may have disemboweled itself—and beyond that, may have endangered the entire interdependent structure of international aid to Africa, of which the U.S. contribution is only one element.

A Strange Case of Calamity

For the past eight years a bizarre and tragic drama has been played out in American politics relating to foreign aid. In the first postwar decade, this major instrument of American foreign policy, which expressed the most profound humanitarian and internationalist instincts of the American people, achieved stunning successes. But it has now lost much of its base of political and popular support at home, has become an object of cynicism in many of the recipient countries, and has produced considerable resentment among other major donor countries—nearly all friends and allies —because of the martyred and self-righteous stance taken by the United States regarding its assistance "burdens." Confusion, disappointment, and disenchantment envelop the entire subject. Adding another curious quality to the story, administration officials, despite the washing-out of domestic political support for the program, over the past eight years have—heroically or foolishly— labored to convert it into something more than an instrument of service to specific American interests and to make it into a broad and long-term effort of support for international development. Yet the Congress, having the final voice, has been moving in precisely the opposite direction, restricting not only the scale of the program but covering it with what David Lilienthal calls "carbuncles" of a more and more nationalistic and narrow-minded kind.

President Kennedy, in his first foreign aid message in 1961, recommended both an increase in appropriations and a restructuring of the program to better serve long-term development needs. His attempt met heavy congressional opposition and was largely defeated. To make matters worse, his own advisers introduced concepts of development planning, resource allocation, and project preparation of such sophistication in the administration of aid that the shorthanded African states could not satisfy the required paper work. As a result, funds did not move; year after year the allocations to Africa were not expended. Not until 1966 did AID recognize that its "banker-like" and reactive posture was not enough and that, if Africa were to be helped, the donor would have to seek out and help prepare projects as an active partner in a common development task.

President Johnson made a second attempt to revamp U.S. aid philosophy in 1967, but he was even more shatteringly defeated. That story and its consequences is pertinent to recount because of its particular connection with Africa. In May 1966, after harrowing difficulties with Congress in connection with the aid bill, President Johnson asked Edward M. Korry, then his Ambassador to Ethiopia, to lead a group to re-examine and make recommendations for a thorough overhauling of the African aspect of the program. Focusing the study on Africa was partly due to the fact that congressional opposition, particularly in the Senate, had taken not only the form of cuts in appropriations but antagonism to "proliferation" and "scatteration." The African aid program was especially vulnerable to this line of attack because of the large and growing number of new states. The recommendations of the Korry Report, which have never been made publicly available in full, are understood to have been reflected in President Johnson's proposals for a new aid policy in early 1967 incorporating four principal goals:

First, to encourage greater and more effective cooperation among donor nations in extending aid to Africa and greater use of multinational agencies;

Second, to encourage greater economic cooperation among African recipients on a regional basis and through regional development projects;

Third, to support development in all of independent Africa and on a long-term basis;

Fourth, to improve and gradually increase U.S. aid to Africa.

To some skeptics, the proposals seemed little more than a clever attempt to deflect congressional opposition and to lay down a smokescreen—through talk of regionalism and multilateralism—behind which to carry out an American cutback. In fact, however, they constituted a serious, indeed a radical, attempt to make long-range development in Africa a governing criterion and central commitment of U.S. policy. In this sense they flew in the face of tradition and of manifest congressional sentiment.

The Korry Report and President Johnson proposed; but the Congress disposed. By its actions in 1967 and 1968 the Congress in effect rejected every one of the new goals outlined by the administration and adopted policies the reverse of what had been recommended. The administration wanted gradually to increase American aid to Africa, but congressional cuts have resulted in a reduced and declining program. From a peak figure for U.S. aid to Africa in 1962 of $487 million, the total for fiscal 1968 has fallen to $337 million.* It was proposed to support economic development in all of independent Africa, but, under the legislation passed, less than a third of the African countries are now permitted to receive capital loans for development. From a program which offered bilateral aid to thirty-five of them in 1967, only ten are now designated as "development emphasis areas" and therefore permitted to continue to receive such AID assistance. By the end of fiscal 1969, bilateral programs in the remaining twenty-five will be ended. They will thereafter be able to receive assistance only by participation in regional or multidonor projects (to which the United States may not contribute more than half the cost) or in the form of Food-for-Peace allocations, Peace Corps volunteers, or small "self-help" awards.

* Of the latter figure, gross AID commitments for bilateral capital loans and grants amounted to $160 million in fiscal 1968, as compared with $315 million in 1962. Preliminary figures for fiscal 1969 indicate that U.S. assistance continued to decline.

Donor cooperation was to be encouraged, but the reduction of U.S. assistance has undercut this goal. Moreover, reduced funds have transformed the effective meaning of the concept of regional cooperation in Africa, which was stressed in the Korry Report. Had adequate U.S. assistance been forthcoming to continue substantial bilateral programs and to support new regional undertakings, an important step toward rationality in African development would have been taken. But given the fact of sharply reduced American aid, regionalism has come to seem little more than a gimmick to spread a reduced amount of aid over an undiminished surface of political interest. It was proposed to strengthen multilateral efforts. But the most 'essential single action requested, namely replenishment of the funds of the IDA of the World Bank, was not even brought to the floor of Congress by the end of 1968.

United States aid administrators, devoted and able as they are, will doubtless be able to pick among the present debris of the program and find useful, limited actions which can be taken to give some encouragement to particular African development projects. But that a calamity has occurred there can be no doubt, and it is of such proportions that a sober attempt must now be made to assess its real consequences for Africa and its meaning and implications for U.S. policy and interests in the future.

It would be difficult to exaggerate the extent of the damage which has been done—of which at least five distinct kinds can be identified. First, by the line its policy has taken, the United States is helping to throw Africa back into utter and destructive hopelessness. At a time of growing need for both capital and technical assistance in Africa, the United States is reducing, not increasing, its response. It has at the same time rejected any commitment to continuing support for African development, despite the obvious and inherent long-term nature of the problem. The shrinking of the American contribution comes at a time of decreased availability of other forms of economic help and therefore makes the negative impact on Africa all the more severe.

Second, by the reduction of aid and by the liquidation of bilateral programs in most African countries, the United States is depriving itself of what unquestionably has been the single most useful instrument of its diplomacy in dealing with the many new African states and in serving its many specific economic, political, and other interests in Africa.

Third, while urging its European allies to maintain their responsibilities and development contributions to Africa, the United States has, by the pattern of its own conduct, provided them with a ready rationale for further reducing their own contributions. By its own miserably poor performance it has lowered the standard which other donors feel they must meet. The fact that Britain and France have not sharply reduced their aid in proportion to American cuts and that some of the smaller donors have actually increased their contributions is particularly to their credit because of the severity of their own economic difficulties in certain cases.

Fourth, the United States has moved from being the leader in strengthening multilateral aid efforts and institutions to being a follower. In the case of IDA in 1968, for example, after the inaction of Congress in renewing the U.S. pledge, a number of other contributing nations, nevertheless, proceeded to make their commitments to keep the program and the institution from disintegration, trusting that the United States might in time follow the responsible course of others.* Even if that proves true, there is no question that the net effect of the paralysis of the American position has gravely undermined multilateral efforts benefiting Africa as well as the other underdeveloped regions.

Fifth, and in some respects most disturbing, by its cutbacks of aid the United States has failed to live up to its own tradition and standards. In American life the accepted measure of a man's ability and obligation to contribute to the welfare of the community is the level of his income, but by this American test the United States is sadly failing in its duties as a member of the world community. The United States is the largest single giver of aid in the world, but judged in relation to its size and wealth it is a below-average donor. The U.S. performance is lower than that of the average Western European nation. Six countries, none as wealthy as the United States, give a larger proportion of their national income in foreign aid. According to the data of the OECD, U.S. governmental and private aid since 1962 has never reached the 1 per cent of national income set as a goal for the Development Decade. Governmental aid has dropped steadily from 0.80 per cent in 1962 to 0.67 per cent in 1965 to 0.57 per cent in 1967. The United States has long prided itself on its generosity

* This, in fact, has happened. On April 25, 1969, Congress appropriated $480 million as its contribution to IDA for the next three years.

and humanitarianism. But, as the 1960s draw to a close, after a period of sustained, unprecedented prosperity and at the zenith of its wealth and power, the United States has callously begun to turn its back on a world filled increasingly with poverty in its starkest form and with the consequent desperation.

What now must be faced, therefore, goes well beyond the need to find new ways to make the best of an inadequate aid policy. Talk about shifting emphasis from capital development loans and grants to technical assistance, about greater "burden sharing" by other developed nations, or about "regionalism" and similar technical devices is almost beside the point. The fate which has befallen the American aid program is only the most manifest symptom of a general condition of American discouragement and confusion about its responsibilities of world leadership in the latter half of the twentieth century. What are called for are new American answers to fundamental questions of national goals and priorities. More simply, a more adequate policy can be achieved only through greater concern on the part of the United States for the problems of the poorer regions of the world, together with greater willingness to contribute resources and to join wholeheartedly and unselfishly in the long-term task. Such a reversal of present trends in American policy would require not only a changed international outlook but also profound changes in American society itself.

THE SOMBER PROSPECT

The world today is a different one even from that of a decade ago, and the way in which the United States sees the world has also greatly changed. In the industrially and militarily powerful nations of the Northern Hemisphere, a technological and scientific revolution is under way which is generating rapid social, economic, and political transformations. Those dynamic states remain the immediate preoccupation of American policy. The huge other part of the global landscape is the so-called Third World—a multitude of new and unstable states staggering under the weight of many burdens. It constitutes the most obscure, unexplored, and unformulated dimension of American foreign policy for the future. Africa constitutes a major part of that huge and forbidding range of problems, and in some ways Africa's essential importance lies in the illumination it throws upon American diplomacy's "heart of darkness."

In attempting to deal with these poor countries, one finds that almost everything is unfamiliar, unorthodox, amorphous, fluid. What is the nature of U.S. interest and responsibility toward them? What means and methods are useful, even relevant, in serving that interest effectively? Where and how can such states be fitted into any rational, workable system of American foreign policy objectives and priorities? The issues they present may not be as directly threatening to U.S. survival as nuclear proliferation and intercontinental ballistic missiles, but there are few even among the most tradition-bound military and foreign policy thinkers who would say that they can for that reason prudently be ignored.

Looking back, it is remarkable how drastically earlier premises and hypotheses framing American policy toward the underdeveloped areas have been altered and, above all, how greatly the mood and way of thinking about them have changed. Only a few years ago, their emergence was viewed with considerable optimism. The political changes taking place were considered positive and promising; the problems of development were felt to be serious but solvable. There was a considerable degree of readiness on the part of both the American public and Congress to provide resources for the task. The launching of the Decade of Development by the United Nations, in 1961, as the result of a suggestion by President Kennedy, was a reflection of the atmosphere of courage the boldness which then prevailed.

Humanitarian motives in supporting development were reinforced by the belief that it was in the enlightened self-interest of the United States in both economic and strategic terms to give substantial help to the poor nations. In anticipation of the growing needs of American industry for supplies of raw materials and for future markets, the mineral resources and the needy millions of such areas as Africa were judged to be of great importance and potentiality. Strategically and politically, likewise, they were considered to be of consequence. The prevailing logic of the cold war was that the United States was engaged in a protracted if not permanent conflict with Communist imperialism, that this conflict would involve every instrumentality of modern diplomacy—military, economic, psychological, political, cultural—and that, in a period of nuclear stalemate and standoff, the emergent nations would become one of the principal arenas of competition. Therefore, in terms of the vital interests of the United States, it was deemed worthwhile, if not essential, to provide assistance to them to promote development, increase political stability, and help prevent Communist penetration and takeover.

Perhaps the most striking characteristics of American thinking during that period were self-confidence and scope. The assumption was unquestioned that, because the United States was a great power, it had great power: that it possessed the economic capability to provide the resources needed to spur development and that, where specific situations required, it could bring to bear the military forces necessary to counter insurgency or prevent aggression. The belief also prevailed that, even though U.S. instrumentalities for propaganda and political warfare were relatively limited and inexperienced, they could provide effective supplementary support to cope with the protracted and all-embracing conflict under way. The Marshall Plan in Europe was taken as evidence of the capacity of American productivity and of the utility of economic aid to shape affairs in that crucial area; the Truman Doctrine testified to the effectiveness of military and economic aid in another region; and events in countries as different as Iran and Guatemala suggested the potency of some of the less familiar instrumentalities of foreign policy in manipulating events.

By the end of 1968 the cheerful mood and the assumptions of the earlier time had disappeared like the mists of morning. Political developments in the Third World had made apparent the innocence and superficiality of earlier expectations of Western-style democratic development. Continuing economic difficulties had revealed the frightening depths and complexities of the tasks of modernization and industrialization. And, as the cold war evolved, it had become less clear that all parts of the Third World would be arenas of active East-West competition. Increasing doubt had therefore arisen as to how vital these various regions might be to American interest and security, and a more relaxed view developed regarding the likelihood of some of the countries' being "lost" to communism. Indeed, the very nature of the Communist threat had come to be viewed differently in the light of changes within the Soviet Union and Eastern Europe and, particularly, of the great rift between the Soviet Union and China—although the shock of the Soviet invasion of Czechoslovakia in 1968 had dissipated excessive earlier expectations for détente.

In sharp contrast to the hope and self-confidence—and perhaps the illusion of omnipotence—of a few years ago, a strong and possibly exaggerated sense of the limits of foreign policy and of American power has come to prevail. The feeling has grown that the United States can no longer afford to give foreign aid on the scale of the past. Doubts have increased about the extent to which political and economic measures available to the United States can make a decisive difference to the development, stability, or political orientation of nations of the Third World. Questions have likewise arisen as to the effectiveness of American military intervention in coping with the type of warfare and the interrelated military and political problems which tend to be presented in these areas, the ability of the United States to control the military escalation which tends to result, and its political and economic capacity to sustain the strains and costs if a stalemate at a high level should occur.

True to a recurrent American habit of thinking that whatever is worth doing is worth overdoing, these specific doubts have led to general skepticism about American capability and the applicability of American power in shaping world events. In its extreme form, the developing mood is one of neo-isolationism based on the beliefs that the Third World has no real importance to America, that the United States has greatly overextended itself everywhere, and that drastic cutbacks in commitment and involvement should now be made. By this reasoning the United States should adopt a stricter scale of priorities and should, if necessary, simply write off whole regions considered to be of lesser significance. Not only can this be done, it is asserted, without great risk or danger, but, even if the United States were to attempt to exercise influence or control, there would be little it could do.

Disappointment with the political and economic performance of the new states and frustration over the war in Viet Nam have obviously contributed to the new frame of mind. But there can be no question that the current impulse to withdraw and the prevalent inhospitality to bold concepts or major international undertakings also reflect developments over recent years within the United States itself.

Only a decade ago the United States was a proud and unified nation. Its material standards of life were the highest in the world and continuing to rise, and, although pockets of poverty existed, these were regarded as inconsequential and in the process of disappearing. The nation's huge commitment to education, it was thought, had virtually eradicated illiteracy and was making Americans the best-trained and best-informed people on earth. The long-neglected Negro problem was being given attention, and, after the Supreme Court decision in the Brown case in 1954, major steps were taken which, it was assumed, would lead to fulfillment of the promise of racial equality and integration. Insofar as concern existed about the youth of the country, it related largely to their distaste for "rugged individualism" and their apparent preference for job security, a good pension plan, and a "gray flannel suit."[3]

But today the nation has become confused, exasperated, divided, and in disrepute. Its complacency has been jolted by a succession of events ranging from political assassinations to a persistent gold drain to the humiliating ineffectiveness of its military and political efforts in Southeast Asia. Within the nation there has come sharp awareness that poverty is an endemic condition of a significant fraction of the population, that the educational system has profound structural and conceptual weaknesses and is not performing effectively, and that new laws and Supreme Court decisions in themselves have not been sufficient to correct the deeply rooted racism which remains one of the realities of the American way of life. Where poverty and racial tension have intersected, as in the central parts of the major American cities, the combination has produced a dismaying series of eruptions of violence and lawlessness, adding further to the nation's unease and its awareness of the number and magnitude of its unsolved domestic problems.

Throughout the country, disadvantaged and formerly docile elements of the population have begun to demand with new militancy a more nearly equal share in the nation's power and affluence. Although these emergent political forces have not yet broken through the crust of existing party hierarchies and other power structures, their influence is clearly on the rise. The revolution in the attitudes and the behavior of American youth has been at least as great as that of Negroes and the poor. Their discontent remains inchoate but it is unmistakable, and its manifestations range from their music, dress, and behavior to campus protests and public disorders. Although their manner is abrasive and their methods are sometimes abominable, their demand to be heard politically cannot very much longer be resisted. Precisely what their impact may be on the future course of the nation cannot yet be discerned. Nevertheless, it is likely to be far-reaching, because what is troubling them is not confined to specific faults of present policies or institutions but extends to the basic values which have become dominant in American life. And, just as their discontent has arisen in part from the domestic impact of international events, so U.S. foreign policies and priorities, as well as domestic

programs, will be affected by the participation of the present
generation of American youth in the political life of the country
in the years just ahead.

Africa, that habitual afterthought of American foreign policy,
may well become the aspect which is particularly modified by
the new atmosphere and the emergence of these new political
forces. As of now, all recommendations for serious action or
commitment by the United States in regard to Africa—whether
for increased aid or for support of black political movements in
the Redoubt—have about them an air of unreality. They have no
chance of acceptance, because as matters now stand there is no
political will in Washington and no effective political base of
support for a change in the policy priority of Africa. Until such
a will and base are created, it is vain to spin out refined schemes
of possible action. But, when they exist, there will be no great
difficulty in identifying concrete measures to which the new political force can be harnessed.*

In this regard there are promising prospects. Signs of an awak-
ening interest in Africa on the part of both youth and Negroes are
beginning to be apparent. For the internationally minded portion
of the younger generation, Africa has much of the appeal and
excitement which outer space and oceanography seem to have for
the technologically minded. For the American Negro community
it is a natural focus of future interest. Hitherto their political
strength in America has been limited, ineffectively organized, and
directed largely and understandably to immediate domestic issues
of political and economic advancement. But the politicization of
the American Negro, like that of the American student, is rapidly
taking place. This fact, plus the impact of demographic trends
on the apportionment of legislative representation over the next
decade, will create major centers of Negro political strength in
most of the industrial cities of the United States. Black congressmen, senators, and chairmen of state political party machinery
will adorn the American political scene in increasing numbers.

---

* To bring about a definite change in U.S. policy toward Africa, only a
marginal shift in the balance of domestic political forces is necessary, since
the problem is not so much one of strong opposition to a different course as
one of general indifference to, and ignorance of, Africa as such. If there were
only some thirty members of the House and Senate with a strong and steady
interest in Africa, and if they were vigorously supported by fifty leaders of
Negro, labor, and church organizations, it would probably be sufficient to
make a decisive difference in U.S. policy on most African issues.

Although their interest and that of their Negro constituencies will undoubtedly continue to be directed primarily to domestic problems, it can be anticipated that they, in the tradition of most American ethnic groups, will develop some parallel interest in foreign affairs. Over the somewhat longer term, therefore, unless quite basic trends in American life should be reversed, there is the prospect of not only a definite but a dramatic shift in the degree of effective public concern about the economic and political progress of Africa. When it comes, a constituency for a new policy line will have been created, and, from that point on, Congress, the White House, and the Department of State will not fail to take notice—nor will African leaders, including those presently in political control of Southern Africa.

But, if such is the historical prospect, the chances for a sudden change in policy in the near future are not excessively bright. At the moment, Africa and everything it represents as a task and responsibility for American policy are counter to the national mood. That continent's problems are unfamiliar and intractable; it is big and complicated; its needs are seemingly endless; its people are mostly brown or black; its tone is disturbing, even revolutionary. What it calls for from the United States is a very high order of faith, commitment, and responsibility—in the implementation of larger, better organized, and more effective assistance programs; in the modification of the world trading system; in the transfer of a far larger volume of resources in the form of private investment to the new states; in the creation of new multilateral structures for security and development purposes; in the facilitation of a process of political evolution in areas where racist and exploitative governments now exist. Both the strangeness and the hugeness of the challenge are forbidding to a weary and discouraged nation, which in recent decades has been called upon again and again to accept great and costly international responsibilities. The pendulum in the United States has therefore swung far toward the extreme of indifference, and, realistically, it may be some time before it returns to a more internationalist middle position—and a willingness to confront the kinds of problems Africa presents.

Before that can happen, measurable progress will have to be made in bringing about some improvement in the condition of American cities and rural slums, in easing racial tensions, in extricating the nation from its predicament in Viet Nam, and in restoring higher degrees of unity, order, and self-confidence.

Though it may take some time before the basic turn comes about—and it is not inconceivable that a period of even more backward-looking and inward-looking policy may temporarily intervene—the turn at some point must come, not only because of dynamic changes occurring in American society which will shift the domestic political balance but also because the character of the nation is what it is. From its beginning, the United States has symbolized belief in freedom and justice, in the possibility of progress and the improvability of the human condition, and in the obligation of the strong to protect the weak.

Decade by decade, those guiding principles have been more and more effectively applied to the internal life of the nation. And historically, there has always been an organic relationship between the character of American society and the character of its foreign policy. Since its earliest days, the United States has seen itself as a social experiment with meaning for all of mankind, as a model, a "standard to which others might repair." This approach has sometimes been overblown with righteousness and pursued with indiscriminate missionary zeal; it has also been used as a cloak to obscure baser motives. But the idealism and the moral sense have persisted, and, given the rising political influence of the Negroes and the new generation of American youth, the "moralization" of American foreign policy, in the sense not of new crusades but of a new fusion of its goals with morally defensible values, is likely to increase. If that is the future tendency, the heightened relevance of Africa is obvious. That continent is a place of great human need, of oppression and injustice, of dramatic struggle by a great branch of mankind for dignity, freedom, and progress. Its problems are specifically related to the values, ideas, and principles upon which American society has been built.

Africa stands, therefore, not only as a test of American foreign policy but also as a challenge to the nation's vision of itself and of its meaning as the dominant civilization in the world of the late twentieth century.

Notes

CHAPTER 1. *The Altered Configuration of Power*

1. Gwendolin G. Cecil, *Life of Robert Marquess of Salisbury*, Vol. 4 (London: Hodder & Stoughton, 1932), pp. 222–24.

CHAPTER 2. *Britain's Decolonization and Post-Independence Relations*

1. See Angus Maddison, *Economic Growth in the West* (New York: The Twentieth Century Fund, 1964).
2. The extent to which Conservative support for the maintenance of colonial control in Africa in that period had disintegrated, is suggested in the autobiography of the white Kenyan leader Sir Michael Blundel. He wrote that, after his talks with Tory Colonial Secretary Ian Mc-Leod and other senior ministers in London in 1960, he came to the conclusion "that the decision had been made to clear out of Africa as soon as possible." M. Blundel, *So Rough a Wind* (Toronto: Ryerson Press, 1964), p. 277.
3. For an excellent and more detailed account of this sequence, see *The Rise and Fall of Western Colonialism* by Stewart C. Easton (New York: Praeger, 1964), pp. 221 ff.
4. W. P. Kirkman, *Unscrambling an Empire* (London: Chatto & Windus, 1966), p. 12.
5. *Board of Trade Journal*, January 26, 1969, p. vii.
6. *Assistance from the United Kingdom for Overseas Development*, 1960, Cmnd. 974.
7. *Overseas Development: The Work of the New Ministry*, Cmnd. 2736.
8. *British Development Policies* (London: Overseas Development Institute, 1966).

406 NOTES

9. Development Assistance Efforts and Policy, 1967 Review (Paris: Organization for Economic Cooperation and Development, September 1967).
10. "Britain's Influence in Africa," Current History, May 1967, p. 279.
11. December 16, 1964, House of Commons Debates, Vol. 704, Cols. 421, 423, 424.
12. For details on the types of assistance and the recipient countries, see Table 13, p. 150 of Chapter 4, summarizing Western European military assistance to the new African states.
13. Quoted in Ali Al'Amin Mazrui, Towards a Pax Africana (Chicago: University of Chicago Press, 1967), p. 153.
14. British Parliamentary Paper, Cmnd. 2901.
15. Cmnd. 3515.
16. Cmnd. 3701.
17. Vol. 211, June 6, 1964, p. 1073.
18. Quoted in Hugh M. F. Caradon, Race Relations in the British Commonwealth and the United Nations (London: Cambridge University Press, Smuts Memorial Lecture, 1967), p. 14.
19. Hugh M. F. Caradon, cited, p. 15.

CHAPTER 3. *France: From Colonialism to Community to Independence*

1. See Michael Crowder, *West Africa Under Colonial Rule* (Evanston, Illinois: Northwestern University Press, 1968). Stewart C. Easton, *The Rise and Fall of Western Colonialism* (New York: Praeger, 1964), pp. 284–302. Ruth Schachter Morgenthau, *Political Parties in French-Speaking West Africa* (Oxford: Clarendon Press, 1964). For excellent coverage of certain particular areas see also Georges Chaffard, *Les Carnets Secrets de la Colonisation* (Paris: Calmann-Lévy, 1965) and Jean Lacouture, *Cinq Hommes et la France* (Paris: Editions du Seuil, 1961).
2. Cited in Virginia Thompson and Richard Adloff, *French West Africa* (Stanford, California: Stanford University Press, 1957), p. 258.
3. *The Overseas Territories in the Mutual Security Program* (Washington: Mutual Security Agency, March 31, 1952).
4. For a clear and more detailed analysis of this question, see Teresa Hayter, cited, pp. 54 ff.
5. OECD, *Geographical Distribution of Financial Flows to Less Developed Countries, 1960–66*, Paris, 1967 (mimeographed).
6. Proper title: *La politique de coopération avec les pays en voie de développement*, published December 1963.
7. OECD, *Development Assistance Efforts and Policies 1967 Review*, pp. 104–5, and OECD *Press Release, July 10, 1968* (Press/A(68)34), p. 15.
8. The number of such *militaires du contingent* in Africa, largely in

teaching positions, increased from none in 1963 to 372 in 1964, to 1,369 in 1966, to an estimated 2,000 in 1967.

9. Vol. 2, p. 89.

10. Although the agreements are in many respects uniform, there are specific and in some cases important variations. For a detailed analysis, see Chester A. Crocker, "France's Changing Military Interests," *Africa Report,* June 1968.

11. *Le Monde,* March 22, 1967, p. 6.

CHAPTER 4. *Other Western European Bilateral Relations*

1. The term "Free World," as used in U.S. government aid publications, includes the nations of Western Europe and the United States, plus Israel, Kuwait, Canada, Taiwan, Japan, and Yugoslavia, as well as various multilateral international donor agencies.

2. See *Africa: Special Report,* October 26, 1956.

3. *Africa Research Bulletin,* Vol. 5, No. 8 (September 30, 1968), p. 1110.

4. Jack L. Knusel, *West German Aid to Developing Countries* (New York: Praeger, 1968), Table XXII, p. 122, and Table XXXI, p. 144. Since then, it has been overtaken by the United Kingdom. If reparations payments and IBRD bond purchases are excluded from the German figures, its aid never exceeded that of Britain.

5. Knusel, cited.

6. The DAC in its sturdily cheerful manner reports in its 1967 Review that a number of the smaller European countries as well as France and Germany, "firmly intend to achieve steady increases in their official assistance programs over coming years"; p. 16.

7. *The Observer,* August 30, 1964.

8. Quoted in *Belgian Administration in the Congo,* Georges Brausch (London Institute of Race Relations, Oxford University Press, 1961), p. 78.

9. "The Speech of Patrice Lumumba on Independence Day" reproduced in Alan P. Merriam, *Congo, Background of Conflict* (Evanston, Illinois: Northwestern University Press, 1961), Appendix IV, pp. 352 ff.; and *Congo, My Country* by Patrice Lumumba (New York: Praeger, 1961), see foreword by Colin Legum, p. xiv.

CHAPTER 5. *Multilateral Relations Through the Common Market*

1. NATO Letter, March 1968, p. 5.

2. In the following description, considerable reliance has been placed on the authoritative analyses of the late Arnold Rivkin of the World Bank on this subject, including Africa and the Common Market (Denver: University of Denver, Monograph Series in World Affairs, Vol. 3, No. 4, 1966); "After the Lagos Agreement" in *Africa Report* of March

1967; and "Africa and the European Economic Community" in *Finance and Development*, quarterly publication of the IMF and IBRD, Washington, June 1966.

3. See *Bulletin of the European Communities*, Vol. 1, No. 6, June 1968.
4. Quoted in Arnold Rivkin, "Africa and the EEC: New Inter-regional Association," in *Studies in Law and Economic Development*, Vol. 2, Study No. 1, May 1967.

CHAPTER 6. *Soviet Relations*

1. Quoted in Colin Legum, "Pan-Africanism and Communism," in Sven Hamrell and Carl Gösta Widstrand (eds.), *The Soviet Bloc, China and Africa* (London: Pall Mall Press, 1964), p. 14.
2. Aimé Césaire, Lettre à Maurice Thorez (Paris: *Presence Africaine*, 1956), p. 12.
3. Colin Legum, "Pan-Africanism and Communism," cited, pp. 20–21 and fn. 27.
4. In the preparation of the following sections of this chapter, the author gratefully acknowledges his indebtedness to Professor Robert Legvold of Tufts University not only for research assistance but also for guidance in the general formulation of the argument. In the phrasing of several key points he has drawn freely on Legvold's writings, particularly his articles: "Lignes de force de la diplomatie Sovietique en Afrique," *Le Mois en Afrique*, March 1967, pp. 30–52; "The Soviet Union in Senegal," *Mizan*, Vol. 8, No. 4 (July–August 1966), pp. 57–66; "Ten Years of Soviet and Chinese Policies in Africa," *Mizan*, Vol. 10, No. 8 (July–August 1968), pp. 107–14; and a manuscript to be published in 1969 by Harvard University Press, *Soviet Policy in West Africa*. This is not to imply, however, that Dr. Legvold is necessarily in accord with a number of the author's interpretations and evaluations.
5. G. Mennen Williams, "Communism's Impact on African Nationalism," *Department of State Bulletin* (June 3, 1963), p. 879.
6. Quoted in Zbigniew Brzezinski (ed.), *Africa and the Communist World* (Stanford, California: Stanford University Press, 1963), p. 12.
7. *The New York Times*, July 13, 1960, p. 7.
8. See *Pravda*, July 14, 1960, p. 3.
9. See Khrushchev's statement in *Pravda*, July 15, 1960, p. 5.
10. *Pravda*, July 15, 1960, p. 5.
11. For a fuller discussion, see Thomas Hovet, Jr., *Africa in the United Nations* (Evanston, Ill.: Northwestern University Press, 1963), p. 88.
12. See, for example, Conor Cruise O'Brien's treatment in his *To Katanga and Back* (New York: Simon & Schuster, 1962, 1963).
13. Richard Lowenthal, "Russia, the One-Party System, and the Third World," *Survey*, No. 58 (January 1966), p. 46.
14. *Pravda*, June 6, 1952, p. 1.

15. Editorial in *Kommunist*, No. 2 (1962), p. 18. See also Y. Dolgopalov, "National Liberation Wars in the Present Epoch," *International Affairs*, No. 2 (1962), pp. 17–21, and V. Matveyev, "Wars of Liberation and Diplomacy," *International Affairs*, No. 3 (1963), pp. 69–72.
16. Same.
17. *Pravda*, April 3, 1963.
18. CCP Central Committee Reply to CPSU Central Committee, *Pravda*, July 14, 1963.
19. For a full discussion of these ideological trends see Uri Ra'anan, "Moscow and the 'Third World,' " *Problems of Communism*, January–February 1965, pp. 22–31.
20. This milestone discussion was printed in the Soviet journal *Mirovaya Ekonomika i Mezhdunarodnyye Otnosheniya*, No. 4 (1964), pp. 116–31; and No. 6 (1964), pp. 62–81.
21. N. I. Gavrilov (ed.), *Nezavisimyye strany Afriki: ekonomicheskiye: sotsial'nyye problemy* (Independent countries of Africa: Economic and Social Problems, Moscow, 1965), quoted in *Mizan*, Vol. 7 (October 1965), p. 6.
22. *Mirovaya Ekonomika i Mezhdunarodnyye Otnosheniya*, No. 8 (1964), p. 84, quoted in *Mizan*, Vol. 7, No. 10 (November 1965), p. 5.
23. One Soviet writer maintained that Houphouët-Boigny was only "an African by the color of his skin" (M. Azembski, "Report on the Ivory Coast," *New Times*, No. 40, 1961, p. 28). Another early reference denounced Houphouët as a "big plantation owner enriched through the exploitation of underpaid African labor" (*Izvestia*, June 14, 1961).
24. IVᵉ Congrès PDCI-RDA, Ministère de l'Information (mimeo.), September 23–25, 1966, p. 17.
25. Lufti El Kholi (editor-in-chief of *Al Talia*), "The Current Phase of the Anti-imperialist Struggle," *World Marxist Review*, Vol. 10, No. 1 (January 1967), pp. 4–5, a view with which the Soviet leadership was in accord. Lufti is an Egyptian Communist; his publication is the ideological organ of Nasser's Arab Socialist Union.
26. See *Pravda*, August 14, 1966, p. 4.
27. "At the Cairo Seminar," *World Marxist Review*, Vol. 10, No. 2 (February 2, 1967), p. 39.
28. Alexander Sobolev, "Some Problems of Social Progress," *World Marxist Review*, Vol. 10, No. 1 (January 1967), p. 13.
29. From *Kommunist*, No. 17 (November 1964), p. 31, quoted in Milton Kovner, "Soviet Aid and Trade," *Current History*, October 1967, p. 222.
30. Michel Ayih, *Ein Afrikaner in Moskau* (Cologne, 1961), pp. 134 ff., quoted in Roger E. Kanet, "African Youth: The Target of Soviet African Policy," *The Russian Review*, Vol. 27, No. 2 (April 1968), p. 172.
31. See *The New York Times*, December 22, 1967.

32. See Stuart H. Schaar, *The Arms Race and the Defense Strategy in North Africa*, North Africa Series, Vol. 13, No. 9, American Universities Field Staff Reports Service, 1967.

CHAPTER 7. *The Chinese Involvement*

1. Cited in W. A. C. Adie, "Chinese Policy Towards Africa," in *The Soviet Bloc, China and Africa*, cited, p. 52.
2. Cited, p. 52, fn. 24.
3. From *Peking Review*, No. 5, January 31, 1964, quoted by Robert A. Scalapino in *Current Scene*, Vol. 3, No. 26, September 1, 1965.
4. Robert Counts, "Chinese Footprints in Somalia," *The Reporter*, February 2, 1961, pp. 32–34.
5. Denis Warner, "China Fans the Flames," *The Reporter*, January 14, 1965.
6. Same.
7. Commentary on CPSU "Open Letter" in *People's Daily* and *Red Flag*, October 21, 1963.
8. Same.
9. Reuters dispatch from Cairo, February 16, and Colin Legum in *The Observer*, London, March 12, 1962.
10. Quoted by William E. Griffith, *Survey*, No. 54 (January 1965), p. 188.
11. Kurt Müller, *The Foreign Aid Programs of the Soviet Bloc and Communist China: An Analysis* (New York: Walker & Co., 1967), p. 140.
12. Lin Piao "Long Live the People's Republic," *Department of State Daily Report*, September 3, 1965. See also the pamphlet "More on the Differences Between Comrade Togliati and Us," reprinted in *Red Flag* (Peking), Nos. 3–4, March 4, 1963.
13. The Central Committee of the Chinese Communist Party strongly reaffirmed this view at its meetings in late October 1968, predicting in its final statement that "imperialism would be smashed everywhere" by the "revolutionary people of the world" led by Communist China. *The New York Times*, November 2, 1968.
14. Herbert Dinnerstein, "Rivalry in Underdeveloped Areas," *Problems of Communism*, Vol. 13, No. 2 (March–April 1964), p. 69.
15. Mao Tse-tung, "Strategic Problems of China's Revolutionary War," December 1956, *Chinese Communist World Outlook* (Department of State, June 1962), p. 6.
16. Cited, p. 7.
17. From *The People's Daily* summarized by NCNA, February 16, 1967, quoted in *Mizan*, Vol. 9, No. 2 (March–April 1967), p. 183.

CHAPTER 8. *The Truman-Eisenhower Period*

1. See, for example, Richard Hofstadter, *The American Political Tradition* (New York: Knopf, 1962), pp. 348–49.

2. Leland M. Goodrich and Marie J. Carroll, *Documents on American Foreign Relations*, Vol. 5, July 1942–June 1943 (Boston: World Peace Foundation, 1944), p. 6.
3. *Department of State Bulletin*, Vol. 7, No. 182 (December 19, 1942), p. 1008.
4. Robert Murphy, *A Diplomat Among Warriors* (New York: Doubleday & Co., 1964), p. 117.
5. OSS Files, letter cited by William L. Langer, *Our Vichy Gamble* (New York: Knopf, 1947), p. 333.
6. *Department of State Bulletin*, Vol. 10, No. 248 (March 25, 1944), p. 276.
7. *Department of State Bulletin*, Vol. 12, No. 308 (May 20, 1945), pp. 929–30.
8. *Department of State Bulletin*, Vol. 12, No. 310 (June 3, 1945), p. 1010.
9. Andrew M. Kamarck, *The Economics of African Development* (New York: Praeger, 1967), p. 201. In some respects, Kamarck's estimates regarding the scale of the use of direct program funds, as well as of counterpart funds, may be conservative. From 1948 through 1951, according to U.S. government data, France alone chose to allocate more than $250 million of the direct French allotment of Marshall Plan aid, plus $100 million of counterpart funds, to finance essential imports for its overseas areas. See *Development of the Overseas Territories Since the War* (Washington: ECA, 1952).
10. See Edgar S. Furniss, *France—Troubled Ally* (New York: Harper & Brothers, for the Council on Foreign Relations, 1960), pp. 162 and 176.
11. Harry S. Truman, *Memoirs, Vol. 2: Years of Trial and Hope* (New York: Doubleday & Co., 1956), pp. 232, 233.
12. Speech before the Foreign Policy Association, Oklahoma City, May 8, 1950, *Department of State Bulletin*, Vol. 22, No. 572 (June 19, 1950), pp. 999–1003.
13. Vernon McKay, *Africa in World Politics* (New York: Harper & Row, 1963), p. 321.
14. Successive American policy declarations are here identified by the name of the official delivering them. That they were, however, not personal but factory products, is made obvious by the constant repetition of many phrases and ideas in virtually unchanged form from statement to statement.
15. See Emmett John Hughes, *The Ordeal of Power* (New York: Atheneum, 1963), p. 209.
16. See *Africa Special Report*, January 28, 1957.
17. *Economic Aid and Technical Assistance in Africa* (Washington: U.S. Government Printing Office, 1957).
18. "The Emergence of Africa, Report to the President by Vice-President Nixon on his trip to Africa," White House release, April 7, 1957.

19. See *Africa Special Report*, May 29, 1957.
20. *Congressional Record*, Vol. 103, Part 8, pp. 10780–88 *passim*.
21. Joseph Palmer, 2nd, "The Problems and Prospects of Sub-Saharan Africa: A United States Point of View," *Department of State Bulletin*, Vol. 37 (December 9, 1957), pp. 930–33.
22. *Department of State Bulletin*, Vol. 38 (May 26, 1958), pp. 857–62.
23. Same.
24. *Department of State Bulletin*, Vol. 43, No. 116, pp. 752–57.

CHAPTER 9. *African Policy Under Kennedy and Johnson*

1. Quoted in Arthur M. Schlesinger, Jr., *A Thousand Days: John F. Kennedy in the White House* (Boston: Houghton, Mifflin & Co., 1965), p. 558.
2. *Department of State Bulletin* (November 27, 1961), p. 887.
3. See, for example, the statement by Jonathan Bingham of the U.S. delegation, June 22, 1962; U.S. Delegation Press Release 4014.
4. *Department of State Bulletin* (August 19, 1963), p. 284.
5. *Department of State Bulletin* (August 19, 1963), p. 308.
6. *Department of State Bulletin* (August 26, 1963), pp. 337, 338.
7. *Kennedy* (New York: Harper & Row, 1965), p. 637.
8. Apropos of Acheson's concept of sovereignty as a kind of absolute property right, compare for example Blackstone's eighteenth century statement in the *Commentaries:* "Regard of the law for private property is so great . . . that it will not authorize even the least violation of it, not even for the general good of the whole community."
9. See, for example, his "Legality and Loyalty in Rhodesia," The *Washington Post*, June 4, 1967.
10. For an extraordinarily sane and analytical statement of the problem and of U.S. foreign policy, see the presentation by Assistant Secretary of State Joseph Palmer, 2nd, before the African sub-committee of the Senate Foreign Relations Committee, Washington D.C., September 11, 1968.

CHAPTER 10. *The Unassembled Triangle: Europe, Africa, and the United States*

1. George W. Ball, *The Discipline of Power* (Boston: Little, Brown & Co., 1968), pp. 240–43.

CHAPTER 11. *Southern Africa: Smoldering Catastrophe*

1. For one careful attempt to calculate the costs of military action against forces of the strength and sophistication of those of South Africa and to think about other unthinkables in this situation, see Amelia C. Leiss (ed.), *Apartheid and United Nations Collective Measures* (New York: Carnegie Endowment for International Peace, 1965).

2. See Vernon McKay, "Southern Africa and American Policy," in William A. Hance (ed.), *Southern Africa and the United States* (New York: Columbia University Press, 1968), pp. 19–24, for a detailed documentation on the structure, activities, and financing of this apparatus in the United States.

CHAPTER 13. *The Linchpin: The U.S. Role in African Development*

1. For a fuller discussion see John W. Evans, *U.S. Trade Policy* (New York: Harper & Row, for the Council on Foreign Relations, 1967).
2. In this there is, of course, nothing in the least unusual. Professor Hans Morgenthau has identified, in terms of purpose, six types of foreign economic "aid" given by powerful nations in the past: humanitarian aid, subsistence aid, military aid, bribery, prestige aid, and development aid. See, for example, his *A New Foreign Policy for the United States* (New York: Praeger, for the Council on Foreign Relations, 1969), pp. 88–106.
3. See, for example, David Riesman's influential *The Lonely Crowd* (New Haven: Yale University Press, 1950).

Index

Acheson, Dean, 318
Adenauer, Konrad, 164
Adoula, Cyrille, 196, 224, 287, 308
Afghanistan, 191
Africa: Brazzaville *vs.* Casablanca groupings, 197; and Communism, 186–206, 238–42; disarmament pacts with (proposed),374–75; economic assistance to (1959–67), table, 145, *see also* under (Britain, France, U.S.S.R., U.S.); Eighteen Associated States, *see* European Economic Community, Eighteen Associated States; factionalism within, 14–15, 16, *see also* African unity, *below*; independence wave, 3, 6–7, 9; internal violence in, 365, 374; intervention in, 118–20, 217, 370–73, 376–78; investments in, 42–46, 144, 383–85; liberation movements, *see* Liberation movements; military regimes, 15; postcolonial problems, 13–17; prospects for, 397–404; "regionalism" in, 394, 397; security problems, 365–66; "socialism" in, 200, 201; strategic importance of, 56–57, 154–55, 159, 263, 331, 366–67, 368, 371; trade union developments, 266–67; unity within, 16, 200–201, *see also* Pan Africanism; and Western Europe, *see* Europe, Western, and individual country entries; *see also*

Central Africa; East Africa; Equatorial Africa; French West Africa; North Africa; Southern Africa; Tropical Africa; West Africa
African Development Bank, 16
Afro-Asian People's Solidarity Conference (1957), 222; (1958), 270; (1963), 228; (1964), 228–29
Afro-Asian People's Solidarity Organization, 228
Afro-Asian Writers Conference (1962), 228
Agency for International Development (AID), 290, 292, 293, 299, 303, 321, 326, 393, 394
Algeria, 44, 123, 127, 169, 204, 267, 271, 282, 289, 344, 351; Chinese economic aid to, 233; and EEC, 168; Evian Agreements, *see* Evian Agreements; FLN, 196; and NATO, 366; and President Johnson, 306; and President Kennedy, 86–87, 268–69, 269–70, 276, 285; Rhodesia, aid to, 12; strategic importance of, 154; trade with China, 232; U.S. recognition of, 291

and France: aid to, 148; economic ties to, 102, 103, 104, 106, 109; military cooperation with, 120–21, 123

and U.S.S.R.: aid to, 208, 213, 214, 215, 242; trade with, 212

415

COUNCIL ON FOREIGN RELATIONS

Officers and Directors

PUBLICATIONS

FOREIGN AFFAIRS (quarterly), edited by Hamilton Fish Armstrong.
THE UNITED STATES IN WORLD AFFAIRS (annual), by Richard P. Stebbins.
DOCUMENTS ON AMERICAN FOREIGN RELATIONS (annual), by Richard P. Stebbins with the assistance of Elaine P. Adam.
POLITICAL HANDBOOK AND ATLAS OF THE WORLD (annual), edited by Walter H. Mallory.
THE GREAT POWERS AND AFRICA, by Waldemar A. Nielsen (1969).

A New Foreign Policy for the United States, by Hans J. Morgenthau (1969).

Middle East Politics: The Military Dimension, by J. C. Hurewitz (1969).

The Economics of Interdependence: Economic Policy in the Atlantic Community, by Richard N. Cooper (1968).

How Nations Behave: Law and Foreign Policy, by Louis Henkin (1968).

The Insecurity of Nations, by Charles W. Yost (1968)

Prospects for Soviet Society, edited by Allen Kassof (1968).

The American Approach to the Arab World, by John S. Badeau (1968).

U.S. Policy and the Security of Asia, by Fred Greene (1968).

Negotiating with the Chinese Communists: The U.S. Experience, by Kenneth T. Young (1968).

From Atlantic to Pacific: A New Interocean Canal, by Immanuel J. Klette (1967).

Tito's Separate Road: America and Yugoslavia in World Politics, by John C. Campbell (1967).

U.S. Trade Policy: New Legislation for the Next Round, by John W. Evans (1967).

Trade Liberalization Among Industrial Countries: Objectives and Alternatives, by Bela Balassa (1967).

The Chinese People's Liberation Army, by Brig. General Samuel B. Griffith II U.S.M.C. (ret.) (1967).

The Artillery of the Press: Its Influence on American Foreign Policy, by James Reston (1967).

Atlantic Economic Cooperation: The Case of the O.E.C.D., by Henry G. Aubrey (1967).

Trade, Aid and Development: The Rich and Poor Nations, by John Pincus (1967).

Between Two Worlds: Policy, Press and Public Opinion on Asian-American Relations, by John Hohenberg (1967).

The Conflicted Relationship: The West and the Transformation of Asia, Africa and Latin America, by Theodor Geiger (1966).

The Atlantic Idea and Its European Rivals, by H. van B. Cleveland (1966).

European Unification in the Sixties: From the Veto to the Crisis, by Miriam Camps (1966).

The United States and China in World Affairs, by Robert Blum, edited by A. Doak Barnett (1966).

The Future of the Overseas Chinese in Souteast Asia, by Lea A. Williams (1966).

The Conscience of the Rich Nations: The Development Assistance Committee and the Common Aid Effort, by Seymour J. Rubin (1966).

ATLANTIC AGRICULTURAL UNITY: Is it Possible?, by John O. Coppock (1966).

TEST BAN AND DISARMAMENT: The Path of Negotiation, by Arthur H. Dean (1966).

COMMUNIST CHINA'S ECONOMIC GROWTH AND FOREIGN TRADE, by Alexander Eckstein (1966).

POLICIES TOWARD CHINA: Views from Six Continents, edited by A. M. Halpern (1966).

THE AMERICAN PEOPLE AND CHINA, by A. T. Steele (1966).

INTERNATIONAL POLITICAL COMMUNICATION, by W. Phillips Davison (1965).

MONETARY REFORM FOR THE WORLD ECONOMY, by Robert V. Roosa (1965).

AFRICAN BATTLELINE: American Policy Choice in Southern Africa, by Waldemar A. Nielsen (1965).

NATO IN TRANSITION: The Future of the Atlantic Alliance, by Timothy W. Stanley (1965).

ALTERNATIVE TO PARTITION: For a Broader Conception of America's Role in Europe, by Zbigniew Brzezinski (1965).

THE TROUBLED PARTNERSHIP: A Re-Appraisal of the Atlantic Alliance, by Henry A. Kissinger (1965).

REMNANTS OF EMPIRE: The United Nations and the End of Colonialism, by David W. Wainhouse (1965).